MUSIC
OF THE
WARAO
OF
VENEZUELA

Music of the Warao of Venezuela

Song People

of the

Rain Forest

Dale A. Olsen

University Press of Florida
Gainesville ○ Tallahassee ○ Tampa ○ Boca Raton
Pensacola ○ Orlando ○ Miami ○ Jacksonville

Library of Congress Cataloging-in-Publication Data

Olsen, Dale A. (Alan)
    Music of the Warao of Venezuela: song people of the rain forest/
Dale A. Olsen.
        p.   cm.
    Includes bibliographical references and index.
    ISBN 0-8130-1390-9 (alk. paper)
    1. Waro Indians—Music—History and criticism.   2. Folk music—
Venezuela—History and criticism.   3. Folk songs, Warao—Venezuela—
History and criticism.   I. Title.
    ML3575.V3047   1996
    781.62'98—dc20   95-46549

Portions of chapter 11, "hoa Magical Protection Songs," were originally published as
"Magical Protection Songs of the Warao Indians—Part 1: Animals" and "Magical
Protection Songs of the Warao Indians—Part 2: Spirits" in *Latin American Music
Review* 1, no. 2, pp. 131–61, and 2, no. 1, pp. 1–10, respectively. Reprinted by
permission of the University of Texas Press.

The University Press of Florida is the scholarly publishing agency for the State
University System of Florida, comprised of Florida A & M University, Florida Atlantic
University, Florida International University, Florida State University, University of
Central Florida, University of Florida, University of North Florida, University of South
Florida, and University of West Florida.

University Press of Florida
15 Northwest 15th Street
Gainesville, FL 32611

This book is dedicated to my wife, Diane,
who shares my life and my loves,
and to my son, Darin.

*Their support and love from the
concrete jungle of Los Angeles
accompanied me to the rain forest
jungle of the Orinoco Delta.*

Cuando yo me muere, la música será guardada por ti, Sr. Diego
[When I die, the music will be preserved by you, Mr. Dale]
Jaime Zapata
Warao Keeper of the Isimoi
10 July 1972

Contents

Figures

Song Texts

Music Examples

Recorded Examples

1. Traveling song with ehuru drum, Talejo Tovar (Juan Mata Ahanoko) (1:18)
2. Two muhusemoi flutes, nahanamu festival music, Juan Bustillo Calderón (Hebu Wabanoko) and Jaime Zapata (Yaruara Akoho) (:49)
3. Two isimoi clarinets, nahanamu festival music, anonymous (Boca de Koboina) (2:02)
4. Ensemble music (muhusemoi, isimoi, hebu mataro, sewei) and dance from nahanamu festival, anonymous (Boca de Koboina) (3:07)
5. Two versions of dakotu dance song "Iboma Sanuka" (3:20)
   a. Silbano Ramírez (Lorenzano Ahanoko)
   b. Melicia Torres (Boca del Sakobana)
6. Dakotu dance song "Naniobo," Pedro Rivero (Lorenzano Ahanoko) (2:05)
7. Two hoerekitane lullabies (2:15)
   a. Florencia Rivero (Yaruara Akoho)
   b. Cirilo Rivero (Yaruara Akoho)
8. Wisiratu shaman curing song (sections A and A^1) with hebu mataro, Bernardo Jiménez Tovar (Yaruara Akoho) (2:15)
9. Wisiratu shaman curing duet (section A) without hebu mataro, Juan Bustillo Calderón (Hebu Wabanoko) and Bernardo Jiménez Tovar (Yaruara Akoho) (3:00)
10. Wisiratu shaman curing song (section B) with hebu mataro, Bernardo Jiménez Tovar (Yaruara Akoho) (1:55)
11. Wisiratu shaman curing ritual with hebu mataro, Bernardo Jiménez Tovar (Yaruara Akoho) (12:53)
12. Bahanarotu shaman apprenticeship song, Antonio Lorenzano (Lorenzano Ahanoko) (2:15)
13. Bahanarotu shaman curing ritual with hebu mataro, Primitivo Sánchez (Yaruara Akoho) (2:08)
14. Bahanarotu shaman "Song of the Creator Bird of the Dawn," Antonio Lorenzano (Lorenzano Ahanoko) (4:50)

15. Hoarotu shaman inflicting ritual (beginning, middle, and ending), José Antonio Páez (Moriki Hana) (3:15)
16. Hoarotu shaman curing ritual (solo), Francisco (Hana Kahamana) (3:45)
17. Hoarotu shaman curing ritual (duet), Francisco and Miguel (Hana Kahamana) (5:03)
18. Hoarotu shaman curing ritual (trio), Gabriel Sánchez, Biwa Tovar, and Gerónimo Velásquez (Yaruara Akoho) (5:43)
19. hoa curing song for hatchet cut, Bernardo Jiménez Tovar (Yaruara Akoho) (1:00)
20. hoa curing song for snakebite, Isaías Rodríguez (Hebu Wabanoko) (1:26)
21. hoa curing song for snakebite, Jaime Zapata (Yaruara Akoho) (1:36)
22. hoa curing song for birth complications, Bernardo Jiménez Tovar (Yaruara Akoho) (2:50)
23. Magical protection hoa song against transformed agouti, José Antonio Páez (Moriki Hana) (2:33)
24. Marehoa magical love song, Pedro Rivero (Lorenzano Ahanoko) (2:32)

Total time 72:40

Tables

Preface

The ideological intent of this book is to extol an important yet often slighted aspect of the South American rain forest—the traditional music and music making of its native inhabitants. The traditional rain forest (that is, undisturbed by outside influences), wherever it is found in South America, is musically as well as ecologically rich. The lower Orinoco River rain forest in Venezuela, for example, is alive with music that enables its primary inhabitants, the Warao native Americans, to maintain their traditional culture. As fragile as the ecological system itself, Warao music survives because the Orinoco Delta habitat remains relatively undisturbed. This could change almost overnight, however, if non-Indian intrusion suddenly determined that the rain forest should serve a purpose other than to support the Warao. In August 1993, for example, the world witnessed the worst type of intrusion in the Amazon rain forest, when Brazilian gold miners (garimpeiros) reputedly massacred many Yanomamö Indians. Media coverage of this tragic event reached the West almost overnight; but numerous indigenous musics and other cultural expressions in the South American rain forest, like thousands of biological species, disappear without the world's knowledge. We will never know what those cultural expressions could have taught us about the people who made them.

Ethnomusicology is the study of a culture's music undertaken to learn something about how that culture thinks about itself and the world in which it lives. Music can be defined as a form of humanly organized sound communication (other than speech and telegraphy). The ethnomusicologist must ask, What can music tell us about a civilization, a nation, a tribe, a village, a person that nothing else can tell us? While approaches to ethnomusicology vary, they usually include some attempt to be interdisciplinary. To "write" the ethnomusicology of a people or a locale, for example, the ethnomusicologist must think of the subject of study as akin to the hub of a bicycle wheel, with many spokes of information and knowledge leading to and supporting that hub. These spokes can include music as sound, music as communication, musical instruments as material culture, musical instruments as symbol, dance as music, religious expression as music, music and myth, a specific music within the world of music, and so forth. Feld (1989, 253) suggests another spoke: "Ethnographies are supposed to be what we ethnographers think about things as much as they are supposed to be accounts of what we think the locals think they are doing." The spokes I have mentioned will be the structural supports of this book, whose hub is the music of the Warao Indians of Venezuela.

The purpose of this book is multifaceted but is centered on the hypothesis that much of Warao existence is held together by Warao music. Nearly all aspects of Warao life include music, and many of them would be unthinkable without it. For the Warao, music is diversion, stability, protection, and power.

This book will, in large part, be "musicocentric" because it is an ethnomusicological study in which music is used to explain aspects of culture. It will also be descriptive with the objective of explaining native Warao music theory and interpretative with the purpose of relating Warao music to Warao life in this world and the next. To understand the essence of shamanistic ritual among native South Americans, for example, it is vital to understand their most important vehicle for communicating supernatural power: music. Geertz (1988, 10) explains that hearing only the words but not the music is insensitive and treats people only as objects. Music helps us understand the function of Warao rituals, for example, because, among the Warao, ritual behavior is musical behavior.

For the Warao certain types of music are elements of spirit as well as human behavior, and musical events cannot be separated from the cultural events that produce them. This book explores Warao music as an aspect of Warao culture by providing emic analysis (what the Warao say about their music and music making) as well as etic analysis (what objective researchers deduce about Warao music and music making through participant observation, description, analysis, comparison, and interpretation). Gilbert Rouget (1985, 33) supports this approach. He discusses "three kinds of information," which can be paraphrased as native interpretations, ethnographic interpretations, and descriptions that enable others to make interpretations. In the course of this book I present these three viewpoints, and the folk evaluations are always separated from the analytical ones (Merriam 1964).

Gilbert Rouget's (1985) broad interdisciplinary study of music as power has additionally encouraged me to place Warao theurgical music (music for supernatural communication, the topic of my dissertation [Olsen 1973]) within a broader musical/cultural picture that includes Warao secular music. To answer the question "What is power in Warao music?" (a major concern of this book), one must explore all avenues of Warao organized sound because not all Warao music has the same type of power to them.

Each chapter of this book includes extensive musical and ethnographic information and analysis about the Warao. Chapter 2 offers detailed information about their cosmological beliefs and practices. Chapter 3 provides background about their musical genres, which I divide into three large categories: music for pleasure, utility, and theurgy. Chapter 4 presents detailed information about their many musical instruments—relating them to mythology, describing them (including numerous photographs), and placing them in a Caribbean, circum-Caribbean, and South American context. Warao entertainment music and dance constitute chapter 5, while chapter 6 studies another type of secular music—lullabies. Chapters 7, 8, and 9 analyze in great detail the apprenticeship, inflicting, and curing songs of the three types of Warao shamans along with the musical behavior of the shamans in their various roles. Another curing genre is studied in chapter 10, while chapters 11 and 12 continue with other types of musical songs for power—magical protection and magical love. A final individual musical expression for power is studied in chapter 13—songs for canoe construction. Individual and group musical expressions are presented in chapter 14 with musical and cultural analyses of Warao religious festivals and related supernatural songs. Chapter 15 addresses the Warao concepts of music as power and power as music by synthesizing all the analyses and conclusions from preceding chapters to support my hypothesis. Finally, chapter 16 returns to the hypothesis that much of Warao existence is held together by Warao music and provides some final thoughts about the future of Warao music and culture within the context of the rain forest. The book presents many musical transcriptions of Warao autochthonous music; and numerous song texts are translated, explained, and analyzed. Additionally, an accompanying compact disc provides audio examples of representative Warao musics, all of which are discussed in this book.

There are many individuals and institutions to thank for making this book possible. I am very grateful to the late Dr. Charles Speroni, former dean of the College of Fine Arts at the University of California, Los Angeles (UCLA), for his support of my first field trip to Venezuela, partially made possible with funds from the Clifton Webb Fund; and to Johannes Wilbert, former director of the Latin American Center, UCLA, for his financial support of both my first and second field trips, which were made possible with funds from the Venezuelan Indian Project of the Latin American Center and the Centro Latinoamericano de Venezuela (CLAVE). My thanks also go to Mantle Hood, director of the former Institute of Ethnomusicology, UCLA, for providing me with professional recording equipment; and to former technician Michael Moore for his help. My third field trip was funded by a summer stipend from the National Endowment for the Humanities, for which I am grateful. I am also thankful to H. D. Heinen of the Fundación La Salle in Caracas for his assistance and encouragement while in Caracas and the Orinoco Delta. I also extend my appreciation to Dr. and Mrs. Max Brandt, Mr. and Mrs. George Hall, and the late Sr. Germán Bracamonte for their help and hospitality during my various stays in Caracas.

To the Spanish Capuchín missionaries in the Orinoco Delta—Monseñor García, Padre Pedro, and especially Padre Damián del Blanco—I am very grateful. I am particularly thankful to Cesáreo Soto of the Guayo (Wayo) Mission for his patience as an expert guide and excellent translator. For help in scientifically identifying many of the Warao animals referred to in song texts I extend my appreciation to Dr. C. Pedro Trebban, curator of the Jardín Zoológico El Pinar in Caracas, Venezuela.

I would like to thank my colleagues Allan Burns, Ter Ellingson, Johannes Wilbert, and the late John Blacking and Charles Boilès for reading earlier drafts of the manuscript and offering valuable suggestions. Thanks also go to the Center for Latin American Studies at the University of Florida and the former Center for Instructional Development and Services at Florida State University for help in the preparation of various stages of the manuscript. Except where indicated in the captions, the photographs and music transcriptions in this book are my own.

I express my sincerest appreciation to my wife and colleague, Diane, for her immeasurable help with various stages of this project. To her and my son, Darin, I lovingly dedicate this book.

Above all, I wish to thank the Winikina-Warao for their hospitality, kindness, patience, and willingness to share an important part of their musical world with me. This will be their musical story, and my only wish is to tell it as enthusiastically as they sang it to me.

Warao Orthographic and Musicographic Transcriptions

Orthographic transcription is the technique of writing words from a spoken language; and orthography is a term commonly employed by linguists, anthropologists, and ethnomusicologists when explaining how a particular phonetic transcription is going to appear. The musical counterpart of writing spoken language is musicographic transcription, which is the technique of notating how a particular musical performance sounded or sounds when preserved on a recording. Both writing words and writing music employ objective techniques peculiar to linguistics and ethnomusicology, and both employ subjective determinants as well—some common to each field and others invented by the authors of particular studies. Because of their common challenges in ethnomusicology, I discuss linguistic and musical transcription together.

Orthographic Transcriptions

All the scholars of the Warao whose writings have been referenced in this book have transcribed Waraoan with Castilian or modified Castilian orthography. Spanish writers such as Barral (1957, 1964, 1969), Turrado Moreno (1945), and Vaquero (1965) often incorporate Castilian consonants such as *j*, *gu*, and *qu* into Warao (Guarao) language transcriptions, while Venezuelan (Suárez), European, and American scholars generally employ the more universal Roman consonants of *h*, *w*, and *k*. In all cases the Castilian vowels *a*, *e*, *i*, *o*, and *u*, with their appropriate pronunciations, are used. Therefore, Warao can be effectively rendered with modified Castilian Spanish, which is more universally called Romanization. The orthographic transcriptions of Warao in this book use standard Romanization to facilitate readability and singability. I have transliterated the song texts phonetically, as I hear them; therefore, spellings may differ from singer to singer.

In addition, when a plural Warao word appears out of context, I will employ only the Warao form of writing its plural form (most commonly written with the suffix -*tuma*) rather than attach an *s* as would be done in English or Spanish. Thus hebu (spirit) becomes hebutuma rather than hebus. This technique differs from Wilbert and other writers, who commonly add an *s* for making a Warao word plural. Even the Warao themselves, however, often add an *s* to Warao nouns when they are speaking Spanish. All translations of Spanish materials (songs texts, interviews, secondary sources) are by me.

Musicographic Transcriptions

Just as standard Romanization functions well for the orthographic transcription of spoken and sung Warao, modified European five-line staff notation, referred to as the "Hornbostel paradigm" by Ellingson (1992, 141), effectively serves for Warao musicographic transcription. All but two of the Warao musical transcriptions have been done by me, and I accept full responsibility for their accuracy. Although I have not been aided by any electronic apparatuses other than several tape recorders, a dictographic machine, a Korg tuner, and an electric metronome, my transcriptions of Warao songs have been made with phonetic detail. Moreover, I wish to render them in such a way that the reader can sing them. For this reason I have written the transcriptions with treble clefs, treble clefs 8 basso (sounding one octave lower than notated), or treble clefs 8*va* (sounding one octave higher than notated). Freedom of tempo is indicated by ca. (circa) before the metronome marking. While there is little tempo fluctuation, internal lengths of notes and rests can only be approximated by the transcriber. The Warao sing the songs with a similar freedom.

The following diacritic symbols appear in the transcriptions:

1. Upward or downward diagonal lines between note heads or between Arabic ciphers indicate glissandi (upward or downward melodic glides).

2. Plus or minus Arabic ciphers below or above the pitches indicate cents deviations sharp or flat (A = 440 Hertz standard).

3. Arabic ciphers (whereby a number corresponds to the placement of a pitch relative to the complete melodic scheme) are used to show musical intervals and melodic movement. These ciphers are

based on European-tempered tuning (100 cents per semitone) as the standard. The pitches are given ciphers according to their distance from the principal tone (PT, referred to as the tonic by many writers [discussed later in this section]). A major third above the PT, for example, is written as 3 while a minor third is written as ꞔ, the downward diagonal line indicating about one-half step lower than 3. The terms major and minor are used even though the intervals they represent are not precisely based on 300 or 400 cents, as in equal temperament. With cipher notation it is possible to compare basic melodic patterns more quickly and effectively than if standard European five-line staff notation is used. Cipher notation is also a transposing technique whereby the PT in any melodic phrase is given the cipher 1 and the other pitches are given corresponding numbers up or down, with a downward diagonal line indicating a half-step flat. A period above or below the cipher indicates the upper or lower register respectively, while the cipher without a period refers to the middle register of the transposition.

4. Arrows above or below the note or incorporated into the "key" signature itself indicate approximate quarter tones (ca. ± 35 to 50 cents) sharp or flat. Likewise, approximate eighth tones (ca. ± 15 to 30 cents) sharp or flat are indicated by arrows within parentheses.

5. Neither bar lines nor time signatures are used except when a definite metrical unit is obvious. Generally melodic and rhythmic configurations are subservient to the song texts. Double bar lines, however, indicate the ends of songs; otherwise, the music continues.

6. The clef sign and x note head employed for percussed instruments of indeterminate pitch (ehuru, habi sanuka, hebu mataro) make absolutely no reference to a particular pitch, even though they are located on a five-line staff.

7. A breath mark (') rather than a rest occasionally indicates a very short pause when the singer or instrumentalist takes a breath.

8. Dynamics or amplitude level (loudness) are indicated with common Italian abbreviations found in European-derived music. These include *pp* (pianissimo, very soft), *p* (piano, soft), *mf* (mezzoforte, medium loud), *f* (forte, loud), and *ff* (fortissimo, very loud).

These are the only Italian-derived abbreviations used in the transcriptions, and they have been selected simply because they are in common use with European staff notation. In addition, a gradual increase in volume (crescendo) is indicated with the symbol <, and a gradual decrease (decrescendo) is indicated with the symbol >. Likewise, accents are written with the symbol > as in European-derived music.

The term *tone system* is commonly employed in this book as an analytical tool. A tone system is an arbitrary arrangement (determined by analytical evaluation) of the pitches used by a singer in a song (song section) or by an instrumentalist in his or her musical performance; additionally, it is used to mean an arbitrary arrangement of pitches of a musical instrument. A tone system derived from a musical performance (as opposed to that of a musical instrument) is usually written in a descending order because a majority of the Warao songs descend rather than ascend. In addition, a tone system is often meant to show a hierarchy of pitches based on frequency of occurrence, melodic movement, and other characteristics derived from analytical evaluation. The most frequent pitch of a song (the pitch that appears most often and which is the musical point of rest) is called the "principal tone" (PT); it is indicated by a whole note (𝅝) and is given the cipher 1. The tone that often occurs just above the principal tone is referred to as the "supporting tone" (ST), indicated by a half note (𝅗𝅥). The PT and ST form what I refer to as the terminating or foundation interval of many forms of Warao music. Other tones that progressively occur less than the PT and ST are secondary supporting tones; they are indicated in the tone systems by a quarter note (𝅘𝅥) or a quarter note without a stem (•).

1 Introduction:
Fieldwork and Musical Contexts

Following a thirty-month tour with the Peace Corps in Santiago, Chile, that lasted from 1966 to 1968, my wife, Diane, and I left the Andes Mountains and traveled throughout the Amazon rain forest in Peru, Colombia, and Brazil. Before returning to the United States, we lived for a while in Trinidad in 1969. I did not realize that another rain forest existed in the Orinoco Delta, just a canoe ride from the southern shores of Trinidad and far north of the Amazon River (figure 1.1); and I was not aware that a large hill in San Fernando in southern Trinidad was a sacred mountain of the Warao native Americans who live in the delta of the Orinoco River in Venezuela. I did not hear of the Warao until a few years later, when I moved to Los Angeles to pursue a doctorate in ethnomusicology at UCLA. One day in 1971, while Diane and I were attending an anthropology class on South American Indians, an intellectual experience with the professor, Dr. Johannes Wilbert, changed my life. In a discussion after class, I volunteered to transcribe a Warao shamanistic rain chant for him (Wilbert 1993, 228–29). He spoke these words: "Why don't you study the music of the Warao?" Why not, I thought; and after another year of studying and acquiring grant money for field work, I left for Caracas, Venezuela.

Field Method

My first encounter with the rain forest of the lower Orinoco River was in 1972, when I went to Venezuela to do dissertation research with the Warao. This book is a result of my musical and cultural experiences during four months in 1972, one month in 1973, and two months in 1974. I spent most of my time with the Warao in the central Orinoco River Delta, where I lived in the extended family village of Yaruara Akoho on the Winikina River (figure 1.2). From there I occasionally traveled to other villages to attend musical events, make new friends,

Figure 1.1. Location of the Orinoco Delta in South America. Cartography by Dale A. Olsen.

or just enjoy the sights and smells of the rain forest with any number of willing Warao young people as guides (figure 1.3).

In 1972 I was in the Orinoco Delta for one purpose—to learn everything I could about Warao music and especially to focus on its role within Warao shamanism. During later field trips I continued my study of Warao music, focusing on other areas of music and magic.

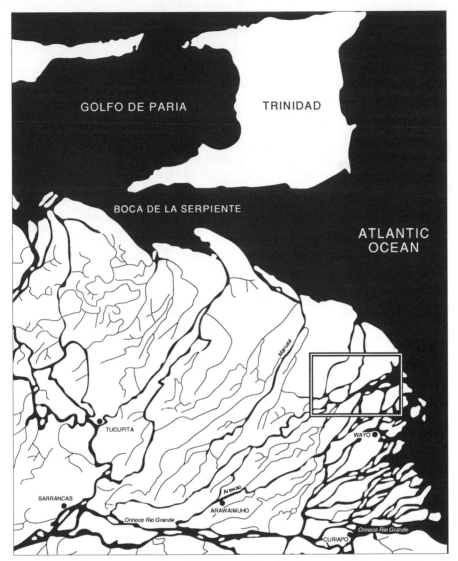

Figure 1.2. The Orinoco Delta of Venezuela (Delta Amacuro Federal Territory) and its proximity to Trinidad. Cartography by Robert R. Burke.

The study of indigenous cultures of Venezuela is an important focus at UCLA, largely because of the work and influence of Johannes Wilbert. Therefore, I knew precisely what I wanted to do in the Orinoco Delta rain forest, although I had several backup topics, such as musical instruments, lullabies, secular music, and so forth. The logistics of my fieldwork were greatly expedited by my association with

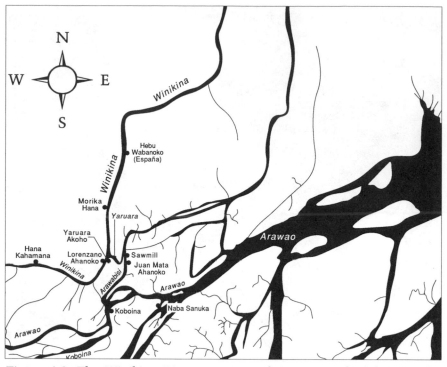

Figure 1.3. The Winikina River area, central Orinoco Delta, showing the Warao villages where research was conducted. Cartography by Robert R. Burke.

Dr. Wilbert. I was told by many Warao in Yaruara Akoho that, because I am a friend of "el doctor Wiber," I am also their friend. During several of my field trips to the delta, Sr. Cesáreo Soto, Dr. Wilbert's personal guide and a Winikina-Warao by birth, met me in Barrancas and transported me to Yaruara Akoho, deep within the rain forest of the central Orinoco Delta.

Rain forest river travel in South America can be very unpredictable, and certain events took place during my field trips that, at the time, I could not describe as perfect successes. Travel to the center of the Orinoco Delta rain forest on a graduate-student budget was frustrating; and mechanical mishaps with outboard motors were common for me, as the following excerpt from a letter to my wife and son attests (dated 30 June 1972):

> I really don't believe it, but here I am. Why don't I believe it?
> It's a long story—21 hours long. The trip from Barrancas (to

the Guayo mission) should take only eight hours, but ours lasted 21 hours. Tell Dr. Wilbert that even his 33 horsepower outboard motor can't compete with the water spirits. Halfway between Araguaymujo (mission) and Guayo (mission) the oil drain screw vibrated loose, all the oil escaped, water entered the shaft, the ball-bearings burnt up as a result, and the motor suddenly stopped. The oil drain screw is at the very bottom of the motor, the part that's in the water, so we couldn't see anything happening. We took the foot apart and saw the bad news. So there we were, 12:00 noon, hot sun, in the middle of nowhere without a motor, and nobody around for miles on either side of us. The current of the river moves fast, and there was a strong wind blowing the opposite direction. Since the boat was big, the wind and current balanced out and we sat still. Finally we hooked up to a large bunch of floating weeds that carried us around the bend in the river where the wind did not reach us; then we paddled—only two paddles for four people. This lasted until the next curve where we picked up more weeds. We finally reached a ranchería—the first Warao settlement—at 7:00 P.M. (it was dark). We rented their small motor—three of the Warao (from that settlement) went along to run the motor, pulling their canoe behind. . . . Cesáreo said it would take another three hours, and it would have had this other motor also not broken down in the middle of a little stream about as wide as Sawtelle Blvd. So there we sat, drifting into weeds, trees, etc. while the muchachos were trying to fix *their* motor. Then it began to rain just as they got the motor going, and it really rained hard. When it stopped raining we putted for a while longer until the motor failed again, this time for good. After almost an hour of trying to fix it, Cesáreo decided we should paddle—we had four paddles now. So the little canoe set out and so did we. We finally arrived (to Guayo) after 2:00 A.M.—the mission was locked and everybody was asleep. Hans (a German student who is accompanying us) and I put up our hammocks on a launch belonging to the padres. Everything was fine until it began to rain, and it rained so hard and so long that the splashing of the water and the rain blown by the wind soaked us. . . . When

we woke up at 6:30 A.M. there were Waraos sitting around on
the dock, I guess to see what we were.

After several days Cesáreo transported me to Naba Sanuka mission
where I spent several additional days with Padre Damián del Blanco.
From there we made our way to the village of Yaruara Akoho on the
Winikina River, where Cesáreo left me. I arrived just one day after the
schoolteacher in Yaruara Akoho left for her home on the Venezuelan
mainland and was thus able to move into the room in the schoolhouse
that she had vacated (figure 1.4). This gave me some privacy (a very
un-Warao concept): I was able to set up my hammock and mosquito
net (figure 1.5); and I even had my own outhouse, although I soon realized it was risky to walk across the rickety footbridge to use the la-
trine (figure 1.6). (Indeed, crossing the walkways from one piling
house to another was dangerous for someone who weighed at least
twice as much as the typical Warao male.)

Just before I left Los Angeles, I was fortunate to meet Dr. Heinz Dieter Heinen, another former anthropology student of Professor Wilbert
and today one of the great authorities on the Warao. (He is highly respected and loved by the Winikina-Warao, who call him "Jaino.") Dr.
Heinen visited me in Yaruara Akoho several times, bringing me news
from home or just offering moral support, as I wrote in a letter to
Diane and Darin (dated 14 July 1972): "It's nice having Heino here. It's
the first English I've used in some time. We just returned from a trip to
what was supposed to be to a Warao village, but because Wilbert's
motor broke down again we putted into the sawmill to have it fixed.
There Renaud (the Creole owner of the sawmill) invited us for dinner.
We also bought a lot of supplies such as eggs, corned beef, milk, etc.
which Heino . . . put on the bill of a (Venezuelan) governmental fellow
who's coming." Indeed, those supplies were gourmet food to me because my usual diet consisted of rice cooked with a variety of canned
sardines. (Three types of canned sardines could be purchased at the
sawmill—in hot sauce, mustard sauce, or oil. I have not eaten a sardine
since!)

I began recording Warao music almost immediately upon my arrival in Yaruara Akoho—beginning, in fact, on my first evening there.
My room in the small schoolhouse became my recording studio. I
made simultaneous recordings with a Nagra III reel-to-reel tape

Figure 1.4. Bernardo Jiménez Tovar and his family on the dock in front of the schoolhouse where I lived in Yaruara Akoho, Winikina River, Delta Amacuro Federal Territory, Venezuela.

Figure 1.5. Warao children inside my room in the schoolhouse.

Figure 1.6. The deck off my room in the schoolhouse and the bridge to the outhouse.

recorder and a Concord cassette recorder. Subsequent evenings of music making and listening to the playbacks were fun social occasions for everybody involved. Someone would sing one or more songs, and I would play the performance back on my cassette recorder, much to the delight of the artist and his or her friends. Then another would sing and so on throughout the evening. The Warao had no fear that the máquina (machine or tape recorder) would capture their words (hence, their souls), as Kenneth Good experienced among the Yano-mamö in the upper Orinoco of Venezuela (Good and Chanoff 1991, 88). During the days I often transliterated and translated the song texts sung during the previous evenings with assistance from the singers or other Warao teachers. After several weeks of such musical evenings I had a very good idea of who the Warao themselves considered to be their best singers and who among them were the most knowledgeable about Warao world view. I then made arrangements to hire those singers and teachers to record their songs individually. Almost all my teachers were shamans, and most were bilingual in Warao and Spanish. I usually made transliterations and translations of the song texts the same day I recorded the songs, working with the singers themselves. For playback I used my Concord cassette recorder to make a work tape of each musical event. While recording the music simultaneously with a Nagra III tape recorder, I used an Electrovoice RE-15 microphone; both the Nagra's and the Concord's microphones were supported by the same table microphone stand, with the RE-15 suspended in a shock mount. For these full-day recording sessions I paid each teacher about double the amount he could earn by working at the nearby sawmill. In several cases I recorded, over a period of many days, all the songs some singers knew. Several times Antonio Lorenzano, a very knowledgeable shaman, requested that we record his supernatural songs at the Spanish Capuchín mission of Naba Sanuka, away from the ears of his family and other villagers. I thought recording at the mission might create a paradoxical situation for him, but the atmosphere did not hinder him. He was, in fact, mission educated—another paradox, I thought, but a characteristic that did not conflict with his traditional Warao cosmological knowledge and beliefs.

I was soon to discover that a study of shamanism is not an easy task. It involves logistic, linguistic, and human communication considerations of the most personal kind as well as an entire realm of intangibles and undiscussables. I realized, however, that music sharing between me and the Warao bridged communication gaps and allowed a musical-cultural rapport to be developed. One of my first tasks in the delta was to learn several Warao secular songs called dakotutuma or dance songs (canciones de baile). Almost every evening, I played these for my new Warao friends on my plastic soprano recorder as we sat on the dock watching the sunset, stars, and satellites. We exchanged songs— they taught me some of theirs and I taught them some of mine. The children called me "Sr. Jingle Bells" because that was their favorite song. In this process of music exchange I became a pupil of several of the Warao musicians and in one situation became a shaman's apprentice (see chapter 9). In those roles I recorded and learned many songs. Therefore, although they were recorded in my studio, the singers' houses, or the Naba Sanuka mission, many of the songs can be considered contextually transmitted because of the student-teacher relationship. Just as his uncle Salvador had taught his supernatural songs to his nephew Antonio Lorenzano, Antonio taught them to me.

As the Warao of the Winikina River became more familiar with me and my commitment to know more about their music, I was invited to attend shamanistic curing rituals and make additional contextual recordings of Warao music. Most of these rituals took place during the evenings, although in some urgent cases they were held during daylight hours (see cover photo). Before the events began, and with the concurrence of the officiating shaman (who was most often a teacher and friend of mine), I hung my microphones from the rafters of the house directly above the patient's hammock. These were placed in a manner that was not obtrusive to the shaman as he conducted his work.

Although I studied Warao before and during my fieldwork in Venezuela, all my research among them was conducted in Spanish because the majority of Warao men speak Spanish. Translation of Warao religious song texts, however, is difficult because of their unusual semantic code: they are often transmitted in an archaic and ritual language. I have chosen, therefore, not to present the majority of the shamanistic song texts literally in this book, although they were usually translated that way. One mistake I made, however, was believing a young Warao man who claimed to know the language of the shamans (which he did not) and hiring him to translate many of the songs I recorded during my first month in the field. (He liked the money.) Most of my second field trip was spent retranslating certain texts, this time in consultation with the shamans themselves, who explained, in current Warao, the meanings of the ritualistic and often archaic words and phrases. I worked closely with Cesáreo Soto, an educated, bilingual Warao who was paid by UCLA to collect, transcribe, and translate Warao mythology for Dr. Wilbert. The song texts were then translated into Spanish by Cesáreo, sentence by sentence, and subsequently translated into English by me. This body of sung literature can be referred to as "shamanic lore . . . a genre pertaining to ritual. It is spoken or chanted by religious practitioners during public ceremonies and in the course of shamanic initiations. Therefore, shamanic lore is not as thoroughly in the public domain as [secular] kinds of narrative but forms part of the esoteric repertoire of the religious elite" (Wilbert 1985, 147). Additionally, because the religious songs are esoteric and the Warao religious elite often come from different villages or learn their knowledge from different teachers, melodic and textual variations often occur.

Following the practices of Wilbert, Heinen, and other scholars of the Warao, I have also used the real names of my teachers in this book. Unlike the Yanomamö and possibly other rain forest cultures of South America, the Warao do not have taboos against allowing people to speak their names. This is because their present names have been acquired by Christian "baptism or by assuming the name of a missionary, nun or 'criollo' they like" (Suárez 1971, 90). Among themselves, the Warao usually use their own kinship terms or, more rarely, nicknames.

Native Contexts for Music

Native South American cultures do not usually conceptualize music and music making as we do, and not all that we call music is music to them. Similarly, many of the native South American's nonspeech aural phenomena are not considered by them to be music. Indeed, much native South American organized sound communication (other than speech) consists of predetermined pitched vocal phenomena (what we would call songs) for curing illnesses or healing wounds and is called by some "falling into a trance" (among the Selk'nam), "reciting" (among the Cuna), "moving the mouth and lips," or "conversing" (among the Warao) (Olsen 1980b, 365).

At a very specific level, native South American musical systems are as diverse as South American Indian languages. It is believed that there were 1,492 different languages spoken when the Spanish arrived in South America (Loukotka 1968, 17). Likewise, the varieties of South America's geography and ecosystem have caused specific and diverse musical systems to develop. Nevertheless, native South American contexts for music making can be generally placed into three large categories: pleasure, utility, and theurgy. The first category, pleasure, is perhaps the smallest of the three, consisting of songs and instrumental music used for amusement and songs for social dancing. The second category, utility, includes more music genres than the first, such as lullabies, songs for social control, music for work, some festival music, and so on. Although reference to the supernatural may be made, it is often secondary to the utilitarian nature of the music. The last category, theurgy, contains the largest number of musical types, including all the shamanistic and nonshamanistic songs that pertain to cosmology or call upon supernatural forces in one way or another. These may include shamanistic songs for curing illnesses or causing illness and death, shamanistic initiation, dreaming, making rain, assuring good harvest or fertility, and other forms of power. The theurgy category may also include nonshamanistic songs for magical protection, magical love or courtship, cutting down trees to build large canoes, healing wounds and certain natural disorders of the human body, funeral and wailing, and many others. While many of these categories are general (and there are exceptions as well as areas where they overlap), shamanism is one the most important contexts for what can be termed music making among native South Americans.

Shamanism and Other Native Musical/Spiritual Specializations

Many scholars agree that the most likely etymology of the word shaman is *saman*, from the Tungus people of Siberia (Eliade 1972, 4, 495; Harner 1973a, xi; Jensen 1963, 214; Lessa and Vogt 1965, 452). Other origins are possible, however, such as the Sanskrit word *scharamana* (Haro Alvear 1973, 9) or *sramana* (Ellingson, personal communication); the Pali word *samana* (Eliade 1972, 495); and others (see Eliade 1972, 495–97). Mihály Hoppál (1987, 91–92) links the Sanskrit term *saman*, meaning "song," to shamanism, as he writes: "This implies that the shaman is literally the person who sings the song, with long genealogies, to cure, to conjure, to heal. He is not simply an 'ascetic,' but also a wise man and poet." This link between singer and wise person is certainly relevant in most South American forms of shamanism. If there is a universal among South American shamans, it is that they sing for power.

Hereafter in this book the masculine pronouns he, his, or him will be used to modify the term shaman. Although in some regions of the Americas female shamans are found, most shamans are male; among the Warao, especially, male shamans are the norm. (See, however, Wilbert 1987b, 2, who writes that among the Warao "most adults, male and female, are shamans of one sort or another. Even the people who excel at particular crafts, such as boat or hammock builders [the latter being women], are shamanic craftsmen.") I do not imply sexism in my choice of the masculine pronouns. If I were writing about the Mapuche, for example, where female shamans are the norm, I would use feminine pronouns. Additionally, if shamans were equally distributed among females and males among the Warao (which they are not, although men and women probably equally engage in some sort of theurgical activity), I would also use feminine pronouns.

Just as the etymology of the word shaman is debatable, so is a definition of shamanism. I consider shamanism to fall broadly within Lessa and Vogt's description of religion (1972, 1):

> Religion may be described as a system of beliefs and practices directed toward the "ultimate concern" of a society. "Ultimate concern," a concept used by Paul Tillich, has two aspects—meaning and power. It has meaning in the sense of ultimate meaning of the central values of a society, and it has power in the sense of ultimate, sacred, or supernatural power which stands behind those values.

I define shamanism specifically as a religious specialist's individual role of bridging the natural and supernatural worlds, using techniques such as direct contact with and transformation into the supernatural via a particular state of consciousness (trance) that often includes flights of ecstasy (out-of-body experiences). This state of consciousness has been called ASC or Altered State of Consciousness (Tart 1969) and, more recently, SSC or Shamanic State of Consciousness (Harner 1987, 3). In this book I call it TSC or Theurgical State of Consciousness. I chose this term because a shaman communicating with the supernatural may not consider his particular state of consciousness "altered"; it may instead be the "normal" state. Moreover, people other than shamans can and do acquire such particular levels of awareness.

The shaman in a TSC mediates between the mortal and immortal, often via ecstatic flights to the cosmic world. Eliade (1972, 4) has defined shamanism as a "technique of ecstasy," and differentiates between the shaman, the medicine man, and the magician. Because of the uncertainty of these terms, as Eliade (1972, 3) explains, other writers have used them "interchangeably to designate certain individuals possessing magico-religious powers and found in all 'primitive' societies." By "technique of ecstasy" he means that the shaman, in a trancelike state, is believed to travel to the outer limits of his or her cosmos (1972, 5), while the medicine man or woman, the sorcerer, and the magician do not. Like the medicine man and the sorcerer, the shaman is also believed to cure and inflict illness. The shaman, however, uses a method of curing that is distinctly his own: through his control of the spirits he is able to communicate with them and seek their help (Eliade 1972, 6). There is, moreover, a deeper level of communication involved between the shaman and the spirits: the transformation of the shaman into a spirit itself. Loeb, writing in 1929, makes a similar distinction between what he called "shaman" and "seer" (cited in Ackerknecht 1971, 66), although he used the term "possession," explaining that the shaman is an inspirational type of practitioner who is possessed and *through* whom the spirit speaks, while the seer is the noninspirational, nonpossessed practitioner *with* whom the spirit speaks (Ackerknecht 1971, 66, emphasis mine). He also explains that the shaman, found in Siberia, Asia, Africa, India, Melanesia, Fiji, and Polynesia, developed later than the seer, who is found as the so-called medicine man of North and South America and also in Australia, New Guinea, and among the Negritoes (Ackerknecht 1971, 66). The distinction drawn by Loeb, however, may be an inaccurate generalization. Some cultures may contain both types of practitioners, as he reported finding in Indonesia and as are found in South America among the native Americans. In addition, there is confusion about the terms possession and transformation. It appears, in fact, that Loeb may have confused these terms. Rouget (1985, 132) has explained three dichotomies between what he calls transformation (shamanism) and possession (such as found in many African-derived religions in the Caribbean and Brazil). Summarized in table 1.1, these three points of contrast serve well for describing the Winikina-Warao of Venezuela, while they may not be useful for other native South Americans. (Hereafter I will use "Warao" to refer to the Winikina subtribe.) Among the Warao, for example, many shamans explained the transformation concept to me as a spirit speaking through the shaman because the shaman *is* the spirit. In other instances, Warao shamans explained that they also speak *with* the spirit.

The term medicine man is applied more frequently to North American native peoples than South American, perhaps because of ethnocentrism among early North American settlers and the fact that using

Table 1.1. Dichotomies between shamanism and possession cult

Shamanism	Possession cult
Journey to the spirits	Visit by the spirits
Control over the spirits	Submission to the spirits
Voluntary trance	Involuntary trance

organic medicine to cure illnesses (very common in North America) is more obvious to whites because it is more easily seen than spiritual medicine. I do not use the term *medicine man* in this book because of its overuse and association with native North American practitioners.

The term *priest,* which is also found in the literature, refers to the religious practitioner who conducts rituals for his community rather than strictly for himself, another person, or a group of people who solicit his aid. Such rituals consist of a body of knowledge that is learned and passed on by inheritance from teacher to apprentice. In some cultures, such as the Warao, it is possible to be a shaman and a priest simultaneously (see also Lessa and Vogt 1972, 381–82, and chapter 7 in this book).

Sorcerer, magician, and *witch doctor* are also unacceptable terms to describe the various kinds of specialists found in South American indigenous cultures. In popular usage these words connote the ethnocentric image of a charlatan who, perhaps by sleight of hand, is able to perform numerous tasks. More specifically, according to Eliade (1972, 4) the sorcerer, magician, and witch doctor do not employ a technique of ecstacy that is associated with the shaman who is contacting the supernatural.

While shamanism should be considered a religion because of its spiritual dimensions, it differs from organized religions because it does not involve the service and adoration of a god as expressed in worship and ritual observances. Michael Harner (1987, 4–5) prefers not to classify shamanism as a religion but as a method related to the religion known as animism. He writes:

> Shamanism ultimately is only a method, not a religion with a fixed set of dogmas. Therefore people arrive at their own experience-derived conclusions about what is going on in the universe, and about what term, if any, is most useful to

describe ultimate reality. . . . It is a method which is often associated with the religion known as animism, but distinct from it. Animism is basically the belief in spirits, and spirits are defined in shamanism simply as those things or beings which are normally not seen by people in an ordinary state of consciousness, but are seen by the shaman in the SSC [Shamanic State of Consciousness]. Moreover, they are entities that the shaman respects, having some sort of integrity or power.

Numerous references discuss the role of accessories used by South American shamans to achieve a state of ecstasy, such as a drum, a rattle, a sacred bench, tobacco, a post that is climbed, and so forth (see Métraux 1944, 217–19 and Eliade 1972, 172–80). Another term used is "psychotechnical expedients," which can include "darkness, monotonous chanting, rhythmical drumming, hours of inertia, solitude, fasting, narcotics of all kinds, physical fatigue, and dancing" (Jensen 1963, 233). Both accessory and psychotechnical expedient, however, imply something secondary; to the shaman who is using an object or action, that object or action is primary and vital to his shamanic powers. The use of a power object or device is often a culturally conditioned means to an end, that end being communication with the supernatural or transformation into a supernatural entity. Words that may better characterize a shamanic object or action include tool, which stresses the work function, or medium, which emphasizes the communicative role.

Many writers have missed the significance of song as a shamanic tool or medium. The most common musical expedient is usually described as monotonous chanting, a term often used to mean a nonspeech form that is regarded (by the outsider) as too simple to be called song. This bias, however, must be discarded. Song can be defined simply as words set to melody, and melody can be single toned (static) or multitoned (active). The term chant should be employed only to mean "to extol" or "to praise," as with the French word *chanter*, and not for suggesting something that is vocally primitive or lacking complexity. According to Eliade, in the realm of shamanic curing, song is the actual evoking of and communicating with the spirits (1972, 96, 100, 227, 290, 303–6). The song text, however, is almost always the focal point that determines the definition of song as used by Eliade and others, and it is the song text that is believed to carry the weight of evoking the spirits and the subsequent communication with them. Therefore, such nonmusical words as chant, oration, prayer, incantation, and recitation are often used. To writers who have little knowledge of music outside the European art tradition, the actual music—the carrier of the song text—is often considered to be secondary.

Music, including pitch, contour, tone quality, and dynamics, however, is a very important and necessary power tool for many kinds of theurgy. Many native South American cultures, in fact, use melody without words during shamanistic rituals. For example, the Yanomamö of Venezuela often buzz their lips rather than sing words; the Pilagá of the Gran Chaco sing "monotonously in rising and falling tones" to a melody that "has no words, although the shaman may order the evil to go away" (Métraux 1946, 362); the Jungle Quichua of the Napo River region of eastern Ecuador use the violin and a bird bone flute plus occasional whistling to contact the supernatural (Whitten 1979); the descendants of the Moche in the Peruvian north coast whistle to communicate with the spirits (Gushiken 1977, 115–16); and the cholos ("urbanized . . . Indians" in Peruvian terminology, according to Katz and Dobkin de Rios 1971, 321) and other inhabitants living in and around Iquitos, Peru, employ whistling as a technique of ecstasy for curing (Dobkin de Rios 1972, 131–33).

The most important function of the shaman, for which song is used either indirectly or directly, is the curing of illnesses. The indirect association of song with curing is often prefatory to the actual physical contact between the shaman and his patient—that is, before he attempts to effect a cure. During this time the shaman usually calls his helping spirits, and song is the most important vehicle for such communication.

Among the Yanomamö and many other cultures, shamans often sing and dance while contacting the spirits; the Warao, however, do not dance while making spirit contact, perhaps because they live and cure where there is no ground upon which to dance. Much of the dance behavior of the Yanomamö is influenced by the use of hallucinogens that enable them to "see" the spirits they become transformed into. Hallucinogens are important shamanic tools in many cultures, although the Warao do not use them. Eliade considers the use of narcotics to be indicative of a decadent form of shamanism, functioning as a substitute for "pure" trance (1972, 401). To ascribe such a bias to the use of drugs in non-European cultures, however, is ethnocentric because among some nations, such as the Mazatecs of Mexico, the hallucinogen actually embodies the divinity (Boilès 1978, 162). While the Warao form of shamanic ecstasy is not dependent upon drugs, many shamans use tobacco smoke from a nonhallucinogenic cigar (wina) as a shamanic tool in addition to song. Nevertheless, song seems to be more important because it is continuous; and a shaman would never inflict or cure illnesses without it. In contrast, inflicting and curing illness without tobacco does occur among the Warao.

Throughout South American autochthonous cultures there are at least three types of shamanistic illnesses, including spirit intrusion, soul loss, and improper balance with nature. The first of these is the only type the Warao possess—the intrusion of a spiritual essence of either an object (believed by the Warao to be the physical quality of the object), an animal, a part of an animal, its movement, a spirit itself, or any combination of these into the body of the patient. Intrusion illness is caused by either a spirit, a shaman acting on behalf of a spirit, or a shaman acting on his own behalf. Song is extremely important in the curing of all these forms of shamanistic illnesses.

Warao shamans employ a complex array of song types, each defined by a distinct melodic formula and designed for a particular use. These songs provide shamans with power for communicating with the supernatural in order to cure illnesses and occasionally cause illnesses and death. In addition, Warao of many ages sing power songs for various reasons, each discussed in particular chapters of this book. Even some nonreligious songs such as lullabies and dance songs have certain attributes of power associated with them, although the latter are disguised as music for pleasure. Why certain types of music have power to the Warao is a most difficult question to answer because it involves the spiritual reality of the Warao and how they relate to it.

2 The Warao:
Canoe People of the Rain Forest

Sometimes first impressions of an area are colored by logistical diffi-
culties, lack of sleep, rain, and other discomforts. In spite of my day
and a half of canoe motoring, drifting, paddling, and getting soaked (it
was the rainy season), my first impressions of the Orinoco Delta were
memorable in a very positive way. In a letter to my family (dated 1 July
1972), I wrote the following perhaps typical graduate-student description of the rain forest from the mission at Guayo (Wayo), deep within
the waterways of the Orinoco Delta:

> I didn't say anything to you about the scenery. [The rain forest
> is] similar to that of the Amazon and its tributaries except
> that the trees aren't as tall. Since we were paddling and
> drifting I got to see it up close and also to hear it. It's beau-
> tiful, and has all kinds of birds including parrots. Towards
> dark we saw big turkey-like birds in the trees and after dark
> we saw several small crocodiles called *babas*. The noises of
> the jungle at night are something else.

The Setting and the People

The tropical rain forest and the intricate maze of waterways of the
Orinoco Delta, known as the Delta Amacuro Federal Territory, are
easily navigated by canoes or other shoal draft boats (see figure 1.2).
There are no rapids or cataracts and few obstacles except for shoals
during low tide or the dry season, fallen trees blocking one's path, and
flotsam. There are few dangerous animals, snakes, or underwater
threats (except for stingrays, electric eels, and caribes [piranhas]).
Wilbert (1980b, 3) writes the following about the Orinoco Delta:

> The Orinoco Delta is a fan of alluvial deposits bounded on
> the south by the Río Grande and on the west by the Manamo
> River which branches off the main river at Barrancas, the

apex of the Delta. From Barrancas it is about 180 kilometers along the Río Grande to the Atlantic Ocean and an equal distance along the Manamo to the Caribbean Sea. Most of this low-lying triangle is a vast tidal swamp, lacking in dry ground and stone. The waters of the Orinoco are discharged through the Delta by the Río Grande, the principal channel, and through eight so-called *caños* known as Merehina, Sacupana, Araguao, Macareo, Tucupita, Pedernales, Cocuina, and Manamo. Connecting these major branches are innumerable smaller *caños* that form a network of navigable waterways over the entire Delta. The region is splintered by these crisscrossing *caños* into a multitude of islands of varying sizes.

He continues with a description of the rain forest itself (1980b, 3–4):

The islands of the Orinoco Delta are covered with macrothermal pluvial forest. The Lower Delta is the growing edge of the swamp, a coastal belt of mangroves. Typical of such environments, the soil is almost always inundated, thus providing ideal conditions for the pioneering red mangrove (*Rhizophora mangle*). Of great importance to the Warao is that mangrove forests die at the center rather than on the periphery, so that the dying core areas can be invaded by such food-producing and otherwise most useful palms as the moriche (*Mauritia flexuosa*), several species of the manaca (*Euterpe*), and the temiche (*Manicaria saccifera*), as well as by other trees and plants. . . . The flora of the Intermediate Delta is otherwise quite diverse. The banks of wide rivers often present asymmetrical forest galleries. Medium-high, twisted trees, smothered with lianas, flank the riverbank that catches the current. On that side semiche, manaca, and macanilla (*Bactris*) palms struggle through the dense mat of *Hirtella*, *Parkia*, and *Bixa*. On the opposite side of such winding rivers, where the water flows more slowly, tall palms and trees shoot up from behind a barrier of Araceae. *Oenocarpus*, *Euterpe*, *Hymenaea courbaril*, *Bombacopsis*, and *Acrodiclidium* are among the giants. Epiphytic plants are less conspicuous on these trees but become more abundant on those along the banks of smaller waterways with little or no current. Here they grow like cobwebs, shrouding the thick palms and other trees which symmetrically flank the riverbanks. *Manicaria, Oenocarpus, Pachira insignis, Ficus, Inga,* and *Bauhinia* are common.

The native inhabitants of this complex delta call themselves Warao, glossed as "canoe people" (*wa* = canoe; *arao* = owners of), a fitting auto-designation for a culture whose only mode of transportation from childhood through death is the dugout canoe (figure 2.1). (A cadaver is "buried" in a canoe.) The majority of the Warao (also spelled Warrau, Guarao, Guarauno; see Kirchoff 1948, 869) group themselves in extended families and live in piling houses along the swampy shores of rivers (figure 2.2). While the Warao refer to each of these settlement villages as a ranchería, I will use the English term village to refer to a cluster of Warao houses forming an extended family nucleus. Because the Orinoco Delta is a web of rivers and streams that dissects approximately 10,200 square miles of one of the few remaining tropical rain forests of northern South America, the Warao are now a riverine fishing people. Before becoming a fishing culture, they were primarily gatherers and occasional hunters, living in the monte or the inner part of many deltaic islands and establishing their villages next to moriche palm groves called morichales. The moriche palm, then and today, has provided the Warao with the essentials of life, including mortal food for themselves and spiritual food for their kanobotuma (literally, "our grandfathers") or gods (figure 2.3). Today they have also added horticulture to their food quest activities. It has always been essential for the Warao to travel through the swampy rain forest by land and later by water, either in search of food or cosmological sustenance or simply to pay a visit to other Warao.

Since before the Spanish Encounter, the Warao have lived in the dense and swampy Orinoco Delta; and until recently their isolation has kept them relatively free from contact with European- and African-derived cultures, as Wilbert (1983, 357) relates: "The Delta of the Orinoco River, home of the Warao Indians, has lain like a boulder amidst this torrent of human migration. Witnessing the havoc which unknown pestilence wrought on the islands, along the coast and throughout the lower Orinoco basin, the Warao withdrew into the sanctuary of the Delta swamps where they weathered the storm of de-

Figure 2.1. Menegildo Paredes and his family leaving in the family canoe. The first task is to bail out the rainwater.

Figure 2.2. Chief Cirilo Rivero's house in Yaruara Akoho, adjacent to the schoolhouse.

Figure 2.3. The sun setting across the Winikina River with a moriche palm at high tide, from the deck outside the back door of my room in the schoolhouse.

sanctuary of the Delta swamps where they weathered the storm of destruction that ravaged the land."

For this reason the Warao are still large in number and rich in their traditional culture. Extensive missionization did not begin until 1925 when Spanish Capuchín missionaries began to establish mission schools in the delta. Even today Spanish missions have control of the area; and Protestant missionization, so common in other parts of the South American tropical rain forest, has not occurred. Other recent acculturative forces include Creole-built and -owned sawmills that attract occasional buyers, sellers, traders, adventurers, and entrepreneurs from the outside; oil-exploration teams; road and dike builders; Creole settlers; and anthropologists and other scientists. Creole is the English form of the Spanish word criollo, meaning in Venezuela "a Venezuelan whose ancestors have interbred for several generations among whites, Indians, and blacks" (Wilbert 1980b, 4n. 1). The anthropologists and other scientists who have studied the Warao for decades include Venezuelans (especially from the Fundación La Salle and the Instituto Venezolano de Investigaciones Científicas), Americans (especially from UCLA), and Germans.

Today the Warao number approximately 19,500 individuals (Oficina Central de Estadística e Informática 1985, 38) grouped into about 250 villages throughout the central Orinoco Delta (Wilbert 1980b, 4; 1981b, 129). They are "socially and politically organized into subtribes, each consisting of several bands from twenty-five to sixty members. Each band is made up of a number of uxorilocal extended families and nuclear family households" (Wilbert 1980b, 7). An additional small number of Warao, known as the "Spanish Warao," inhabit the swampy coast lands of Guyana between the Orinoco Delta and the Pomeroon River (Wilbert 1970, 21). They have mixed with the Spanish and are today an acculturated group. The total number is large, as Wilbert (1980b, 4) explains: "This makes the Warao one of the largest tribal societies of Lowland South America, inhabiting, surprisingly enough, a geographical area which otherwise has been depopulated of Indians since the Discovery."

According to Joseph Greenberg (1987, 106), the language of the Warao (Warrau) belongs to the large Chibchan-Paezan phylum, making them distant relatives of the Amazonian Yanomamö with whom they also share religious and musical characteristics. This linguistic affiliation, however, is strongly debated, as other scholars claim an independent status for Warao.

The most isolated and also the most unacculturated Warao are those who live in the central delta of the Orinoco, on the Winikina River. They are also known as hoanarao, "people of the black water," because of the dark color of the low-oxygen river. (The Warao of the Arawabisi River, however, are of the same subtribe as the Winikina River Warao, according to Heinen [1972, 23], and together they form the Winikina-Arawabisi subtribe.) The most important villages along the Winikina River are Yaruara Akoho, also called Winikina Hanokoida and Barranquilla; Lorenzano Ahanoko, also called Ohidu Sanuka and Ori Kayanuka; Hana Kahamana; Moriki Hana; and Hebu Wabanoko, also called España (Wilbert and Layrisse 1980, 13–47, 168–76) (see figure 1.3). My principal teachers, their birth dates, and their residences in 1972 are given in table 2.1.

The Warao are culturally considered part of northern South America or the Caribbean, depending upon their cultural ties. They

Table 2.1. My principal Warao teachers, their birth dates,
and their residences in 1972

Name	Birth date	Residence in 1972
Juan Bustillo Calderón	1921	Hebu Wabanoko
Bernardo Jiménez Tovar	1929	Yaruara Akoho
Antonio Lorenzano	1914	Lorenzano Ahanoko
José Antonio Páez	1922	Moriki Hana
Menegildo Paredes	ca. 1945	Yaruara Akoho
Silbano Ramírez	1943	Lorenzano Ahanoko
Chano Rivero	1931	Lorenzano Ahanoko
Cirilo Rivero	1917	Yaruara Akoho
Florencia Rivero	ca. 1950	Yaruara Akoho
Pedro Rivero	1928	Lorenzano Ahanoko
Santiago Rivero	1937	Yaruara Akoho
Tirso Rivero	1951	Hebu Wabanoko
Isaías Rodríguez	1903	Hebu Wabanoko
Gabriel Sánchez	1907	Yaruara Akoho
Primitivo Sánchez	1947	Yaruara Akoho
Talejo Tovar	1911	Arawabisi
Melicia Torres	ca. 1940	Boca de Sakobana
Gerónimo Velásquez	1944	Yaruara Akoho
Jaime Zapata	1909	Yaruara Akoho

have a closer proximity to the Caribbean islands than any other native South American culture. Trinidad, for example, is only a short distance north of the Orinoco Delta. Still, because of cultural differences, anthropologists have designated the Warao as a tropical forest rather than a circum-Caribbean culture (Steward 1963, 1:12)—specifically as a "tribe of the Guianas" (Steward 1963, 3:xxvi). Nevertheless, many aspects of extant Warao culture are similar to the historical accounts of the Caribbean native Americans, especially the Taino or Island Arawak. Music, rituals, and the shaman's power seem to be similar; and the musical instruments of the Warao and the ancient Taino may have had commonalities (see chapter 4).

Warao Cosmology and Religion

For several decades, Johannes Wilbert has studied the Warao concept of their universe. Nevertheless, he explains his explorations into Warao metaphysics with this admonition (Wilbert 1975a, 163): "it is well to bear in mind that regional variations in cultural patterns do exist among the hundreds of local groups of the [Warao] and that the facts as described . . . best fit the Winikina. Furthermore, the information. . . is the result of interviewing many different religious practitioners, none of whom would necessarily know all of the data presented. . . . Much of this lore is based on the dream experiences of individual shamans, and differs in descriptive detail from informant to informant." My overview of Warao cosmology summarizes many of the data presented by Wilbert in conjunction with those of other scholars, including myself (Wilbert 1971, personal communication; 1972b; 1975a; 1979; 1981a; 1983; 1985).

Certain aspects of Warao cosmology may be influenced by natural geographic and astronomical phenomena visible in the Orinoco Delta and adjacent areas. For example, the Warao view their world as surrounded by water, which it nearly is. In the middle of their cosmic sea is the land mass upon which they live, flat and disk-shaped. Beneath their earth lies a lower world inhabited by a double-headed snake (Hahuba) that encircles the earth, exposed at times like a sandy beach with its two heads spaced apart to create an opening toward the east, just as the mouth (Boca Grande) of the Orinoco River creates an opening into the Atlantic Ocean. Hahuba's movements are believed to cause the ebb and flow of the tides. Beneath this "snake of being" is the goddess of the nadir, believed to be a four-headed serpent with deer horns on each head (Wilbert 1975a, 165). Humans have little or no contact or communication with these two supernatural creatures.

The Warao live at the center of this land mass, while at each of the cardinal and intercardinal points, across the water and at the very ends of the world (aitona), are sacred mountains or pillars upon which certain deities dwell. At the very edge of earth are smaller mountains where other deities live. These supreme beings are known as kanobotuma (plural of kanobo), which literally means "our ancient ones." (While the word is sometimes translated as "our grandfathers," Barral [1964, 35] points out that the designation has a much greater significance than that translation implies.)

The most powerful of the kanobotuma is Uraro, the god of the southern mountain in the aitona—geographically inspired, perhaps, by one of the central Guyanan tepui, or high mesas or table mountains south of the Orinoco Delta (Wilbert 1985, 151). Living nearby on a smaller hill on the edge of earth is Karoshima, Uraro's companion and near equal. Dr. Wilbert and I visited this hill (latitude 8°25′ N; longitude 61°19′ W; altitude 150 m; Wilbert 1979, 139) just south of the Río Grande of the Orinoco River in 1973. At that time it contained a mine (Venezuela's first commercial iron mine, dating from 1883), with electric lights adorning the opening of the mine shaft and visible from the river. The Warao elders in Yaruara Akoho told us of the voices of Karoshima (voices of the miners?) and his glowing eyes (lights in the mine shaft?) and warned us of sickness if we ventured too close. During that trip Dr. Wilbert's new fifty-five horsepower outboard motor broke down, and we drifted for hours on the Orinoco River, slowly being carried toward the Atlantic Ocean. We were finally rescued and towed to a Catholic mission, where I recuperated for several days from too much sun. (Was this the wrath of Karoshima?)

The kanobotuma of the south resemble toads in their godly states, although they can also assume human forms. They reside on their mountains in great mansions, with many subjects, golden horses, and several wives (Wilbert 1975a, 166).

At the opposite end of the Warao cosmos, on sacred mountains in the north, live Warowaro and Anabarima. The former is believed to be a supreme butterfly living on the northernmost sacred mountain in the aitona, while the latter lives on Nabarima Hill at the earth's northern-most edge—inspired, no doubt, by the actual Naparima Hill on the western coast of southern Trinidad (latitude 10°17´ N; longitude 61°28´ W; altitude 192 m; Wilbert 1979, 138). Anabarima is known as the "Father of the Waves," and his abode contains a cave where Haburi, the culture hero, lives with his mothers.

The kanobo of the eastern cosmic pillar in the aitona is Ariawara, the unapproachable god of origin whose geographic equivalent does not exist because it is in the Atlantic Ocean (Wilbert 1979, 148). Ari-awara's son, Mawari, called the "Creator Bird of the Dawn" by Wilbert (1972b, 65), is represented by a swallow-tailed kite (*Elanoides forfi-catus*) (Wilbert 1985, 151). Because it is situated at the end of the uni-verse where the sun rises, this easternmost cosmic zone (called hokonamu in shamanic texts) is most sacred to the Warao. The realm of light, it is misty like dawn and tobacco smoke and is the cosmolog-ical sector associated with bahanarotu shamanism. In the eschatology of the Warao it is a highly sought-after place to spend eternity.

The western extreme of the Warao universe is the world pillar of Hoebo, the god of the underworld and the supreme Hoa spirit. Hoebo is embodied by a deified scarlet macaw (*Ara chloroptera*) (Wilbert 1972b, 73), while his soul resides closer to earth at the edge of the celestial dome. This cosmic world is the ominous end of the universe where the sun sets, symbolized by the fiery sky of dusk, the bright feathers of the scarlet macaw, and the redness of human blood. It is the eternal place of death and darkness. Hoebo's body is forever cut off from the rest of the Warao cosmos; nevertheless, thirsty for human blood, he hungers for Warao souls and appears in dreams to hoarotu shamans, asking them for human food. There is no hope for those hu-mans who die of Hoa sickness.

At the intercardinal points of the southwest and the southeast re-sides a female supreme being, Dauarani, mother of the forest. Her body dwells on a mountain in the southwest and her soul on a moun-tain in the southeast. Also known as the goddess of the light, she is the patron of male artisans, especially canoe makers (Wilbert 1975a, 167). Astronomically, Dauarani's abodes correspond to the midsummer sun-rise and sunset. Likewise, at the points of the winter sunrise and sunset are sacred mountains that respectively house Aruarani, the mother of moriche flour, and Oriwakarotu, the god of the dance. Wilbert (1975a,

167) refers to these places as "the world mountains of sustenance and fertility deities," identified also "with the Natue, the Grandmothers, patronesses of the moriche palm."

Covering this complex Warao universe of water, land, sacred mountains, serpents, light, and darkness is a celestial dome shaped somewhat like an Indonesian knobbed gong, connected from its apex to the center of the earth by an *axis mundi,* or central pathway embedded from beneath the earth like a celestial tree. Warao shamans ascend the dome via the central pathway and travel to the world mountains via celestial roads. The apex or knob of the dome is inhabited by lesser-ranked kanobotuma. The most important of them is Yaukware, the god of the center of the world (Wilbert 1975a, 167). Yaukware was the first wisiratu shaman, who ascended the axis mundi with his sacred hebu mataro rattle and other ritual instruments and paraphernalia. With his son as his constant companion, he has never left his celestial home.

Also at the zenith of the celestial knobbed gong of the Warao is a supernatural guide, an eternal psychopomp who leads spiritual travelers to the east. Nameless, his exact location is also unknown. The third and final resident of the celestial knob is the soul of Hoebo. It is through his bloodstained house that doomed souls pass on their way to the eternal darkness of the west, only to be devoured by Hoebo.

Wilbert (1975a, 168) summarizes the Warao universe with such thoroughness that I will quote him in full:

> Thus we can distinguish five cosmic strata in the Warao universe: (a) the flat surface of the earth, (b) the cardinal and intercardinal gods on the world mountains at the horizonal ends of the world, (c) the gods residing on the imaginary belt mid-high around the bell-shaped cosmic vault, and (d) the gods and spirits of the center of the world at the zenith. Below the earth and the ocean is (e) the almost featureless and dark realm of the Goddess of the Nadir. This realm below is solid; it supports the earth, serves as the bottom of the ocean, and carries the world mountains. On the latter rests the cosmic vault which in its center is supported by the world axis.

Warao religious practitioners (wisiratu, bahanarotu, and hoarotu shamans) frequently travel the celestial paths in the Warao universe.

Without their supernatural knowledge the Warao would have no life after death, and their lives on earth would be meaningless. Additionally, the souls of the kanobotuma, known as hebutuma (plural of hebu) when they visit earth, can cause sickness and death to the Warao. Shamans are the only mediators between the mortal and immortal, and with their powers and knowledge they can cure illness and maintain stability in the Warao world.

Warao religion can be divided into two large areas: shamanism and Kanoboism. Wilbert (1972a, 113) refers to the latter phenomenon as a "temple-idol cult," and Heinen and Ruddle (1974, 125) call it a "kanobo cult." While there is much overlap, and the expertise of a particular shamanic type, the wisiratu, is employed in both, shamanism is more widespread throughout the Orinoco Delta than is Kanoboism (Heinen and Ruddle 1974). The origin of Kanoboism goes back to the primordial mythical times of the first Warao. Because of an overabundance of pain, suffering, and death among the Warao at that time, a religious elder traveled to the outer reaches of the cosmos to appeal to the gods, begging a supreme being or kanobo to come live with the mortals and bring an end to human suffering. The kanobo agreed to abide with humans in the form of a sacred stone (Wilbert 1972b, 62). To this day certain Warao villages in the central Orinoco Delta follow Kanoboism and have temples (a thatched-hut sanctuary for the patron kanobo is called kwaihanoko in Warao) that are devoted to a particular kanobo who is represented by a sacred stone. There the wisiratu priest-shaman spends much of his time with his sacred hebu mataro rattle, and there the sacred yuruma starch is stored until the nahanamu ritual complex occurs (see chapter 14). The practice of using a stone as a representation of a supreme spirit, coupled with the fact that a wisiratu can be a shaman and a priest at the same time, shows a possible connection between the Warao and their ancient neighbors to the north—the Taino of the Caribbean (see Olsen 1979). The ancient Taino shaman-priests presided over a cult in which stones carved into triangular figures called zemi were worshiped (Métraux 1949, 599).

Although shamanism and Kanoboism are simply different levels of understanding the same Warao universe, I believe that the former is older than the latter among the Warao. The unique characteristics of Warao religion are complicated by the fact that shamanism and Kanoboism are tremendously intermingled. We will see that music is one of the microscopes (or telescopes) for deeper understanding of these religious phenomena.

Warao View of Life and Death

The most frequent shamanistic context for song among the Warao—the curing of illnesses—points to one very important function of the music: to furnish the singer with power. This power is essential to the Warao because of their preoccupation with death and dying. In their language, for example, death takes prominence over life: they have words for dying and dead but no word for living (Wilbert 1975a, 169). If death is inevitable, then why is so much emphasis placed on the curing of illnesses? As Wilbert (1975a, 169) explains, "what matters to the Indian is the survival of his soul, *mehokohi.*" A preoccupation for curing illness exists among the Warao because of the uncertainty of the causes of illness; it is necessary to discover the cause because of what happens to the soul after death. Again, Wilbert (1975a, 169) explains: "All Warao hope for a life after death and arrange their affairs teleologically toward an existence in the heaven of their predilection." Although death is inevitable, it is still seen as an interruption to an individual's immanent end, especially if the individual is a child.

Most, if not all, Warao deaths are believed to be caused by the actions of supernatural powers. There are three levels of supernatural causes—hebu, bahana, and Hoa, with the last being the most deadly. Wilbert (1983, 358) provides the following overview of Warao spiritual sickness:

> Most often, illness is believed to be the result of mystical retribution and spirit aggression. Illness of the former kind is incurred by the individual through acts in violation of moral injunctions. Aggressive supernaturals vent their wrath through punitive illness whenever they feel offended by human negligence. This means, of course, that far from being self-sufficient, Warao gods are quite dependent upon man, not so much for reasons of vain admiration but, most basically, for their sustenance. And herein lies the crux of man's relationship to these lords: upon suffering the slightest want in food or drink, the Supernaturals retaliate with illness and death. For both sides, then, health and well-being are guaranteed by

a contract of compelling mutuality, and neither party can
withdraw from this partnership as long as the ground rules
that govern heaven and earth remain unchanged.

According to the eschatological beliefs of the Warao, almost all dead
souls are destined to go to a particular place, depending upon the dead
person's occupation during life. Two exceptions to this are adults believed to have been killed by Hoa, and children who, until adolescence,
are *possibly* believed not to have souls (Wilbert 1975a, 178). The largest
number of deaths among the Warao is among the children; the infant
mortality rate, at 49 percent, is especially high. Wilbert has shown
that, among eighty-five deceased children, more than half were believed by their parents to have been killed by Hoa, "claimed as food for
the spirits of the Underworld" (1975a, 177). The deaths of the others
were believed to have been caused by either hebu or bahana spirits.

The death of a Warao child is not taken lightly by the members of
the child's village; all the villagers are related to the deceased by either
blood or marriage. When I arrived at the village of Yaruara Akoho in
the summer of 1974, a child had just died. The entire village was in
mourning, many of the men were (ritually) drunk, and the women
were wailing. After several days of quiet observation on my part, and
when the village seemed to have returned to normal, I noticed a
number of women leaving by canoe. My male friends explained to me
that the women were going to check the canoe in which the deceased
child was buried to see if there were any bird tracks in the mud within
which the body had been encased. According to Wilbert (1975a, 168),
a corpse (waba in Warao, meaning "dead") is wrapped in a hammock,
placed in a dugout canoe, and packed in mud. The canoe coffin is
placed above the ground on poles in a Warao cemetery, not too far
from the village. According to Warao belief, a certain bird will visit the
burial place and leave its tracks in the mud if the deceased was killed
by Hoa. To the Warao the canoe is a vaginal symbol, and dying and
burial symbolize a return to the womb (Wilbert 1975a, 168); nevertheless, if death is determined to have been caused by Hoa, all is lost.

Thus, the ability to cure illnesses is extremely important to the
Warao, and powerful shamans who can communicate with and pla-
cate the supernatural are a vital necessity. Under the leadership of a

shaman, the kanobotuma are annually placated during the nahanamu ritual complex, as Wilbert (1983, 359) explains:

> To keep the lords of the North, South and East satisfied the members of a band and subtribe are pledged to procure a sufficient supply of moriche sago which serves the Supernaturals for ablutions and drinking water. The god of the West is a cannibal who demands human livers and blood which are provided for him by sorcerers. But the others, after they have used the ritual "water," release the sago and will it to be doled out as emergency rations throughout the rainy season of scarcity (Heinen and Ruddle, 1974). In other words, averting malnutrition and starvation through ritual compliance actually staves off sickness and death among the faithful and verifies a basic tenet of Warao ethnopathology.

Concern about life and death, therefore, is of utmost importance to the Warao. In spite of more than seventy years of contact with Roman Catholicism through the Spanish Capuchín order, Warao traditional eschatological beliefs prevail. Christianity has functioned mainly as a parallel pathway for assuring a happy life after death rather than replacing the more ancient and traditional Warao ideology.

3   Musical Background of the Warao

Warao people enjoy music, and they especially like to sing. Men and women sing while they work, children sing while they play, and Warao of all ages often sing while relaxing in their hammocks. Shamans sing while they cure illnesses and contact spirits, other religious leaders or elders sing ceremonial songs during rituals, and anyone can sing certain magical songs for protection or healing. Most of my singing friends and teachers were men (although women also sang songs out of context for me), and most were shamans (figure 3.1).

Among the Warao the three musical categories—pleasure, utility, and theurgy—overlap: utilitarian songs can also be pleasurable, and theurgical songs can also be sung (with certain items omitted) to while away the time.

Music for Pleasure

The most common type of music for pleasure among the Warao is called dakotu, which is glossed into Spanish as canción de baile and into English as dance song. The dance context, explained in detail in chapter 5, has disappeared; and today dakotutuma (the plural form) are sung individually for pleasure by women while they work or take care of their children and by men while they work, canoe, relax in their hammocks, or (more rarely) drink. Although some of these contexts border on the utilitarian, the main difference between dakotutuma and work songs in other cultures is that their rhythm is incidental to the activity they accompany. There is one exception, however: when dakotutuma are sung by a group of men as they collectively paddle a canoe. Then the pace of the song and the paddling is the same. Dakotutuma are most often sung individually, although they were sung collectively during their original dance context.

Dakotutuma are occasionally performed instrumentally on a handmade violin or sekeseke. At other times they may be accompanied by a wandora (a Venezuelan cuatro), a small four-stringed guitarlike instrument.

Figure 3.1. Two of my major teachers and best friends, Antonio Lorenzano on my left and Jaime Zapata on my right, in Yaruara Akoho, Winikina River. Photograph by Johannes Wilbert with my camera (1973).

Music for Utility

The primary utilitarian song type among the Warao is the lullaby, or hoerekitane, which actually has two functions. First, the lullaby soothes the child—not so much by its delivery, which is harsh and loud by European-derived standards, but by the presence of a familiar person (mother, father, brother, sister, grandparent, and so on) whose continued presence is assured by a familiar voice. More important, however, the lullaby functions as a vehicle for informal education. Functionally similar to the lullabies of the Cuna of Panama (McCosker 1976), the texts of Warao lullabies are improvised to predetermined melodic patterns and address certain areas of Warao mythology and daily life.

Although the Warao have developed as a riverine culture and are considered Meso-Indian fishermen, remnants of their food-gathering past linger in other utility songs, such as moriche starch gathering songs and land songs sung while traveling in the rain forest to and from the moriche palm groves. The traveling songs are often sung individually to the accompaniment of the ehuru drum.

Music for Theurgy

Theurgy means "supernatural communication," and the majority of Warao music can be included under this category. Theurgical music can be further divided into group and individual genres determined by performance practice (that is, number of performers).

In the first subgroup are the musical genres of two Warao dance festivals known as habi sanuka and nahanamu, both part of a larger nahanamu ritual complex (Barral 1964, 1981). Habi sanuka is a fertility dance, while nahanamu is a harvest festival. Both are occasions of joy as well as supernatural communication, and nahanamu is the only context for group instrumental performance.

The most frequent contexts for theurgical music among the Warao are shamanistic curing and other mostly individual expressions of musical power by one person for another person or a group. The Warao term for this type of expression is wara (guara), which means both theurgical speech discourse ("word, conversation, speech," according to Barral 1957, 86) and theurgical music discourse ("song" or "singing"). Wara is a type of Warao singing that is supernatural conversation,

and there is a different term for natural or everyday speech discourse—dibu. Musically, the distinction between wara and dibu is
clear to the outsider because the former is definitely singing in a European-derived sense as opposed to speaking in a European-derived
sense. With some South American indigenous cultures, distinctions
between singing and speech cannot be made (Sherzer and Urban 1986,
9); but with the Warao, the musical aspect of the singing transports the
words. There are many vehicles or song formulas for wara, and Warao
shamans and other singers *must* use the correct one for their particular musical journey.

According to the Warao world view there are three types of cosmological practitioners who can be classified as shamans—wisiratu, bahanarotu, and hoarotu. They function as mediators and cosmic specialists. "During their lifetime the spirits of [Warao] shamans travel
routinely in trance states and in dreams to their respective heavens"
(Wilbert 1975a, 169). The Spanish translations that the Warao gave me
for their shamans are doctor or piache for the wisiratu, and brujo for
both the bahanarotu and hoarotu. Doctor translates into English as
doctor or curer, piache is a Carib Indian word for priest-doctor (Roth
1915, 329), and brujo means male witch or wizard. One of the most
important duties of the shaman is curing illnesses. Through a technique of ecstacy that is culturally induced with the aid of music and tobacco smoke (less of the latter than the former), the shamans are
transformed into powerful beings who are able to sustain contact with
the spirit world (which can be dangerous) for the purpose of reestab-
lishing order and balance in Warao society.

Just as there are three types of shamans, there are also three types
of shamanistic curing events. Wilbert explains that the wisiratu cures
hebu sickness "caused by the introduction of a metaphysical essence,
such as an ancestor spirit, into a person's body, thereby causing internal pressure"; the bahanarotu cures "physical ailments caused by
bahana . . . by the introduction of some material object into the body
of a victim"; and the hoarotu "cures patients who suffer from hoa. . . .
[This] sickness is caused by the introduction of hoa essences, which
are the specific properties of all plants and animals" (1970, 24). According to the curing song texts, however, it seems that the intrusion
illnesses of wisiratu shamanism are caused by the spiritual essences of
any living object or parts of objects except humans, those of baha-

narotu shamanism are caused by the spiritual essences of any material object, and those of hoarotu shamanism by the spiritual essences of almost anything. I will present more details about these spiritual essences in chapters 7, 8, and 9, which deal respectively with each type of Warao shaman.

In addition, there is a fourth type of infliction among the Warao that requires curing—a physical and often external ailment of the body. I use the term infliction rather than affliction because these ailments, such as knife and hatchet wounds, bee and scorpion stings, animal bites, bruises, and certain internal problems that may occur during childbirth, are believed to be caused by supernatural powers that possess, empower, or otherwise persuade the objects or animals and cause them to harm humans. These inflictions are neither shamanistic nor caused by intrusion. Therefore, they do not require a shaman for healing because there is no direct communication with the supernatural; communication is directed only to the inflicting material object or animal or to the blood, pus, or swelling.

The curing music for these four kinds of illnesses include song groups for the shamanic types and prayerful songs called hoatuma (plural of hoa) for the nonshamanistic type. The three classes of shaman employ music for communication with good and evil spirits, and distinct musical characteristics exist for those and other functions in shamanism. The most important power element of Warao shamanistic curing is the naming of the illness-causing spirit essence. While curing, hoarotu shamans and, to a lesser degree, wisiratu shamans may sing alone or in small groups of two or three. The small group, which is used when the patient is an important person, results in a complex multipart texture. The power of music can also be used malevolently. Only the hoarotu shaman, however, inflicts illness or death through his song; and this genre employs distinct musical characteristics.

The wisiratu and some bahanarotu shamans commonly employ two material tools in their curing ceremonies: they always use the wina cigar and often use a container rattle. The hoarotu shaman, however, uses only the wina. The importance of the wina cigar in Warao shamanism cannot be overstated (see Wilbert 1972b, 55–83; 1987b), and the ceremonial role of tobacco in general has been elaborated upon by many ethnologists and anthropologists (Wilbert 1987a). The role of the shaman's rattle, however, is equally important as a ceremonial tool related to the shaman's power; and for the wisiratu shaman the rattle may even surpass tobacco in its frequency of use during his curing rituals.

Within the Winikina subtribe of the Warao culture, then, there are three different types of shaman, with different forms of song patterns existing for each. These differing song patterns or melodies are determined by particular functions. Nevertheless, there are unifying factors that make up what can be termed an overall Warao shamanistic song style. Analysis of the melodies and texts of the songs reveals structural patterns that have important functions within Warao cosmology. This structural basis is found in not only the shamanistic songs but also other songs associated with the supernatural, such as the nonshamanistic hoa songs, which are used to cure outer and some inner body ailments not caused by intrusion.

Another type of hoa is used for magical protection against supernaturally altered animals and ogres. These songs also rely on the power of naming the danger, reinforced by the appropriate melodic aspect of the song itself. As with other Warao theurgical songs, these are characterized by individuality of melodic pattern. An additional type of hoa, called marehoa, is used by men for magical power associated with courting and sexual love.

Many other theurgical songs are sung individually by the Warao for communicating with supernatural forces during shamanic initiation, after dreams containing supernatural messages, for cutting down trees to build large canoes, for causing rain (Wilbert 1981b), and during other contexts when private or collective spiritual communication is necessary.

Certain types of musical instruments are used as tools within the performance contexts of some theurgical songs and dances, and other types are played in musical contexts for nonritual pleasure. Other musical instruments are remembered but no longer owned or played. The next chapter explores the diversity of Warao sound-producing instruments and analyzes several of them in depth.

4 Musical and Sound-producing Instruments

The Warao possess fifteen musical and other sound instruments that are used in shamanistic rituals, nonshamanistic ceremonies, signaling, and entertainment. (I use the conventional terms for musical-instrument classification: idiophone or hard-material sounder, membranophone or stretched-skin sounder, aerophone or air sounder, and chordophone or stretched-string sounder.) The fifteen instruments are classified in table 4.1, which shows their names in Warao and their corresponding type and context in English.

My detailed descriptions of Warao musical instruments are based on my fieldwork and on information derived from historical, folkloric, ethnographic, and mythological sources. I will use these data to help contextualize all Warao music and music making. In addition, I will draw conclusions about the cultural contexts of similar but ancient Caribbean musical instruments that were in use during the time of the early Spanish explorations of the circum-Caribbean region. This methodology, derived from ethnographic analogy as used in archaeo-musicology (see Olsen 1990), compares the musical material culture of a surviving culture (the Warao) with musical material culture used in the past within the same geographic region. The goal of the approach is to create a musical-cultural history of the greater Orinoco Delta. Let us first examine the Warao instruments and their origins in the order found in table 4.1.

Descriptions, Origins, and Myths

Sewei

The sewei, a strung rattle idiophone consisting of numerous small hooves, seeds, nuts, fruits, or beetle wings strung on a string (all difficult for the Warao to obtain), is one of their most sacred sound makers. A sewei is traditionally worn on the ankle of the shaman or male nonshaman dancer's right leg while another is attached to the top

41

Table 4.1. Musical and other sound instruments of the Warao

Warao Name	Type	Context
Idiophones		
Sewei	Strung rattle made from seeds fastened to fiber string	Nahanamu and habi sanuka festivals; worn on ankles or strung to pole; sacred
Habi sanuka	Small container rattle made from calabash, wood, and seeds	Habi sanuka festival; bahanarotu shaman; sacred
Hebu mataro	Large container rattle made from calabash, wood, and quartz	Wisiratu shaman; nahanamu festival; sacred
Moriki	Small container rattle made from woven tirite and seeds	Toy and tourism; secular
Membranophones		
Ehuru	Double-headed drum made from wood and monkey skin	Nahanamu festival and traveling in rain forest; sacred
Aerophones		
Muhusemoi	Vertical flute with notched mouthpiece; made from deer tibia	Nahanamu festival and traveling in rain forest; sacred
Hekunukabe	Vertical flute with notched mouthpiece; made from stem	Nahanamu festival and traveling in rain forest; sacred; nearly extinct
Daokohota (daukoho)	Vertical whistle made from crab pincer	Crab fishing; sacred; extinct
Harehare (harihari)	Horizontal flute; made from cane	Extinct
Isimoi	Heteroglottal clarinet; made from calabash, cane, plant stalk, and beeswax	Nahanamu festival; sacred
Heresemoi	Trumpet made from conch shell	Signaling; sacred
Bakohi	Trumpet made from bamboo, wood, or cow horn	Signaling; sacred
Chordophones		
Sekeseke	Bowed lute or European violin	Entertainment; secular
Wandora	Plucked lute or Venezuelan cuatro	Entertainment; secular

of a pole during the sacred harvest dance known as nahanamu. As an anklet rattle, the instrument's sound enhances the rhythm of the nahanamu dance; and as a pole rattle, the sewei "is played by the [shaman] only during the mysterious dance of *Hatabo*, which takes place in the festival of *Nahanamu*. Each time he strikes it to the floor marks the beginning of a phase of the dance" (Wilbert 1956, 12). The sewei is never used by a woman.

According to two pictures that appear in Cruxent and Rouse (1963), anklet-strung rattles were worn by both Arawak and Carib dancers but on both legs rather than one. Indeed, the strung-anklet or leg rattle is one of the most common sound instruments among native Americans and, as Izikowitz (1970, 33) points out, its construction probably evolved from the common necklace. According to Vaquero (1965, 132), the word sewei comes from the Cariban language. Wilbert (1956, 12–13), however, suggests possible northern Andean provenance for the instrument itself because of the use of metal bells by the Warao Mariusa subtribe (1956, 9–13).

According to Warao folklore, as Antonio Lorenzano told me, the sewei was the gift of a kanobo who appeared to a wisiratu shaman in a dream and instructed him how to make it:

> This is from the kanobo, because it is very ancient, according to the ancestors. None of us saw the birth of the . . . sewei, where [it] came from. Now, the ancients, who were the first to die, according to how it is said, learned how to make [it] from a dream. According to the story, a wisiratu slept and had a dream. When the wisiratu woke up, at dawn, he told his people and he sang, "Look, people, last night I slept and I dreamed about a . . . sewei." Then the wisiratu said, "I'm going to see."

In the narrative, the wisiratu shaman left and later returned with about forty small fruits (probably retamo fruits, which do not grow in the vicinity of the central Orinoco Delta) with which he made his sewei. As a gift from a kanobo, the sewei is an instrument of great value; and only people of importance, such as the chief or the shaman of a village, are allowed to own one. In addition, the Warao believe that the sewei possesses a spirit called hebu oriwaka aroto (Wilbert 1956, 10), or "spirit owner of the festival."

Habi Sanuka

During the same trip, according to Antonio's narrative, the wisiratu also returned with approximately one hundred to two hundred small seeds that he placed inside a small calabash before inserting a stick into it for a handle. This was the first habi sanuka rattle, a container idiophone. Turrado Moreno (1945, 223) explains that the calabash is the fruit of the tirite while the rattlers inside are small stones and pieces of shells. The habi sanuka rattle in my possession, however, which Antonio made, is made from the fruit of the calabash tree (*Crescentia cujete* [figure 4.1]) and contains 120 small black seeds about the size of buckshot (figure 4.2). This rattle also has an ornamentally incised container and moriche-fiber topping, while some other examples I have seen are undecorated (figure 4.3). The overall length of the habi sanuka rattle in figure 4.2 is 23 centimeters (excluding the top tuft of moriche) and the container's circumference is 20.5 centimeters, while the approximate length of those in figure 4.3 is 20.4 centimeters. Habi sanuka rattles are traditionally sacred instruments played by Warao men and occasionally women, usually with the bahanarotu shaman as their leader. These musicians dance with their small instruments during the fertility festival also called habi sanuka (Wilbert 1956, 16).

Antonio said the following about his habi sanuka rattle, explaining how he obtains one and how the small rattle differs from the large rattle of the wisiratu shaman:

> I have to make one. When I go up river I look for a good dry calabash so I can make a rattle. I do not look for a very large one; since I am a bahanarotu I can use a small one. The maraca of a wisiratu is large and very long, but the maraca for the bahanarotu when he is singing for bahana is a maraca like this [he indicated its size with his hands], with feathers from a konoto bird so it looks pretty.

During a lengthy description of the habi sanuka song about a headless snake (see chapter 14), Antonio had the following to say about the construction of a habi sanuka rattle, which he calls korokoro:

> Korokoro is the name in Warao, while in Spanish it is maraquita [little maraca]. The little calabash comes from the hills, not from here. The local calabash is not used for habi sanuka dancing. The proper little calabash comes from

Figure 4.1. A calabash tree (*Crescentia cujete*) growing behind the house of José Antonio Páez, in Moriki Hana, downstream from Yaruara Akoho on the Winikina River.

Figure 4.2. A habi sanuka rattle constructed by Antonio Lorenzano from Lorenzano Akoho, just across the Winikina River from Yaruara Akoho. Olsen Collection.

> outside, from the highlands, and it is that type which pertains to the dance of habi sanuka. For this reason you have to look there, in the hills. You have to collect them, or if you know someone you can ask for them as a gift; or if that is not possible, you can buy from twenty, forty, to sixty little calabashes. They are brought here where we take out the insides, prepare everything, and insert little grains or seeds from a local indigenous fruit into the little calabashes.

Antonio also explained that although he used to play a habi sanaka rattle, he stopped after a Spanish missionary told him that he should no longer play it. The missionary warned him, in fact, that he should not be a shaman either because he is a mission-educated Indian. Antonio may have stopped playing the habi sanuka rattle, but he continues to make them; additionally, he is still the most knowledgeable bahanarotu shaman in the region.

The habi sanuka is the most important sound instrument associated with bahanarotu shamanism. From the very beginnings of the belief in bahana, the habi sanuka was present, first played by Mawari, the Creator Bird of the Dawn, with his right wing (Wilbert 1985, 147). From that primordial time the habi sanuka has been the power tool of the bahanarotu, perhaps not used for curing but for singing for bahana and accompanying the fertility festival known also as habi sanuka. Its very shape symbolizes fertility, as Wilbert (1985, 155) writes:

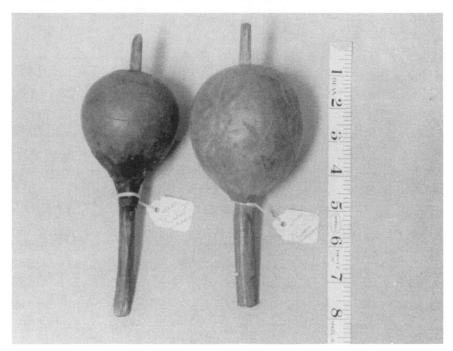

Figure 4.3. Two Winikina habi sanuka rattles from the museum of the Fundación La Salle, Caracas, Venezuela.

Like the bow and arrow, the rattle is a composite symbol consisting of a phallic axis and a uterine calabash denoting conjunction. This finds linguistic expression in the word for calabash, *mataru* or *mataruka*, "hymen," a word that refers to a virgin womb that is deflowered by a *mataruka aiwatu*, "someone who pierces a calabash." The natural model of the [habi sanuka] rattle is the ovoid termitary or apiary built around the branch of a tree and whose rustling interior teems with termites' known reproductive power.

It is no surprise, given these Warao vegetable and animal metaphors plus the seeds within the pierced calabash, that the habi sanuka rattle is the preeminent sound instrument for their fertility ritual.

Hebu Mataro

No instrument among the Warao compares in size, sound, profundity, and power with the wisiratu shaman's sacred container rattle known as hebu mataro (figures 4.4 through 4.9). The literature on the Warao reveals numerous names for this large instrument. Turrado Moreno (1945, 223), for example, gives the following three terms: dioso a mataro (the god's rattle), jebu a mataro (hebu's rattle), and mataroida (the large rattle). Barral (1964, 175; 1972, 282; 1981, 136) calls it mari-mataro; and Wilbert (1956, 13) refers to it as hebu amataro, the name closest to the term the Warao gave me (hebu mataro).

Like the habi sanuka, the hebu mataro is a spiked-vessel or -container idiophone that is fabricated from the fruit of the calabash tree known as mataro or totuma in the Orinoco Delta; the fruit (the calabash) has the same names. According to Padre Gaspar Ma. de Pinilla (1943–44, 145), "the totuma is a species of calabash from the tree named totumo, tapara or guira." Wilbert (1979, 146) explains that the calabash tree capable of producing a large enough fruit suitable for hebu mataro rattles grows only on higher ground outside the lowland delta area. While I did see calabash trees growing in the delta near Warao houses (see figure 4.1), these were bearing only small fruits suitable for drinking containers or the smaller habi sanuka rattle of the bahanarotu shaman.

The finish of the calabash for the hebu mataro is natural, although two vertical and two horizontal slits always appear in the sides of the container. At times rectangular depressions are cut around the slits, and these may be painted with the sap of the Warao iburu tree (sangrito in Spanish), giving them a very dark brown color that contrasts with the light brown tone of the natural calabash. At other times straight lines or geometrical motifs are burned into the calabash. Wilbert (1974, 90) explains the slits and the ornamental depressions around them: "These slits are called the mouths of the head of the *hebumataro* rattle. Frequently the 'mouths' are bordered by bands of triangular or rectangular designs, representing its teeth. Some rattles are also decorated with symbols representing humans, animals (especially insects), and the Sun."

The spike that pierces the calabash, forming both the uppermost projection and the handle of the rattle, is made from a stick of wood called haheru (also himaheru) in Warao (apamatillo in Spanish). This is the same type of wood used by the Warao for their fire-making drills (Wilbert 1974, 92).

The stones inside the container are small quartz pebbles (hoyo in Warao; also kareko, referring to their spiritual properties) that are not found in the central delta but must be brought from Tucupita, the capital of the Territorio Federal Delta Amacuro, or "acquired either from metamorphic rocks on offshore islands or in the piedmont region of the Sierra de Imataca, in the south" of the delta region (Wilbert 1979, 146). These small stones vary in shape from perfectly round to oblong and irregular, and in size from approximately one to 0.3 centimeters in diameter. The number of pebbles in a rattle also varies. Wilbert (1956, 16), for example, first writes that from sixty to seventy are used and later (1979, 146) that some 120 to 200 are needed; one of my wisiratu teachers, however, said he uses fifty-three pebbles, while another said 160. It appears, therefore, that uniformity in number is not a major concern. As Wilbert points out, however, the greater the number, the greater the power (1974, 90–91):

> The shaman blows tobacco smoke impregnated with a fragrant resin over scores of small quartz crystals and places these one by one into the hollowed-out gourd, invoking for each a particular ancestral spirit believed by the Warao to be embodied in the stone. These quartz crystals are his familiar spirits who assist him in curing and other ritual endeavors; indeed, he refers to them as his "family." Obviously, the greater the number of crystalline spirits, the more potent the instrument.

At times, when the hebu mataro belongs to a powerful wisiratu priest-shaman (as opposed to a less powerful wisiratu shaman who has not yet inherited the position of priest in Kanoboism), the instrument will be adorned with bird feathers at the apex of the wooden spike that protrudes from the calabash. Selected red and yellow tail feathers taken from a live cotorra parrot (*Psitacidae*) are sewn into a long sash that is wound around the tip of the stick. In a Warao narrative entitled "Origin of yuruma and of the moriche worm" (Wilbert 1970, 330, narrative 154), a wisiratu adorns his "mari mataro" with tufts of cotton.

The construction of a hebu mataro rattle is not easy, given the difficulty of obtaining the required materials; and the shamans employ special songs for a rattle's consecration. These songs empower the

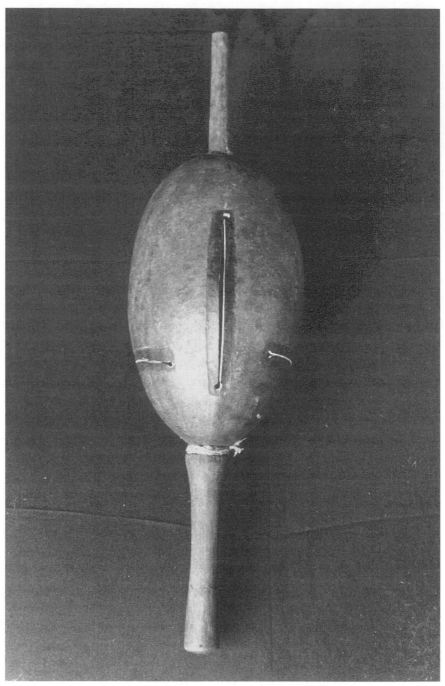

Figure 4.4. A hebu mataro rattle belonging to Bernardo Jiménez Tovar, showing one of the two vertical slits.

Figure 4.5. Another hebu mataro rattle belonging to Bernardo Jiménez Tovar, showing one of the two horizontal slits.

Figure 4.6. A hebu mataro rattle (showing one of the two vertical slits) belonging to Juan Bustillo Calderón, with wina cigars inside a torotoro basket. Olsen Collection.

Figure 4.7. Another hebu mataro rattle (showing one of the two horizontal slits) belonging to Juan Bustillo Calderón, with wina cigars inside a torotoro basket. Olsen Collection.

Figure 4.8. A Winikina hebu mataro rattle from the museum of the Fundación
La Salle, Caracas, showing one of the vertical and one of the horizontal slits.

Figure 4.9. Another Winikina hebu mataro rattle from the museum of the Fundación La Salle, Caracas, showing one of the two horizontal slits.

hebu mataro rattle in the early stages of the nahanamu ritual by naming and describing the rattle's parts during its construction (Briggs n.d., 33).

Because the hebu mataro rattle is large, varying in total length from about 45 to 70 centimeters, it must be gripped and shaken with both hands. It is held in a variable playing position, depending on the particular task it is being used for. During a curing ceremony, for example, the performing wisiratu will first sit on a bench (cover photograph) and hold his hebu mataro at an angle over the patient; then he will later stand to lean over his patient, shaking his rattle in a horizontal position (see chapter 7). During the wisiratu's ecstatic voyages to the cosmos, which take place on the hohonoko or dancing platform, he will hold his rattle vertically to enable his soul to journey straight up the axis mundi, symbolized by the central shaft of the hebu mataro (Sullivan 1988, 430). Only men, wisiratu, and occasionally bahanarotu shamans (see chapter 8), use the hebu mataro; and they value it highly. The entire Warao society, in fact, places a high value on the hebu's rattle; and those who use it are also highly esteemed by their peers. The maker of the rattle is usually its performer unless the instrument has been handed down from teacher to apprentice.

The hebu mataro has a low indeterminate pitch because of its large calabash and numerous stones. It is capable, however, of a wide range of dynamic levels. During a curing ritual to remove a hebu spirit, the wisiratu firmly grips the handle of his rattle with both hands and revolves it clockwise over the patient, beginning slowly and proceeding slightly faster until a very loud sound is produced. Between each curing song section, as if performing a type of transitional passage, he stands and furiously shakes his instrument inches above his patient who lies in a hammock before him. (I explain the functions of these curing sections in chapter 7.) The sound of the hebu mataro is very loud during almost all parts of a wisiratu's curing ritual, especially to the patient and others lying in their hammocks nearby. The number of rattle shakes fluctuates from 96 to 210 per minute while the wisiratu is singing (although Wilbert [1987b, 5] writes that "underlying the rattling and chanting is a rhythmic pattern of sixty beats, which approximates a relaxed heartbeat"). The number of shakes increases during the transitional sections, when the shaman is not singing, to 244 shakes per minute (recorded example 11).

Physical characteristics of hebu mataro rattles are determined by individual choice and ritual usage, as figures 4.4 through 4.9 clearly show. The first instrument (figures 4.4 and 4.5) belongs to Bernardo Jiménez Tovar, a wisiratu shaman from the village of Yaruara Akoho and my neighbor during my tenure in the delta. Bernardo and I became friends, and I had many opportunities to attend his curing sessions and record him with his hebu mataro. The second rattle (figures 4.6 and 4.7) was the property of Juan Bustillo Calderón, another wisiratu who befriended me and allowed me to record him during his curing ceremonies. Although Juan is from the downstream village of Hebu Wabanoko, he is related to the people of Yaruara Akoho. His instrument is now in my possession—a gift, in a way, from one musician to another. The third hebu mataro (figures 4.8 and 4.9), a specimen in the museum of the Fundación La Salle in Caracas, was collected on 20 August 1954 in Winikina (possibly Yaruara Akoho). Although not playable because its stones are missing, its size and proportions have been studied for purposes of comparison and contrast with the two 1972 examples.

The hebu mataro in figures 4.4 and 4.5 is unique in its almost complete lack of ornamentation. It has neither feathers at its uppermost end nor decorative incisions on its body, except for the slight rectangular depressions around the vertical and horizontal slits. The lack of feathers means that the wisiratu owner is not yet a priest in charge of the Konoboist temple (see chapter 14). The application of the painted rectangular depressions makes this rattle very similar to the 1954 specimen in figures 4.8 and 4.9. Conversely, the instrument pictured in figures 4.6 and 4.7 has a completely different form of ornamentation surrounding the slits. It reveals a series of incisions crossing the slits at ninety-degree angles, with little or no paint added. There is apparently no uniformity of slit decoration among hebu mataro rattles, judging from additional examples pictured by Suárez (1968, 163–64, 179), Barral (1972, 282), and Wilbert (1956, 15; 1974, 90). Likewise, there appears to be great diversity of general exterior calabash decoration, with the greatest contrast seen between the rattle in figures 4.4 and 4.5 and those presented by the authors I have just mentioned. Bernardo's hebu mataro has vertical slits that are open approximately 3 centimeters in their middle while the horizontal slits are open only a hair's width and in one area are completely closed. When questioned about

Table 4.2. Dimensions of three hebu mataro rattles (in cm)

Figure nos.	Overall	Calabash	Circumference	Handle	Spike	Vertical slit	Horizontal slit
4.5, 4.6	58.3	26.7	52.2	18.4	13.3	15.8 15.5	12.6 15.5
4.7, 4.8	66.7	26.6	64.0	18.9	20.8	16.5 14.9	13.9 15.2
4.9, 4.10	45.6	29.5	47.3	9.2	12.0	13.3 13.3	11.1 12.4

this, he said that the vertical slits are made well and the horizontal slits are not, adding that he could fix them if he felt it necessary. (They were made well enough to serve their purpose.) Table 4.2 compares the sizes of these three instruments.

Juan's hebu mataro (figures 4.6 and 4.7) is the largest of the three examples; Bernardo's rattle (figures 4.4 and 4.5) is smaller; and the third and oldest instrument (figures 4.8 and 4.9) is the smallest. The greatest difference between the museum rattle and the other two is the length of its handle, which is extremely short for the two-handed playing technique of the instrument.

The hebu mataro rattle is one of the most powerful musical instruments in the practice of Warao religion, both for curing hebu illnesses and in individual and group religious practices of Kanoboism. Historical accounts first attest to its power as observed by outsiders, as Josa (1888, 40) wrote in the nineteenth century:

> The Waraus . . . are the most renowned as sorcerers. The huts which they set apart for the performance of their superstitious rites are regarded with great veneration. A missionary once visited a Warau settlement, entered one of those huts, not being aware of the offence he was committing, and found it perfectly empty, with the exception of the gourd, or "mataro," as it is called by that tribe. There was in the centre of the hut a small raised place fire [that] had been made for burning tobacco. The sorcerer being asked to give up the gourd, peremptorily refused, saying that if he did so his "two children would die the same night."

Today, approximately one hundred years after Josa's account, the hebu mataro is still a powerful instrument of high value. When I expressed the desire to purchase a rattle from Juan Bustillo Calderón in 1972, the price asked was one hundred Bolívares, the approximate equivalent of twelve full days of work at the nearby sawmill. It is even more surprising, however, that a master would consider selling his prized curing tool; for, according to Turrado Moreno (1945, 163), the hebu would punish the Warao if a rattle got into the wrong hands. He writes: "These sacred rattles . . . are hereditary and pass from one wisiratu to another. When it happens that there is no successor, the relatives of the last wisiratu burn them or throw them into the river. If the rattles pass

over to profane hands, there is a great danger that the hebu may become irritated and send punishment, pestilence, hunger, and even
death to the tribe." When I was finally able to purchase a hebu mataro
rattle from Juan in 1973, he warned me not to spill gasoline, oil, or
kerosene on it. Such disrespect, he explained, would make the spirit of
the rattle angry and it would then appear to him in a dream demanding tobacco smoke or moriche-palm starch (yuruma) as com-
pensation. Juan, however, had no hesitation about selling me his personal sacred rattle, which I interpret as an act of friendship—he
trusted me to care for it and knew I needed it to complete my study of
Warao music and shamanism.

The main function of the hebu mataro rattle is to provide the
wisiratu shaman with sufficient power while curing hebu-caused illnesses. In fact, a wisiratu would not be able to function as a shaman
without it. How the wisiratu and the hebu mataro achieved this special
power is related in a narrative entitled "Komatari, the First Medicine-
Man," collected and translated by Roth (1915, 336–38). Those portions
of the tale explaining the origin, construction, and function of the
hebu mataro are so enlightening that I quote them in full:

> Komatari . . . built a *piai*-house [a temple for the piai, a term
> for shaman that Roth borrows from the Cariban language],
> and going round his field, looked out for a calabash tree; he
> found one full of gourds. He took one, but on turning round,
> he saw a Hebu, who, after asking whether it belonged to him
> and getting "Yes" for an answer, said: "All right. So long as the
> calabash is yours you may have the whole tree. I have a name,
> but will not tell it to you. I want to see whether you learn the
> piai business well. If you do, you will be able to find it out for
> yourself." On reaching home with the calabash, Komatari
> started cleaning it out. When cleaned, another Hebu came
> along and asked him what he intended doing with it, but Ko-
> matari would not tell him. You see this particular Hebu was
> the one who comes to kill people and was afraid of the power
> of the *maraka* (rattle), which is made from this very calabash.
> After scooping out and cleaning the calabash, Komatari went
> into the bush and, traveling along, came upon a creek with
> swiftly flowing water: it was here that he cut the timber from

out of which he next shaped the handle for the rattle and cut the sticks to make his special fire with. (The timber always employed for these two purposes has a milky sap, and is found in places such as described, that is in the forest, along the banks of swiftly flowing creeks.) Returning home once more, he fastened the handle in the gourd, but was not satisfied with the result: the rattle did not look as it should. So he hung it up on the beam of his piai-house, and went once more into the bush, where he again met the killing Hebu, who repeated his question as to what Komatari intended doing with the rattle, but as before, the latter would not tell him. Passing along, and hearing a noise as of many people talking, Komatari proceeded in the direction from whence the sound came, and found a number of Hebus fastening various parrot feathers into cotton twine. How pretty this ornament would look tied on his calabash left hanging up at home, was Komatari's first thought when he saw what they were doing. On asking, the ornament was given him. The Hebu who gave it to him said: "I have a name, but I will not tell it to you. You can find it out for yourself, if you should ever become a good piai-man." . . . Komatari went home now, and arranged the feathered cotton on top of the calabash, when who should put in an appearance again but the killing Hebu. When he again asked Komatari what he intended doing with the calabash, the latter refused to tell him, as before. But Komatari was not satisfied even now, because when he shook the gourd it did not rattle. As yet it had no stones in it. So Komatari went into the bush again, and followed creek after creek, and at last came to a big river. There he met another Hebu, who got the proper stones that were wanted. When he had given them to Komatari, he said, like the others: "I have a name, but I will not tell it to you. You must find it out for yourself when you are a medicine-man." Komatari again made his way home and put the stones into the calabash. Just as he was finishing the work the killing Hebu again appeared, asking him as before, what he intended doing with the calabash. The answer was, "This is to kill you with, and to prevent you killing other people," and as Komatari shook the calabash, which was now a finished *maraka* rattle, the Hebu began to tremble and stagger, and almost fell, but he managed to pick himself up and get away just in the nick of time. He ran to his Aijamo (head-man, chief) and said: "There is a man who has an object with which he nearly killed me and I must get my payment (i.e., my revenge). I am going back to kill him." "All right!" said the Aijamo, "I will go with you." So they went together, and brought sickness to a friend and neighbor of Komatari's; for they were afraid of attacking Komatari himself. However, his sick friend sent for him. Komatari went, and played the maraka on him, and took out his sickness. So the killing Hebu made another man ill, but Komatari took the disease out of him also. The Hebu next afflicted a third victim, and again Komatari was victorious. But when he attacked a fourth one, Komatari was out hunting. When he returned, the poor fellow was in a bad enough condition: so strong did the sickness come, that Komatari could not cure him—he had "stood too long." The killing Hebu then explained to Komatari that it would always be thus: some patients he (Komatari) could save, and other patients he could not. Of course Komatari had been able to find out the names of all the Hebus that had lent him assistance in the manufacture of his maraka, and it is to these different Hebus whom the present-day medicine-men are said to "sing" and call on when they cure the sick.

Although this narrative came from the Pomeroon River Warao of British Guiana (Guyana) in 1913 it is, nevertheless, a valuable source of information about the hebu mataro rattle as it is found throughout the Orinoco Delta. From it we learn that the calabash, the stick, and the pebbles come, respectively, from a calabash tree, wood with a milky sap that grows along the banks of fast-moving creeks, and a big river. But, more important, we learn of the supernatural helpers that give the instrument its power. The calabash itself, as a gift from a good hebu, has the latter's blessings incorporated into it. The pebbles were also given to the shaman by a good hebu. According to the Reverend W. T. Veness quoted by Izikowitz (1970, 107), the stones contained within a shamanic rattle are "fragments of rock crystal (Maraweri diamonds, or Calicut stones, as they are called) brought from the mountains of the interior and supposed to possess some hidden virtue." According to Warao belief, the pebbles inside the rattle (the physical form of the kareko spirits) are more than simply symbols of various helpful spirits; they *are* the spirits. Barral refers to kareko in the Spanish language plural form when he explains how the wisiratu, before he begins curing, gives a large amount of tobacco smoke to the karekos in the rattle (1964, 187); during this time the shaman says to the spirits within the hebu mataro, "Karekos, my children, obey me, I rule over you: you are wise, you are powerful: give me your help this minute."

Likewise, the parrot feathers are a gift from the hebutuma and, although used as ornaments, they possess magical powers. Izikowitz (1970, 104–5) mentions the magical significance of feathers among several Indian tribes who attach them to their rattles. Among the Warao the parrot is a sacred shamanic bird because it inhabits the two realms of heaven and earth; the parrot's feathers are an additional shamanic tool that enable the wisiratu shaman to fly to the outer firmament of his cosmos. One of my shaman friends explained that the feathers must be taken from the tail of a live bird. If the bird is not alive, the rattle will have no curative power and the patient will die. In addition, each feather is believed to be a helping hebu spirit. Finally, the narrative emphasizes the importance of naming, which occurs in the song texts of shamanistic songs as the epitome of power.

Another Warao narrative collected by Roth and included in a collection by Wilbert (1970, 225, narrative 106: "The hummingbird with tobacco for the first piai") tells how the calabash for the hebu mataro rattle comes from the east side of the calabash tree. The east, hokonamu, the place of light and the origin of life, casts its power on the side of the calabash tree that first receives the sun's morning rays. Whether or not these calabashes are physically stronger because of their easternmost placement on the tree, they are certainly spiritually more powerful, as the following excerpt from the narrative suggests: "The brother . . . next sent him for the *hebu-mataro* [rattle] and he brought gourds of all sizes, but at last he returned with a calabash that he had picked from off the east side of the tree: this was the very thing."

The vertical and horizontal slits that always appear cut into the hebu mataro rattle are also power symbols. The vertical slits symbolize female while the horizontal slits symbolize male gender. The sexual symbolism of the slits is functional during curing sessions because the wisiratu breathes into the vertical slits that are held over a female patient and into the horizontal slits that are held over a male. Likewise, when the wisiratu extracts the illness-causing hebu, he places one vertical slit on the female patient and sucks the evil hebu into the rattle by sucking into the opposite vertical slit. The same procedure, using the horizontal slits, is employed when the patient is a male. Although he does not discuss sexual symbolism, Turrado Moreno (1945, 164) gives a different explanation for the function of the slits. According to him, the hebu enters through the slits into the rattle and, with the help of the sacred stones, leaves again through the same slits to go into the body of the patient for the purpose of curing him or her. This, however, is not consistent with the belief that the benevolent helping hebu possesses the rattle and gives the kareko stones their strength (see chapter 7).

Wilbert (1974, 90–91) explains that the sacred hebu mataro of the priest-shaman is a "head spirit," with its handle as the leg, its calabash as the head, its slits as the mouths, its geometric decorations around the slits as the teeth, and its feathers as the hair of the spirit. This idea is confirmed in chapter 7: the wisiratu curing song texts reveal that the sound of the rattle *is* the voice of the helping spirit.

Wilbert (1974, 90–91) writes a further interpretation of the joining of the hebu mataro's handle within the calabash: "Once his spirit family is assembled inside the 'head' of the rattle, the shaman inserts a central shaft through the openings at either end of the fruit. The handle is called the rattle's 'leg,' but this act is actually a symbolic union of male and female symbols. And this, in turn, is related to the fertilizing power believed to adhere to the completed instrument."

An additional symbol of power is the hebu mataro's capability to produce sparks when vigorously shaken by a wisiratu during a curing ritual. Experiments by Wilbert (1974, 92; 1987b, 24–25; 1993, 137) have proven this phenomenon, although the sparks were too dim for photographic documentation (Wilbert 1977, personal communication). When a wisiratu shaman shakes his rattle during the instrumental part of his curing séance (between sections A and B, as explained in chapter 7), the quartz pebbles repeatedly strike against the wood that projects through the center of the calabash, producing a fine dust. According to Wilbert, the wood of the central shaft of the rattle has a low flash point; and its dust is ignited by the heat produced by the pieces of quartz striking together. This has a tremendous psychological effect on the patient who sees the glow through the slits of the rattle, as Wilbert (1974, 92) writes: "How much more profound must be the effect on his [the patient's] fevered mind, and on his kinfolk who attend the healing séance, when the rattle actually begins to emit a shower of brightly glowing sparks as it whirls ever more rapidly in the shaman's hand to summon the denizens of the spirit world to his assistance!" I was not able to confirm this phenomenon while in the field in 1972 and could see no glow coming from the slits of the rattle at a distance of approximately eight feet. Wilbert (1987b, 24) explains why the sparks cannot be seen by observers:

> Now if you are only an observer, rather than in the hammock, under the rattle, you will never see that. The shaman, of course, produces the actual rain of sparks. They are not really sparks but sort of glimmering particles, and they are immediately extinguished once they meet the colder atmosphere. The shaman produces them by swinging the rattle first and then changing the rhythm through a sudden up-and-down movement, in which phase the rattle is called the "club" or "mace of the god." Then, by producing a different sound, he forces this powder out through the slits of the rattle. He knows that he is producing this and that is how he knows that the spirits are there. Because he is above the rattle he does not see the sparks either. But he does know that because of the change in rhythm and the stones inside, he is producing these sparks.

During additional field research in March 1973, I learned from one of my wisiratu shaman teachers that the hebu mataro does indeed produce sparks. His interpretation, however, was that the sparks are produced by the quartz pebbles striking against each other. According to Wilbert (1993, 137), quartz pebbles do not spark when struck together but only produce heat. When asked about a fine dust, my shaman friend explained that, when new, a rattle does produce dust made by the quartz hitting the inner wooden shaft; but this is not desirable because dust may clog the breathing passages of the patient. To wisiratu shamans, then, the quartz clearly produces the sparks. Nevertheless, in shamanism the product—the light—is important rather than the process of how the light is produced. And this light, the rattle's glow, is one visible sign of the wisiratu's power as reinforced by his hebu mataro rattle.

It is not only in the wisiratu's curing role where the hebu mataro is important; it is also with him during his individual séances with his supreme beings, as Wilbert (1987a, 178–79) writes:

> In addition to the spirit helpers in his body, the priest-shaman also feeds a family of tutelary spirits which inhabit his sacred rattle in the form of quartz pebbles. The rattle spirits serve the shaman as a means of communication with the cardinal gods and with the world of Supernaturals at large. . . . Warao shamans retire frequently to their temples to feed the rattle spirits by blowing tobacco smoke into the orifices of the instrument. Seating himself on his stool or box, the shaman lights one of the long cigars that are kept in the temple for this purpose, holds the rattle with both hands up to his mouth, and blows the smoke through the mouth slits into the calabash. As the interior of the "head" of the rattle fills up with tobacco smoke it begins to "awaken." The shaman shakes it three times vertically and then swings it horizontally. The rattle is now fully awake, its spirit stones inside satisfied and ready to help the shaman communicate with the gods.

The hebu mataro is traditionally stored within a special basket called a torotoro (see figures 4.6 and 4.7). This is a large rectangular basket with a cover, both of which consist of inner and outer woven layers of wicker with palm leaves between them. Such a double thickness and inner core provides a practical cushion and protection from the rain for the hebu mataro. Citing Wilbert (1975b, 63), Guss (1989, 235) writes about the shaman's preparation of the basket and his appropriate song:

> When a Warao shaman prepares a torotoro to receive a rattle,
> he first lines the inner walls with caranna incense and chants:
>
>> "See here, my rattle.
>> This basket is for you.

You can occupy this *torotoroida*.
No longer
Do you have to lie on the floor
Wrapped in a piece of cloth.
Now you have a house of your own."

Along with the hebu mataro, the wisiratu will place a number of wina cigars within his torotoro. Thus prepared, the shaman is properly outfitted for his many religious obligations.

Given these many uses and functions and its large size, the question of the hebu mataro's provenance is perplexing. The Pemón to the south of the Orinoco Delta, for example, shake a bundle of leaves while curing illnesses; the Yekuana in the upper Orinoco use a smaller calabash with a carved handle depicting two shamans back to back in ecstasy; the Yanomamö use no rattle at all. Historical sources, however, describe calabash container rattle types among Guiana tribes. Bolingbroke (1947, 103–4), in his travelogue written between 1799 and 1806, describes a gourd or calabash rattle that is common to all indigenous people in the Guiana area: "This is a hollowed calabash, with a few seeds and stones enclosed in it, and a stick thrust through it. With this instrument he [the shaman] rattles, singing meanwhile a prayer to the yawahoo who is supposed to be offended." Likewise, Reverend Brett describes a "sorcerer's" rattle in 1868:

> They [shamans] are each furnished with a large gourd or calabash, which has been emptied of its spongy contents, and has a round stick run through the middle of it by means of two holes. The ends of this stick project—one forms the handle of the instrument, and the other has a long string, to which beautiful feathers are attached, wound round it in spiral circles. Within the calabash are a few small white stones, which rattle when it is shaken or turned round. The calabash itself is usually painted red. It is regarded with great awe by the heathen Indians, who fear to touch it, or, even to approach the place where it is kept.

Likewise, Izikowitz (1970, 115) writes: "it is not surprising that the use of the gourd rattle among the Warrau resembles that of the neighboring Arawak and Carib tribes." The large Warao rattle may, in fact, be similar to a large rattle that existed among the Taino or Island Arawak during preconquest times. Lovcn (1935, 494), for example, describes the shamanistic rattle of the Taino of Haiti as being so large that it required both hands of the shaman to grip it while playing it. Its sound was also very loud, like that of the hebu mataro. Unlike the single-handled rattle of the Warao, however, the Taino rattle had a double handle (perhaps similar to the Yekuana instrument). Further similarities and differences are impossible to ascertain because the Taino culture no longer exists and ancient examples have not been preserved.

Moriki

The Warao have another vessel idiophone, the moriki (figure 4.10), which is about the same size as the habi sanuka. It is a woven-container idiophone, however, and is constructed from filaments of tirite (*Ischnosiphon arouma,* according to Suárez [1968, 51]; *Junco americano,* according to Barral [1957, 185]), which is a vegetable fiber similar to willow (sarga in Spanish) or wicker (Suárez 1968, 60). Today a child's toy, the moriki may have been used during sacred ritual dances long ago and may have been imported from another culture; very little is known of its background. Evidence for its ritual-dance use

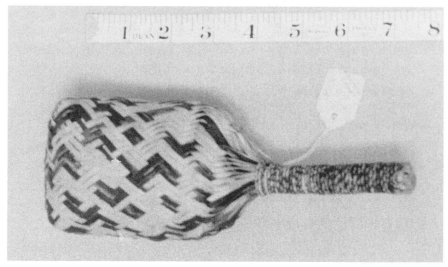

Figure 4.10. A moriki woven rattle from the museum of the Fundación La Salle, Caracas.

is suggested by the narrative "Usirumani, the woman of the hog plum tree" (Wilbert 1970, 377–78, narrative 172), which mentions that the basket rattle is performed in ensemble with several flutes at the house of Hokohiarotu, the Lord of the Sun. Today, in the village of Yaruara Akoho, the wicker rattle is most often made to sell to tourists in the Venezuelan towns of Tucupita and Barrancas. The construction of the instrument is noteworthy, nevertheless, as its crisscross style of weaving is extremely fine. Suárez (1968, 60–61) notes that there are two shapes for the moriki: one cylindrical and the other cubical. Both types have moriche strings wound around their tirite handles. The two examples in my possession measure approximately 22 centimeters in length and 28 centimeters in circumference.

Ehuru

The only membranophone belonging to the Warao is a double-headed skin drum known as ehuru (also eruru) (figure 4.11). Fashioned from a hollowed log cut into an hourglass shape, the ehuru has two heads that are usually made from the skin of the howler monkey (arawato),

Figure 4.11. An ehuru drum with drumstick. Olsen Collection.

although deer skins (Wilbert 1956, 9) and jaguar skins (Im Thurn 1883, 308) have also been used. Each drum head is dried around a hoop that is held in place by a wooden rim, and each rim is secured to the drum's body with moriche-fiber thongs that hold the skin heads in place somewhat in the manner of a European military drum. The end opposite the playing end includes a snare made from twisted moriche-fiber string containing a thorn about the size of a small toothpick inserted between the fiber strands. Because of the tension of the twisted strings, one end of the thorn presses on the drum head and vibrates against it when the opposite head is struck with the player's single drumstick. The ehuru in my possession measures 36.5 centimeters in length; the diameters of its heads are approximately 27 centimeters each; the circumference of the widest part of the body is 85 centimeters; and the circumference of the narrowest part of the body is approximately 73 centimeters. To play the instrument, the male drummer holds up his ehuru in one hand by a small moriche-fiber strap and strikes the head with a drumstick held in his other hand.

The most common Warao explanation for the ehuru's musical role is that it is used by a man while he is walking through the rain forest either on his way to the moriche palm grove to gather yuruma starch in preparation for the festival of nahanamu or simply as a means of diversion while traveling. As a sound maker, it may accompany song in the latter context while also letting those behind the drummer and those ahead at the destination know where their companions are. Schad (1953, 417) explains that the drummer is last in line, and he plays continuously. Turrado Moreno (1945, 227) writes that it is used to frighten off the jaguars and evil spirits that lurk in the rain forest when the Warao go off to gather yuruma. The roaring sound of the ehuru with its buzzing snare and howler-monkey skin is said to be caused by the spirit of the howler monkey; it is believed that the use of the skin gives the drum the "power of emitting the rolling roaring sounds for which this monkey is celebrated" (Im Thurn 1883, 308–9). Wilbert (1956, 10) suggests yet another use for the ehuru with his publication of a photograph of a nahanamu festival in which the drum is used along with several bone flutes. Today, however, the ehuru is no longer played during the nahanamu ritual complex, having been replaced by the hebu mataro rattle.

Talejo Tovar, a wisiratu shaman from Juan Mata Ahanoko, sang a traveling song with the ehuru as an accompanying instrument (recorded example 1). The drum rhythm he played was not steady, as one would expect for walking; instead, it was gradually accelerated, a characteristic that he did not explain, and one that naturally effected the tempo of the entire song, causing it to speed up. Music example 4.1 is an excerpt from his song with ehuru in which the drum acceleration (and, consequently, the acceleration of the singing) is indicated by the variable metronome markings and the symbol <.

Music Example 4.1. Song with ehuru (Talejo Tovar). Olsen Collection 72.8-137.

Muhusemoi

One of the most frequently seen and heard aerophones of the Warao is the muhusemoi (muhu = bone, semoi = wind instrument), a ductless, edge-blown flute made from the tibia of a deer (figure 4.12). Many Warao men possess and play muhusemoi flutes, and several of my Warao friends made them for me. Antonio Lorenzano taught me how to play it by giving me weekly lessons (figure 4.13).

While the muhusemoi belongs to a subcategory of edge aerophones with a notched mouthpiece, it does not possess an actual notch but more of a saddle-shaped cut where the flutist focuses his airstream. As such, the muhusemoi mouthpiece is more similar to that of the Japanese shakuhachi than the Peruvian kena. But an instrument that may be an archaeological prototype of the muhusemoi, an ancient bone flute from the La Cabrera style in Venezuelan archeology, has an actual U-shaped notch (pictured in Cruxent and Rouse 1963, plate 38A). Both this archaeological artifact and the muhusemoi have three finger holes and no thumb hole.

As I observed, personal preference dictates which fingers cover which holes. Juan Bustillo Calderón, for example, uses one finger of his left hand for the top hole and two fingers of his right hand for the bottom two holes (figure 4.14), while Antonio Lorenzano uses a two plus one combination (figure 4.13). The Warao flutist has a unique and standardized way of fingering his muhusemoi, however, making the technique unlike any other method of fingering in the known world of flutes. The typical Warao method is to open the bottom finger hole, close it, open the middle finger hole, close it, and open the upper finger hole and close it. In other words, only one hole is open at a time. This technique produces a scale unlike any other known to me; and to

Figure 4.12. A muhusemoi bone flute made by Antonio Lorenzano. Olsen Collection.

Figure 4.13. My flute teacher, Antonio Lorenzano, playing the muhusemoi.

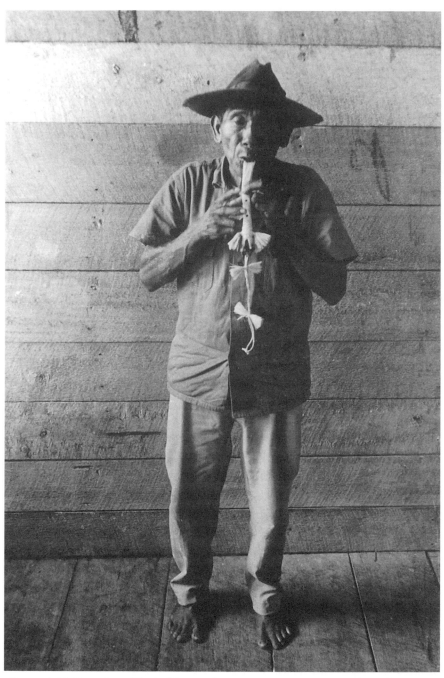

Figure 4.14. Juan Bustillo Calderón playing Antonio Lorenzano's muhusemoi.

understand it more deeply, I took muhusemoi lessons from Antonio, a master muhusemoi player and maker. Additionally, I collected fifteen bone flutes in the central Orinoco Delta (some were made especially for me, and some were old), studied three muhusemoi flutes from the museum of the Fundación La Salle in Caracas, and analyzed six more from the Fowler Museum of Cultural History at UCLA (figure 4.15). Thus, I had a total of twenty-four that I tonometrically measured in search of information about Warao tuning; these data are presented in table 4.3. I found that the most typical tone system, placed in cipher notation, is 1 ♮ 4 6, occurring in seven of the twenty-four muhusemoi flutes or in 29 percent of the total studied (see table 4.4). A minor third (♮ 1) foundation interval occurs in 67 percent of all the muhusemoi flutes studied, while the major third (3 1) occurs in 4 percent, the major second (2 1) in 25 percent, and the minor second (♮ 1) in 4 percent (see table 4.5). Although several of the flutes I studied have nearly identical tone systems, this seems only coincidental because most often (when playing together) Warao flutists choose several instruments of varying lengths and thus of differing pitches (recorded example 2). The only standard that exists is an approximate one, and variations on the tone system I have indicated are common.

The method of muhusemoi construction explains the lack of tuning standardization. After he has selected the proper deer tibia, the maker opens both ends of the bone and removes as much marrow as he can with his knife. Then he places the bone in a place out of the reach of dogs but within the reach of cockroaches, which eat out the marrow within several days. After the bone is hollowed and dried, the maker forms the saddle-shaped mouthpiece with a knife. Then he places the mouthpiece edge within the crotch between his thumb and first finger, using his fingers as rulers for finger-hole placement. Where the tip of his first finger falls he will drill the bottom finger hole with the sharpened point of a harpoon in the fashion of a fire drill (figure 4.16), a technique requiring only about one minute of effort per finger hole depending on the sharpness of the harpoon point. The maker then measures the distance for the second finger hole with the back of his thumb (from the tip of the thumb to the first joint) and drills it with similar ease. The same techniques are used to determine the placement of the third finger hole and drill it out. Because Warao hands and Orinoco Delta deer tibias all differ in size, there is naturally a difference in the

Table 4.3. Muhusemoi tone systems

Tone system	Warao maker	Warao village	Item	Collection/ID no.	Date
7 4 3 1	P. Rivero	Lorenzano Ahanoko	1	Olsen/M-1	1972
7 4 3 1	J. Calderón	Hebu Wabanoko	9	Olsen/M-9	1972
7 4 3 1	J. Moraleda	Yaruara Akoho	14	Olsen/M-14	1973
7 4 3 1	—	—	16	Fund. La Salle/a	—
7 4 3 1	—	Wayo	22	UCLA/X65-6240	—
6 4 3 1	C. Rivero	Yaruara Akoho	2	Olsen/M-2	1973
6 4 3 1	J. A. Páez	Yaruara Akoho	7	Olsen/M-7	1973
6 4 3 1	J. Moraleda	Yaruara Akoho	13	Olsen/M-13	1973
6 4 3 1	—	Naunoko, Winikina	18	Fund. La Salle/c	1954
6 4 3 1	—	Wayo	20	UCLA/X65-6241	1965
6 4 3 1	—	Wayo	23	UCLA/X65-6239	1965
6 4 3 1	—	Wayo	24	UCLA/X65-6238	1965
7 4 2 1	A. Lorenzano	Lorenzano Ahanoko	3	Olsen/M-3	1972
7 4 2 1	A. Lorenzano	Lorenzano Ahanoko	4	Olsen/M-4	1972
6 3 3 1	C. Rivero	Yaruara Akoho	5	Olsen/M-5	1973
6 3 3 1	C. Rivero	Yaruara Akoho	6	Olsen/M-6	1973
4 3 2 1	J. Calderón	Hebu Wabanoko	8	Olsen/M-8	1972
5 3 2 1	J. Calderón	Hebu Wabanoko	10	Olsen/M-10	1973
7 6 3 1	J. Moraleda	Yaruara Akoho	11	Olsen/M-11	1973
7 3 2 1	J. Moraleda	Yaruara Akoho	12	Olsen/M-12	1973
6 4 3 1	J. Moraleda	Yaruara Akoho	15	Olsen/M-15	1973
3 3 2 1	—	Sarewabanoko	17	Fund. La Salle/b	1952
6 3 2 1	—	Wayo	19	UCLA/X65-13712	1965
2 4 3 1	—	Wayo	21	UCLA/X65-6237	1965

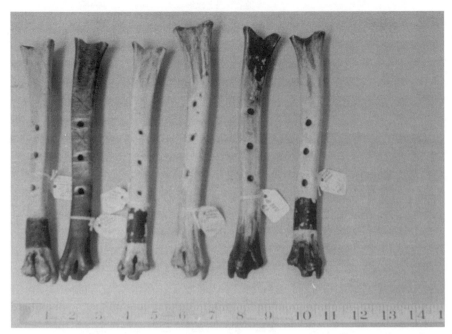

Figure 4.15. Six muhusemoi bone flutes from the Fowler Anthropology Museum of the University of California, Los Angeles.

Table 4.4. Occurrence rate of muhusemoi tone systems

Tone system	No. of items	Item nos.	%
7̌4 3̌1	5	1, 9, 14, 16, 22	28.8
6 4 3̌1	7	2, 7, 13, 18, 20, 23, 24	29.4
7̌4 2̌1	2	3, 4	8.3
6 3 3̌1	1	5	4.15
6̌3 3̌1	1	6	4.15
4̌3 2̌1	1	8	4.15
5 3 2 1	1	10	4.15
7̌6̌3 1	1	11	4.15
7̌3 2 1	1	12	4.15
6̌4 3̌1	1	15	4.15
3̌3̌2 1	1	17	4.15
6 3̌2 1	1	19	4.15
? 4 3̌1	1	21	4.15

Table 4.5. Occurrence rate of muhusemoi musical terminating patterns

Terminating pattern	No. of items	Item nos.	%
3 1	1	11	4
3̌1	16	1, 2, 5–7, 9, 13–16, 18, 20–24	67
2 1	6	3–4, 10, 12, 17, 19	25
2̌1	1	8	4

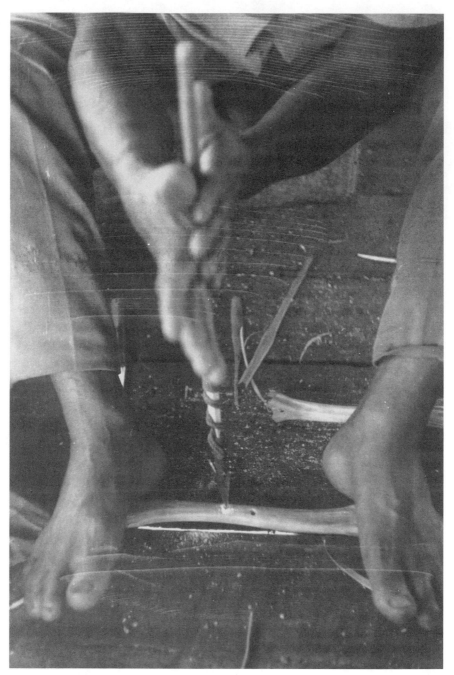

Figure 4.16. Cirilo Rivero drilling a finger hole in a muhusemoi. Olsen Collection.

tone systems of the final products. Another construction technique often includes the fabrication of moriche-fiber tassels that are attached to the distal end of the flute (see figures 4.13 and 4.14). According to several flute makers, such tassels are for ornamentation only, although occasionally they are made into lengthy loops used for suspending the instruments around the necks of the players.

Muhusemoi flutes are played in several contexts, as my Warao flute teachers explained. A muhusemoi and an ehuru, for example, are often played together for contentment while going into the rain forest to cut down sangrito trees to make face paint. Another Warao musician explained that two muhusemoi flutes, or a muhusemoi and a hekunukabe (a plant-stalk flute), occasionally accompanied by an ehuru drum, are played in the morichal by several men while other family members fell moriche palms, cut out the pith, and prepare yuruma starch for the patron kanobo during the preparation-gathering segment of the nahanamu ritual complex (see chapter 14). The nahanamu dance sequences provide the major contexts for bone-flute playing when several muhusemoi flutes, two isimoi clarinets, several hebu mataro rattles, perhaps a habi sanuka rattle or a sleigh bell, and sewei anklet and pole rattles make up the orchestra (recorded example 4). A different melody is used for each of these muhusemoi contexts. Music example 4.2 is an excerpt of the melody performed while preparing yuruma. It emphasizes the approximate minor third (from a B-flat to a G) as a terminating or foundation interval. Recorded example 2 features two muhusemoi flutes playing together as they would during a nahanamu festival dance; notice how the two instruments are pitched a fourth apart and how they play the same melody in a type of canon, each giving free reign to individual expression while maintaining a similar pulse.

In spite of the fact that the muhusemoi is used during the preparation and gathering of the sacred yuruma starch and is played during the nahanamu dance festival, it has very little power, as Antonio explained. Nevertheless, according to Warao mythology, it is an ancient musical instrument that first appeared in antiquity as an instrument belonging to Haburi, the Warao culture hero and the inventor of flutes. Before Haburi there was no music in the world at all, and he is credited with inventing both the muhusemoi and the harihari flutes.

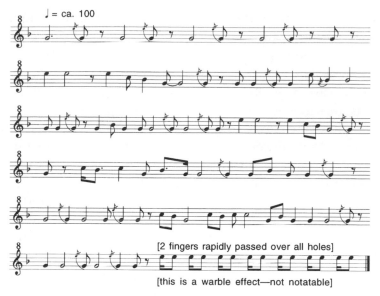

Music Example 4.2. Muhusemoi melody for yuruma gathering (Pedro Rivero).
Olsen Collection 72.8-289.

Hekunukabe

Another ductless vertical flute, similar to the muhusemoi but constructed from a plant stem (wana), is the hekunukabe (also waro,
according to Wilbert 1956, 3). This instrument also has a saddle-
shaped mouthpiece and three finger holes and is played exactly like the
muhusemoi (figure 4.17). It derives its name from the Warao word for
a burning piece of carbon because the flute's finger holes are pierced by
an ember stick (Barral 1957, 111). The prefix, hekunu, means fire in
Warao.

Like the muhusemoi, the hekunukabe is played in ensemble with a
muhusemoi and occasionally an ehuru during yuruma preparation;
but by contrast the hekunukabe is destroyed while the muhusemoi is
saved and used over and over again, year after year. Antonio explained
that the hekunukabe is used for serenading to while away the time. In
1666 the chronicler Rochefort (cited by Stevenson 1975, 52) wrote
about a similar role for cane and bone flutes among the Taino and Island Carib: "In the morning, as soon as they are up, they commonly
play on the Flute or Pipe; of which Instrument they have several sorts,
as well polish'd and as handsom [sic] as ours, and some of those made

Figure 4.17. Juan Bustillo Calderón playing a hekunukabe plant-stalk flute. Olsen Collection.

of the bones of their Enemies. . . . While they are playing on the Flute, the Wives are busie in making ready their breakfast."

Daokohota

Another ductless vertical flute, daokohota (daukoho semoi), also said by the Warao to be used for entertainment, is similar to the muhu-semoi and hekunokabe because of its saddle-shaped mouthpiece. But virtually nothing is known about this instrument except that it is made from the pincers of the blue crab (congrejo) and can produce only one tone. If the daokohota was indeed used for entertainment, it would be a most unusual instrument for that context because of its limited melodic capabilities. Usually one-toned instruments are used for signaling. The Warao narrative "Usirumani, the woman of the hog plum tree" (Wilbert 1970, 377–78, narrative 172) contains a passage that refers to the daokohota and another flute: "When he [the religious practitioner named Imanaidarotu, Lord of the Dark Night] returned in his canoe, he heard music nearby, music of flutes and fifes of the Warao *esemoi daukoho, esemoy harihari* and others, accompanied by dance (basket) rattles. Imanaidarotu approached the place of the music that turned out to be the house of the other shaman, Hokohiarotu, Lord of the Sun." This narrative suggests a ritual-dance use for the daokohota, in ensemble with the harihari flute and basket rattles, possibly morikituma.

Harihari

Another Warao aerophone no longer used today is a ductless, cross-blown, horizontal or transverse bamboo flute called harihari (hari = toucan) (figure 4.18). It is also referred to as hariharisemoi or esemoi harihari, the "flute of the toucan," because its sound is similar to the song of the toucan (Barral 1957, 79). The harihari is the principal musical instrument of Haburi, the Warao culture hero, and other spirits, an association that may also be suggested by its name: the Warao identify the toucan as a "witch bird" (Barral 1957, 108). In spite of the instrument's etymology, these mythical references are the only association of the harihari with the toucan—it is not constructed from toucan parts, nor does its shape resemble that of a toucan or toucan parts. Another Warao narrative associates the harihari with vultures, as in the following excerpt from "The man with a vulture wife" (Wilbert 1970, 343–44, narrative 161):

> There were once three brothers. The middle one was a very good hunter, and this story is all about him and his bird wife. While out in the bush one day he came across a large house wherein people were "sporting." These people were very fair, much like white persons, a thing not to be wondered at, because they were really vultures . . . who had taken off their feathers just for the occasion, to hang about the place and decorate it. They were dancing and singing the *makuari* tune on all sorts of musical instruments, from the *harri-harri* flute to the rattle.

Figure 4.18. A harihari flute made by Antonio Lorenzano. Olsen Collection.

The harihari flute is mentioned again later in the narrative; however, it is then played by the man, alone in his hammock, as he thinks of the beautiful vulture girls.

The harihari is a unique edge-type aerophone because both ends of its bamboo tube are closed and its cross-blown embouchure hole is placed between the finger holes—one finger hole is to the left of the embouchure hole and two finger holes are to its right. This particular construction gives the instrument a rather low fundamental pitch and a dark tone quality. (When I play it, the tone is soft, dark, and slightly breathy.)

The harihari is almost completely unknown among today's Warao. Antonio Lorenzano knew how to make one by remembering how his uncle Salvador used to make it, but he did not know how to play it. The harihari he constructed for me measures 40.5 centimeters in length. Like the muhusemoi, this instrument had a serenading function and was usually played by bachelors for entertainment. When questioned about a possible magical love-charm capability (which is suggested in the previous narrative, when the man plays the flute while resting in his hammock), as with some native North American flutes, Antonio assured me it had none. He insisted it was simply an instrument played by happy and contented young men in the morning, the afternoon, or at midnight, even when people were sleeping. He also explained that it was the most important instrument associated with Haburi, the culture hero and inventor of all flutes. Several Warao narratives about Haburi describe situations when he is playing a harihari (Wilbert 1970, narratives 140 and 144), a muhusemoi (Wilbert 1970, narrative 141), and an unidentified flute (Wilbert 1970, narrative 139). Its entertainment function is suggested in the following excerpt from the narrative called "The story of Haburi" (Wilbert 1970, 286, narrative 140):

Wau-uta [a female shaman] made the child [Haburi] grow all at once into a youth, and gave him the *harri-harri* to blow and the

arrows to shoot. As the mother and aunt were returning with
the cassava, they heard the music playing and said to themselves, "There was no man or boy there when we left the house;
who can it be? It must be a man playing." And though ashamed
they went in and saw the youth blowing the *harri-harri*.

This narrative is important for another reason: it does *not* credit
Haburi as being the inventor of the flute (as stated by Antonio), although he may have been its first player. Rather, the narrative suggests
that Wau-uta, a woman, was the possessor and perhaps inventor of the
flute before a man. Because flutes among today's Warao are exclusively
men's instruments, this narrative suggests a reversal of the social
order. A similar reversal of gender roles also occurred among the
Brazilian Mundurucú, according to their myth about the origin of
their sacred trumpet called karökö, which the women originally
owned and played but was taken away from them by the men (Murphy
and Murphy 1974, 87–95).

   In still other narratives the harihari is a favored instrument of supernatural male beings (Wilbert 1970, narratives 52, 55, 144, 161, and
172) as well as of certain mortal men who play melodies that enable
their female loved ones to identify them from afar, as the following two
excerpts from Warao lore attest:

> When night came on, she heard the *harri-harri* [flute] playing
> in the river, and the sound gradually coming nearer and
> nearer. Recognizing it as her husband's, she turned to her
> child and said, "That tune is like what your father used to
> play. Perhaps he alone was saved when all the others were
> killed." [from "The woman killed by her husband's spirit" in
> Wilbert 1970, 139, narrative 52]
>   . . . When he left, Mayakoto carried with him a kind of
> flute, *harihariesemoy,* or "flute of the toucan," as it was called
> by the Indians. And when he returned from fishing, he blew it
> from a long distance to tell his wives that he was coming back
> bringing *morocoto* [fish]. Upon hearing the sound of the flute,
> the women got up and lit the fire in the kitchen. Afterwards
> each of them set up her *diri* or wooden grill in order to broil
> the fish as soon as Mayakoto arrived.
>   But one day when Mayakoto had left very early in the

morning, the evil spirit Hahuba appeared to him while he was fishing. Hahuba snatched the *morocotos* from him and swallowed Mayakoto as well. Afterwards he got in the canoe of Mayakoto and went to the latter's house. Hahuba, the evil spirit, did not know how to play the *harihari* or flute of the toucan, and so upon arriving at the house, in place of playing the flute as Mayakoto was accustomed to doing, he called to the women, "Hey, my wives! Where is the road, one can't see anything here." The women looked at each other strangely and said, "Hmmm. Who will this be that doesn't know the road. Mayakoto knows it very well, and besides he played the flute of the toucan." [from "The Warao legend (Haburi)" in Wilbert 1970, 301, narrative 144.]

These suggestions of flute music as a type of personal identification are similar to one of the functions of the kena flute among the Incas, as Garcilaso de la Vega (1961, 79) wrote in the late sixteenth or early seventeenth century: "The story is told of a Spaniard who, one evening, upon meeting an Indian girl of his acquaintance on a Cuzco street, urged her to come home with him. 'Señor,' she replied, 'kindly let me go my way. The flute you hear is calling me with such tenderness and passion that I can't resist it. Leave me, for your own life's sake; my love is calling me and I must answer him, that he may be my husband and I his wife.'"

Izikowitz (1970, 300–301) discusses several transverse flutes that have notable similarities to the Warao harihari, especially a flute of the Palikur people (Arawak speakers who inhabit the border area between Brazil and French Guiana) and other cultures in Guyana (formerly British Guiana). The relative proximity between the Warao and native American (Arawak) cultures in French Guiana and Guyana suggests cultural borrowing, perhaps from the ancient Arawak who passed through the delta and possibly continued eastward as well as northward.

Isimoi

A Warao aerophone that has been called everything from a trumpet (Heinen and Ruddle 1974, 130; Wilbert 1975a, 177; Suárez 1968, 175), to a large flute (Turrado Moreno 1945, 226), to an oboe (Schomburgk, cited by Roth 1924, 461) is actually a heteroglottal,

single-reed, concussion aerophone (clarinet) called the isimoi
(esimoi) (figures 4.19 and 4.32). This instrument, used during many
of the events associated with the nahanamu ritual complex, is the
most sacred aerophone among the Warao. It is the sole property of
the isimoi arotu or "owner of the isimoi," who is both the maker and
the player of the instrument. The Warao believe that the isimoi has a
spirit that is the same as the kanobo who is the patron of the village.
Jaime Zapata was the owner of the isimoi when he related the following origin myth to me:

> The origin of the isimoi is this: a wisiratu named Yauware
> bought a kanobo, and as payment for the kanobo he gave two
> Warao, like exchanging kanobo for Warao. When the kanobo
> arrived here in this land and to Yauware's house he said: "You
> have to make an isimoi." And Yauware made an isimoi. This is
> the knowledge that the wisiratu held so that fewer Warao
> would die, like they were dying then. "Now you have to make
> an isimoi," was the command. The wisiratu Yauware thought:
> "With so many Warao dying, we cannot continue like this. We
> have to do something so that so many will not die. For this
> reason we are going to make an isimoi. This is my knowledge."
>
> These are the desires, the thoughts, the beliefs of our
> grandfathers whom we do not see. These were their desires
> and this was the knowledge they had, in order to keep the
> Warao from dying. Yauware made the isimoi, and here is the
> isimoi. Then the people also thought to celebrate a nahanamu
> ritual. Thus, they held a nahanamu, using the isimoi while
> dancing. This isimoi was made by them so that people can
> dance in the festival of nahanamu.
>
> Those who made this isimoi died. And many others died.
> But now the isimoi is always with the Warao, and it will stay
> forever with us. Now, I was called to be in charge of the isimoi.
> And the day when death touches me, I will die too, and an-
> other person will become in charge of the isimoi. This is the
> desire of the Warao. Thus, you must not lose the isimoi, be-
> cause if you do, everybody will die—women, men, even the
> Creoles will die. If the isimoi is played during times of pesti-
> lence among the Warao when many people are dying from ill-
> ness (which is not often the case with the Warao today, be-

cause today's Warao die from witchcraft caused by other Warao), then they do not die. And, neither does the kanobo. When an illness from the kanobo does hit a Warao, however, then a wisiratu comes and sings a song to cure him.

Thus, the origin of the isimoi went like that, and one should not die now with an illness brought upon by a kanobo. If an illness does come, however, we cure with a wisiratu song. And thus we go on like this forever, and we continue our customs. All of us are going to die, including me. All the people here at this moment will die. But the isimoi will remain forever, for us and the Warao who will follow us. The isimoi must not be lost, because we must avoid death for the Warao. This is a Warao belief. For this reason we want to keep it, and we have the right to guard the isimoi well. Losing it, we lose all Warao existence. This dance, this song of the isimoi, is forever. And the nahanamu that we dance is forever. It cannot be lost. This custom is for everybody. It is for us at Winikina, for those at Arawabisi, Arawao—all are the same. The day I die, whoever replaces me, will do the same. And presently there is little illness, since I am in charge of this.

Thus, we are here as Warao, and this is how we think. And just like that our grandchildren and great-grandchildren continue the beliefs of our ancients who have died. This isimoi will continue forever, for our grandchildren and our great-grandchildren. The isimoi will never be lost for the Warao because we received it from our grandfather and before that from our great-grandfather. Thus we, the grandchildren, continue with the same custom.

The nahanamu ritual cycle itself, as it relates to Kanoboism will be discussed later; the isimoi is employed throughout numerous portions of that cycle, as Antonio Lorenzano explains in detail as he narrates his stories about nahanamu in chapter 14. During the final day, which includes the main dancing festival of nahanamu, two or more of a pair of isimoi are played, one larger than the other (recorded example 3). They are usually performed along with one or more muhusemoi flutes, one or more hebu mataro rattles, and several sewei strung rattles (recorded example 4). The isimoi is held with one hand only when played.

Figure 4.19. One of the isimoi players at a nahanamu festival, warming up his instrument; Koboina Akoho, Arawao-Koboina River.

Each isimoi is reconstructed yearly before the collecting and preparation of the sacred moriche starch (yuruma) for the patron kanobo. When the owner of the isimoi returns to his house from the moriche grove in the rain forest where he performed during the yuruma gathering, he must hang his instrument in a basket above his hammock until he needs it again for the main dance of the nahanamu ritual complex. When the festival is over he breaks his isimoi by dismantling it. This involves removing the wax, detaching the reed sounding device, and cleaning the small calabash. If any of these parts are not broken, he saves them because they belong to the patron kanobo.

Jaime Zapata, the Winikina isimoi arotu, constructed two isimoi clarinets for me in 1972. Figures 4.20 through 4.32 document the various stages of the construction. The commentary of the process is by Antonio Lorenzano, whose respect for his friend is summarized by these words: "When he blows into it, it sounds. For him it sounds. When I try it, it doesn't sound. It is very difficult. Some others can play it, but the most knowledgeable is Jaime. He is the only one." In the following discourse, Antonio's descriptions are followed by my additional comments and interpretations:

Figure 4.20: "It has a small stick inside that has to have a hole made in it from here to here." This is the internal sounding device tube, to

Figure 4.20. Jaime Zapata making an isimoi clarinet. He is holding the internal sounding device to which he will affix the single reed.

Figure 4.21. Jaime Zapata wrapping the reed to the internal sounding device.

which is affixed the reed. It is made from ohiyobotoro wood, according to Jaime (ojioboto, young moriche shoot, Barral 1957, 174).

Figure 4.21: "Then he makes a thing called eruko from the palm called deao or ao." This term is probably eruru, meaning "noise maker," although the word is usually applied to the membranophonic drum, ehuru (Barral 1957, 79). In this picture Jaime is wrapping the reed to the internal sounding-device tube. Jaime explained that he makes the long reed from the leaf of the sehoro (*Junco americano;* tirite in Spanish, a willow commonly used in basket making, Barral 1957, 185; this plant is scientifically known as *Ischnosiphon arouma*, according to Suárez 1968, 51).

Figure 4.22: Here Jaime is holding the completed internal sounding-device tube with its reed attached; the long portion of the tirite will protrude from the bell of the instrument without an acoustic function.

Figure 4.23: "Then he takes a small fruit called trist or triste, made from amaro amaro (calabash)." The long palm reed is inserted into the open calabash, and the base of the internal sounding device is fastened inside the proximal end of the calabash that has the smaller opening.

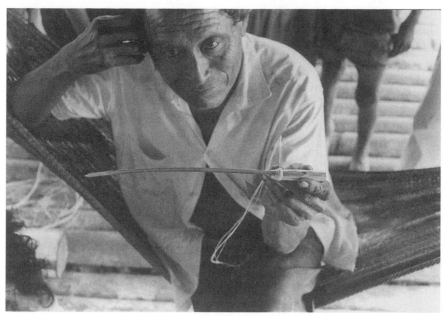

Figure 4.22. Here Jaime is holding the completed internal sounding device with its reed attached.

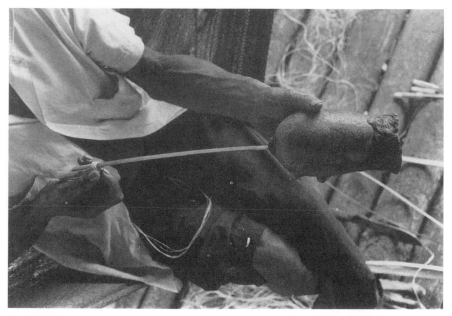

Figure 4.23. The long reed is inserted into the smaller end of the open calabash.

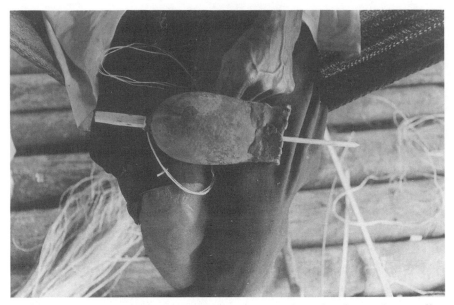

Figure 4.24. The completed sounding device protrudes from the smaller opening of the calabash.

Figure 4.24: The completed internal sounding device protrudes from the smaller opening of the calabash, while the nonacoustical free end of the reed protrudes from the larger distal-end opening of the calabash.

Figure 4.25: Like any fine reed musician, the maker of the isimoi scrapes and adjusts his reed until it sounds good.

Figure 4.26: "Then he blows. When he blows into it he has to see if it is good."

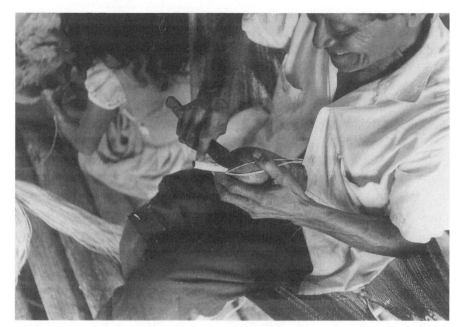

Figure 4.25. Jaime adjusting the reed of the clarinet.

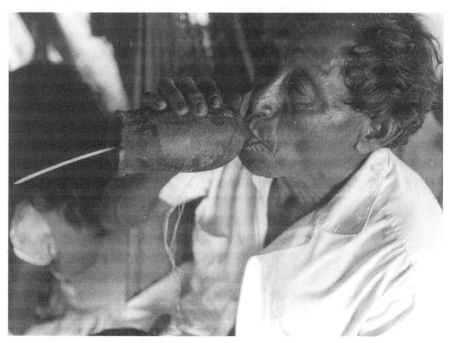

Figure 4.26. Blowing into the instrument to test its reed.

Figure 4.27. Fabricating the external air duct by cutting a section from a long piece of moriche palm stem.

Figure 4.27: Jaime fabricates the air duct, or batoko (meaning pendant, according to Barral 1957, 48), by cutting a section from a long piece of moriche palm stem. This tube is also called nahawaha arototo, referring to the hole inside the moriche stem.

Figure 4.28: The hollowing out of the moriche stem is started with a knife. "The mouthpiece (duct) is made open, with a hole." The stem is converted into a tube by first piercing it with a red-hot metal rod.

Figure 4.29: "The hollowing out of the stem is continued and completed with a piece of burning ember until it is completely hollowed out." Jaime actually started a small fire within the tube, blowing into it until the insides were completely burned out.

Figure 4.28. Hollowing out the solid moriche stem with a knife to make an air duct.

Figure 4.29. Hollowing out the tube with a burning ember.

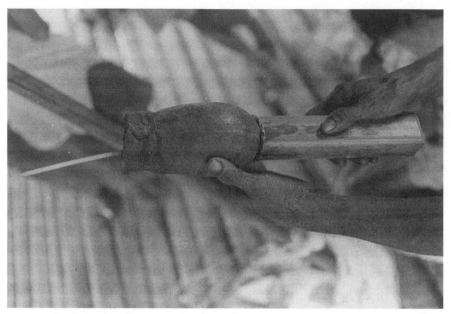

Figure 4.30. The external air duct is placed over the internal sounding device, jutting up to the calabash.

Figure 4.30: "And then here the batoko is placed over the mouthpiece, and with its batoko the isimoi is almost ready."

Figure 4.31: The nearly completed isimoi and a number of components and tools are placed within a torotoro basket. In the middle of the basket a completed heteroglottal reed attached to its internal sounding-device tube can be seen, while underneath are several additional internal sounding-device tubes. All that is lacking to complete the isimoi is the wax (abi in Warao, cera in Spanish), which is packed tightly around the joint between the duct and the calabash, and the ornamental isimoi arokoihi, the "beard" according to Jaime.

Figure 4.32: These are the two completed isimoi heteroglottal single-reed concussion aerophones constructed by Jaime Zapata.

In summary, the isimoi internal single-reed sounding device never touches the player's lips. Instead, it is placed in a small hole in the calabash and enclosed within a tube or duct made from a moriche palm stem that functions like a cap on a European Renaissance krummhorn. The long extension of the reed protrudes from the open distal

Figure 4.31. The nearly completed isimoi and a number of components and tools are placed within a torotoro basket. In the middle of the basket is a completed heteroglottal reed attached to the internal sounding device, while underneath are several other internal sounding devices.

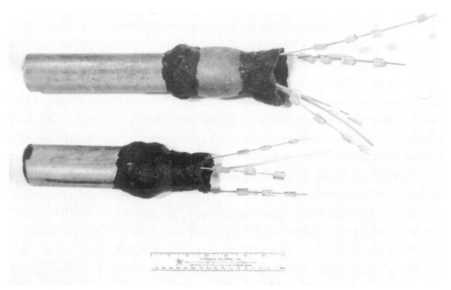

Figure 4.32. Two completed isimoi clarinets built by Jaime Zapata. Olsen Collection.

end of the calabash and is acoustically nonfunctional as are the attachments stuck into the wax at the distal end of the instrument. Both types of extensions were explained as being merely ornamental. The wax, however, forms a bell like the distal end of a European clarinet, and this may have an acoustic effect on the isimoi. Although the isimoi does not have finger holes, the owner of the isimoi is capable of producing two distinct notes and limited microtonal glissandi by increasing and decreasing his air pressure (recorded example 3). The isimoi's two main pitches, like the first interval produced by the majority of the muhusemoi flutes and like Warao shamanistic curing music, are at the interval of an approximate minor third (3 1). Music example 14.3 (included in chapter 14) is a transcribed excerpt of nahanamu instrumental music during a contextual performance; the two isimoi parts constitute the middle staves. The music for each instrument clearly demonstrates the prevalence of the approximate minorthird interval, while the two isimoi clarinets are pitched a fourth apart. Recorded example 4 is from a portion of that nahanamu festival recorded at Boca de Koboina on 27 July 1972. The free but metered polyphony is clearly heard in the two sections that constitute a dance cycle (see chapter 14).

Other native American cultures in Venezuela and adjacent areas also have heteroglottal single-reed (clarinet-type) instruments somewhat related to the isimoi. The Carib-speaking Wai-Wai in nearby Guyana, for example, have a similar instrument, as do the Venezuelan Amazonian Yekuana, also Carib speakers. Among the latter group, their bamboo clarinets known as tekeyë (tekeya) or wanna (wana) are more than a meter in length and are always played in pairs, with one instrument considered male and the other female. The Warao do not make a gender distinction between their pair of isimoi. Another clarinet-type instrument is found among the northwestern Venezuelan Guajiro, who are Arawak speakers. Theirs, however, is an idioglottal clarinet with finger holes. The Warao's ancient neighbors to the north, the Taino and the Carib in the Caribbean islands, did not possess single-reed instruments, nor did any other pre-Columbian culture according to Izikowitz: "In South America the clarinet is never found archaeologically. . . . It is therefore possible that the clarinet is a post-Columbian instrument in South America" (1970, 262). This analysis, however, does not consider the fact that, if there were pre-Columbian reeds, they were made from perishable materials and no trace would be left of them. This is the situation, for example, with the Greek and Etruscan auloi (plural of aulos). The perishability of the reeds is what makes it so difficult to arrive at conclusions concerning the precise nature of sound-producing devices and other ancient musical instruments when the vibrating parts have long since disintegrated (see Olsen 1990). Therefore, archaeologically discovered tubes in South America that have been thought to be trumpets or flutes could actually have been single- (or double-) reed aerophones whose reeds have not survived. In addition, the rich ritualistic folklore surrounding the isimoi and other sacred clarinet-type instruments in the South American rain forest strongly suggests their pre-Columbian origin. Nevertheless, the question will always remain moot.

Heresemoi

The heresemoi is a Warao lip-concussion aerophone (trumpet) made from a conch shell (figure 4.33 and Furst 1965, 6, figure 1a: these photographs are of the same instrument). It is an important instrument, primarily used for signaling and giving directions to canoes at night. Related uses include signaling the departure and arrival of the crabbing canoes, announcing the death of a tribal member, signaling the

Figure 4.33. Heresemoi conch-shell trumpet from Yaruara Akoho. Olsen Collection.

annual trek to the moriche groves in preparation for nahanamu (Wilbert 1956, 5–6), announcing the completion of a newly made canoe (Furst 1965, 27), and "herald[ing] each new phase in the process of felling, trimming, and scooping out . . . the trunk" of the tree from which a canoe is built (Wilbert 1976, 329).

The conch used by the Warao for the heresemoi belongs to the species *Strombus eieas Linne* (Furst 1965, 5), which is not local but must be acquired from as far away as the island of Margarita or purchased in nearby Tucupita. The heresemoi's mouthpiece is made by cutting off the end of the conch shell with many short chops of a machete. Because this is the hardest part of the shell, the maker sometimes has to repair a damaged embouchure hole with wax.

The heresemoi is usually played by a shaman or other high-ranking Warao male. It was played for me by Bernardo Jiménez Tovar (figure 4.34), a wisiratu shaman, whose playing technique included portamento or note bending caused by an increase and decrease of air pressure. This style is indicated in music example 4.3. (The portamenti are represented by the graphics in the notation.) Another heresemoi playing technique, used to signal grief at the time of death of a Warao, is to make three long blasts (Wilbert 1956, 5).

The shell-trumpet concept in the central and southern regions of the Americas is pre-Columbian; and ancient Caribbean, Mexican, and Andean cultures had shell trumpets (Furst 1965). Those from ancient Peruvian coastal cultures, for example, especially the Moche, were highly venerated for their interior spirals; the concept was so important for them that they even manufactured replicas from ceramic when natural shells were not available. No information about such conch-shell internal spiral symbolism was provided by the Warao for their conch-shell trumpets.

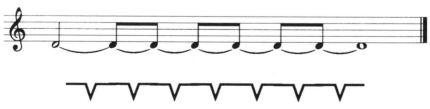

Music Example 4.3. Heresemoi melody for signaling (Bernardo Jiménez Tovar). (No recording.)

Figure 4.34. Bernardo Jiménez Tovar playing a heresemoi conch-shell trumpet in Yaruara Akoho.

Bakohi

A lip-concussion aerophone that has replaced the heresemoi in many areas of the Orinoco Delta is the bakohi (also known as the warra, according to Wilbert 1956, 6), a trumpet of either thick bamboo, wana wood, or cow horn. The word *bakoi* comes from *baka* (*vaca* in Spanish, meaning cow) and *ahoi* (horn). Although a conch shell is preferred because its sound carries over greater distances, the bamboo or wooden bakohi is occasionally used to announce the crabbing season in a way similar to that described for the heresemoi. Likewise, it can also be used in place of a heresemoi to send signals between villages—announcing, for example, a serious illness or a death. In an ethnographic description about Warao canoe building, Wilbert (1976, 341) writes: "Next the conch shell trumpet must be readied. They are rare instruments hard to come by and if one is not available a wooden trumpet made from the bark of a piece of mangrove aerial root may be substituted." In 1847 Schomburgk (cited in Wilbert 1956, 6) mentioned that several bamboo trumpets were played together in an "orchestra" for the festival of nahanamu, although he undoubtedly confused the instruments with the isimoi clarinets, which look like trumpets to the untrained eye, perhaps sound like trumpets to the untrained ear, and to this day are still confused with trumpets, as I have mentioned.

When the bakoi is made from cow horn (figure 4.35) in parts of the central Orinoco Delta, it occasionally serves as a substitute for both the heresemoi and the bamboo or wooden bakohi. It is used to signal events within a short range because its sound is not nearly as loud as the conch shell, bamboo, or wooden varieties.

Other Trumpets

In earlier times a double-chambered ceramic trumpet in the shape of a figure 8 was used by the Warao (Schomburgk, cited by Roth 1924, 452). Although this clay trumpet was never mentioned to me by my Warao musician friends, I photographed at the British Museum the very instrument that Schomburgk collected among the Warao at the turn of the century (figure 4.36).

Early writers about the ancient Caribbean mention only conch-shell trumpets, although a picture of a Carib war dance shows two shamans or priests holding long tubes to their mouths that resemble spiral trumpets (after Picard, reproduced from Fewkes 1907 and pictured in Rouse 1963b, plate 95). Also with reference to the ancient Caribbean, Fred Olsen (1974, 96) has suggested that the conch-shell trumpet had a ceremonial function because the protuberances on the shell are similar in shape to the zemis or Taino idols. The triangular shapes of these protuberances may, according to him, symbolize a volcano or sacred mountain; and to carve a zemi into this particular form may capture the supernatural power of the mountain. To carry this symbolic interpretation one step further, the voice of the conch-shell trumpet may be

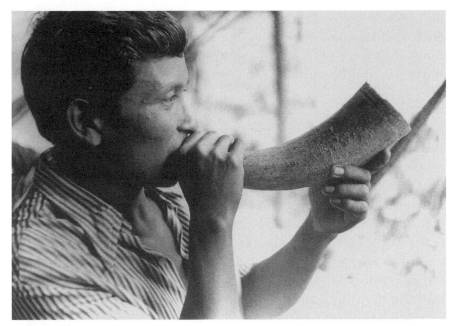

Figure 4.35. Segundo Rivero playing a bakohi cow horn trumpet in Yaruara Akoho.

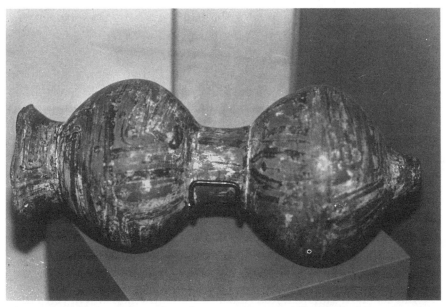

Figure 4.36. An hourglass-shaped Warao trumpet collected by Schomburgk at the turn of the century and now in the British Museum, London.

the symbolic voice of the mountain spirit or the voice of the volcano. Such sound symbolism was also common among the Inca, who blew conch-shell trumpets to intimidate their enemies and scare away evil spirits during eclipses of the sun (Vega 1961, 73, 167).

Sekeseke

Stringed instruments or chordophones have been documented for the Warao since the nineteenth century. Hilhouse (1834, 329), for example, described a struck musical bow that is no longer used among the Guyana Warao: "and then was proclaimed a general dance. This was merely stamping round in a ring to a simple monotonous song by the women, accompanied by beating on a monochord, being the skin of the arm of an eta leaf, raised by a bridge from the pith, not quite so musical as Paganini's." Bernau (1847, 44–45) gave a more complete description of this or a similar chordophone in 1847: "The eta tree is very useful to the Warraws, and grows chiefly in swampy places . . . [by] stringing a few fibres over a piece of the hollow bough, and placing a bridge under them, they make a rough viol, to the music of which they dance." The instrument so described is an idiochord (the string is taken from the same material as the body of the instrument), but Roth (1924, 461) later wrote that both the Guyana Warao and the Arawak used a heterochord (the string is made from a different material than the body of the instrument) that they called a tarimba. He explains (1924, 462) that this instrument, a mouth bow that is plucked (struck) with a plectrum (stick), may have had an African origin. Regardless of the particular provenance of this ancient Warao chordophone, the concept of a string instrument has been so embedded into Warao culture that today they consider their European-derived violin, called sekeseke, to be one of their traditional instruments. This phenomenon also prevails among the Mexican Huichol, who claim that their violin is as ancient as their culture (personal communication with the late Ramón Medina Silva, a Huichol shaman). As explained by the Huichol and as I interpret its presence among the Warao, a musical bow was the forerunner of the violin in both cultures. With the arrival of the Spanish the violin replaced the musical bow as a sound maker, while the musical bow's ancient function as a shaman's instrument remained among the Huichol and disappeared among the Warao.

    Although the Warao made no mention to me of an ancient musical bow, its use in Warao primordial times is suggested by Wilbert (1985, 155) with his interpretation of the origin myth of bahanarotu shamanism:

> Upon approaching the oval house in the sky, the journeying novice became fascinated by the music making inside the house where the creator bird played his musical bow. In a similar fashion the Warao hunter uses his bow and arrow as a lure to attract his prey. Holding the bow with the hand of his outstretched left arm horizontally and pointing away from him, he takes the free end of the bow between his teeth while his right hand taps the string with an arrow to produce a series of twanging sounds. With the animal in shooting range, the hunter quickly converts the musical bow into a deadly weapon and lets fly.

If this myth reflects reality among the Warao, then the luring and hunting technique would be similar to the way the Jívaro (Shuar) shaman in Ecuador uses a struck mouth bow to lure back his spirit helpers, to the manner in which a Shuar father plays the musical bow to attract a girl for his teenage son (Harner 1973b, 3), and to the individually performed musical method of sexual invitation by the Yukpa men and women of Venezuela and Colombia as they play their mouth bows to lure a mate (although the latter culture scrapes the bow with a stick—a bowed-lute rather than a struck-lute technique). Wilbert (1985, 155) carries the function of the musical bow a step further when he suggests that the musical use of the bow and arrow within the mythology of bahanarotu shamanism is a replacement for the shaman's drum: "it merits pointing out that within the shamanic context of the myth the kite's bow and arrow becomes a symbol of magical flight and transcendence. Replacing the shamanic drum of other regions, it attracts a sorcerer's pathogens like game. But it also prepares, through music and dance, the trance experience of the shaman's arrowlike flight across the celestial bridge, prefigured in the bow, to the sky house of *bahana*." Yet another related musical substitution occurs among the Warao, this time a hammock chordophone substituting for the sound of a rattle. While the musical instrument's function is also luring, the musician is a jaguar, as seen in the narrative "The 'rattle' Jaguar" (Wilbert 1970, 463, narrative 199):

Some Indians were walking through the forest one day, and heard a sound as though someone was playing the rattle. They went toward the place where the sound came from, and found a jaguar wrapped in a hammock. With the cords he was making a sound as though playing the rattle.

Each Indian armed himself with a club, and together they carefully crept near, and when they were close enough they hit him with the intention of killing him. But the jaguar gave a leap and went off into the forest.

That jaguar had eaten many people, as was proved by the signs thereabout. He carried on in that way, playing on the hammock cords like a rattle, with the idea of attracting the people who might be passing and eating them. He was an evil spirit jaguar.

These many examples suggest an ancient chordophonic tradition among the Warao, with roots in the historical and mythological past and comparable traditions among several other native American cultures. I asked Antonio Lorenzano about the musical bow among his ancestors, and he replied, "The only bow is the hunter's bow, used with arrows. Only the ehuru has a string across it." He had no knowledge of a Warao stringed instrument before the sekeseke. The present Warao sekeseke chordophone, in fact, is quite different from the historical and mythological prototypes and ethnographic analogs that I have mentioned.

The Warao sekeseke is usually a crude representation of a European violin, although the instrument used by Menegildo Paredes in Yaruaro Akoho is a fairly close copy (figures 4.37 and 4.38). The bow that is drawn across the sekeseke's strings, however, generally resembles a European Renaissance viola da gamba bow rather than a modern violin bow because of its convex rather than concave curve and the lack of a nut to tighten the hairs (figure 4.39). In addition, the playing technique of the sekeseke resembles European Renaissance bowed-lute technique (figure 4.40). Roth (1924, 463) writes that "sekke-sekke" is an onomatopoeic word used by the Warao to describe their bowed lute and any European violin.

According to Warao folklore, the violin was first built and sent to the Warao in a ship by a monkey named Nakurao from a far-off land. This creature, who had the upper torso of a man and the lower torso of a monkey, learned how to make the violin in a dream. Antonio related the following narrative to me about the origin and magical protective power of the sekeseke:

This is the story about the origin of the sekeseke which was made by a monkey. The monkey dreamed one night, and in the dream he made a sekeseke. During the dream the monkey cut a piece of wood from afar, not here but found over there. It was a piece of cedar, similar to the cedar found around here. He cut it with a machete, and with his knife he made the little head and the place where the strings go. Thus the monkey dreamed, and when he woke up he knew how to make the sekeseke. He said, "Wow, what a great dream I had. Today I'm going to make a sekeseke like I made in my dream last night. I'm also going to make a boat, a very large one, because people from other countries have never seen this." Then the monkey got up and began to make the sekeseke. First he cut a piece of cedar, similar to the wood from afar. The wood that he used in the dream is not the same as the wood of the earth. Now, during the day he cut wood that is from this world; he cut cedar. He carved it well, and with his knife he refined it and made the little holes on each side. He made the little head and made a little hole behind it. Then in the middle, where he made the double holes on each part, he attached the bridge. Over this he placed the strings—the first, second, third, and fourth—four strings. Violin—four—sekeseke. Now, as he did in the dream, he made a bow. Then the monkey tried it out. It sounded good when the bow was drawn across the strings. All the songs sounded good. Therefore, it was ready.

The tiger [jaguar] didn't know anything about this. He is dumb, lazy, and is good for nothing. He doesn't know anything and is a brute. The tiger thought, "Hey, tomorrow I am going to kill and eat the monkey." Then he slept, and when it was about dawn he sent a message to the monkey: "Look, friend monkey, be prepared. You know that today I am going to kill you and eat you."

The monkey said, "Who's going to attack me today?"

"The tiger," was the answer.

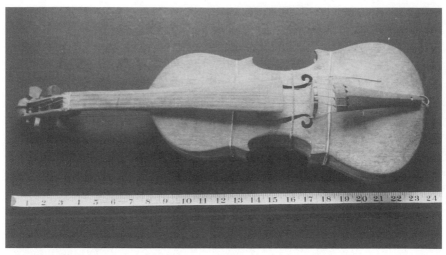

Figure 4.37. Front view of a Warao sekeseke violin built by Menegildo Paredes.

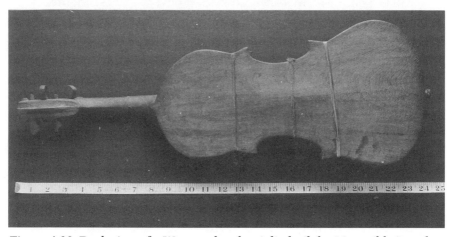

Figure 4.38. Back view of a Warao sekeseke violin built by Menegildo Paredes.

"Aha," said the monkey, "now that I have my violin already made, it's okay, let him come. If he kills me and eats me, it doesn't matter. It's not important to me. But before he kills me and eats me I am going to play some beautiful music for him. After that he can kill me and eat me."

The tiger said, "Now is the time. At eight or nine o'clock I will arrive there, precisely to kill this monkey and eat him, nothing more." So, at eight or nine o'clock the tiger came. But

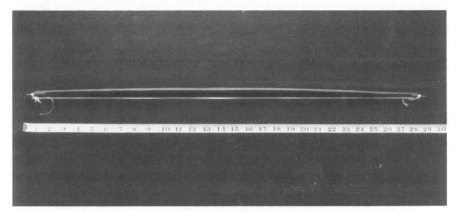

Figure 4.39. Sekeseke violin bow built by Menegildo Paredes.

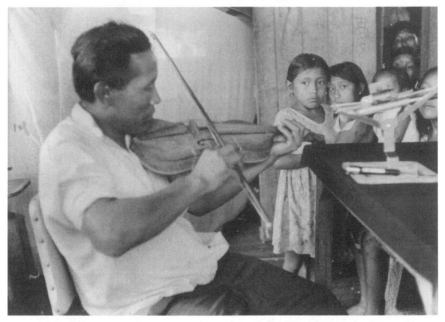

Figure 4.40. Menegildo Paredes playing his sekeseke in my room in the school-house at Yaruara Akoho.

before he arrived, the music was all prepared by the monkey. When the tiger got there he said, "Well, monkey, today is the last day of your life. Pretty soon I am going to kill you and eat you."

The monkey answered him, "Just one little minute, tiger;

before you kill and eat me I'm going to play some music for you. Afterwards you can kill me and eat me." Thus, the monkey passed his bow over his violin and the music was the best ever heard. The tiger, the deer, the agure, the howler monkey, and all kinds of birds gathered around the monkey. When the bow passed over the strings of the violin all the animals stood up and began to dance. The tiger danced, the birds danced, everybody danced, and the music they heard was the most beautiful ever. They danced until they were tired of dancing.

"It's good, stop, we're tired. Ah, such beautiful music!" said the tiger. "Good, my monkey friend, it's all right. I thought you were a brute and that you didn't know anything about music."

Yes, my friend tiger," replied the monkey, "I am your friend, your cousin. I have been a musician from the time I was very little. I am the one who made this sekeseke, the strings, the bow, the song, everything. Now you must not eat me."

"Certainly not," said the tiger, "because you are a musician."

This is the end of the story, my friend.

It has been suggested that this monkey from a faraway land was actually a person of African descent from the island of Trinidad (personal communication with Wilbert). When I questioned Antonio about this, however, he emphatically said no and gave the following explanation:

This is a monkey from another world, from the other side of here. I don't know exactly from where, I don't know the place, this country where the monkey comes from. In Warao he is called nakuarao or naku-arao. He is the same as people. He has the body of a man, and from the waist down he is a monkey. He is the one who fabricated the sekeseke and also the wandora, but not the guitar because the guitar has many strings. This monkey made a very large boat. After all the animals and birds had danced, a large boat with two masts arrived. The sekeseke embarked in this ship and arrived from afar. Nakarao made it and passed it to us. The sekeseke was placed aboard the ship, and the ship set sail, took to the breeze, and sped straight for all the countries of the world.

Thus, the sekeseke arrived here. Now, the people from here saw everything of the sekeseke that came from the outside. The people of Winikina are no good [*son brutos*, are brutes] at making the sekeseke. They do not know how. Today's best makers of the sekeseke are the people around Naba Sanuka up to Koibona. Over there, their forefathers, their grandfathers, they knew everything about it. Between there and here, nothing. The song "Seke Sekeima" also arrived from the ship. When the boat came here from another country, the sekeseke was theirs. Our people knew nothing. They themselves made the sounds, sang, and played just like the monkey did in the story I told you. They played over and over again, and the Warao thought, "How beautiful is the sound of this sekeseke." The Warao became interested in playing the sekeseke.

Among the present Warao, the sole use of the sekeseke is for entertainment. It is most often performed by an individual male for his own satisfaction, with family members nearby tending to their chores. Its repertory primarily includes dance songs (dakotu) for listening pleasure rather than dance (see chapter 5).

Wandora

According to Antonio, the wandora (cuatro in Spanish) was fabricated by the same monkey because it also has four strings like the sekeseke. But the monkey, he explained further, had nothing to do with the invention of the guitar because it has more than four strings. The number four is sacred among the Warao as it is among many native American cultures, and this perhaps explains why four-stringed instruments rather than the six-stringed guitar have entered into Warao mythology.

The wandora is derived from similar European Renaissance instruments that first arrived with the early Spanish and Portuguese explorers. Its construction is almost identical to the Hawaiian tenor ukulele, which is a pan-Pacific version of the Portuguese braga (Roberts 1967, 10). It is a small, four-stringed guitarlike instrument; and, as Chase says in his discussion of early Iberian examples, "of the four types of guitar, the oldest was that with four strings" (1959, 53).

The wandora's role is to accompany the Warao as they sing modern

Warao dance songs (see chapter 5) or Venezuelan popular and folk songs. These songs are often imported or derived from Creole culture through transistor radios, and the wandora is used to provide basic European strummed harmonies. In many cases, however, European functional harmonic progressions are disregarded in favor of a continuous tonic chord. In other cases, the basic tonic and dominant chords are played whenever the musician feels the urge. The wandora is not a popular instrument among the Warao except in regions where outside influence is felt, such as at the Catholic missions of Wayo (Guayo) and Arawaimuhu (Araguaymuju).

Other Musical Instruments

Throughout many Warao narratives there are references to musical instruments such as "flute" (Wilbert 1970, narratives 42, 139, and 151) or "bamboo flute" (Wilbert 1970, narrative 71). One narrative, collected by Roth (cited in Wilbert 1970, 195–97, narrative 88, "The story of Okoo-hi") mentions a wind instrument—the kahabassa—and includes a great deal of cultural information but no physical description of it. Wilbert (1970, 196) explains in a footnote that "from indirect evidence, ROTH is inclined to believe that this obsolete or little known musical instrument was some form of a 'cow-skull' gourd-flute, the Warao *bure-akwa.*" The following passage is an excerpt from "The story of Okoo-hi" in which the nephew of Okoo-hi and a young woman are returning from a walk in the rain forest:

> Just before reaching home, she said: "We are going to have drink when we get in. Can you play the *kahabassa?*" "Yes, I can play it a little," was the reply. When they got back to her place Assawako gave him a whole jugful of drink all for himself, and this primed him for playing the music: and he played beautifully, making the *kahabassa* sing *Waru-huru-tea.* They sported all night, and next morning Okohi made ready to leave. Of course poor Assawako wanted Waiamari to remain with her, but he said: "No! I cannot leave my uncle. He has been good to me, and he is an old man now." So she began crying, and between her sobs told him how sad she felt at his going away. This made him feel very sorry also, and he

consoled her by saying, "Let us weep together with the *ka-habassa.*" And there and then he sang *Heru-heru,* etc., on the instrument, and thus comforted her before he left.

Although the narrative provides no clue about the construction of the kahabassa, we learn much about the power of the musical instrument, especially its ability to bring comfort and consolation. This power, however, is secular rather than religious, judging from the all-night entertainment ("sporting") and drinking associated with the instrument. The final sentence of the narrative excerpt refers to singing on a musical instrument. Other Warao narratives also make it clear that musical instruments are often thought of as extensions of or substitutes for singing voices insofar as musicians "sing" particular songs on them. This is not to suggest that any Warao musical instruments are "singing gourds" (as are found in Africa) but that musicians often play songs on their musical instruments that have texts associated with them. In other words, most of the music of the Warao is vocal in origin; words, although not heard aloud during performances on musical instruments, are "heard" mentally.

Masters of Musical Instruments

Many cultures have a particular status for musicians, who stand out or are venerated as performers on musical instruments. In most European and American countries, for example, such musicians are referred to as artists or professionals, which are levels determined by skill (most often virtuosity), number of concerts or recordings made, or amount of money earned. While the Warao do not have those particular levels (although one could argue that skill is apparent), another level is very important—power. Power is invested in many musical instruments, as we have seen in this chapter; but, even more, power is attributed to particular musicians who are the masters of the musical instruments. These musicians are the Warao professionals. In the following excerpt from the Warao narrative "The wrong rattle, the bush-hog, and the baby" (Wilbert 1970, 82–85, narrative 27), we can see how the power of certain rattles, when in the wrong hands, can be disastrous:

Siwara [a hebu bush spirit posing as a Warao male human] . . . proved himself a very good husband and son-in-law, and always returned from his hunting expeditions well loaded with game. He also took the trouble to teach his wife's brothers how to shoot bush-hog. Formerly, whenever these two fellows went out and brought back a bird, they would say they had brought back bush-hog. You see, they did not know what a bush-hog really was. So he took them out one day, and when they reached a suitable spot, he shook his *maraka* (rattle) and bush-hogs came rushing up in obedience to the summons. "This is hog; shoot," said Siwara, but the two brothers, who had never seen one before, were frightened and climbed up a tree, so he had to kill three or four by himself, and these they subsequently took home.

Time passed, and, his wife having presented him with a baby, Siwara became a recognized heir of her family's possessions, and removed his own property, which he had hitherto kept in the bush, into his father-in-law's house, which henceforth became his own hearth and home. Among the property which he brought with him to his new home were four rattles used for bush-hog only. There are two kinds of hog, the timid (*eburi*) and the very savage (*eburi-oriassi*), and there were a pair of *marakas* for each kind: one rattle to call the beast, the other to drive it away. So after he had hung them up Siwara warned his wife's people that on no account must they touch these *marakas* during his absence, because trouble would be certain to ensue. Siwara soon afterward went away to cut a field; during his absence one of the brothers-in-law came home, and, seeing the prettily feathered rattles all in a row, could not resist the temptation of taking one down and scrutinizing it closely.

While absorbed in its contemplation, he forgot all about the injunction, and started shaking it. Good Lord! It was the wrong rattle—the one for the wild bush-hog! And now these savage beasts came trooping in from near and far, leaving the poor mother, her two brothers, and the old people barely time to escape with their lives up the nearest trees. In the hurry and excitement, however, the mother had forgotten her baby, which the hogs tore in pieces and devoured. On seeing all this happening below, the fugitives yelled and screamed for Siwara to come quickly and get rid of all these beasts, so that they might descend in safety. Siwara came and, shaking the proper rattle, drove the brutes away. When they had all dispersed, and his relatives had joined him, he looked for his baby, but of course did not find it. He blamed them for disobeying his orders, and was so angered that he left them. It is very hard for them to get food now.

There are many morals to this story, and many ways in which the narrative can be analyzed. (Wilbert lists nine categories for motif content.) Musically, the power of the rattles is obvious (motif D1440, "Magic object gives power over animals," according to Wilbert); but even more important is the power of the professional musical-instrument performer—Siwara, the bush spirit cum human musician. Without his skill (that is, his knowledge), the musical instrument (the rattle) cannot be performed correctly. As we see, the result is not a bad review or lack of payment but death. Crossculturally, perhaps, these are the same; that is, a bad review or lack of payment for a Western professional musician could be analogous to death for a Warao "professional" or master of a musical instrument.

Crosscultural Correlations

We have seen how a number of Warao musical instruments resemble descriptions of instruments in use in the Caribbean Basin during the time of the first Spanish explorations (early sixteenth century). Such similarities can be the result of parallel development or diffusion. Because of the close proximity of the Orinoco Delta to the islands of the Caribbean, diffusion is a valid theory for similarities of material culture. Fred Olsen, in his book *On the Trail of the Arawaks* (1974), suggests that the migrating ancient Arawak may have had prolonged contact with the ancient Warao in the Orinoco Delta. In his excellent archaeological overview he mentions the possible existence of Colombian, Ecuadorian, and even Peruvian travel routes over jungle rivers that may have been used by the ancient Arawak in their migration northward. He discusses one particular route that they may have taken on their way to the Lesser Antilles: from Colombia to the Rio Negro, up the Rio Negro to the Orinoco River, crossing to the latter during flood stage, and then down the Orinoco (1974, 262). Basing his hypothesis on archaeological evidence, he shows how an ancient people known as the Saladoids once made their homes on the upper Orinoco River. They later lived on the banks of the lower Orinoco just above the present Venezuelan town of Barrancas at the edge of the Orinoco Delta (today the site is called Saladero) and were probably forced to leave that area by less peaceful invaders known as Barrancoids. In their flight, which probably took several centuries, the Saladoids very likely continued down the Orinoco to its mouth and from there to Trinidad. According to Fred Olsen, "good paddlers leaving Saladero could probably have reached the mouth of the Orinoco in a few days. But the truth is, we have no idea how long they took on the journey. All we can say is that Arawak Saladoids left the apex of the delta possibly before 900 B.C. and were in the Lesser Antilles a thousand years later, about A.D. 100 to 300" (1974, 233). It is very possible that these ancient Arawak intermingled with the peaceful Warao living in the delta of the Orinoco River and taught them, perhaps informally or indirectly, how to make various musical instruments. This is a question that can never be answered completely, however, because artifactual evidence does not exist.

In the following chapters, some of the Warao musical and other sound-producing instruments will also be seen to play important roles in traditional music making. Other musical genres, however, will not use any musical instruments. It will be noticed that the theurgical musical forms have fairly strict rules governing which instruments will or will not be used, while Warao secular music has fewer rules. Let us next look at the Warao musical forms that can be placed into the category of music for pleasure, where musical instrument usage varies to such a degree that musical instruments can be viewed as accompaniments rather than essential tools.

5   Songs for Pleasure

According to the Warao, only one type of nonspeech aural activity is considered to be music—dakotu—while the terms hohomare and maremare (which are the same thing) refer to the now extinct accompanying dance form. The Warao translate dakotu as canción de baile or dance song. Although the plural term, dance songs, does characterize dakotutuma (the plural form) because they are metered, today it may be more accurate to call them entertainment songs or songs for pleasure; for the dance function has all but disappeared. To remain consistent with the Warao translation of dakotutuma, however, I will call them dance songs. Today, Warao dance songs are sung by women while they work and tend to their children and by men as they work, canoe, relax in their hammocks, or drink.

Several authors have written about Warao dakotutuma. The earliest source is Mons. Fray Angel Turrado Moreno (1945, 215), who calls them "profane songs" used by the Warao during "profane dances, the hunt, while fishing, while traveling, while gathering, relaxing in the hammock, and so forth." He presents five dance-song texts in Warao and Spanish with annotations, which he collected in the 1940s at the Guayo Mission in the central part of the Orinoco Delta.

The largest collection of Warao dakotu songs in print is by Padre Basilio María de Barral (1964), who presents 371 songs in notation and transliteration, with some translated into Spanish. Padre Barral melodically transcribed from memory all the Warao dance songs he collected (1972, personal communication). Moreover, many of them were collected at missions, which is probably why most of his transcriptions resemble Spanish folk songs. More important, however, he categorized and discussed them in groups relating to subject matter, such as songs about flowers, animals, birds, fishing, love, boating, and so on. One of his missionary colleagues, Padre Julio Lavandero, has also transcribed, translated, and analyzed numerous Warao dance songs, usually publishing one in each issue of *Venezuela Misionera*, a monthly illustrated journal of the Catholic missions in Venezuela. His musicographic and orthographic transcriptions are done with extreme care, and his conclusions are often insightful.

María Matilde Suárez (1968) is another source. A Venezuelan anthropologist, she includes six dance songs as filler in her book about the Warao. Although the melodies of the songs are carefully transcribed and the song texts translated into Spanish, she neither discusses them nor gives credit to the ethnomusicologist who made the transcriptions.

None of these Spanish and Venezuelan authors analyze Warao dance songs in a comparative manner with other Warao nonspeech oral expressions (that is, other types of "song"). Therefore, this chapter is an ethnomusicological study of Warao dance songs based on one hundred songs that I have collected plus those in the sources I have mentioned. In addition, I discuss the hohomare dance within the context of other Warao dances described in ethnographic sources and from personal observation, and in similar structural terms as outlined for the dance songs. I attempt to show how these genres have music, dance, and other cultural characteristics that separate them from Warao musical and dance forms such as nahanamu, habi sanuka, and others that the Warao do not consider to be music or dance. I further argue that the function of dakotu is somewhat analogous to the now extinct game form known as nahakara, in which pent-up hostilities were released. The dakotu of the Winikina subtribe of the Warao functions as a musical release of pent-up frustrations associated with various factors resulting from acculturation.

Dakotu Song Styles and Culture Dynamics

Dakotutuma are built on what can be termed "true" melody. In the words of David Morton (1980, 79), they are "true songs, . . . independent of linguistic control factors." They are not, in other words, text bound; that is, their melodies are not subservient to their words. The dakotu songs, however, all have titles; and a comparison of multiple examples of songs with similar titles, even from differing villages and collected by different people at different times, reveal that many have similar melodies and tone systems despite numerous variants. The majority of the songs are strophic (that is, the verses of each song are sung to the same melody or a variation of the first presentation of the melody). Lavandero (1969, 249) explains that a song can have an indefinite number of verses, "depending on the talent, good humor, and inspiration of the moment." This technique contrasts greatly with other types of Warao songs, such as lullabies and theurgical songs, where the term "through composed" (that is, the words and the music constantly unfold) can loosely be applied within the constraints of the songs' individually determined melodic patterns based on culturally determined tone systems. Overall, the melodies of each dance-song verse descend with a certain amount of reverting movement (that is, ascending and descending) during their gradual descent. In addition, there are as many different melodies as there are titles to the songs, and nearly as many tone systems as there are melodies. Because the dakotutuma are based on melodies rather than melodic patterns, I have made melodic analyses rather than tone-system analyses of representative samples. Some of the melodic characteristics of Warao dance songs strongly suggest European-derived influence, and the Warao themselves distinguish between older dance songs (canciones mas antiguas), newer dance songs (canciones mas modernas), and dance songs from recordings (canciones de disco).

Dakotutuma song texts most frequently have semantic referents, although some include two types of vocables, "kwanera nera" and "na na na," both functioning as beginning and ending filler material. Unlike the Suyá (Seeger 1987, 45), who refer to their vocables as "song words," the Warao do not have a general name for them. Antonio Lorenzano explained that "kwanera nera" refers to male context, while "na na na" refers to female context. I found both sets of vocables used in the same songs, however, making his statement perhaps only theoretical. Warao song vocables may be derived from an archaic language, but in no other way do the texts of dakotutuma consist of any type of secret or old language as do the theurgical songs.

Dakotutuma are rhythmical, although applying European-derived meter to them is too restrictive and does not adequately represent their temporal freedom. Nevertheless, sections of some songs make use of triplet figures that approximate compound-duple (such as $6/8$) European-derived meters, while at other times sets of sixteenth notes seem to approximate Western duple meters. Because all the songs were recorded outside their original dance context (the dance is extinct), rhythmic freedom or elasticity is quite common. Likewise, variation from one verse to the next is the norm, affecting melody as well as rhythm. (For the sake of consistency, my comparative notations are all made from the first verse of each song.)

Finally, dakotutuma are always sung in a natural voice. They are never masked, and amplitude is generally high (that is, they are loud). Freedom of expression is standard, and never will a singer stop and start over if he or she feels a mistake has been made.

Melodic, pitch, rhythmic, and textual variations are common because of freedom of expression influenced by outside factors such as work, family distractions, alcohol, and so on. Lavandero (1969, 249) writes that "one has to remember that the Warao dance songs, although each has a determined nuclear theme and a known melodic line, receive their final form when performed, in the moment of interpretation." While the product is always recognizable to the Warao, the performance process often determines the interpretation of the product. In spite of the many interpretations of the songs that exist, the dakotu repertory is very dense among the Warao of the central Orinoco Delta. Nettl (1983, 195–96) has defined "the density of a repertory" as "the degree to which separate units of a repertory are similar."

These culture dynamics can first be seen by comparing the melodic and rhythmic aspects of one of the best known examples of dakotu, a song entitled "Iboma Sanuka." Three versions of "Iboma Sanuka" are notated for comparison, and two of them are included in recorded example 5. Music example 5.1 was sung by Silbano Ramírez, a man from Lorenzano Akoho (song text 5.5 and recorded example 5a); and music example 5.2 was sung by another man, Tirso Rivero from Hebu Wabanoko. Music example 5.3, however, recorded some distance away in 1970 by Padre Damián del Blanco in the village of Omuana, was sung by Melicia Torres, a woman (recorded example 5b). These three versions of the same song display only slight rhythmical, melodic, and textual differences, and they have many similarities. To show even further how dense this repertory is, table 5.1 includes the opening melodic phrase of fifteen versions of the same song; these variants clearly indicate how personal interpretations make the melodic and rhythmic aspects of dakotu music dynamic yet constant to a certain degree. Thus, "Iboma Sanuka" (with variant song titles) is an example of a dense tune family.

The dynamics of culture can also be seen in the great variety of song texts for "Iboma Sanuka." Turrado Moreno (1945, 219–20) and Barral (1964, 402), for example, have each made translations of this song ("Iboma Sanukidarone," a variant title). Their respective versions are included here as song texts 5.1 and 5.2:

Song Text 5.1. "Iboma Sanukidarone" (Turrado Moreno 1945, 219–20)

Although the girl is small, she is beautiful, wow.
Although the girl is small, she is beautiful, wow.
Although you are a small girl, come and pursue me, wow.
Although you are a small girl, come and pursue me, wow.
Little girl, I want you. Little girl, I will carry you away.
Little girl, I will gather you up; gathered up as you should be,
    I will carry you away.
Little girl, you will go with me, with me you go, and we will
    be married.

Music Example 5.1. Dakotu "Iboma Sanuka" (Silbano Ramírez). Olsen Collection 72.8-235.

Song Text 5.2. *"Iboma Sanukidarone" (Barral 1964, 402)*

Young girl, although small, pretty; just like me.

Single girl, that is the truth, unmarried. I do not have a husband.

Although I am a small girl, I am very pretty.

Although they see me as a little girl, in pursuit of my tracks, I am a girl who, although small, is very beautiful.

Although I am very beautiful to me . . . the man from Wirinoco, when he came, to me, without seeing me, rejected me.

Although I am a little girl, and neighbor of the man from Wirinoco, I came, I came to this festival.

Little young girl, I want you. Little girl, I will gather you up.

Little girl, I will take you for my wife. When I take you for that, I will bring you.

Little girl, I will walk with you; when I walk with you, we will marry.

Both versions use the Warao term tanainé (Turrado Moreno) or tanáine (Barral), which I translate as "wow" in the first song text. Turrado Moreno does not translate the term but explains it as follows: "above

Music Example 5.2. Dakotu "Iboma Sanukida" (Tirso Rivero). Olsen Collection 72.8-233.

Table 5.1 Song Variants of "Iboma Sanuka" (transposed to C = principal tone)

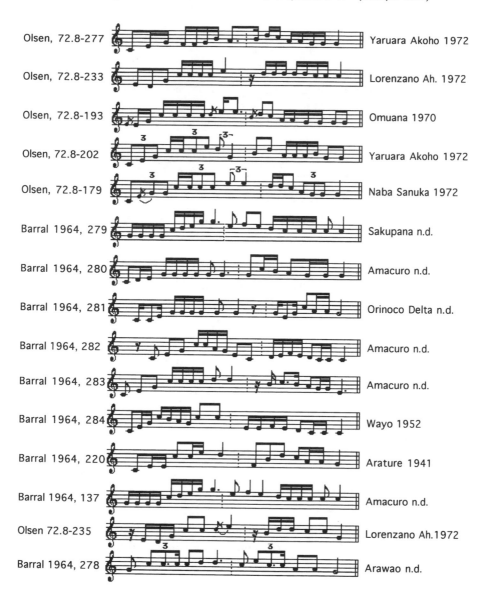

Olsen, 72.8-277   Yaruara Akoho 1972

Olsen, 72.8-233   Lorenzano Ah. 1972

Olsen, 72.8-193   Omuana 1970

Olsen, 72.8-202   Yaruara Akoho 1972

Olsen, 72.8-179   Naba Sanuka 1972

Barral 1964, 279   Sakupana n.d.

Barral 1964, 280   Amacuro n.d.

Barral 1964, 281   Orinoco Delta n.d.

Barral 1964, 282   Amacuro n.d.

Barral 1964, 283   Amacuro n.d.

Barral 1964, 284   Wayo 1952

Barral 1964, 220   Arature 1941

Barral 1964, 137   Amacuro n.d.

Olsen 72.8-235   Lorenzano Ah.1972

Barral 1964, 278   Arawao n.d.

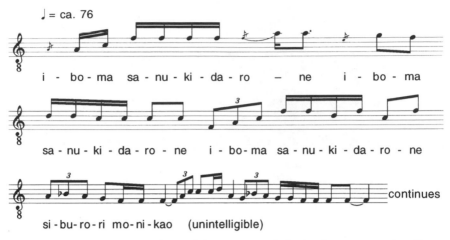

♩ = ca. 76

i - bo - ma sa - nu - ki - da - ro — ne i - bo - ma

sa - nu - ki - da - ro - ne i - bo - ma sa - nu - ki - da - ro - ne

si - bu - ro - ri mo - ni - kao (unintelligible) continues

Music Example 5.3. Dakotu "Iboma Sanuka" (Melicia Torres). Olsen Collection 72.8-193.

all, this seems to be an untranslatable vocable, an expression of happiness and love, an explosion of the heart, like the Spanish word *olé*." Barral (1964, 402–3) writes the following about his translation:

> This song has two parts. The first is a self apology that is about the attractive physical characteristics of a Warao maiden who, single and baring her teeth, tests the winds to find a husband; and then with the plan of a conqueror [conquistadora] she comes to Wirinoco, another village where a *casiri* or drunken festival is being celebrated at which the unmarried Warao youth try to find spouses. . . . There is nothing that can better connect these sentimental cables and start a fire between the two poles of the human species than the vibrant, noisy, enthusiastic, and jocular atmosphere of these reunions with their local fermented drinks, mixed songs, choruses, and exciting ancestral dances. The second part of the song is about the victory of the conqueror. . . .
>
> In the following verses the poor unmarried pretty girl laments the bad taste and brutality demonstrated by the boy from Wirinoco who also came to the festival and, rather than building her up as being pretty like she wishes, rejects her. . . .
>
> The three verses of the second part demonstrate to us that

the girl does not waste her time and tries to interest the heart of a third boy who, with endearing words, promises to take her as his wife.

Several of the "Iboma Sanuka" versions I collected are extreme variations of the boy-meets-girl or girl-meets-boy theme. In song text 5.3, sung and translated by Menegildo Paredes, a particular girl named Mercedes has many favorable attributes, including the ability to sing well:

Song Text 5.3. "Iboma Sanuka," Menegildo Paredes (Olsen Collection 72.8-215)

The girl named Mercedes, it's the truth that she is a girl.
The Mercedes girl is the mistress of eyebrows. That's it, when we are looking, it is the truth that she is the mistress of eyebrows, good eyebrows.
The girl named Mercedes comes from Merehina.
It is the truth that she is the mistress of song.
Miss Mercedes is the mistress of Merehina and the mistress of song.
When her song is heard, it makes everybody happy.
Miss Mercedes, the mistress of song, makes us joyful when we listen.
The girl named Mercedes knows many songs.
Miss Mercedes has a beautiful necklace worth lots of money.
She will give it to us so we can buy alcohol so we can sing.
When we buy something to drink, then we can sing.
It is the truth that she is the mistress of song.
When you hear her sing you become happy.

The subject of this song, "Iboma Mercedes" or Miss Mercedes, is a very stylish woman within Warao culture. Menegildo explained that, because Warao women have very little facial hair and practically no eyebrows (barihisa), they sometimes use eyebrow pencils purchased in Tucupita to draw them in. Miss Mercedes is, therefore, physically attractive to Warao men. In addition, she is desirable because she is a pleasing singer whose songs bring great happiness. Finally, she is wealthy, as suggested by her elaborate necklace known as dowáe (literally, "neck's teeth"), which, if sold, would provide enough money to buy alcohol. Originally fabricated from teeth, shells, bone, or seeds, Warao necklaces are commonly made today from red, blue, and white glass beads purchased or traded for in Tucupita or brought as gifts by outsiders (Wilbert 1972a, 71).

In several other "Iboma Sanuka" songs that I collected, the girl looks good from afar but when seen up close she is not attractive to the boy, as in song text 5.4, sung by Tirso Rivero:

Song Text 5.4. "Iboma Sanuka," Tirso Rivero (Olsen Collection 72.8-233)

Although the little girl is said to be pretty, and when she is seen from a distance she is good, when she is seen up close she is bad.
Although the little young girl is said to be pretty, she turns her back on me.
She is the mistress of Ayarina [that is, from Ayarina].

As the song title suggests, the little girl from Ayarina is not so pretty to Tirso. However, when his friend, Silbano Ramírez, sang his version of "Iboma Sanuka" (recorded example 5a), the girl from Ayarina is the prettiest girl around, as we read in song text 5.5.

Song Text 5.5. "Iboma Sanuka," Silbano Ramírez (Olsen Collection 72.8-235)

This little girl, she is the prettiest girl in Ayarina.
That's right! Kwaneranera [vocables]
From there she comes to my side, the prettiest girl in Ayarina.
After I drank some booze, then I talked and sang.
The little girl came to my side when she arrived, kwanera.
The prettiest girl in Ayarina is now the owner of the house, kwanera.
She greeted me, I took her hand and we danced, kwanera.

In spite of the textual variations of "Iboma Sanuka" (including the titles), the relative similarities of subject matter, such as male attitudes about women, activities relating to love or physical attraction, and so forth, also link the songs into an example of dense repertory based on text.

"Iboma Sanuka" can be classified as a modern song, primarily because no singer ever commented on its being old as singers were sure to do with some of the other songs. In addition, its melodic line fits within the framework of modern European-derived folk song. Furthermore, it can be readily harmonized and accompanied by a wandora using tonic, subdominant, and dominant harmonies. Indeed, the younger Warao men will occasionally strum a wandora while singing some of their canciones mas modernas.

One dakotu that was distinguished as being old (una canción mas vieja) is entitled "Naniobo," meaning "Frog." Two versions of this song were sung by two of the eldest and most knowledgeable of my Warao teachers: Pedro Rivero sang music example 5.4 (recorded example 6), and Antonio Lorenzano performed music example 5.5. Both men come from the village of Lorenzano Ahanoko, and in spite of the proximity of their homes, their songs are very different; neither version displays any European-derived characteristics as previously discussed for "Iboma Sanuka." Barral (1964, 332–33) includes two more distinct versions of "Naniobo" and provides the following commentary about them:

> These songs try to evoke a certain peculiar custom of these batrachians: the frog approaches a Warao house, attracted by the lights of the cooking fires or kerosene lamps, and seeks out a place at the walls or the corner poles of the house, which are their guideposts. A lighted wall or corner pole attracts the frog, and the animal attempts to get closer in order to hunt insects. And when it tires of the hunt, or, if we may say, when it rests between acts, it gets together with other frogs, who form the rear guard of the corner poles or walls. Together they expand their lungs, as bagpipers fill their bags, and sing the glories of the Lord with the fervent tribute of their unconscious psalmody. This constitutes the dakotu vakerá-ja, the agreeable song of the big warty frog.

Melodically, the four songs entitled "Naniobo" differ tremendously from the songs that the Warao describe as modern; moreover, the four songs are different from one another. Therefore, the "Naniobo" tune family is lacking in density and can be considered "sparse" (Nettl 1983, 195). Overall, the melodies used in the "Naniobo" versions descend

Music Example 5.4. Dakotu "Naniobo" (Pedro Rivero). Olsen Collection
72.8-219.

while containing internal motifs that are reverting. The melodies
cannot be harmonized with basic Western European chords, suggesting they belong to an archaic repertory. Additionally, the "Naniobo"
songs are very rhythmical, stressing a dance characteristic that the
more modern "Iboma Sanuka" songs do not have. Moreover, the texts
of the "Naniobo" songs sung by Pedro and Antonio are filled with
rhythmical vocables such as "na, na, na," "kwanera nera," and "dere."

Music Example 5.5. Dakotu "Naniobo" (Antonio Lorenzano). Olsen Collection 72.8-266.

The first two have already been explained; and the third, representing the sound of the frog, provides rhythmic energy by accenting sudden stops in the overall rhythmic pulse. I include only Pedro Rivero's version of "Naniobo" for analysis. To show the vocables and repetitions, the texts are presented in Warao and English. Listen to recorded example 6 and follow along with song text 5.6, which is a transliteration and free translation of his frog song.

Song Text 5.6. "Naniobo," Pedro Rivero (Olsen Collection 72.8-219)

naniobo dere naniobo dere naniobo dere naniobo dere
Frog croak frog croak frog croak frog croak

na na na na na na na na na na na na na na . . . na na na na na
na na na na na kwanera nerane kwanera nerane kwanera
nerane kwanera neranera ta na na na na na na na ta na na na
na na na na ta na na na na na na na na na na na na na na
na na na na na

naniobo dere naniobo dere naniobo dere . . . iobo dere
Frog croak frog croak frog croak frog croak

hanoko anamuna yaruhunae tiane, hanoko anamuna yaru-
hunae tiane, hanoko anamuna yaruhunae tiane
He is sitting under the house on a piling, he is sitting under
  the house on a piling, he is sitting under the house on a
  piling

naniobo dere naniobo dere . . . bo dere naniobo dere
Frog croak frog croak frog croak frog croak

hanoko anamuna yaruhui tanera, koitaturu tayaha tiyanera
He is sitting under the house on a piling, he is thinking about
  singing

sia enchoro aisiko oriyahorabane koitaturu tayaha tane tiyane-
nana
He has a companion, and they are both thinking about
  singing

naniobo dere naniobo dere naniobo dere naniobo dere
Frog croak frog croak frog croak frog croak

ta na na na na na na kwanera nera nera kwanera nerane
kwanera nera nera ta na na na na na na ta na na na na na na
kwanera neranen kwanera nera nera ta na na na na na ta na
na na na na na . . . na na na ta na na na na na na

naniobo dere naniobo dere naniobo dere
Frog croak frog croak frog croak

hanoko anamuna yaruhunae tiane, yaruhunae tiane
He is sitting under the house on a piling, on a piling

ta na na na na na na ta na na na na na na

Because "Naniobo" is a secular dance song, there is no apparent theurgical content. This is implied by the nonreligious aspect of the song text (although a frog could be a hebu spirit or associated with the habi sanuka festival; see chapters 7 and 14) and is also suggested by the absence of microtonal rising or "upward drift." (This phenomenon will be interpreted in the following chapters as an indicator of Theurgical State of Consciousness or TSC; see especially chapter 15.) The dance aspect of this song is heightened by its many rhythmical vocables, which, in Pedro's interpretation, are highly repetitive and almost percussive.

The Dakotu Dance Context: Hohomare (Maremare)

Hohomare means "happy dance" or "dance of joy" (hoho = dance, mare = joy) (Barral 1964, 576); therefore, the other word for the same phenomenon (maremare) means "joy, joy" (Turrado Moreno 1945, 233). Because of the purely entertainment function of hohomare, I refer to it as "dance as dance." This traditional dance context for dakotu is extinct and has been replaced by Western couple dancing among the youth, especially in villages that have close contact with Catholic missions. Fortunately, Turrado Moreno (1945, 229–34) and Barral (1964, 575–83) have provided detailed descriptions of hohomare; and much of the following information is condensed from their works.

One reason for the demise of hohomare is the social change brought about by the missionization of the Delta Amacuro Federal Territory since the early twentieth century. Its disappearance, however, is not due to religious infiltration but to ridicule from the outside. Partially responsible are attitudes such as the following (Barral 1964, 575): "To the Warao, exotic dance falls poorly to them, even to the point of being ridiculous. The Warao is a bumpkin when it comes to movements. He lacks grace and agility because of evolution. His feet are heavy because of a lack of exercise, and, in addition, they are very deformed and twisted: parrot feet, as we have the habit of calling them." These seemingly ethnocentric comments are based on the truth that the Warao, being a riverine culture, do not exercise their lower bodies. As a result, their physical attributes (noted from the late 1880s through the middle twentieth century) are characterized by a well-developed upper torso (owing to muscles developed from paddling canoes) and a disproportionate development of the lower body (Gardner 1980, 153). Recent scientific measurements of muscular strength have revealed that the Warao have low leg strength and powerful upper-body strength— "better understood when one considers the lack of 'solid ground' in the Warao environment for walking and running" (Gardner 1980, 156). Nevertheless, the Warao used to perform hohomare with as much enjoyment and finesse as any culture performs its dances of joy. But unaided by the strength of their traditional religion or life cycle, as nahanamu and habi sanuka were, hohomare disappeared.

Barral (1964, 578) explains that the hohomare dancers were young people who would form themselves into one row of men and another row of women, these being also the two choruses that sing the dance songs. With one row facing the other, the dancers would entwine themselves by placing their arms around their neighbor's neck, back, or waist. Barral writes: "Placed in the form described, and having drunk sufficient amounts [of casiri, warapo, or aguardiente] to stimulate their enthusiasm, the Warao begin to keep time by softly moving their right feet forward and back, while the forward part of the left foot stays in place on the floor, moving only the heel up and down. When the right foot moves forward the left heel is raised, and when the right foot returns to its place the left heel hits against the floor." After a short time the Warao dancers begin to sway forth and back and soon begin to take steps forward and backward again. At this time the singing begins among dancers and spectators alike. Both rows then turn to face the two groups of chiefs and elders, men and women of importance known as idamotuma, seated to the sides of the dancers. The dancers bow to greet the elders and then rotate back to the same position from which they began. Now the dance proper begins; and as the drinking progresses, the elders may join in song and dance with the young people. Barral (1964, 581–82) gives the following detailed description of how the dance ensues:

> The dance is continued with the same rhythm [as before]. The women gently oscillate forward and backward, conserving their natural posture, although they are slightly inclined forward. The men, on the other hand, become more and more frenzied, inclining themselves profoundly forward and arching themselves later to the back, violently moving their hair, whose long locks in front of them violently fall over the napes of their necks. This action may sufficiently provoke dizziness or drunkenness in them, even though they may not have been drinking. Singing does not stop during the dance but continues with all its variations of rhythm, fieriness, and frenzy; or else repose and serenity. . . . After the first ten or fifteen minutes of the dance . . . both choruses initiate a type of race forward and backward. One group advances, making it necessary that the other chorus recedes or recoils until they reach the edge of the dance floor. Then they repeat the race in reverse, that is to say, with the other chorus advancing, causing the other to retreat in the same manner. These races are repeated three or four times, always without losing the rhythm or stopping the singing. After this the choruses return to the center of the dance floor as before and the dance continues . . . as it began. With the fourth rhythm, which is like a type of trot, both choruses perform winding maneuvers among themselves in a rotating movement, each one describing two circumferences, rolling or coiling up and then uncoiling themselves, arriving as they were until finally each chorus is situated in the place where the other was, forming in this last case a type of spiral with one another, and having thusly changed sides. Sometimes they maneuver in this way only once; at other times, two, three, or more times. And on

occasion they vary the general situation of the dance, with both choruses placing themselves in the direction which before was at their sides. This, more or less, is how the hohomare, the secular dance of the Warao, can be described. When they feel tired they will rest for a few minutes, will drink to warm themselves up again, and will continue the dance. The festival will not end as long as the drink lasts or until all fall into drunken stupors. In such a way to call this a bacchanal festival is not an exaggeration.

These detailed descriptions show that the hohomare had an entertainment function. At one time, however, it also had the secondary function of releasing pent-up emotions and frustrations, much like another type of entertainment—the nahakara. Nahakara was a form of mock battle, a test of strength and group duel between neighboring villages (Wilbert 1972a, 99). Not unlike Japanese sumo, the objective was to push one's opponent away or down, although the Warao used rafted wooden combat shields. Like hohomare, this form of entertainment has disappeared. But two elements of hohomare remain—drunkenness and dakotu singing—and both have become substitutes for nahakara and hohomare. Drunkenness is increasing among young Warao men, providing a release of pent-up hostility and frustration; dakotu singing is a release of emotion and an expression of joy. Dakotu singing is usually a spontaneous form of individual or collective celebration that, when individually performed, can bring inner contentment. As a communal event within a particular social group, such as young men, the more modern songs are sometimes accompanied by the wandora; for individual expression, a young man may perform dakotu on a sekeseke, and no singing is involved. In every situation, however, the dakotu is the most frequent type of music for pleasure.

The following chapter analyzes another form of pleasurable music, the lullaby, which derives its pleasure more from its primary utilitarian function of making a baby go to sleep than its secondary function of entertainment. We shall see, however, that a division between utility and pleasure is not clearly distinguished by Warao singers, and that the lullaby even approaches the category of theurgical music. In addition, it is an indispensable tool for enculturation or informal learning.

6   Lullabies: Songs for Utility

Among the Warao the term used for lullaby is hoerekitane, which means "to rock"—that is, to swing back and forth in a hammock or a mother's arms. In Spanish the genre is known as canción de cuna or cradle song, although Barral calls it canción infantíl or infant's song (1964, 389–97), a better term because a Warao infant's only cradle (except for human arms) is his or her hammock.

Barral (1964, 389–97) transcribes twelve lullabies from various regions of the Orinoco Delta; and only one of them, recorded in 1940 at the ranchería del Bagre (village of Bagre), somewhat resembles the thirty-seven that I recorded from the Winikina region. Many of Barral's examples melodically resemble Spanish lullabies, suggesting they were perhaps learned by the Warao from the Spanish missionaries and mission teachers and recorded at Warao villages adjacent to or on Capuchín missions in the Orinoco Delta. Textually, however, Barral's examples and six others translated by Vaquero (1965, 290–92) conform to the style I recorded in the Winikina village of Yaruara Akoho. This textual style is characterized by its reference to Warao everyday and mythological situations, making the hoerekitane a vehicle for informal education. Because of their textual consistency throughout the delta, lullaby texts are less conducive to change than are their corresponding melodic fabrics.

Hoerekitane Song Style

Melodically, Winikina-Warao hoerekitane songs are characterized by a tone system that contains three basic pitches, emphasizing the intervals of an approximate minor third and the fourth, as indicated in the sequence in Western and cipher notation in music example 6.1. Additionally, short upward glissandi are often employed as an individually determined stylistic characteristic at the $\hat{3}$ 1 and 4 1 points of rest. Music example 6.2, lasting only twenty-seven seconds and sung by Florencia Rivero, typifies the culturally determined melodic pattern of the Winikina-Warao lullaby (recorded example 7a).

135

Music Example 6.1. Hoerekitane melodic sequence.

Music Example 6.2. Hoerekitane (Florencia Rivero). Transcribed by Herman Kamrowski. Olsen Collection 72.8-142.

In addition to the upward glissando inflections, many of the performances include a microtonal rise in pitch or "upward drift." Listen, for example, to the lullaby on recorded example 7b, which is transcribed as music example 6.3. This song is sung by Cirilo Rivero, a grandfather, who microtonally rises in pitch 160 cents in one minute and forty seconds. In fact, all the lullabies sung by Cirilo Rivero rise in pitch, while all those sung by Florencia Rivero do not. Additionally, an equal proportion of the remaining lullabies sung by other men or women either do or do not reveal upward drift. Therefore, microtonal rising is not gender specific. Its presence or absence, however, is always consistent

Music Example 6.3. Hoerekitane (Cirilo Rivero). Transcribed by James Amend. Olsen Collection 72.8-149.

among singers, suggesting that it is an individually determined characteristic perhaps based on tension or concentration. A comparison of the textual content with upward drift also suggests that there may be a correlation between the textual content of the lullaby and its microtonal rising, as some singers rose in pitch when they sang about dangerous spirits or animals that may harm the infant (see chapter 15). None of the lullabies were recorded contextually; therefore, tension or concentration causing upward drift could be affected by other factors.

Hoerekitane Song Texts

The majority of the texts of Warao lullabies from the Winikina area are improvised (individually determined) to the predetermined (culturally determined) melodic pattern I have already described. The songs are usually sung by an adult member of the family, often a parent or grandparent, and begin with commands addressed to the baby, telling it to go to sleep and not to cry. Following these introductory supplications are several textual themes, such as reference to the absence of a parent who is away working in the rain forest, gathering yuruma, or searching for food. The following lullaby, sung by Cirilo Rivero (also appearing as music example 6.3 and recorded example 7b), tells about parental roles regarding food quest and infant feeding requirements:

Song Text 6.1. Hoerekitane Lullaby, Cirilo Rivero
(Olsen Collection 72.8-149)

Don't cry, go to sleep, my little child
Your mother went to look for food; she is looking for moriche
    grub worms.
When she returns we are going to eat.
Your mother has not returned yet from there.
When she returns we will not give you anything because you
    don't know how to eat yet.
Your father went without us.
Don't cry, go to sleep.

Another, sung by a mother, Florencia Rivero, explains how the child's father is in the rain forest gathering food, how the baby cannot yet eat solid food, and when dinner is served:

Song Text 6.2. Hoerekitane Lullaby, Florencia Rivero
(Olsen Collection 72.8-145)

Don't cry, go to sleep, my little child.
Your father is far off gathering yuruma for our dinner.
We are going to eat and we will not give you food because you
   are very little.
We are going to eat in the afternoon.
Don't cry, go to sleep, my little child.

Most of the Warao hoerekitane song texts, however, describe animals
and spirits of the rain forest. Included among the thirty-seven lullabies
I recorded are nine about birds, two about deer, three about monkeys,
eleven about tigers (tigres in Spanish, which are actually jaguars;
tigers are not found in the Americas), four about spirits, two about all
the animals, one about an unidentified animal, and two about unidentified entities called "it." Because all these songs were sung outside
their natural context, many are of short duration. Others, however, are
long with texts referring to several topics.

   The following lullaby, also sung by Florencia Rivero, is about a
singing bird that follows the current of the river at high tide:

Song Text 6.3. Hoerekitane Lullaby, Florencia Rivero
(Olsen Collection 72.8-146)

The bird from above knows when the river is full and grown.
The bird is preparing its throat to sing.
There it is; it knows the full tide.
Since it knows, it is following the current.
After this it begins to sing.
When it sang it broke its throat and became hoarse.

Another, sung by Antonio Lorenzano to his grandson, makes references to several birds in addition to food quest and eating habits:

Song Text 6.4. Hoerekitane Lullaby, Antonio Lorenzano
(Olsen Collection 72.8-167)

Don't cry; go to sleep, my little grandson.
The large bird from above, the arucu bird, is singing from the
   top of the moriche palm where it is sitting.

Go to sleep.

Your mother is working, gathering yuruma.

Don't cry, go to sleep, my little grandson.

I am your grandfather and I am rocking you.

When your mother comes at midday we will eat.

Go to sleep, my little grandson.

The ahia aromu and the karao sanuka are hearing that you are good. It will eat shells, and it is singing until it is hoarse, this shell eater.

The wacharaca bird and the red cachicamo tree bird sitting above us are singing together.

The dove, also from a cachicamo tree, sings above in the leaves.

Go to sleep, my little grandson.

The birds mentioned by Antonio in this lullaby (arucu, ahia aromu, karao sanuka, wacharaca, red cachicamo tree bird, and dove) have not been identified. Antonio explains that ahia aromu is the name for birds that are from other places; and this agrees with Barral (1957) who writes that ajía means "in the direction towards the headwaters of rivers" (26) while aromu or domu means "bird" (38). Barral (1957, 127) defines karao sanuka only as carrao, bird of the tropics (sanuka means "little"). He (Barral 1967, 87–88) identifies wacharaca (guasaraka, guacharaca) as *hortalis motmot,* a scientific name that is not found in *Aves Venezolanas* (Deery de Phelps 1954), a reference book about Venezuelan birds.

The majority of the animal lullabies are about jaguars (tigres). Some refer to the physical characteristics of the jaguar, as Jaime Zapata (Olsen Collection 72.8-165) sang: "The tiger is walking and nobody hears it because its paws have cotton padding beneath its feet." Other lullaby texts about jaguars, however, address certain aspects of Warao mythology in a way that would seem to frighten the baby, who is told to go to sleep or be eaten by a supernatural jaguar (or some other infant-eating animal or spirit). Bernardo Jiménez Tovar sang the following lullaby for his infant son, about a boneless jaguar:

Song Text 6.5. Hoerekitane Lullaby, Bernardo Jiménez Tovar (Olsen Collection 72.8-154)

Nearby in the rain forest the tiger is listening to us.

The head of the tiger has no bones, it is pure flesh.

The tiger is near, and it has a good head [is smart] and can
learn and speak Warao.

It is learning my words and my family's words.

My son, I am your father.

The tiger thinks well in order to learn my words.

It is listening to us. Go to sleep.

Your mother went to look for food this afternoon.

If she brings food we'll eat.

If not, we'll go to sleep without eating.

Antonio sang the following lullaby for his grandson in which he explains
about a jaguar, a monkey, and a spirit—all potentially dangerous:

Song Text 6.6. Hoerekitane Lullaby, Antonio Lorenzano (Olsen Collection 72.8-166)

Don't cry, go to sleep, my little grandson.

You are crying, and maybe the tiger will come.

You are crying, and maybe the tiger will come, little
grandson.

Don't cry, go to sleep.

The tiger comes from the rain forest and is nearby watching
us.

It comes watching us, and it can eat you raw.

Your mother is working. When she finishes working at noon
we will eat soup.

Off to our one side the tiger comes from the seashore, passing
by the Carib people and the fishermen.

Don't cry, go to sleep, my little grandson.

The monkey comes looking for us from the tree tops where it
travels.

The spider-eating monkey comes.

Don't cry, go to sleep, my little grandson.

A spirit is nearby; it is standing there and watching us. It would like to take you away.

Don't cry, go to sleep, my little grandson.

A spirit is there nearby, hearing that you are crying.

Therefore, don't cry; go to sleep.

You are crying, and it will also cry, this evil spirit, it will also cry.

This spirit doesn't have flesh, it is pure bones, and it is there at the tree top.

It can cry just like you, this spirit of the tree tops, and it can eat you from within.

Your mother is still working, and will soon finish.

Go to sleep, my little grandson.

After singing this song, Antonio gave this explanation:

Hoerekitane in Venezuelan Spanish means "to rock" (mecer), from Warao hoere. This is so the child can sleep. Manatoro sanuka means "my little grandson." Ubau means "go to sleep." I sing, "Go to sleep without crying, and beware of the tiger that can come here, hearing these cries." Because the tiger is very bold and daring, when it knows and hears someone crying, or someone doing something, then it comes close to that person. When the tiger comes close to someone, it begins to watch that person over and over. It has the capacity to eat someone. Therefore, I sing, "Go to sleep without crying, little grandson." Now, from midday, from midday to one or two o'clock, we eat and drink. Another thing, I sing like this: "the tiger, when you are crying, will pass the fishermen, will pass near to us, from there to here, from the beach, the salt flats. . . . Therefore, it will pass between us when you are crying. Thus, don't cry, sleep, don't cry, little grandson. I am rocking you. After this, go to sleep, little grandson, because a monkey will come from there." This monkey is a little animal that is very daring. This little monkey can close in on us and when it does it will touch a person, regardless of whether that person is alive or dead, because this little monkey is very bad, very energetic. Because it is not afraid of anyone, this monkey can do anything to anyone. If the person is alive, the monkey can stick its finger in the person's eye, or in his nose, his mouth, in both eyes, wherever, because this monkey is a very bad little animal. Therefore, I sing, "Go to sleep little grandson, don't cry; I am rocking you because I am your grandfather. You are my little grandson. Your mother is working. Go to sleep without crying." You don't know if a tree, a tree branch torn from its roots, carries a spirit, a thin one, which has no flesh, but is pure bones. A child's cries can attract it. Thus, I sing, "Go to sleep, quietly. I am rocking you. I am your grandfather." This is for when I accompany the child, and because of the evil spirit of the branch, when it becomes bad. The child could get sick, and when you get very sick you could die. Therefore, I sing, "Go to sleep quietly and don't cry, my little grandson. I am rocking you."

To a non-Warao, the texts of the Warao lullabies may appear overly frightening for children. The idea of "go to sleep or else," however, may be more recognizable to North Americans and Europeans if we think of this familiar cradle song:

> Rock-a-bye, baby, on the tree top.
> When the wind blows the cradle will rock.
> When the wind blows the cradle will fall,
> And down will come baby, cradle and all.

McCosker (1976, 29) writes that many other native American lullabies also seem frightening, "scaring the children to sleep by threatening descriptions of bogeys," while the lullabies of the Panamanian Cuna Indians are generally positive. In a similar way the Warao lullabies can be thought of as positive rather than frighteningly negative because they informally educate the older children who are nearby in their hammocks listening, subconsciously being prepared by their elders for the supernatural part of their world and its dangers as well as indirectly educated about parental chores, eating times, the types of food an infant cannot eat, and so forth. This enculturation or informal learning is apparent because the infants are too young to understand the complexities of the lullaby texts. The Warao distinguish between infancy (first twelve months), childhood (from one to twelve years old), and adolescence (from thirteen to seventeen years old). While some informal learning takes place during infancy, learning by listening to songs (the sung language) takes place during childhood and adolescence as the children themselves learn to speak and comprehend the Warao spoken language.

Although the Warao lullabies warn young children about supernatural dangers, the Warao cosmic world is so full of potential threats toward young and old alike that warnings and preventive measures can only go so far. The next three chapters discuss how the Warao treat supernaturally caused illnesses. The cosmological and musical healing knowledge of the three classes of Warao shamans—wisiratu, bahanarotu, and hoarotu—are crucial to the physical and mental health of every Warao individual.

7   Wisiratu Shaman Songs

The wisiratu (wisidatu, wishiratu, güisiratu) is the highest-ranking Warao shaman. He is the overseer of the cosmic upper realm; guardian of the kanobotuma's earthly manifestations; leader of the sacred rituals; healer of great pains; great communicator of the beyond; and, in many ways, village leader.

The Wisiratu Teachers

Although the ideas I explain in this chapter are derived from the explanations and interpretations of numerous Warao teachers, the knowledge of three particular men stands out. In terms of the ethnographic present, they are ritual specialists in their forties, each living in a different village on the Winikina River. Bernardo Jiménez Tovar lives in Yaruara Akoho, Chano Rivero lives across the Winikina River in Lorenzano Ahanoko, and Juan Bustillo Calderón comes from the downstream village of Hebu Wabanoko. I also consulted three other shamans, all elders who were two or three generations older than Bernardo, Chano, and Juan: Isaías Rodríguez of Hebu Wabanoko, the powerful priest-shaman of his village; Talejo Tovar of Juan Mata Ahanoko on the Arawabisi River; and Antonio Lorenzano, chief of Lorenzano Ahanoko, who is not a wisiratu but a bahanarotu with a deep understanding of wisiratu shamanism that he learned from his uncle Salvador. The song language used by all these men is typically archaic and ritualistic but is not beyond the individual understanding of the singers; therefore, the translations of the songs are their own.

Wisiratu Shamanism

Padre Barral (1964, 144), one of the greatest authorities on the Warao native Americans, explains that the word wisiratu is "composed of three words: *güisi* (pain), *era* (much), and *arotu* (master), meaning güisi-(e)ra-(aro)tu, grand master of pain." "Wisi" can also be translated as "poison," according to Turrado Moreno (1945, 146), another member of the Catholic order and a respected authority on the Warao. He writes: "*Güisi*—poison, and *daotu*—rich, [mean] abundance of poison." Wilbert (1974, 92) defines wisiratu as "master of fire," perhaps an appropriate meaning for "wisi" because the wisiratu makes almost exclusive use of the spark-producing hebu mataro rattle. Another possible meaning for the "wisi" prefix comes from the language of the maroon river cultures of Surinam (the Bush Negroes) with whom the Warao may have had contact. (On the other hand, the Surinam maroons could have borrowed the term from the Warao.) To the maroons, wissi is an evil spirit capable of entering the body and causing damage (Dark 1970, 15). The Warao also refer to the wisiratu in his curing role as hebu arotu or "master of hebu," and the prefix to that appellation is similar in usage to the maroon term wissi because hebu is also a spirit capable of causing pain or illness. The Warao themselves gloss wisiratu as doctor in Spanish, meaning one who practices healing.

The wisiratu shaman has many roles, as Turrado Moreno (1945, 146–47) writes:

> He is a wizard, a doctor held in the highest esteem, the most feared by all, and the person of highest consideration; because he is medical doctor and priest at the same time, his principal duties are the following:
>
> a) to remove the hebu spirits from the bodies of patients;
>
> b) to recite and sing hoas, psalms, and prayers during curing, while playing the sacred rattle and smoking wina cigars at the same time;
>
> c) to place yuruma, tobacco, and tobacco water (in some parts of the Delta) within the sanctuary of the Supreme Hebu;
>
> d) to consult their god in times of epidemics, fevers, and illnesses, in order to appease the god and do what he asks;
>
> e) as a priest, he is the only person who has the right to enter into the house of the Supreme Hebu to recite, appease, listen to, and even threaten the god; therefore, in times of epidemics, the wisiratu spends a lengthy time in the temple, reciting and singing hoas and psalms, playing the sacred rattle, and murmuring to the god so that he will remove the illness from the village;
>
> f) if the god asks for a dance, the wisiratu organizes the sacred dances of *nahanamu* and *habi sanuka* in honor of and

promise to the Supreme Hebu, and respectfully takes out and carries the sacred rattle from the sanctuary to be played during the dances;

g) when there is a tempest, the wisiratu along with an *aidamo* or elder who helps him if he makes a mistake, conjure up and drive away the clouds by forcefully blowing at them, waving their hands at them, making grimaces at them with their eyes, and chanting the following hoa: "uf, uf; naha naru, naha naru, naha ekoranu, naha ekoranu," which means "uf, uf, go away rain, go away rain, stop rain, stop rain."

In this chapter I discuss the wisiratu as a healer of hebu-caused ill-nesses—that is, in his curing rather than his priestly role. Because he is a healer of persons suffering from hebu or ancestor-spirit sickness, the wisiratu is loved by all Warao. As a wisiratu matures, and if his vil-lage has a hebu ahanoko (also called kwaihanoko), a temple that houses a sacred kanobo stone (the material representation of a patron supreme spirit or kanobo), he will inherit the important position known as kanobo arima—father of the kanobo. This double function as a priest-shaman gives the wisiratu extremely high status in Warao society.

Presently, only men are wisiratu shamans. Warao mythology, how-ever, suggests that in ancient times women may also have been holders of the powerful office, as the following narrative excerpt, entitled "The Mother of the Forest and the First Canoe," implies (Wilbert 1976, 337–38):

Haburi [the culture hero] invented the dugout canoe, and es-caped [from the treacherous frog woman] with his mothers [with whom he committed incest] to the northern world mountain, at the edge of the earth. . . . The canoe, however, transformed itself into a giant snake-woman and the paddle into a man. They returned as the red cachicamo [tree] (canoe) and the white cachicamo [tree] (paddle), to the center of the earth, where the Warao had since come into ex-istence. The cachicamo woman became Dauarani, the Mother of the Forest. She was the first priest-shaman (*wishi-ratu*) on earth. Eventually she departed from earth to take up residence on a world mountain at the end of the universe in the southwest (where her body lives) and in the southeast (where her soul remains). The paddle stayed in the center of the earth with the Warao.

The frog woman referred to in the narrative is Wau-uta, or Wauta, who, before she was changed into a frog, was a female shaman who sang with her rattle (Wilbert 1970, 285, narrative 140, "The story of Haburi"): "While going along, they heard Wau-uta singing. Wau-uta was a woman in those days, indeed she was a *piai* woman, and she was just then singing with her *shak-shak* (rattle). The two women went on and on, quickly too, for they knew that once they arrived at Wau-uta's place they would be safe." Today there are no female wisimo among the Warao in the Winikina area. (Wisimo is the plural form of wisiratu; when capitalized, Wisimo refers to the spirits of the deceased wisiratu shamans who have hung their hammocks next to their konobotuma in the great beyond; in the lowercase it refers to living and practicing wisiratu shamans. [See, however, chapter 9 for another interpretation of wisimo.])

Wisiratu Apprenticeship Songs

The initiation period of the wisiratu is strenuous, requiring several days of fasting, smoking tobacco, and learning songs from a master wisiratu teacher. During a deep trance state brought about by lack of food, ingested tobacco smoke, singing, and cultural conditioning, the initiate embarks upon a celestial journey to the house of Yaukware at the top of the cosmic vault. From there he continues to travel to the cosmic mountain of his choice (except to the westernmost abode of Hoebo) to visit a kanobo who will become his patron (Wilbert 1975b, 63–65). The path is arduous and dangerous, filled with temptations that include cooked meat, sensuous women, bottomless pits, clashing gates, serpents, and other tests of the initiate's endurance. If successful, he will reach the kanobo's home where he will eventually have his own abode after death (that is, where he will hang his hammock) and will awaken from his trance reborn as a wisiratu shaman with six wisi spirit helpers residing in his chest. He will also gain the power of additional helping spirits within his hebu mataro rattle.

Antonio Lorenzano sang a wisiratu apprenticeship song for me that he learned from his uncle Salvador. A portion of it is transcribed as music example 7.1, and its complete song text (song text 7.1) is transliterated and translated word for word because that is the way this bilingual Warao man of knowledge taught me. Additionally, the translation emphasizes the extensive use of repetition and demonstrates Warao word order and something of the abstract nature (to us) of the apprenticeship song (recorded in Naba Sanuka).

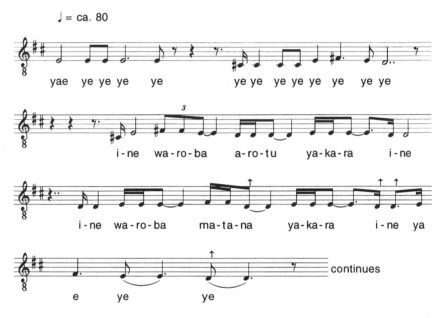

Music Example 7.1. Wisiratu apprenticeship song (Antonio Lorenzano). Olsen Collection 72.8-46.

Song Text 7.1. Wisiratu Apprenticeship Song, Antonio Lorenzano, 20 July 1972 (Olsen Collection 72.8-46)

yae ye ye ye

ine waroba arotu yakara ine ine waroba matana yakara ine yae
　ye ye
I throat master good I, I throat other side good I, yae ye ye

ine waroba diawarae ine ine waroba yakara ine ine
I throat was born I, I throat good I, I

ine waroba matana ine ine waroba matana yakara diawarae
    ine
I throat other side I, I throat other side good was born I

ine mehori diawarae ine ine mehori matana diawarae ine
I chest was born I, I chest other side was born I

ine yobotaru yakara diawarae ine ine mehori yobotaru matana
    diawarae ine
I waist good was born I, I chest waist other side was born I

ine mutu diawarae ine ine mutu diawarae ine
I together was born I, I together was born I

ine warao diawara ine ine warao diawara ine
I was born Warao I, I was born Warao I

ine yakara ine ine yakara ine ine yakara ine ine warao diawarae
    ine
I good I, I good I, I good I, I was born Warao I

ine yerebatu ine ine yereba mukwarotu ine ine yereba arotu ine
I eater I, I food (?) head owner I, I food owner I

ine mutu diawarae ine ine ine saba diawarae ine
I looker was born I, I, I for was born I

ine hiahokorima tane hiahoko obonoya ine ine hiahoko aisiko
    ine diawarae
I your dawn father he is your dawn thinker I, I your dawn
    with I was born

ine yae ye nohotu ine ine ine waroba nohotu yakara ine
I yae ye one who has hunger I, I, I throat one who has hunger
    good I

ine waroba matana nohotu ine yakara ine ine waroba nohotu
    yakara ine

I throat the other side one who has hunger good I, I throat
one who has hunger good I

ine mehori nohotu ine ine ine mehori yakara nohotu ine ine
I chest one who has hunger I, I, I chest good one who has
hunger I, I

ine mehori matana nohotu ine ine ine mehori matana yakara-
nohotu ine
I chest the other side, one who has hunger I, I, I chest the
other side good, one who has hunger, I

ine yobotaru nohotu ine ine ine yobotaru yakara nohotu ine ine
I waist one who has hunger I, I, I waist one who has hunger
I, I

ine yobotaru matana nohotu ine ine ine yobotaru matana
yakara nohotu ine
I waist the other side one who has hunger I, I, I waist the
other side good one who has hunger, I

ine waroba nohotu ine ine ine ine nohotu yakara yae ye ye ye
I throat one who has hunger I, I, I, I one who has hunger
good, yae ye ye ye

ine mutu diawarae ine ine ine hiahoko arima tane ine
I looker was born I, I, I your dawn father he is, I

ine koroba ine obonatu ine ine koroba seno bahate ine
I tobacco, I thinker I, I tobacco (?) will smoke, I

ine mahoko mahoko arahe nasaribu karamunae ine ine
I my dawn brothers impression trembled I, I

ine ine diawarate ine ine diawarae ine ine ine diawarate ine yae
yae ye ye ine
I, I was born I, I was born I, I, I was born I, yae yae ye ye I

ine masaba ine masaba,ine warao diawarae ine warao diawara
ine warao diawara diawarae ine
I for me, I for me, I Warao was born, I Warao was born, I
  Warao was born was born, I

ine mutu diawarae ine ine hiahoko arima tane ine ine di-
awarate ine ine hiahoko arima tane ine diawarae
I looker was born I, I your dawn father he is I, I was born I, I
  your dawn father he is, I was born

ine warao diawarae ine yakara diawarae ine
I Warao was born, I was born well

ine yereba kwarotu ine yereba ine yereba kwarotu yakara ine
yereba nahorotu ine waeyae yae yae
I food head owner I, food I food head owner good I, food
  owner of dispersion I, waeyae yae yae

ine ine yerebatu ine ine yereba kwarotu ine ine yereba ahoko
sabasabana ine diawarae ine yereba ahoko sabasabamo di-
awarae
I, I eater I, I food head owner I, I food dawn towards I was
  born I food dawn towards was born

ine nahorotu ine nahorotu yakara
I master of dispersion I good

ine ine horera diawarae ine ine ine horera diawarae ine ine ine
horera diawarae ine
I, I good water was born I, I, I good water was born I, I, I good
  water was born I

ine warao diawara ine ine warao diawara horera diawara ine
I Warao was born I, I Warao was born good water was born I

ine mutu diawara diawarae ine yae yae ye ye
I looker was born was born I yae yae ye ye

Antonio explained the text of this wisiratu apprenticeship song in a way that clarifies the meaning of its word order and abstraction. In the song text he is addressing his spirit helpers or spirit "sons," who are in the process of entering his body. In his commentary, however, another point is very clearly revealed, one that is not often discussed in the literature about the Warao—the economics of shamanism. Antonio's explanation does not stress the philosophical or eschatological reasons for wanting to become a wisiratu but rather the practical ones:

> In Spanish this means the following: *ine*, I am myself [soy yo]. Now the throat comes in, as I sang, "Come in, arrive in my throat. In the other part also." I am the one who wants because I want.
>
> Then I sang the following: "Come in through my chest also. Also come in through the other side of my chest. After this, come into me through one side of my waist, and also the other side. This is because I thought of believing in you. I want you."
>
> From the very beginning, that which the old Wisimo learned, those who died, they are the ones who wanted to learn. In the same way I want to learn, just as those who first died. I want it so I do not have to spend my money. I understand, because I can see, that one has to pay to have his son, wife, or fellow man cured when he is sick. For this reason I realize that I want to learn, so I do not lose that which I have saved. When members of my family get sick I do not want to have to call upon another person. You understand that when someone gets sick you have to call someone else, and it is hard to say what is happening. For this very reason I want to learn to become a wisiratu, the same as the first ones who have died. I want everything that comes.
>
> Then I sang this: "I am that which is converted to blood. I am. I like to eat and drink water. I am innocent. I am a Warao, and a great eater, and you a spirit. You neither eat nor drink water. The only food that you have is tobacco smoke from a wina cigar."
>
> This is the signal of learning everything about becoming a wisiratu. Now, when one learns, he does not have to work any

longer. Now he does not have to call upon a companion. Now,
you know that a person, after he has learned to cure everything, will not have to work when his family, his sons get ill.
So I say to the person who will teach me, "My brothers," or
"my uncle," or "you, my older brother, you know that you are
the best wisiratu, so teach me well. I want to learn that what
you have learned, just as you learned it. In exactly the same
way I want to learn to be the same as you. I want to be able to
cure just like the others. Already you know I am seeing a
person who is sick, and about that I feel very sad. I want to
learn everything about them [shamans], especially all the
things about the wisiratu. Why? Because I need this. The
most principal things I want to learn. Thus, I will sing like
you." This is the end, my friend.

Antonio stresses the apprentice's desire to learn the business of
wisiratu shamanism so life will become easier for him. If he can cure
his own family, then he will not need to pay a wisiratu with expensive
tobacco or whatever fee an outside curer will charge. While I have no
more information on the economics of wisiratu shamanism beyond
this, Wilbert (1985, 168–69) explains that the bahanarotu shaman (see
chapter 8) exacts a high price for the curing of female disorders. For
example, the bahanarotu shaman has supernatural powers enabling
him to treat gynecological problems that may require repeated ceremonies. If the patient or the patient's family has no means of payment,
she may be required to provide ateho wabia or "selling of the body,"
placing her into a type of familial, nonsexual bondage with the bahanarotu for life. Similar types of payment for repeated and successful
curing rituals in wisiratu shamanism undoubtedly exist. Indeed,
Warao shamans are usually the wealthiest members of their villages,
just as medical doctors and psychotherapists are among the wealthiest
members of European-derived societies.

Hebu Illnesses: Their Causes, Symptoms, and Treatments

What is a hebu? Padre Damián del Blanco, a Capuchín missionary at
the mission of Naba Sanuka in the central delta and a student of
Warao cosmology, explained to me that in his opinion a hebu is an

ancestor spirit. Wilbert (1970, 24), likewise, says that a hebu is "a metaphysical essence, such as an ancestor spirit."

It is easier to determine what a hebu is like. Suárez (1968, 157), for example, quotes one of her elder informants: "Hebu is like the wind, like the smoke, like the rain. Hebu is everywhere: the roof has hebu, the earth has hebu, the trees have hebu. When hebu is hungry he makes a boy sick, he enters into his stomach." Likewise, one of my wisiratu teachers explained that "hebu comes from everywhere, the sun, moon, water, earth, wind, house, canteen, drum, any object; but, not a person." Hebu can also come from any animal, such as a deer, a snake, a tapir, or a bird, according to one of my elder shaman teachers. Based on information learned from the many wisiratu curing song texts that I collected, hebu is an ancestor spirit that can place itself into or take the shape of any object or animal with the purpose of inflicting illness on the Warao.

Hebu illnesses can be inflicted in three ways: by an ancestor spirit himself; by an ancestor spirit who has had the idea suggested to him by a malevolent living wisiratu (Wilbert 1970, 24; 1972b, 65); and by the supreme spirits, the kanobotuma, who live at the cardinal and intercardinal points of the universe (excluding Hoebo in the west and possibly Mawari in the east). These Warao lords may individually become angry if neglected by the wisiratu for a long period of time and "send wishi pains and death down to earth" (Wilbert 1972b, 61). The disorders they cause are sent via hebutuma, the ancestor spirits who correspond to particular kanobotuma and materialize into or take possession of a particular animal, a breeze, or a noise. Moreover, they can enter into a victim's body directly. Thus, to ward off hebu illnesses, the wisiratu priest-shaman must constantly keep the kanobotuma fed with tobacco smoke and once a year must offer yuruma cakes during the nahanamu ritual complex (see chapter 14).

The ancestor spirits are often Wisimo (the souls of deceased wisiratu shamans) who send illness and death to earth, as the following narrative, "The wisiratu who sends sickness from the clouds," suggests (Wilbert 1970, 184–85, narrative 80, collected by Barral):

There was a *wisiratu* who lived with his wife, his mother, and his younger brother. This youngster went to the *moriche* grove every day, taking with him his sister-in-law, the wife of the *wisiratu*. I do not know why the *wisiratu* began to suspect but one day, without either of them knowing about it, he followed them and discovered them in transgression. Without letting himself be seen, he returned to his house, carrying with him a handful of *manaca* palm bark, the kind that the Indians use to roll their cigars. Arriving at the house, his mother asked him, "Son, with whom did you see your wife in bad ways?"

The *wisiratu* did not answer her. Absorbed in thought and with head down, he set out for the sanctuary, took out the sacred rattle called *mari-mataro* and placed it in the center of the *hohonoko* or dance plaza. He rolled half a dozen magic cigars in the *manaca* palm bark that he had brought from the *moriche* grove, and he placed them next to the rattle. His mother, still more worried, asked him again, "Son, what are you planning to do? Are you going to climb to the clouds and leave me alone?"

The *wisiratu* answered, "Mother, I will not climb up leaving you alone." His mother insisted, "Son, if your wife has failed you, calm anger for now and leave this case to be solved later."

But the *wisiratu* could not find peace. He lighted one of the cigars and filled his mouth with smoke, blowing it out toward the sky, resolved to go up to the clouds among the scrolls of smoke.

His mother said plaintively, "Son, calm your anger, my son!" And she held him around the waist, clutching him.

. . . [T]he *wisiratu* freed himself from the earth and began to rise through the air in the direction of the clouds. "Mother," he cried from above, "I will not send death to you, but the others will soon die." Saying this, he continued climbing, going up and each moment appearing smaller, until he was no longer visible except for a black point, like the head of a pin.

The clouds tore apart, and the black dot disappeared in the hole. The clouds reunited, leaving once again the closed sky, smooth as always. In the later afternoon, the two Indians, brother and wife of the one who disappeared, returned from the *moriche* grove. When they found out that the *wisiratu* no longer lived on the earth, they considered themselves man and wife, and hung up only one hammock in which to sleep. But the next morning they were dead. The Indians say that the *wisiratu* who went up to the clouds remains angry and that once in a while, from above, he sends sickness to the villages.

The symptoms of hebu-caused illnesses are varied. Turrado Moreno (1945, 160) explains that a hebu illness is always accompanied by a fever such as that in malaria, typhus, and measles. Wilbert (1983, 359) relates fever diseases to the kanobo of the southern world mountain, Karoshima, the toad god. He writes: "the cardinal god of the South, the Toad, is perhaps the mightiest of them all. His special scourges are febrile diseases like 'the fever of many granules' (small pox and measles), 'the shivering spirit' (malaria) and 'the hot skin' disease (yellow fever)." My personal observations among the Warao suggest that a wisiratu will attempt to cure any illness whether a fever is present or not; if he is unsuccessful, however, he will recommend that a bahanarotu or hoarotu be brought in, explaining that the patient does not have a hebu sickness. In addition, I also observed bahanarotu and hoarotu shamans attempting to cure patients with high fevers, thus suggesting that illnesses with fevers are not restricted to the wisiratu.

Oramas (1947, 85) studied the role of Warao shamans in 1947 and concluded that the wisiratu does not cure diseases contracted from foreigners, such as measles, catarrh, and influenza. More recently, however, both the common European (and possibly African) illnesses known as influenza and catarrh (the latter is a major killer among the Warao) have become part of a Warao shaman's duty to cure. It does not take very long before outside physical and spiritual maladies are absorbed into Warao ethnopathology.

Respiratory diseases are presently included in the domain of the wisiratu and are attributed to the kanobo of the northern world mountain with whom the wisiratu is able to communicate during his celestial travels. Wilbert (1983, 360) explains in this way: "The god of the North, the owl-face Butterfly . . . travels with the speed of light that reflects in his mirrors and in the cold northwinds that blow from his mountain. His specialty are respiratory ailments like 'the bad cough' (bronchitis), 'the hurting lungs' (pneumonia), and, above all, the 'cough of the howler monkey' (whooping cough)." Warao illness is often described in terms pertaining to air (W. Wilbert 1986), as Briggs (1994, 149) writes:

> A vehicle of transmission is believed to bring a pathogenic odor into the victim's body; detaching itself from the transmitting agent, the *ahaka* (wind, air) becomes lodged in a particular part of the body. Since this odor or wind has physical as well as intangible, invisible attributes, a curer can locate illness in a patient by using his hands to discern the size and relative hardness of the spirit (which serve to distinguish hebu from hoa and bahana) as well as to feel the movement and heat it produces.

In a curing ritual a wisiratu "feeds" his spirit helpers, which reside in his throat and chest and inside his hebu mataro rattle (which are manifested as kareko spirits embodied as quartz pebbles). Strengthened by their tobacco-smoke food from a wina cigar, the wisiratu's spirit helpers are ready to overcome the illness-causing hebu that has intruded into the patient's body. To effect a cure, the wisiratu must name the correct hebu or the animal or object whose essence has become embodied by the hebu. He names through song (wara); and with his hebu helpers and the power of his hebu mataro rattle, he takes control of the malevolent hebu, removing it by massage into his hand. Then he shuffles his feet and forcibly blows into his raised fist, thereby sending the evil hebu into the wind, admonishing it to return to the place of origin from whence it came. Naming is the essence of the shaman's power; and this is one of the reasons why the Warao call this type of singing wara, which means "communication."

A wisiratu curing session generally occurs in the early evening, although it may begin later and last until the early morning. Only rarely, in very serious cases, will a wisiratu conduct a curing ritual during the day (see cover photograph). A wisiratu's curing tools include his hebu mataro rattle and a supply of wina cigars, both items measuring up to three feet in length. As he seats himself on a bench or pile of wood next to the patient in his or her hammock, the wisiratu is usually joined by a number of village men who are also prepared to smoke their long cigars. Because there is no electricity in a typical Warao village, the only light is from the burning coals of the central fire, the glow of the wina cigars, perhaps a dimly lit kerosene lantern hanging at one end of the house, and occasionally the moon.

Normally only one wisiratu attempts to cure at a time; however, if an illness is extremely serious or if the patient is a very important or wealthy person, two or more wisimo may be hired to conduct the ritual together. Although I recorded two wisimo singing together in duo, the performance situation was noncontextual and neither man played a hebu mataro rattle (recorded example 9). The singers explained that during an actual curing performance they would both sing with their rattles.

The wisiratu begins his curing ritual by deeply inhaling smoke from his wina cigar, nourishing his helping spirits within his chest. He slowly releases the smoke and his spirit sons from his mouth with a masked voice, often producing the gravelly sounds "o, oi" (or "owai, yae, yae") and "e e e e e." These masked vocables "reflect the difficulty that the spirits encounter in passing through the larynx and pharynx" and are viewed by the Warao not as "invocations of spirits, signs addressed to invisible audiences, but audible traces of the participation of spirits" (Briggs n.d., 21). While the tobacco smoke gives a physical presence to the wisiratu's breath, the masked vocables give it an acoustical presence. After this introductory smoking ritual he will not need to smoke his cigar again during the curing ritual. In fact, holding his wina is impossible during most of the ritual because he needs both hands to manipulate his large rattle, which he shakes unceasingly while singing with his raspy masked voice.

Voice masking, physiologically produced during the wisiratu's curing ritual by a constriction of his vocal chords, is believed to be caused by the wisiratu's spirit helpers within his chest and throat. Therefore, it is believed that only a wisiratu can do it. When the wisiratu is alone on the hohonoko (dancing platform) for the purpose of ecstatic flight, voice masking can be physiologically aided by the inhalation of a vapor from melted resin of the takamahaka (in Warao) or curucay (in Spanish) tree. In its solid form, called sibu in Warao and caraña in Spanish (*Protium heptaphyllum*) (Wilbert 1993, 118), this resin is melted with the burning end of a wina cigar as the wisiratu begins to call his helping spirits. The vapor, mixed with tobacco smoke, passes through the cigar into the chest of the wisiratu, coating his vocal chords in such a manner that it enables him to produce loud, low-pitched, resonant sounds that are characteristic of his spirit-helper releasing voice. Professor Richard Evans Schultes, director of the Botanical Museum at Harvard University, has written about the use of protium as an incense for coca among the Peritome Tanimuka of Colombia (1957, 241). He personally experienced a hoarseness of his voice as a result of chewing coca that had been incensed with pro-tium (personal communication between Richard E. Schultes and Jo-hannes Wilbert, 26 November 1973). The primary purpose of the in-cense among the Warao wisiratu, however, is to feed the kanobo; and for spiritual reasons it is not employed while curing illnesses. Addi-tionally, it is not used during curing for practical reasons because only the first part of the wisiratu curing cycle uses the technique of voice masking. During the complete cycle of curing (that is, one complete curing sequence), three main musical and functional sections are used; and two of them are sung with a normal (unmasked) voice quality. Therefore, the wisiratu must be able to change immediately from a masked voice to his normal voice during the flow of his perfor-mance. We shall soon see that voice masking has a precise function for the wisiratu during his curing cycle.

Wisiratu Curing Songs

The wisiratu curing songs that I studied include twenty-three perfor-mances: fifteen were recorded noncontextually, and five were recorded during actual curing rituals. (I will interchangeably refer to a contex-tual curing event as a ceremony or ritual.) Each of the twenty-three performances contains one or more musical/textual sections that would make up an entire curing cycle. These sections differ musically and textually, and for analytical purposes I label them A, A¹, B, and C. Of the noncontextual performances, twelve consist of a single section each, and three are made up of several contrasting sections. One of the five actual curing ceremonies is incomplete, but the other four are complete. One additional cycle was attended but not recorded; the con-trasting sections, however, were noted, and the pitches were deter-mined with an A-440 tuning fork and written down while the wisiratu was performing. Table 7.1 lists the performances, their contrasting sec-tions, and the performers of the wisiratu curing music. In the examples

Table 7.1. Wisiratu curing songs

Olsen Collection no.	Section(s)	Performer(s)
Noncontextual performances		
Without hebu mataro		
72.8-26	A	Chano Rivero
72.8-27	A A¹ C	Chano Rivero
72.8-28	A A¹ C	Chano Rivero
72.8-47	A¹	Talejo Tovar
72.8-29	B	Chano Rivero
72.8-30	B	Chano Rivero
72.8-31	B	Chano Rivero
72.8-32	B	Bernardo Jiménez Tovar
72.8-33	B	Bernardo Jiménez Tovar
Uncataloged	B	Bernardo Jiménez Tovar
72.8-35	B	Antonio Lorenzano
72.8-34	B	Talejo Tovar
With hebu mataro		
72.8-36	A	Bernardo Jiménez Tovar
72.8-37	A A¹	Bernardo Jiménez Tovar
72.8-38	B	Bernardo Jiménez Tovar
Contextual curing performances		
with hebu-mataro		
No recording	A B A B A B A B A A¹ (no text)	Bernardo Jiménez Tovar
72.8-39	A B (no text)	Bernardo Jiménez Tovar
72.8-40	A B A B (no text)	Bernardo Jiménez Tovar
72.8-41	A B C A B C A A¹ C (no text)	Bernardo Jiménez Tovar
72.8-42	A C A B C (text A C only)	Juan Bustillo Calderón
72.8-43	A B C A B C B A A¹ C (no text)	Juan Bustillo Calderón
Noncontextual performances (two wisimo)		
72.8-44	A	Bernardo Jiménez Tovar and Juan Bustillo Calderón
72.8-45	A¹	Bernardo Jiménez Tovar and Juan Bustillo Calderón

indicated with "no text," the words were not decipherable because of the overpowering sounds of the rattle.

Section A is the only portion of a wisiratu curing ritual that uses voice masking (recorded examples 8 and 9). The use of voice masking and the section's introductory position within the cycle of the ritual indicate that the shaman is summoning supernatural help. Suárez (1968, 167) writes that the wisiratu "sings and invokes the helping hebu so that the latter helps the shaman to cure" and that the wisiratu's voice is changed (masked) because the invoked helping hebu has become the owner of the wisiratu's voice. This interpretation suggests possession; however, the wisiratu is not possessed by the invoked helping hebu but transformed into it. Furthermore, the wisiratu does not invoke his supernatural helpers (there are usually more than one) through song but releases them with tobacco smoke and vocables. Because his spirit sons dwell within his chest, they and the wisiratu are one entity during spiritual affairs such as curing; and the wisiratu's masked voice *is* the hebu's voice. Warao shamans themselves say that there is no spirit possession in Warao shamanism, only transformation and oneness between mortal and immortal. Therefore, the spirit helpers living within the chest of the wisiratu are summoned with tobacco smoke and waratuma, the shaman's words. The first sounds the wisiratu makes during a curing ceremony are "oi, o, e e e e e e," which function as the sonic carriers of the released shaman's breath (tobacco smoke) and the spirit helpers that slowly exit from deep within the wisiratu's chest and out his mouth. The first word of the wisiratu shaman's curing song is "owai," which has several interpretations. Within the context of the beginning of the song, it is usually followed by "wai," which literally means "name" (Barral 1957, 83, guai = name), referring to the name of the helping spirit(s) that are released with the shaman's breath. "Owai" is also a vocable reserved for the shaman (used by the bahanarotu and hoarotu) and is glossed by Barral (1957, 171) to mean "I will try to cure you" (oae). These vowel sounds are masked, and the wisiratu continues to sing with a raspy voice, speaking through song to the spirits that are either his internal helpers, his hebu mataro spiritual helpers, or the malevolent illness-causing hebutuma. Juan Bustillo Calderón, explaining exactly what was taking place during each section of the texts of the curing songs that he sang (Olsen Collection 72.8-42, 72.8-44, and 72.8-45), told me that when the wisiratu speaks to the hebu spirits in song and the spirits answer through him, he becomes transformed into a hebu himself.

The vocal range of the wisiratu during his curing song cycle is typically within the normal parameters of the male voice (that is, it is neither forcibly high nor low). The average tone-system range of the A section, however, is always at the singer's lowest level. Section A¹ is either the same or at the next highest level, section B is higher still, and section C reaches the highest pitch of wisiratu singing (based upon a comparison of principal tones).

The principal tone of section A of a curing song cycle is almost always approached from above by another tone at an interval of an approximate minor third (♭1). This constitutes what I analytically refer to as the most common Warao foundation interval. Additionally, there are occasional variations, such as a major second alternating with the minor third, as heard in the beginning of recorded example 8 and seen in music example 7.4. Above the foundation interval, one or two additional tones (either 4 or 3, or both) may be sung, as seen in the notations of the most common tone systems (transposed to D as the principal tone) in music example 7.2. Music example 7.3 is an excerpt from the beginning of the A section of a curing ritual performed by Juan Bustillo Calderón on 27 July 1972.

Song text 7.2 is from a different moment of the same ceremony, but it typifies the wisiratu curing song A section. The context of this performance was an early-evening attempt to cure Luís Jiménez, a prominent Warao leader who was suffering from a stroke (see also chapter 9). The ritual took place during the second evening after the patient became ill.

Music Example 7.2. Wisiratu curing song, section A, tone systems (transposed to D as the principal tone).

Music Example 7.3. Wisiratu curing song, section A (Bernardo Jiménez Tovar). Olsen Collection 72.8-43b.

Song Text 7.2. Wisiratu Curing Song, Section A, Juan Bustillo Calderón, 27 July 1972 (Olsen Collection 72.8-42)

I was born for you.

My action is with you.

My action for the hebu is that I am the same as him.

I, with my body, I was born in this body to guard you, hebu.

I was born for you. Thus I was born.

My word is that I was born with your body.

My action is with the body of the rattle.

I am the rattle.

My action is that I am together with the rattle. I grab for you, rattle.

Now I know what you have, patient.

I remember Our Grandfather and the rattle.

Now I know what you have.

I am a good practitioner.

I am one who loosens.

I am going to begin just in order to see, to cure.

I am going to shake you, rattle.

I am going to put my hand over you, rattle.

The following interpretation is based on the free translation of the song by the singer himself and my analytical evaluation of his translation. Juan explained that the motif "I was born for you" refers to the wisiratu's initiation when he experienced symbolic death and rebirth. Being "born well" means he is well prepared to be a wisiratu and that he had a successful apprenticeship. He now is a powerful and transformed Warao who has knowledge and wisdom. As a mortal being, his body is not only his own but also the body of his spirit helpers who were born with him during his initiation ritual. At the end of the wisiratu's successful apprenticeship, his helping spirit sons are "born" into his chest via the tobacco smoke of the master wisiratu's wina cigar. The motif "my action is with you" is the translation of "ine makaramuna hiahokwa aisiko," in which makaramuna is, in this context, a word of musical importance. Ma means "my" and karamuna translates here as "noise," according to Barral (1957, 127). Because one of the functions of the helping spirit sons is to aid the wisiratu while curing, the major noise that occurs during a wisiratu curing session is the shaman's shaking of the hebu mataro rattle, during which time the kareko stones, which are also helping spirits, strike the interior of the body of the rattle. The wisiratu is the owner of the hebu; he also owns the kareko spirits and, in fact, the entire rattle because it, too, is a hebu. Thus, "my action is with the body of the rattle" refers to the action of the wisiratu as he makes the rattle speak. "I am the rattle" refers to the wisiratu's spirit transformation when he becomes a spirit himself.

Often, the idea of transformation is misinterpreted as possession, as Suárez (1968, 170) does when she explains that both the wisiratu and the hebu mataro become possessed by the helping hebu and that the latter takes over the voices of both the wisiratu and the rattle (1968, 167). Her interpretation negates the wisiratu's role as owner and master of the hebutuma. The total control over the hebu is epitomized by the wisiratu's transformation into a spirit, and to call this possession lessens the wisiratu's power role as master of the hebu spirits.

"Our Grandfather," the translation of kanobo, refers to any one of the ancient Wisimo who, after death, has become deified. Kanobo also refers to any one of the four supreme spirits that lives at the ends of the cosmos, plus those at the intercardinal points and the zenith of the celestial vault. The wisiratu remembers the kanobotuma or kano-bowitu (glorified form) from his initiation when he visited one or all of them in their cosmological homes. Because a kanobo is a hebu, the transformed wisiratu is like a kanobo. The wisiratu is also the one who calls upon the other kanobotuma for their help. Juan explained that "Our Grandfather" is an old Wisiratu, an ancestor, who is called upon to help cure. Finally, the motif "I am one who loosens" refers to the wisiratu's power to free the patient from the grips of the illness-causing hebu. This is often done physically either with massage, with the help of pressure applied by the hebu mataro rattle when it is force-fully pressed against the painful place on the patient's body and sud-denly pulled away (thereby pulling away the malevolent hebu with it), or by the shaman's feet stamping in rhythm with his shaking of the rattle during the climax of the A section. This final action, with its loud rattle shaking and foot stamping, is referred to as "spanking the hebu." With musical and sometimes physical force the transformed shaman loosens the evil spirit's grip on the patient and makes the soon-to-be-identified hebu easier to be removed (Briggs 1991, 19).

Music example 7.4 is a complete transcription of a wisiratu curing song, sections A and A[1], as sung by Bernardo Jiménez Tovar, a man who loves to sing curing songs. Every morning at about 5:30 A.M. Bernardo's voice could be heard as he pleasantly awakened the rest of the village with his music. He sang and recorded these A and A[1] curing song segments noncontextually in my room, and their complete song texts are included here as song text 7.3. (The parentheses around cer-tain words indicate that the shaman was shaking his hebu mataro rattle while singing those portions of the text.)

Song Text 7.3. Wisiratu Curing Song, Sections A and A[1], Bernardo Jiménez Tovar, 25 July 1972 (Olsen Collection 72.8-37)

Section A
(*wai wai wai yae wai wai yae ye ye wai yae*)
(name, name, name, yae name, name, yae ye ye name yae)

ine yamoniyana diawarai hinu; ine yamoniyana hinu
I do not forget you were born with breath; I do not forget you
   with breath

ine saba owatu ine hinu ine hioko saba owatu ine hinu
I am for you I with breath I am to grab for you with breath

wai wai yao wai yae yae (owai wai yae)
name, name yao name yae yae (owai name yae)

ine hebu yamoniyana ine; ine owatu ine hinao; ine hioko saba
   yamoniyana diawarae (owai)
I do not forget you hebu I; I am for you with breath; I do not
   forget you were born (owai)

ine ahokwanobutuma morabu yamoniyana (owai yae yae)
I for Our Wonderful Grandfather do not forget your hand
   (owai yae yae)

(saba owatu ine) yao wai wai yao yao wai yae yae oyao yao wai
   (wai)
(I am for you) yao name name yao yao name yae yae oyao yao
   name (name)

ine ine hebu owatu ine ine; ine owatu anobowatu ine (ine, ine)
I, I am for hebu, I, I; I am for Our Grandfather, I, (I, I)

ine anobotuma kobokatu ine, ine; ine ahokwanobutumawitu
I, Our Grandfathers are lifting up, I, I; I, Our Wonderful
   Grandfathers

(owai wai yae ine wai yai) wai wai (wai) e oya oi
(owai name yae I name yai) name name (name) e oya oi

Section A[1]
o oi oi o oi

ine orediawara naboinai ine hebu naboinai
I, it was born, I, the hebu

[rattle alone]

ine warao diawara; ahoko sanitatuwana (o e)
I was born Warao; the hebu does not help (o e)

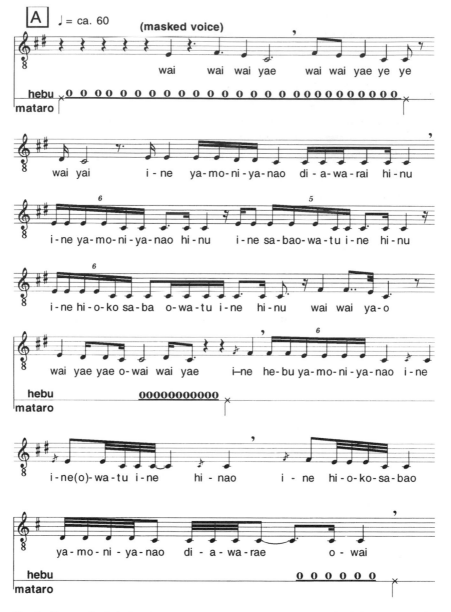

Music Example 7.4. Wisiratu curing song, sections A and A¹ (Juan Bustillo Calderón). Olsen Collection 72.8-37. See music example 7.9 for key to symbols.

Music Example 7.4 (*continued*)

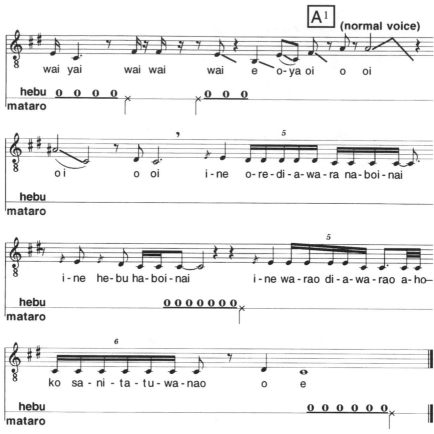

Music Example 7.4 (*continued*)

As you study this example and listen to recorded example 8 you can recognize Bernardo's melodic freedom. He begins his song with the foundation interval of a major second prevailing; very soon, however, he alternates it with the more common pattern based on the minor third as the foundation interval. (Section A[1] is often a musical contrast to section A and will soon be discussed in detail.) In sections A and A[1] of his curing song Bernardo is expressing his control over his helping spirits and singing about how they were born with his breath and how he, the wisiratu, was born for the kanobo (Our Grandfather, deity). Section A is a preparation for the removal of the illness-causing hebu, and during it the singer is being transformed into a spirit himself by oneness with his helping spirits from within his body and his rattle (the kareko spirits, in the form of quartz pebbles).

On rare occasions more than one wisimo will sing together in duet fashion. The historical precedents for this technique are discussed in chapter 15, but now we can listen to multipart shamanic singing in recorded example 9 and study the words in song text 7.4 (sung non-contextually).

Song Text 7.4. Wisiratu Curing Song, Duet, Juan Bustillo Calderón and Bernardo Jiménez Tovar, 28 July 1972 (Olsen Collection 72.8-44)

Juan Bustillo Calderón:

oya oi oi oi oi e e e e e e e e owai wai yae

I was born for him, I was born for him. I was born well, *wae yae*

I was called, I was born for your body. I was born well.

I called myself, I, with the breath, I, with all my body.

I, with a good dream, *wae yae wae owae e e e e e yae yae*

I, with your body, I was born well.

My word is that I want my mother with all my body.

I was born. I am one who guards. I was born for your body. I was born well. We were born.

I am called, my name is [unintelligible]. I know everything.

I am called because I know everything.

I am not the owner of knowledge. I am not the owner.

I remove, I remove well, I well.

I was born for you, to know everything, and not to forget anything.

I am for you, I am, *wae wae wae e e e e e e e e e e e e e e e e e e e e e e e e e e e e wae*

Bernardo Jiménez Tovar:

oya oya oi oi wai wai

I was born for you. I was born with you.

I do not forget anything. I know everything. I was born for you.

When I was born, I knew the name. I was born. I know the spirit inside.

When I touch, for him I know. I am the body of the spirit.

wae yae yae yae owae wae

I was born. I care for your body.
My name, I know you well. I am for you.
I am for you, my father, I know you well.
I am not one who will forget you, my father.
I know for you. I am for my father.
I am not forgetting anything.
I was born well. I know you well. I know and I am born.
wai wai wai oi oi e e e e e e e o

The shamans explained that the helping spirit (alter ego) of each wisiratu is singing. The transformation has taken place, as indicated by the words. Bernardo's and Juan's words and singing styles are similar because both men studied with the same wisiratu master teacher at the same time and because the variants of wisiratu shamanistic singing in the Winikina area are few. Their performance style, heard in recorded example 9, clearly demonstrates the helping-spirit releasing technique employed by wisiratu shamans, both at the beginning and end of the duet. Even in a noncontextual performance such as this one (that is, noncuring but nevertheless contextual because it is instructive; this is how the two men learned it), the wisimo must release their helping spirits with the vocables "oi, o, e e e e e e" or variants that function as the acoustical embodiments of the shaman's breath. The physical embodiments of the shamans' breath (released tobacco smoke) were not present in this performance because the singers did not smoke before or during the event. Only Juan's and Bernardo's vocalizations accompanied their spirit helpers, which slowly exited from deep within their chests and out their mouths.

Fourteen motifs are emphasized in the texts of the eight translated A sections (excluding A¹) from the Olsen Collection. These are listed in table 7.2 with their variants, according to their approximate order of appearance in the songs. The motifs are examples of the wisiratu speaking as a transformed and powerful being, and they establish his identity as master of all hebutuma while proclaiming his loyalty to his own helping hebutuma.

A wisiratu sings the curing song section that I refer to as A¹ after his transformation and oneness with his helping spirits. Each wisiratu approaches this continued musical conversation in a manner he finds most suitable, depending upon either his own personal style or the

Table 7.2. Motifs used in section A of Wisiratu curing songs

I was born
    well
    with you
    with your body
    together with you
    for you (him)
    to know you
I am with you
I am your body
I am
    one who cares for you
    your guardian
I am healer
My action is with
    you
    the body of your rattle
I am your father
I
    am the one who calls Our Grandfather
    am your Grandfather (hebu)
    remember Our Grandfather and the rattle
I
    am not forgetting you
    know
        you (hebu)
        this hebu
        what you have (to patient)
I grasp
    you
    your body
    the rattle
I know how to
    blow
    cure
I
    am the rattle
    own the rattle
I, your father, make a dream together with you
I am one who loosens

style he learned from his wisiratu master. An analysis of several wisiratu A¹ sections reveals a variety of musical characteristics, suggesting individual choice. For example, the section may or may not employ voice masking. (Notice how recorded example 8 reveals voice masking in section A and normal voice in section A¹.) It may be based on as few as two pitches or as many as four (or more if the yells are included), as indicated in the two notations in music example 7.5. Because section A¹ is melodically similar to section A, and because it follows it, A¹ functions as both a conclusion to A and a transition to B. Its greatest melodic variation occurs when it does not employ voice masking. A¹ sections usually begin with a sustained yell, which is approached from below by an upward glissando and terminated with a downward glissando. (See music example 7.4 and listen to recorded example 8.) Analytical evaluation suggests that the wisiratu's section A¹ is transitional, and its infrequent use (it does not always occur) suggests that it is either optional or dependent on particular healing contexts. When employed, section A¹ always follows section A and is itself followed by either section B or C. The content of section A¹ also depends largely on individual choice. Bernardo explained that it is the helping hebu who speaks in this transitional section.

Music Example 7.5. Wisiratu curing song, section A¹, tone systems (transposed to D as the principal tone).

The main part of a wisiratu curing song cycle is section B. It has the widest range in wisiratu music, occasionally consisting of as many as eight pitches. Its basic tone system is 5 4 ♮ 1, as indicated in music example 7.6 and heard in recorded examples 10 and 11. This descending pattern is fundamental to naming in Warao shamanistic curing. Not only does it appear in section B of wisiratu curing songs, but also in section C of bahanarotu curing and throughout hoarotu curing. These melodic patterns iconically indicate that the shaman is in the process of naming the illness-causing essence. At times the naming motive is melodically varied with elongation, augmentation, or diminution. Its most common elongated form includes the pitches 5 4 ♮ 1 4 ♮ 1 ♮ 1; it may be expanded to 6 5 ♮ 1, 6 4 ♮ 1, or more; or it may be contracted to 5 4 ♮ 1. Additionally, the basic minor-third interval may be expanded to nearly a major third (3 1). The variations that include expansion can especially be seen during contextual wisiratu curing rituals when the shaman is in a Theurgical State of Consciousness (TSC) (music example 7.7 and recorded example 11).

Music Example 7.6. Wisiratu curing song, section B, tone system (transposed to D as the principal tone).

Music Example 7.7. Wisiratu curing song, section B (Juan Bustillo Calderón). Olsen Collection 72.8-43b.

The song discourse of a wisiratu in section B of his curing cycle is quite monothematic: it consists primarily of the shaman's attempt to name correctly the illness-causing hebu. The wisiratu has great power through song because he is no longer a person but a supernatural being. The transformed wisiratu, with supernatural abilities gained from his helping spirits (including his hebu mataro rattle), now goes after the malevolent spirit, disabling it by naming it through song and removing it by massage or force from the hebu mataro rattle. Table 7.3 lists thirteen different hebutuma or animals transformed into hebu spirits that were named in the eight curing song examples that I recorded and translated. While this is a small figure, the actual number of possibilities that a wisiratu can name are endless because an illness-causing hebu can take the form of anything except a normal-looking human being. There is even shamanic world crossover as many of the named spirits or animals are found in all the Warao cosmic realms. For example, two birds listed in table 7.3, maisikiri and yoromahore, are evil spirits associated with bahanarotu shamanism; maisikiri is often translated by the Warao as ánima sola, a bad spirit found throughout Venezuela that is associated with fire and tobacco smoke. During a wisiratu curing ritual a shaman will name several or numerous spiritual essences that are believed to be causing the patient's illness. The following song texts demonstrate the variety of spirits and the complexity of song discourse employed by several Warao shamans.

Bernardo Jiménez Tovar's noncontextual section B of a wisiratu curing sequence (music example 7.8) is transliterated and translated in full as song text 7.5. (The words in parentheses indicate that the shaman was shaking his hebu mataro rattle while singing those portions of the text.) Unlike the translations by Antonio Lorenzano, Bernardo's translation is not word for word but is slightly paraphrased.

Table 7.3. Types of Hebutuma appearing in B sections of
Wisiratu curing song cycles

Hebu	Olsen Collection no.
Maisikiri bird	72.8-29
Hebu in the image of a one-legged Warao	72.8-29
Yoromahore bird	72.8-30
Manobo (My Grandfather)	72.8-31
Something sunning itself on the bank of the river	72.8-32
Manatee	72.8-33
Hebu like the shadow when the sun sets	72.8-35
Hebu of the floor	72.8-35
Hebu of the rafters	72.8-35
Water snake	72.8-35
Hebu without a name	72.8-34
Tonina fish	72.8-38
Hebu of the long river	Uncataloged

Music Example 7.8. Wisiratu curing song, section B (Bernardo Jiménez Tovar). Transcribed by Dale A. Olsen (Olsen Collection 72.8-38).

Song Text 7.5. Wisiratu Curing Song, Section B, Bernardo Jiménez Tovar, 25 July 1972 (Olsen Collection 72.8-38)

[rattle alone]

yai ye yai ye ye

ine warao warao diawarae sanuka diawarae sanuka diawarae inese

I was born a Warao, I was born poor, I was born poor

ye ye sanuka hakore sanuka hakore mahoko yawaitu himuwe-
   buna abanae tane tiane tane tiane

ye ye, I am poor, I am poor, my spirit watches with its sight,
   this is it, this is it

(yai ye yai ye ye yai ye ye yai ye)

hokwaraisa emusaba narunonanu; hokwa adamotuma ahoko
   yaroko horebekwanae
our companion, remove yourself; the remedy of our noble elders has sent it away

(tane   tiane):   barawa   yariya   waratu   barawa   aremuria
   orenowakatu
(this is it): it is born in the river, and is swimming in the
   bottom of the river

[rattle alone]
barawa atoni barawa atoni barawa atonina atonina
[name of hebu]

[rattle alone]
yai ye ye (yai ye ye ye ye)

mahokwaraisa emusaba narunonano (yai ye ye ye ye)
our companion, remove yourself (yai ye ye ye ye)

Bernardo's example begins with discourse in which he continues to
proclaim his power. He then names a hebu called barawa atoni, a spirit
that looks like a fish, is born in the river ("barawa yariya waratu"), and
is swimming in the bottom of the river ("barawa aremuria
orenowakatu"). Bernardo then admonishes the hebu to remove itself
and go away. In actual curing, the shaman at some point would pro-
ceed to "spank the hebu" with the heavy noise of his rattle, the
stomping of his feet, the pressing of his rattle onto the patient's body,
and so forth. This cycle of events continues as the transformed shaman
effects his cure.

The next section B text clearly reveals the transformation aspect of the wisiratu shaman that has already taken place. In song text 7.6 the wisiratu, Chano Rivero, speaks to his spirit helpers, the malevolent hebu, and the patient. The cultural context is a studio performance that occurred on 10 July 1972 in Yaruara Ahoko.

Song Text 7.6. Wisiratu Curing Song, Section B, Chano Rivero, 10 July 1972 (Olsen Collection 72.8-30)

This is the rattle.

You, my rattle, what is it you are going to grab?

It will be with my rattle, together with the kareko stones and the wisiratu.

That's how the dream was made for me.

There, in hokonamu, the hebu was born. That is where we were born. That is where we are.

That is where you were born. The hebu was born where the sun is born.

This is the call of a wisiratu. I was born there, in hokonamu.

This is how it is; this is what you are doing.

Separate yourself, let go of my grandson.

You are Our Grandfather; go to one side, go away.

With the body of the wisiratu, I have transformed myself into a hebu.

I am a hebu who is seeing and cutting the evil illness with my power.

You will not die, little grandson.

You were made to kill, but he will not die.

You are not an illness, Our Grandfather, you who have been transformed in hokonamu.

Separate yourself from my little grandson. Turn around and go away, from where you first appeared, from where you were transformed.

During his performance of section B, the wisiratu shaman tapped his foot and bounced his leg incessantly. I did not ask if this was a result of extreme concentration, tension, or nerves or if it was a shamanic technique. I assume that such motor activity is related to the singer's TSC or extreme concentration. Even though the recording situation was noncontextual, the shaman was clearly exhibiting a deep TSC as he named a powerful spirit, Our Grandfather, a kanobo spirit born in hokonamu, in the east where the sun rises. The shaman tells the hebu, "You are not an illness, Our Grandfather, you who have been transformed in hokonamu."

Song text 7.7 includes the naming of numerous hebutuma. The singer, Antonio Lorenzano, performs this song noncontextually, singing directly to various hebutuma. (The text was paraphrased by the singer.)

Song Text 7.7. Wisiratu Curing Song, Section B, Antonio Lorenzano, 20 July 1972 (Olsen Collection 72.8-35)

The hebu looked in from the hole in the roof of the house by the rafters in order to make a boy sick.

You put your sight over my brother's grandson so that he would be rigid.

You, the evil that my brother's grandson has, that makes his hands and feet stiff, loosen yourself. Loosen your grip.

Although I do not know your name, I am going to name you. When I name it, hear me!

This hebu is from the house where you sleep.

If you are here in the house, leave my brother's grandson quiet. Go away!

This hebu is like the shadow that passes during the time when the sun goes over us and sets. This is what grabbed my brother's grandson.

It is you who made my brother's grandson ill.

Although you are not a hebu, you made yourself like a hebu who lives at the end of the earth.

And, by doing this, you grabbed my brother's grandson.

You are the hebu of my floor which is made of manaca wood, and who grabbed the grandson of my brother.

You, and the evil that my brother's grandson has received which makes his hands and feet stiff, go away!

With my very own tongue I say go away from my brother's grandson. Go away to where your leaders are.

This is a hebu of the rafters who grabbed my brother's grandson.

You, who gives fright, I tell you to go from whence you came.

This hebu, who is in the rafters, is silent and does not speak.

It is he who grabbed my brother's grandson.

This hebu, who is sitting on the top of the manaca poles, who does not talk and who sits with his head bowed, it is he who grabbed my grandson.

You have your arms and all of your body rigid.

It was this hebu who grabbed my brother's grandson.

With my very own tongue I say, go away from my brother's grandson. Go away to where your leaders are.

It is you, the hebu, who does all of this; you, who came from the head of the hebutuma.

This is your name, even though I do not know it.

This is the hebu of a pole that fell in the water.

It is that which is on the top of the pole sunning himself, and which raises his head. I am going to name you.

You are a hebu who sleeps when the sun's rays hit you.

It is a water snake which sleeps on the top of the pole that has fallen in the water.

When the sun's rays hit him he dreams.

You looked at the neck of my brother's grandson and it is there where you did the damage.

Although you have your arms, your legs, your body rigid, I ask you to loosen yourself, grandson.

Loosen your hands and go away from whence you came.

With my very own tongue I say, go away from my brother's grandson.

Upon sending you, you will go to where your leaders are.

Ah, it is you who is doing the bad deed of making my brother's grandson afraid.

Although you produce fright, I send you away from whence you came.

Although you have your hands grasped hard, loosen yourself and go away.

With my very own tongue I say, go away from my brother's grandson.

Go away to where your leaders are.

This is your name, you are a water snake.

> Upon saying your name you will go away to the house of your
> leaders, from whence you came.

Unlike Bernardo's section B song, where a specific hebu (barawa
atoni) was named, or Chano's song, where a specific spirit (kanobo
from hokonamu) was named, Antonio refers to numerous entities in
various degrees of vagueness. Not until the end of his song does he
specifically name particular hebutuma. Throughout his song, however,
he presents many clues about the illness-causing entities. First, he
sings about where the hebu is from and says, "This hebu is from the
house where you sleep." Or, speaking directly to it, he says, "You, who
came from the head of the hebutuma." Then Antonio describes how
the hebu got there: "Although you are not a hebu, you made yourself
like a hebu who lives at the end of the earth." What the hebu is like is
explained: "This hebu is like the shadow that passes during the time
when the sun goes over us and sets." What the hebu does or did is carefully described: "The hebu looked in from the hole in the roof of the
house by the rafters"; "This hebu, who is in the rafters, is silent and
does not speak"; and "This hebu, who is sitting on the top of the
manaca poles, who does not talk and who sits with his head bowed."
Finally, Antonio tells who the hebu is by either indirectly or directly
naming it: "You are the hebu of my floor which is made of manaca
wood"; "This is a hebu of the rafters"; "This is the hebu of a pole that
fell in the water"; "It is that which is on the top of the pole sunning
himself, and which raises his head"; "You are a hebu who sleeps when
the sun's rays hit you"; "It is a water snake which sleeps on the top of
the pole that has fallen in the water, when the sun's rays hit him he
dreams"; "This is your name, you are a water snake"; and "This is your
name, even though I do not know it." It is understandable that specific
names of hebutuma are not always given in song, for their endlessly
large numbers mean that they are not always known. This song, however, displays an even more important aspect of the naming technique
that will become obvious in other realms of singing for power: prefatory naming. Before the hebu itself is identified by its particular name,
certain physical attributes are named in preparation. Thus, this example shows how Antonio has presented many clues in his shamanistic detective work.

Such variety displayed in the wisiratu song texts indicates the individualism of each shaman and the vastness of the shamanic realm. Because each TSC is an intimate and individual experience in which only the transformed shaman can take part, one shaman's communication with the spirits will often differ from another's and will often differ from the same shaman's next TSC as well.

Section C of wisiratu shamanistic curing is a dialogue between the transformed wisiratu, the shaman's various helping spirits, and the evil or angry hebu. During the C section the illness-causing hebu speaks for the first time. Voice masking is not employed, although the shaman's vocal range (one-note recitation) is the highest of the ritual. Song text 7.8 is typical of a section C from a wisiratu song cycle; the singer is Juan Bustillo Calderón, the context is an actual curing ritual that occurred on 27 July 1972, and the free translation is by the singer.

Song Text 7.8. Wisiratu Curing Song, Section C, Juan Bustillo Calderón, 27 July 1972 (Olsen Collection 72.8-42)

Here before you is your father, and I speak to you.

I am speaking as you like. Do not stay there; you are nothing more than I am.

I speak to you. What I say is that I will touch my hands over your body and look at you with my eyes.

Here in my chest, rest yourself in one side of my chest. Rest here in the body of your father.

I am not poor, I have power, and since it is like this, I speak to you, father.

I speak to you. I speak to you even though you do not believe me. They are words, so you know.

You come from afar. Even though you are from afar over there, I would say nothing to you.

I speak the truth to you, oh Diawaratuma.

When I see you, you are not of me. This is bad. I say to you that you are not part of me.

This body that is here, this was another thing, it was not of me. It is bahana. This was made by another, a bahanarotu.

Thus it is so, father. That which I say unto you is the truth. You are our father.

I am going to act according to your name. Now I will begin with your words.

Even though I don't know much, I will act in this way, as
   wisiratu.
Like I am doing, I will continue. You are our father.

Juan explained that he was talking with the angry spirits that he believed were causing the illness of his patient. These angry spirits were
the kareko stones inside his own hebu mataro rattle; and they were
probably angry, he explained, because he had not fed them tobacco
smoke for some time. Therefore, they were taking revenge by making
one of the important Warao leaders, Luís Jiménez, ill. Juan then called
upon his own helping spirit and invited it to rest in his chest, thereby
giving him more power to cure ("Here in my chest, rest yourself"). The
hebu helper, Juan explained, talked to him, saying it would help ("I am
not poor, I have power"). The transformed wisiratu began his diagnosis with his spirit helpers, including the angry hebu spirits ("You
come from afar") addressed as Diawaratuma or "lords of hokonamu";
and together they determined that the real cause of the illness was not
an evil hebu spirit but a bahana spirit. This discourse is followed by
the helping hebutuma's telling their wisiratu father that their diagnosis is the truth ("Thus it is so, father"). In the dialogue, however, the
wisiratu told his helpers that he was going to try to name the evil spirit
("I am going to act according to your name"). This section was followed by another section A, another section B in which he attempted
to name the evil spirit, and finally another section C. The formal structure of this cycle was A C A B C.

   A comparison of the section C principal tones reveals that in all
cases except one their pitches are the highest within the curing song
cycles. Because a conversation or dialogue is taking place in section C
between the wisiratu, the helping spirits, and the evil or angry hebu,
clarity of text may explain why a single-pitch recitation is employed.
The feeling of heightened speech is often increased by the response of
the shaman's helper, who recites, at the same high pitch, either the
ending portions of the wisiratu's phrase, the entirety of each line, or a
different word. This answering, called saba dibuyaha, is believed to be
the voice of the hebu; and a wisiratu may himself represent the hebu's
voice through ventriloquism if an assistant is not present. The effect of
saba dibuyaha is intense—a climax in the dialogue between good and
evil. During a noncontextual performance that rivaled an actual curing

ritual because of its intensity, Chano Rivero officiated while his uncle Pedro Rivero performed saba dibuyaha with him (indicated within parentheses). Song text 7.9 represents the shamanic dialogue that occurred during that performance, recorded on 10 July 1972. (I include Warao and English to emphasize the use of saba dibuyaha.)

Song Text 7.9. Wisiratu Curing Song, Section C, Chano Rivero and Pedro Rivero, 10 July 1972 (Olsen Collection 72.8-28)

ine hinobo (hinobu) aisiko diawara (diawara)
I am your Grandfather (Grandfather) with him I was born (was born)

ahotana ine (ahotana) ahotana aisiko (aisiko)
from the beginning I am (from the beginning) from the beginning with him (with him)

saba oriwakahu (saba oriwakahav) saba ubanunaha (nunaha) aisiko diawara (diawara) hoi (ihi nomihae)
for him I am happy (for him I am happy) for him he is without dream (without) with him I was born (was born) hoi (it is the truth)

taiseke mateho (hiteho) hinobotuma mateho (kokotuka mateho) hinobotuma (hokotuka) ateho aisiko (aisiko) nokokitane (obonoyara) obonoyara hoi
this is my body (your body) my body of your Grandfathers (with all my body) with your Grandfathers (with all) with his body (with him) listen (it wants) it wants hoi

yakera bahema (yakera) moniyana hisubu oko (moniyana) ya nokonae tane (tane tate yana)
return good [go away] (good) do not be sick, liven up, adjust (do not be sick) it is hearing (like this)

hemaribu ya nokokitane (nokokitane) manasaribu ya nokokitane (ya nokokitane) obonoya akua naturo (obonoya) homuniya ine (obonoya) hoi

hear my words (hear) hear my words (hear) that's all you
want, old woman, (you want) I am "crazy water" (you
want) hoi

ahoko aisiko (aisiko oba) ubanunaha (ahotana) ahotana ine
(ahotana) akua (akua)
with him (with him want) without a dream (from the beginning) I am from the beginning (from the beginning) that's
all (that's all)

This powerful exchange of words in a heightened level of speech-song
is impressive. To hear the words as if emanating from the rafters creates a climax to the curing event (even though it is noncontextual in
this particular example). The song text clearly indicates that the
wisiratu is the transformed being and that the voice of Pedro from the
audience (as if from the rafters) is like an echo of the spirit's voice.
Chano, in his transformed state as the evil hebu, reveals himself as homuniya, a hebu called "crazy water," a word that Barral (1957, 118)
translates (jo-muni from jo moni) as "impossible water," "crazy water,"
"water spout in the river," and "whirlpool." Indeed, the currents, back
currents, and swirls in the rivers of the Orinoco Delta are capable of
creating fear in anyone who traverses them in a small canoe. In this
type of C section the evil hebu has already been grabbed, subdued, and
removed from the patient and is about to be returned, via the shaman's
breath, to its place of origin. It is indeed the climax of the wisiratu
curing event.

   During the course of a curing song cycle the wisiratu may also sing
to the illness-causing hebu, saying that he knows what the evil hebu is
because it was revealed to him in a dream. The wisiratu's helping
spirits frequently appear to their father in dreams, telling him the
cause of an illness or simply complaining that he, as the master and
the one who cares for them, is not feeding them enough tobacco
smoke. Therefore, the wisiratu, speaking to the malevolent hebu
during a curing song, often tells the evil spirit that it is not of the same
stock as he, the master wisiratu who is good. The latter sings, "I am not
the guardian of this" (Olsen Collection 72.8-27) and "with my preferred rattle I do not guard you" (Olsen Collection 72.8-28).

   Occasionally during his curing cycle, a wisiratu will discern that the evil spirit is not a hebu at all but a bahana or a hoa spirit. During Juan's contextual curing ritual (Olsen Collection 72.8-42), for example, the transformed wisiratu determined that the cause of his patient's illness was not a hebu but a bahana over which he as owner of hebu has no power. At the termination of his attempt to cure his patient, Juan explained his diagnosis to his patient's family; and immediately plans were made to hire a bahanarotu shaman.

A Wisiratu Shaman's Curing Ritual Performance

Throughout this chapter I have referred to the contextual performances that took place when Luís Jiménez suddenly became ill. (The context is also discussed in chapter 9.) This unfortunate event produced many extraordinary performances of Warao curing rituals because of the political importance of the individual, who was the former governor (kobenahoro) of the area. This section of the chapter presents one of these performance events—the wisiratu curing rituals that occurred during the first evening of the patient's illness. The event is presented in the ethnographic present (that is, the present tense) to show its individuality and reality.

The Ethnographic Present

It is nearly midnight on 26 July 1972, and there is a slight commotion throughout the village of Yaruara Akoho. I struggle to get out of my hammock, unzip my mosquito netting, squeeze through the zippered opening, and go out onto the dock in front of the schoolhouse to see what has happened. The word is that Luís Jiménez has suffered an attack of some sort this evening and my neighbor, Bernardo Jiménez Tovar, is going to Luís's house to "sacar hebu" or take out a hebu. I am invited to go along. I quickly gather up my recording equipment and get into a little dugout canoe not much longer than my height. It is dangerous because the darkness, my weight, my bulky equipment, and the excitement of the boys who are paddling could cause the small keel-less dugout to turn over like a floating log. The Luís Jiménez house, however, is only several hundred yards upstream. When we arrive about 12:05 A.M. Bernardo has already begun to sing and rattle his hebu mataro. Not wanting to intrude, I sit with friends, listening, observing as best I can in the moonlit darkness, and taking occasional notes. The wisiratu sings for about half an hour until 12:30, and I make note of ten musical sections during that first event. This is what I write, not seeing what comes out of my pen:

1. Growling with rattle. Singing notes F and D (these pitches are compared to an A-440 tuning fork). Shaman stood up and furiously shook his rattle over the patient (inches from him—I was seated eight feet away and the sound was deafening). I saw no light coming from the hebu mataro. This shaking of rattle marked the end of part 1 and was a transition into part 2—call part 1 "A."
2. Part 2 or "B" began with growling again and with rattle. He sang notes B, A, G, E.
3. Return to "A"—same order except notes sung were E-flat and C. Again the shaman stood and furiously shook the hebu mataro inches above the patient's body.
4. "B" section, same notes of B, A, G, E, with E the principal tone and G the supporting tone.
5. Return to "A," same notes of F, D, with D as the principal tone. Same format.
6. Return to "B" section with same B, A, G, E and format.
7. Return to "A," same notes of F and D, etc.
8. Return to "B" section with notes changed to C-sharp, B, A, F-sharp. Same format.
9. Return to "A" with notes being E-flat and C, with C as the principal tone. Same format.
10. New section, "C," with notes being A-flat and F.

Following this first curing event, Bernardo begins a second ceremony to take out another hebu. At the ritual's end Luís tries to talk but no coherent words come out. During the second ceremony I quietly begin to set up my recording equipment, feeling in the darkness for my tapes and threading the Nagra's takeup reel in total darkness. Only the placement of the microphone remains to be done. After the second session I ask Bernardo's permission to record him, and he agrees. I quietly place my microphone and shock mount slightly behind, above, and to the right of the shaman, hanging them from the rope that ties one end of the patient's hammock to one of the house poles. It is a fairly good angle, and I wish I could be as close as my microphone, seeing all the details that my microphone is picking up. The third ritual begins at 1:10 A.M. and lasts exactly twelve minutes (recorded example 11). I also record the fourth session, but about two minutes are wasted because the tape runs out. Recording with five-inch reels on a Nagra means only fifteen minutes of music, and trying to judge tape lengths and timings in absolute darkness is something I never practiced at UCLA. The evening finally ends, and we slowly and quietly return to our homes. The curing will continue after several hours of sleep. Luís had several hebu spirits removed, and perhaps he will be better tomorrow. I will never forget this evening—the full moon casting an eerie white glow on the wide-leaved rain forest foliage outside Luís's house; the dimly lit kerosene lantern at one end of the room, casting a slightly yellowish glow and creating flickering shadows within the room; the quiet comments of family members; an occasional whimper of a baby; the continuous chirping of crickets and other rain forest insects; and the incessant rattling of the hebu mataro while the shaman sings, yells, growls, and communicates with the supernatural.

Analysis

I analyze in second-by-second detail the third wisiratu curing session in Bernardo's cycle of four to determine the formal structure and role of the hebu mataro rattle. Wilbert (1987b, 25) suggests that these details of a performance event are relevant to the curing ritual: "There are different styles of rattling which produce different kinds of noises, different kinds of rhythms, all in one seance. . . . We record the rattle and all of these things, but we very rarely penetrate deeply enough into the meaning of different rhythms or song patterns." Briggs (1991, 17–19), however, has penetrated into the meaning of the rattling during a wisiratu curing ritual:

> Four types of variation are evident in the use of the rattle as a percussion instrument during each section of the performance: tempo, loudness, relationship to the singing, and distance from the patient's body. At the beginning of each section of the song, the rattle is moved slowly and quite regularly in a circular fashion at the rate of 1 revolution per second. The rattle is used by itself at the beginning of the performance, but

the singing and rattling begin simultaneously in subsequent sections. . . . [They] signal a change that is reflected in the use of the rattle; during 7 seconds in which the singing is absent, the tempo increases to 5 revolutions per second and the loudness of the rattling is augmented as well. . . . [Then] the singing ceases for 20 seconds, the first 10 of which are characterized by the rapid tempo and the last 10 by the slow, 1 revolution per second tempo. This pace is continued until . . . close to the end of the segment, at which point the rapid tempo is resumed.

What is the role of the rattle in the performance and what is the meaning of this variation? . . . Using the rattle enables [the wisiratu] to draw out his own spirit powers as well as to gain control over the *hebu* inflicting the patient.

. . . The slow tempo rattling enables the *kareko* in the rattle—who are the shaman's helpers—to establish contact with the *kareko aurohi* "the fevers of the stones" in the child, and this part of each section is referred to as *dokotebuyaha* "starting up the song." The fast tempo rattling that follows is termed *hebu nayaha* "spanking the *hebu*." Here the shaman either leans forward or crouches above the patient so that the rattle is directly above his body. With the increase in tempo and the intensity of the movement, the revolutions become more ellipsoidal than circular, with rapid downthrusts constituting the blows to the *hebu*. This "spanking" loosens the *hebu's* grip on the child, paving the way for its extraction.

. . . With a return to the slow tempo in the third section of the song, the voice of the *hebu* emerges from the rattle through the words sung by the shaman. The final period of rapid tempo marks the process of sending the *hebu* through the air back to their homes near the mountaintop dwellings of the *kanobo* spirits.

Briggs's detailed analysis concerns a curing ritual performed by a wisiratu shaman of the Mariusa subtribe, who live some distance from the Winikina. I include it for comparison and will apply Briggs's four-part structure to my analysis of Bernardo's third session (transcribed in music example 7.9). In my analysis I have provided the precise seconds for when each rattling action begins and ends; given the exact number of rattle shakes for many performance figures; and transcribed the rattling passages with symbols or figures that indicate loudness, increase and decrease in volume, acceleration, and duration. While Briggs found four areas for analysis, including "tempo, loudness, relationship to the singing, and distance from the patient's body," I have found several other rattle-performance details that are important by virtue of their existence and repetition. I transcribe these characteristics using the symbols in the key at the beginning of music example 7.9 and include (1) accelerated circular motion at one shake per second with rapid increase, (2) continuous up-and-down motion between two and three shakes per second, (3) shakes that begin softly then increase and decrease in loudness (that is, crescendo and decrescendo from p to f, (4) accent, or suddenly loud (f) shaking that becomes immediately soft (p), (5) one abrupt shake, and (6) silence. In other words, the wisiratu uses many gradations of speed (tempo), including accelerated, slow, medium, and fast rhythm. Related to speed is the physical motion of the rattle-performance technique, including circular motion, up and down, abrupt shake, and nonshake (silence). All these motions create contrasting timbres or tone colors. Loudness includes not only soft and loud but increasing and decreasing gradations of loudness and sudden accents. According to Briggs (1991, 18), the beginning rattle music of the wisiratu's curing ritual (what I call the A section and he calls dokotebuyaha ["starting up the song"]) uses a "slow tempo rattling" for establishing contact between the shaman's helping spirits and the hebu intrusion essence within the patient. But there is much more than just "slow tempo rattling"—there is circular motion rattling, one abrupt shake rattling, accelerated rhythm rattling, increasing-decreasing loudness rattling, and steady-shake rattling within the A section alone; and all are embedded within a framework of repetition. What are the reasons for these sonic variations and repetitions? As we have seen from textual analyses, the wisiratu curing ritual's A section is the crucial time of spirit communication and shamanic transformation; and these sonic variations are cultural identifiers of the shaman's preparation for his transformation into the supernatural and his deepening TSC. The circular rattling motion is essential in this section because it creates a sustained pulsating sound. Additionally, the shaman gives his rattling an arrhythmical quality

Key to Symbols for Hebu Mataro Rattle Shakes

1. ○ ○ ○ ○ ○○○○○○○○ = accelerated circular motion at 1 shake per second
   with rapid increase

2. ∿∿ = continuous up and down motion at 2-3 shakes / second

3. ↑ = one abrupt shake

4. $f > p$ ∿∿ = strong accent, suddenly loud and immediately soft

5. $p < f > p$ = crescendo and decrescendo, increase and
   decrease in volume

6. ⸙ = silence

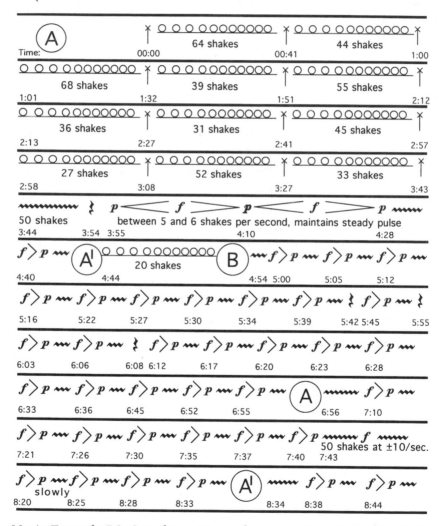

Music Example 7.9. Complete wisiratu shaman curing ritual—formal structure and hebu mataro rattle sequences (Bernardo Jiménez Tovar, 27 July 1972). Olsen Collection 72.8-40.

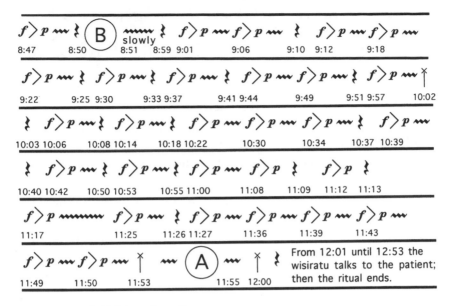

Music Example 7.9 (*continued*)

The technique of pulsation-acceleration-interruption is close to being a sonic universal for bridging natural and supernatural worlds. From Comanche peyote rituals of the Native American Church (Isaacs 1969) to Japanese Zen Buddhist ceremonies of communal penitence (Harich-Schneider 1967), the technique is part of the nonvocal sonic language of communication between humankind and the gods. Bernardo brings his A section to a close by steadily shaking his rattle for approximately fifty seconds (from 3:55 to 4:44) with several increases and decreases of amplitude. When analyzed with Briggs's model, this corresponds to the section he calls "spanking the hebu": there is no singing and the rattling is louder and more intense, with a more brilliant tone color because of the up-and-down motion of the shaking. The illness-causing hebu has not yet been named, however, and the "spanking" of the hebu is intended to weaken its hold on the patient.

Bernardo continues his ritual with an A[1] section at 4:44, which is identified by his unmasked yell of the vocable "hoi" and a final circular-accelerated rattling pattern. This lasts only ten seconds; he then moves directly into his first B section (from 4:54 until 6:56), which is characterized by unmasked singing and a new rattling pattern featuring medium and heavy rattle accents at approximate five-second intervals. In this section he names the first illness-causing hebu.

At 6:56 Bernardo again masks his voice and sings another A section, but this time he continues the rattling pattern established during the B section. At 7:43, however, he stands and furiously shakes his rattle fifty times at approximately ten shakes per second. This is another "spanking of the hebu," performed after the shaman has named a hebu in the B section. He has now returned to another A section for assistance from his spirit helpers. This is also the point at which the rattle would emit its glow (which I could not see; it was also not confirmed by the shaman) because heat is created only when the hebu mataro is shaken with extreme vigor.

Bernardo then sings another transitional A¹ passage, now with his customary accented rattling passages (from 8:33 to 8:50). This is followed by another B section, which lasts for three minutes (from 8:51 until 11:52). This second attempt to correctly name another illness-causing hebu was unsuccessful because there was no "spanking" of the hebu, and the ritual ended on a final shortened A section. As my analysis in music example 7.9 shows, Bernardo's final B section is laden with accents followed by silences, a start-stop activity that was consistent but not explained. Interruption or breaks in sound are also found in many ritual musics around the world. Boilès (1978, 160), for example, writes about similar interruptions during the Ihamba curing rituals of the Ndembu in Zambia: "The main series of Ihamba curing rites are characterized by a start-stop activity. Consisting of singing and dancing with alternated verbalization of anxieties and animosities, the starting and stopping has the effect of causing the congregated villagers and kinsmen to feel a unanimous craving for the cure of the patient, an emotional ambience carefully contrived and augmented by the curer." Although Boilès is writing about dancing as well as singing, the function of the interruptive technique may be similar to that of the Warao. Rouget (1985, 80–81) also describes similar techniques in music (especially drumming) that may trigger trance. Therefore, the persistent use of a start-stop or sound-silence technique on the hebu mataro rattle, when viewed within the broader spectrum of other cultures, can be seen as a significant and perhaps powerful musical characteristic. Stopping and starting (sound and silence), rhythmic accelerating, accenting, increasing and decreasing of sound, and tone coloring, all common hebu mataro performance

techniques during the wisiratu curing performance event, are culturally produced identifiers of the wisiratu shaman's power to control
cosmic forces.

The following chapter continues the Warao musical curing drama
with an analysis of the bahanarotu shaman, his music, and his musical performances. We shall see how all the Warao shamans share
musical performance as a powerful tool for curing illness.

8   Bahanarotu Shaman Songs

Unlike the wisiratu, the bahanarotu is capable of bringing harm to the Warao. Nevertheless, like the wisiratu he is a highly respected and essential member of the Warao shamanistic hierarchy, particularly because of his association with the powers of the eastern cosmic realm, his resulting ability to cure certain types of supernaturally caused illnesses, and his association with the habi sanuka fertility ritual.

The Bahanarotu Teachers

During the summer of 1972 I recorded the music of three bahanarotu shamans: Antonio Lorenzano, Gerónimo Velásquez, and Primitivo Sánchez. Much has already been said about Antonio, the knowledgeable and respected bahanarotu elder from Lorenzano Ahanoko who was Johannes Wilbert's major teacher and my closest associate. Gerónimo, a much younger man who lives in Yaruara Akoho, is also considered an excellent bahanarotu. In spite of his youth, he has cured many people. Primitivo, another young man from Yaruara Akoho, is a novice bahanarotu who often uses a hebu mataro rattle that he borrows from the village wisiratu.

Bahanarotu Shamanism

The bahanarotu shaman is a Warao religious practitioner who has special ties to the eastern cosmic realm called hokonamu, where the sun rises. His affinity with the cosmic space of Mawari, the kanobo of the east, the Creator Bird of the Dawn, inspired Wilbert (1972b, 58) to refer to the bahanarotu's practice as "light" shamanism, an association inspired by the brightness of dawn, the lightness of morning fog (represented by tobacco smoke), and the "goodness" of the realm. Even though bahanarotu shamanism is associated with the "good" side of the cosmic space, the bahanarotu evokes some fear among the Warao who refer to him as brujo in Spanish, meaning "wizard." This is because he not only communicates with the supernatural but is also a "doer": he directly handles supernatural objects by making them appear. Bahanarao is the plural form of bahanarotu. When lower-cased in this book, bahanarao refers to the living and practicing bahanarotu shamans. When capitalized, however, Bahanarao refers to the spirits of the deceased bahanarotu shamans who have gone on to spend eternity with Mawari in the eastern cosmic realm.

Bahanarotu literally means "owner of bahana" (arotu = owner). What is a bahana? There are several meanings or interpretations. According to Turrado Moreno (1945, 147), bahana means "lesser witchcraft" (bajana = brujería pequeña); while to Barral (1964, 149) it is the past participle of bajá, meaning "to suck" (chupar in Spanish) or to extract something with the mouth. In his dictionary Barral (1957, 44) also writes that the meaning of bajá is "to smoke." According to my bahanarotu consultants, bahana is an object made powerful by a bahanarotu in order to cause harm to other Warao. By blowing tobacco smoke upon an object, the bahanarotu transforms it into a magical arrow that can be sent through the air to be lodged in a victim to make him or her ill. The bahanarotu himself, as master or owner of bahana, transforms the object into an arrow. Therefore, he is also known as hatabu arotu, which literally means "owner of the arrows." In his malevolent role a bahanarotu can shoot magical arrows, which are essences of material objects (believed by the Warao to be the material objects themselves) into a victim; and in his benevolent role he is the only shaman who can extract bahana arrows from, and thus cure, a person who was the target of another bahanarotu's harmful actions.

Bahanarotu illnesses are physically characterized by gastrointestinal maladies, as Wilbert (1983, 360) explains: "The cardinal god of the East, the Bird of Origin, controls gastrointestinal disorders like hookworm, enteritis and other diarrheal diseases. But the most devastating and frightening among the avian god's weapons is cholera with its overwhelming dehydrations, enormous water stools and large vomits. Generically, these diseases of the eastern god are referred to as the 'big pains.'"

Another common bahana sickness is seizure, or sinaka illness. Sinaka is defined by Barral (1957, 189) as a nervous breakdown or an epileptic fit. Antonio sang a sinaka-curing song for me, after which he explained the force of the sinaka:

> Do you know what an attack (sinaka) is? It is when someone does not feel anything, has a hard hand, his whole body is stiff, and his eyes are blank. He does not talk at all. You try to shake him, but he is completely rigid, absolutely stiff. If by chance his tongue was caught between his teeth, it gets cut off and he does not realize it. That is the force an attack has.

Antonio insisted that sinaka illness is cured by a wisiratu shaman who sings throughout the night with his hebu mataro rattle. Wilbert (1987a, 160), however, maintains that sinaka is a bahana illness and is cured, therefore, with bahanarotu shamanism. He writes: "known in Waraoan as *shinaka,* the noun for this phenomenon is derived from *shinakakitani,* 'to cause someone to fall down,' and is extended to mean . . . any sickness of abrupt onset, including epilepsy." Wilbert (1987a, 160–61) also explains that the wife of a bahanarotu shaman has special powers to cure seizure illnesses, especially those caused by nicotine. Given the title shinakarani or "Mother of Seizure," the wife of the first bahanarotu shaman passed down her special curing powers to other bahanarotu wives. Infrequently a bahanarotu shamaness is summoned to cure her husband (or any other male patient) of a nicotine seizure, which she does by touching, restraining, and soothing him while mentally communicating with the tobacco spirits believed to be causing the convulsions. The following story, a portion of the origin myth of the bahanarotu shaman that Antonio Lorenzano gave to Wilbert, mentions sinaka and the female shaman's role in curing it (Wilbert 1972b, 69):

> They began to fast so as to lighten their bodies. They smoked and smoked and after eight days the *bahanarotu* ascended. His wife followed shortly, but when they entered the House of Smoke, the Supreme *Bahana* suffered a seizure. "I know how to help him," said the woman. Walking up to the Supreme *Bahana* she transformed herself into a beautiful black sea bird (probably the Magnificent Frigate Bird, *Fregata magnificens,* also known as the Man-of-War Bird, with a wingspread of seven or eight feet). She spread out her wings, shook them like rattles, and, while blowing tobacco smoke

on the epileptic body of her patient, soothed him gently with her plumes. The Supreme *Bahana* recovered. "You are a *bahanarotu* indeed," said he. "Remain here, *Sinaka Aidamo,* spirit of seizures." So there they are, the *bahanarotu* and his wife, smoking, rattling, and chanting in unison with the *Bahanarao.*

Because the same teacher rendered two different explanations to two different people about sinaka illness, there are possibly two types of sinaka illnesses cured by either the wisiratu or the bahanarotu, or there is substantial overlap between the two types of shamanism. Possibly Antonio, who has studied both forms of shamanism, was uncertain about the domain of sinaka illness. I feel that, with certain types of illnesses, there is substantial overlap, as we shall see with the crossover role of the hebu mataro rattle.

According to Antonio's narrative, bahanarotu shamanism is the only Warao religious practice currently to accept women as shamans, albeit infrequently. Unlike her bahanarotu husband, however, the shamaness does not sing while curing.

The origin of the bahanarotu's power is also related in Antonio's story, which continues from the previous excerpt (Wilbert 1972b, 69–70):

Much time elapsed, and when many people appeared in the center of the earth, they knew nothing about *bahana* and the bridge that reached from their village to the House of Tobacco Smoke. For this reason the *bahanarotu* rolled a cigar with two *bahana* inside and aimed it at a young man whom he had chosen to receive them. He sent Smoke for the right side of the youth's chest, and Rocks for his left side. Smoke became the Elder Brother, Rocks the Younger. When they struck the youth he fell over as if dead. The *bahana* spirits entered his body and became his helpers. But when he woke up displaying his weapons and rattle of tobacco smoke, the people vanished from sight. They were transformed into River Crab people and became the Masters of Earth.

Finally many Warao appeared in the center of the earth. Again the young *bahanarotu,* who was himself a Warao, shot the same pair of *bahana* spirits down to earth from the House of Smoke. The young man who received them survived and learned how to travel the bridge of tobacco smoke in the sky. Here he received much advice on how to preserve his *Bahana* spirits and how to use them.

That is why *bahana* continued on earth to the present day. It is not so perfect or so powerful as it was long ago, when the first *bahanarotu* received four spirit helpers. Nevertheless, *bahana* prevails. And it is still very strong among the Warao.

Bahanarotu Apprenticeship Songs

Bahanarotu shamanism is the most popular individual religious practice among the Warao today. Learning it can vary in depth and commitment, but the traditional Winikina way involves days of fasting and learning the proper songs with a knowledgeable bahanarotu master.

Antonio sang an apprenticeship song for me in which he used a tone system and melodic contour unique in Warao theurgical music. As music example 8.1 shows, his song is based on a five-note descending pattern that includes whole and half steps; and his use of vocables between each verse outlines a slightly disjunct melodic contour that seems to prevail throughout the composition. His bahanarotu apprenticeship song can be heard in its entirety in recorded example 12, and it is partially transcribed in music example 8.2. Antonio himself provided a free translation of his apprenticeship song, which he said is a dream song. It is included here as song text 8.1.

Music Example 8.1. Bahanarotu apprenticeship song, tone system and melodic contour (Antonio Lorenzano).

Song Text 8.1. Bahanarotu Apprenticeship Song, Antonio Lorenzano, 20 July 1972 (Olsen Collection 72.8-95)

Yae ye ye ye ye ye ye
I am your father. I, your father, was born a Warao.
I was born Warao. I will sing with you.
Yae ye ye ye ye ye ye.
I say to you, that I was born of Warao blood.
I am one who eats bahanarotu food only.

Yae ye ye ye ye ye ye

I am your father in my house, and I am with you.

Yae ye ye ye ye ye ye.

I, your father, sleep with a new fire.

For this reason you make a dream for me.

Yae ye ye ye ye ye ye.

When I dream with a new fire, you make up a good dream for
    me.

You are Bahanarao.

Yae ye ye ye ye ye ye.

I, your father, will name you.

Yae ye ye ye ye ye ye.

Although I do not name very well, you will hear my words
    when I name you.

Yae ye ye ye ye ye ye

This is your name, just as I am now naming you.

Yae ye ye ye ye ye ye

When I am naming you with greetings, you, as Bahanarao,
    hear my words.

You are Bahanarao with good hands and with good sight.

With all of this, upon naming you, you hear me.

Yae ye ye ye ye ye ye.

With this I will sing, naming you, Bahanarao.

Yae ye ye ye ye ye ye.

You, Bahanarao, have your house there where the sun rises.

Yae ye ye ye ye ye ye

Even though you are the Bahanarao of Mawari, I will sing to-
    gether with you

Yae ye ye ye ye ye ye.

When I sing with you and make myself happy, hear my hap-
    piness and my song, my sons.

Yae ye ye ye ye ye ye.

[Spoken] Now the bahanarotu is going to speak to the Baha-
    narao so they go away to their house.

[Sung] Do not look at me, go to one side, do not become wild.
    I am your Warao father. I was born poor.

I do not want to make myself sad.

Be careful that you do not think of me with bad intentions,
    because I do not want to cry.

Yae ye ye ye ye ye ye

Music Example 8.2. Bahanarotu apprenticeship song (Antonio Lorenzano).
Olsen Collection 72.8-95.

Antonio gave Wilbert (1972b) a lengthy explanation of bahanarotu apprenticeship in which he explained that the traditional bahanarotu teacher fashions a wina cigar with four pieces of tobacco, each representing four spirits that will dwell in the chest of the novice. Wilbert (1972b, 70) retells it this way:

"Smoke this," he [the master teacher] says. "It contains four *bahanas* who come to open your chest." These four *bahanas* are Black Bee, Wasp, Termite, and Honey Bee. Black Bee hits hard when the smoker inhales the first charge of tobacco. Then Wasp, Termite, and Honey Bee tear painfully into his body. . . . The novice falls into a trance; the Indians say, "He dies." And in this state, "All of a sudden it happens." The unconscious apprentice perceives the sonorous vibrations of the four *bahana* insect spirits. Louder and louder they grow, until the trees of the forest are transformed into gigantic rattles, swinging and swaying and emitting sounds that are most agreeable to his ears. He feels exalted and, euphoric with the marvelous sound, embarks on his initiatory journey across the celestial bridge and its rainbow of colors. . . . Awakening at last from his ecstasy, the new *bahanarotu* clutches his chest which encloses the gift of *bahana:* White Smoke and White Rocks.

The bahanarotu apprentice awakens from his ecstatic trance with the gift of bahana spirits in his chest. These are the new shaman's spirit "sons" and he is their new "father." As a mortal father must feed and care for his children, the bahanarotu must feed his sons tobacco smoke, their only food. He must also abstain from sexual intercourse, contact with blood, and odors of certain foods. His transformation into the shamanic realm slowly begins when a small hole appears in the palm of each hand, functioning as the end of a tube extending through each of his arms to his chest, the abode of the spirit sons (Wilbert 1972b, 71). The spirit sons will assist their father during curing rituals by exiting through these holes in the bahanarotu's hands. (This contrasts with the wisiratu shaman, whose spirit helpers are released through his mouth via vocalizations and tobacco smoke.)

The novice's apprenticeship continues, as Wilbert (1972b, 71) explains using Antonio's words:

"Now swallow this small stick," orders the master. "Let your *bahanas* transform it." The stick travels past the spirit in the chest and through the arm of the new *bahanarotu* and is "born" white through the mystical hole in the palm of the hand. A second stick is swallowed which exits as a white stick through the other hand. "Now swallow the white sticks," orders the master. This act produces the final proof of a successful initiation. Now the white sticks travel past the *bahanas* in the chest and through the arms, this time to be born as white crystal beads. "The *bahana* spirits are beginning to play," observes the teacher. He is satisfied. He blows tobacco smoke over the arms of his young colleague and bids him go, with this warning: . . . "Do not send your arrows to cause evil."

Some bahanarotu shamans, however, *do* cause illness and even death to other Warao. They are either instructed to do so in dreams by ancestor Bahanarao, or they do so on their own accord. At night a malevolent bahanarotu's magical arrows can be seen by other bahanarao as fiery projectiles, as Wilbert (1972b, 71) writes:

> They know that somewhere a malevolent *bahanarotu* has swallowed a piece of glass, a twig, a human hair, a rock, or some other object and sent it on its way to enter the body of a victim and make him sick. This is done in the following way: the *bahanarotu* ingests the chosen object and lets it pass by his *bahanas* in his chest and through his arms to the wrist. Here it waits, moving slowly toward the exit hole in the hand. Now the *bahanarotu* takes a deep pull at his cigar, lifts the hand with the magic arrow to his mouth, belches out a ball of smoke and sends the projectile on its way. A *bahanarotu* shooting magic arrows of sickness in this fashion is known as a *hatabu-arotu,* "master of the arrow."

Not all bahanarotu shamans, however, agree to the demands of the ancestor wizards. Antonio, for example, sang and explained another dream song to me in which he was asked by the supernatural to bring illness to someone. (A portion of this song is notated as music example 8.3.) Unlike his other song, which is associated with learning bahanarotu shamanism, and unlike the bahanarotu curing songs, this example is based on a descending five-note tone system featuring half steps (that is, five consecutive notes of a chromatic scale). In the course of his performance, he microtonally rose in pitch 100 cents or one half step. Antonio sang this dream song with great tenderness, as

♩ = ca. 72

yae ye ye ye ye ye   yae ye ye   yae ye ye ye yae ye ye ye ye

ka-sa-bu-ka-ri-te   ya-tu   ka-sa-bu-ka-ri-te ya-tu

i - sa i - ne   yao   ya-tu aho-ko(a) - ri -ma   i -ne

ya-tu aho-koa-ri-ma i-ne   i-ne di-a-wa-rae   i-ne   continues

Music Example 8.3. Bahanarotu dream song (Antonio Lorenzano). Olsen Collection 72.8-97.

if he were actually singing it in a dream (a Theurgical State of Consciousness). In the song he reminded the bahana spirits that he is their bahanarotu master and father and they must obey him:

> The song that I just finished singing means this about a bahanarotu:
>
> I said [sang], "I am your father and you are my children. How is it possible for you to appear in a dream? The dream that you have caused has not done anything to me, but when I had it I became afraid." Thus, after this dream I thought— thinking, thinking, guessing how it is, how it is possible.
>
> I said [sang], "So you are going to make me cry, to make tears fall? As you already know, I am poor, and my children, my family, we are all poor. They are all poor children. This poor child [the object of the request] wants to live in this world. How come you told me in this dream to do this evil thing? This bad thing cannot be. You know that I am your father and you are my children: you are my younger and older brothers. So, look my children, I am going to say something to you, and you heed well. Now, the situation is not like this. It is like this. You have to do as I say because you do."

You understand that all Warao in this world reprimand their children when they are bad; if they are their mother and father, they reprimand their children when they do something bad. If they have heard something bad they ask, "Why, my son, have you talked like this? Is it true?" Now, if it is the truth the son says "true," and if it is not the truth he says, "No, it is a lie." If it is the truth the bahanarotu speaks like that to his spirits who appeared in a dream.

I said [sang], "Well, my children, you know that I am your father and you are my sons. You do not have to think this bad thing because we all want to live in this world. The people who live here are contented and happy—they get up, eat, work, earn a living, make bread each day. Now you say that you are going to do evil, do a bad thing? And I say no! Now you have to hear my voice and my words. Why? Because I heard you talking and did not like it. I became afraid. I became afraid believing the truth. What do you say? Are you going to harm me, do bad things to me, or is this a lie that I heard in my dream?"

They said [sang], "No, my father, this is a game. Talking this way is our joke. We are talking and playing."

I said [sang], "Tell me, do you know where you live? I do not know where your house is. Your house is standing out in the sun. You live there, and I live here. When you appear in my dream, I always give you tobacco, a wina, then you go away. You do not eat like people, you eat nothing but pure tobacco smoke of a wina cigar. Thus, when I smoke a wina of tobacco, one for each of you as you like, when you are satisfied, feeling good, you go. Therefore, I send you away and you have to go to your house, to your place, to your door. I speak, and you know that I am your father. So do not come again and speak in the manner that you spoke before. You know that I always get along well with you. In the same manner you must get along well with me. Now, if you ever see me doing bad things against you, then you should not do or say bad things or words. You should say the following good words: 'Our father wants it like this, so it will be like this.' I can speak with my wife. She is like your sister, so I speak to her about everything that you said to me in my dream: 'Look, the dream said this and that to me.'"

Thus, I have to think, and we have to go into the moriche grove. There we have to gather two, three, or four basketfuls of yuruma for these spirits [gente = people], because they have arrived to me speaking something bad. Thus, we have to do this for them, so they do not do anything bad against us, so they do not make us ill. These spirits do not always remain contented with us. You know that when it is hebu it is hebu, and when it is bahana it is bahana, and nobody sees it. It is like the wind or a breeze, and you do not see it. You do not see its body. But during a dream you see its body, you speak with the spirit, conversing, telling a history, and when you need something you ask, "Well, I need this, and this, and this, and this." The dream speaks. But here, as we are talking, outside the dream, in this world, nobody sees anything. Nobody sees that which is bahana diawara [born bahana] since it is a spirit.

I said [sang], "For this reason, my sons, we have to try above all to do this. What do you say?"

They reply, "Yes, we will do it."

I said [sang], "Now I am occupied. A few days from now when I am no longer occupied we will go to the moriche grove and take out three, four, five baskets of yuruma which will serve you, us, and above all the Bahanarao for the festival of habi sanuka, which is yours and which pertains to all of us."

That is the end, my friend.

The learning experience of Gerónimo, a novice bahanarotu, was very different from the traditional method of learning bahanarotu shamanism as related by Antonio (in Wilbert 1972b). Gerónimo explained, for example, that he underwent his apprenticeship and learned his bahanarotu songs in Tucupita, the capital of the Amacuro Federal Territory. There, at the Casa Indígena (government-owned free housing project for the Warao), he spent five days studying with a forty-five-year-old master bahanarotu. During his apprenticeship he did not smoke traditional Warao wina cigars because the necessary manaca palm leaves were not available in Tucupita; instead, he smoked common Venezuelan filtered cigarettes. In addition, Gerónimo explained that he, like Primitivo, also uses a wisiratu's hebu mataro rattle while curing bahanarotu illnesses.

Gerónimo sang an apprenticeship song for me in which he explained that Mawari, the lord of the east, becomes the spirit representative of the spirit son that lives within his chest. The spirit sings that it is he who arranges his father's (the shaman's) throat and chest and who fabricates the temple, which is the body of the bahanarotu. One of the characteristics he acquires through his apprenticeship song is the power of divination. The curing bahanarotu, through the divining power invested in him by his spirit helpers, is able to know the origin of the malevolent illness-causing bahanarotu and his spirit helpers. This is clear in the text of his apprenticeship song (Olsen Collection 72.8-72) where he sings "I am the one who calls the helpers. Therefore, I know."

During my research in the spring of 1973, Antonio Lorenzano explained more about the practice of bahanarotu inflicting. In the old days, he said, some Warao had dolls with faces and arms that were used for killing people. A bahanarotu shaman with the special knowledge of the dolls is known as daunonarima, and through song he can make the doll dance and sit and can send it over great distances through the air and into his victim to kill him or her. Unlike the bahanarotu's method for sending magical arrows through the air, the shaman does not have to swallow the doll to send it off. The daunarima can also cure this type of illness by removing the doll from the patient with suction and massage but not with song.

Bahanarotu Curing Songs

Song is an important tool for the bahanarotu during his regular curing rituals, although some scholars state or infer that he does not sing while curing. Suárez (1968, 192), for example, writes that "the bahanarotu does not have a rattle and does not sing magic formulas; he fundamentally uses suction." Likewise, Turrado Moreno (1945, 161) explains that "the 'bahanarotu' generally neither sings nor chants, except mentally." In the same fashion, Wilbert mentions neither music nor musical instruments as being among the bahanarotu's curing techniques and paraphernalia. Barral (1964, 231), however, writes that "their orations are simply recitations," suggesting that the bahanarotu's music is something less than song. These are, perhaps, the interpretations of most nonmusical researchers, who do not consider the bahanarotu's orations to be music because the most common bahanarotu curing song formulas consist of two or three pitches, fewer than the curing songs styles of other types of Warao shamans. On the other hand, José Antonio Páez, a very knowledgeable hoarotu who says he can also cure other shamanic illnesses, explained in 1973 that the bahanarao who are really knowledgeable do not have to sing but the younger ones do. This was confirmed by Antonio, who explained that the bahanarotu does not have to rely upon song as he becomes older and more knowledgeable.

Similarly, the scholars I have mentioned seem to agree that the bahanarotu does not use a rattle while curing illnesses. I found, however, that some bahanarotu shamans occasionally use a hebu mataro rattle while curing, borrowing one from a wisiratu because the hebu's rattle is not the usual power tool for a bahanarotu. I witnessed an occasion when a hebu mataro rattle was used by a bahanarotu for curing and recorded interviews when other bahanarao stated that the wisiratu's rattle is used to remove any object that is either large or long and flexible, such as a wire or a cable. The hebu mataro rattle functions as the bahanarotu's helper, much like a "key to open a door," as Gerónimo explained, a strange metaphor for a culture that does not normally use locks and keys. The bahanarotu places the rattle over the patient's body where the object (the bahana) is diagnosed to be, and the rattle itself extracts the object. The same hebu helping spirits (kareko) inside the rattle help the bahanarotu to extract the bahana; and for this reason, according to Gerónimo, the rattle *always* has to be a hebu mataro. Antonio explained that the use of a hebu mataro rattle in bahanarotu curing depends on the skill of the shaman. After a young bahanarotu develops sufficient expertise in extracting the magical arrows (bahanatuma), he no longer needs to rely upon the added power of the hebu mataro. This was also confirmed by José Antonio Páez in 1973.

The customary bahanarotu rattle, the small habi sanuka (see chapter 4), has no part in shamanistic curing, although it is often used by a bahanarotu to aid him in contacting the bahana spirits for other purposes (see chapter 14). The many references to rattling sounds in Warao mythology (Wilbert 1972b), related previously in the explanations of bahanarotu cosmology, suggest the importance of a rattle in bahanarotu shamanism. This importance is physically represented by the habi sanuka rattle, which the bahanarotu uses during the habi sanuka fertility ritual and at other times during his celestial journeys.

Analytical evaluation reveals that a complete bahanarotu curing sequence, like the complete cycle for wisiratu curing, consists of three musical-textual sections. I will again call these A, B, and C, although their functions differ from the A, B, and C sections used by the wisiratu. Musical and song-text analyses reveal, for example, that during the A section of a bahana curing song the bahanarotu masks his voice and conjures up his spirit helpers (which he also considers to be his spirit sons) for three purposes: to express loyalty to them, show control over them, and ask them for help. Therefore, during the A section the bahanarotu communicates with his spirit sons; and his masked singing voice becomes his spirit sons' singing voices. At this time some young bahanarotu shamans will occasionally use a borrowed hebu mataro rattle for additional power. Textual analysis further reveals that after having called his helping spirits, the bahanarotu begins his B section in which he names the evil spirit(s) responsible for bringing illness to his patient. In the B section the bahanarotu may also use a hebu mataro rattle if he is a novice, but he does not mask his voice because the helping spirits have already been communicated with and the bahanarotu is already transformed into a powerful entity. Section B is directly related to the curing process because it addresses the evil bahanatuma and is often followed by suction, when the bahanarotu actually extracts one or more material objects from the patient. Section C, without a rattle or voice masking, is employed only if section B does not help the patient. The C section of the bahanarotu curing sequence is melodically and textually similar to the B section of a wisiratu song and also to the curing song of a hoarotu, as we shall see in chapter 9. In the C section the bahanarotu shaman attempts to name the object within the patient that is causing the illness. In bahanarotu shamanism the magical arrows are believed to have been sent through the air by a malevolent bahanarotu with the assistance of the spirits themselves. Another reason for section C, according to José Antonio Páez, is that the material objects are flexible, like pieces of rope or reed, and only the C section can assist in their removal.

The following interview with Gerónimo (G.V., the singer) and Menegildo (M.P., his friend and translator) helps to clarify the tripartite structure of a bahanarotu curing cycle. (D.O. is me.) The interview took place shortly after Gerónimo noncontextually sang several bahanarotu curing songs (Olsen Collection 72.8-88, 89, 91, 92) and the day following Primitivo's nocturnal curing ritual (Olsen Collection 72.8-90). I played back Gerónimo's songs to him and Menegildo, and we discussed the music and its significance.

> *D.O.* [after playing back a recording of section C, a naming section]: What is this music for?
>
> *M.P.* This is for taking out or removing.
>
> *G.V.* It is for taking out a bahana. For example, if a person has something here [points to a part of his body], such as a cabulla [reed or rush], or if a neighboring person does harm, you begin like this to take care of it. Well, this song is the same as bahanarotu. That which the old man from Hana Kahamana sang during the day is about Hoa proper. For example, this song is for if a man has pain, then you ask him, "Where do you hurt?" If he hurts here, then you have to sing. For example, if he has a cabulla inside of him, you name it like a Hoa is named.
>
> *M.P.* This song is about the first communications, about what the master of bahanarotu named; it is not of Gerónimo.
>
> *D.O.* I see. Another bahanarotu named.
>
> *M.P.* Yes, another bahanarotu, in order to make someone sick.
>
> *D.O.* Therefore, only another bahanarotu can take out the arrows.
>
> *M.P.* Yes, now another comes to cure the patient, to name the arrow: "This is one." And if it is one, then it more or less moves.
>
> *D.O.* And a hoarotu cannot do this?
>
> *M.P.* and *G.V.* No!
>
> *M.P.* A hoarotu does not know what the patient has inside of him. He does not know. Therefore, a bahanarotu has to sing for him. He knows, in his hand.
>
> *D.O.* Are there lots of songs of this type?
>
> *M.P.* There are, but Gerónimo says they are all the same type of music. For example, by learning one song I would know enough to take out bahana. I would know how to name the bahana because the songs are all the same.
>
> *D.O.* So this song [section C] is for removing bahana. Now, those songs [sections A and B] that you sang earlier, what are they for?

G.V. This is also for taking out bahana; it is another song.

M.P. It is also for taking out bahana. The first song is for calling the bahana spirit which lives way over there. And when the spirit arrives here, the bahanarotu knows and recognizes it. He knows it because he is the owner of it. When the spirit comes then he, the spirit, touches the patient with his hand, on the spot where the patient has the pain. Meanwhile the bahanarotu sings. He who is touching with his hand is the spirit of the hand, or the hand of the spirit. He knows what the patient has inside of him. With the spirit himself, the bahanarotu will pull out the object. With the spirit himself, the bahanarotu will remove the object. It is the spirit who takes out the bahana.

D.O. First, you sang to name?

G.V. Yes.

D.O. Second, you sang a song for removing the bahana?

G.V. Yes.

M.P. That which he sang is another type for naming the bahana. The bahana more or less has a name. He has to look for the name. He is looking for the method of naming the bahana, and when he has the name it moves, more or less. Then, with the hand it is loosened and is removed.

D.O. Then there are only these three types of songs?

G.V. Yes, for calling, for naming, and for taking out or removing.

M.P. The third type is also for sending the bahana off and away. It is for seeing what the bahana is. After the bahana has been taken out, it is for seeing what it is when it is leaving for the outside. We have to be careful because some day it might come back.

D.O. Last night, did Primitivo sing like that?

M.P. He sang only the calling, the call. It arrived, and then he said he was going to remove it. "I am a good remover," he sang.

D.O. And he removed objects too.

M.P. Yes, he took out a nail and a piece of nylon rope.

D.O. But he did not sing after that.

M.P. No.

D.O. So it isn't always necessary to sing after the removal?

M.P. No. The patient didn't have a witch [bahana] that had a name. There is a witch [bahana], but it doesn't have a name, a call. He had to remove the object by talking, more or less. There is no name. That which has a name is the witch that is put in the head, and it more or less moves. The head shakes. Thus, when you loosen the object without saying the name, it does not come up and out. You have to give its name. When you say its name, it loosens the object that is tied inside, and when you have loosened it, then it has to come on out, because you have loosened it.

In addition to clarifying the tripartite form of bahanarotu curing music, Gerónimo and Menegildo describe and verify the power of naming. According to them, the C section is sung when the patient has a bahana or witch (that is, the spirit of a malevolent Bahanarotu) in his or her head. This type of bahana illness is very serious, and to cure it the naming melody (section C) must be used. They also emphasize the importance of laying on the hand. As Menegildo explains, "he who is touching with his hand is the spirit of the hand, or the hand of the spirit." From the hole in each of the bahanarotu's hands the spirit helper(s) exit and enter the patient's body to diagnose and effect a cure. Laying on the hand is not massage but is focusing and application of power.

The bahanarotu curing songs presented in this chapter include two performances of each of the three sections used for curing and one example sung when the illness-causing bahanarotu sons appear to the curing shaman (see table 8.1). Section A has a very limited range, consisting of a principal tone and a supporting tone, most commonly at the interval of a major second (2 1), as indicated in music example 8.4. This type of reciting melody is an effective vehicle for communication between the bahanarotu and his helping spirits because the text is not obscured. In addition, both recorded examples of section A include an interlude pitch whose only musical function seems to be to break the monotony of the repeated principal tone and occasional supporting tone. This one-pitch recitation, lower than the principal tone, employs only the words "owai, yae, yae," glossed as "name" and two vocables of exclamation that emphasize the fact that the master's name has been called. Throughout the A section the bahanarotu masks his voice by producing a gravelly tone quality, which Gerónimo considers a rev-

Table 8.1. Bahanarotu shamanistic curing songs

Olsen Collection no.	Function	Performer	Situation	Texture
72.8-88	Curing A	Gerónimo Velásquez	Studio	Solo
72.8-89	Curing A	Gerónimo Velásquez	Studio	Solo
72.8-90	Curing B	Primitivo Sánchez	curing	rattle
72.8-91	Curing B	Gerónimo Velásquez	Studio	Solo
72.8-92	Curing C	Gerónimo Velásquez	Studio	Solo
72.8-94	Curing C	Antonio Lorenzano	Studio	Solo

Music Example 8.4. Bahanarotu curing song, section A, tone system.

erent voice. The two performances of section A included in this analysis, performed noncontextually by Gerónimo, are actually a continuation of one performance during which the bahanarotu is calling upon several of his spirit helpers. The first helper is his spirit son who lives within his chest, according to the words in song text 8.2. As the father of his spirit son, the bahanarotu proclaims his loyalty to and oneness with the spirit. He also shows control over him as a father does over a son, while at the same time asking for his help. Gerónimo stated at the beginning of his performance that during an actual curing ritual he would use a hebu mataro rattle for additional power. The following text is from Gerónimo's complete section A bahanarotu curing song (translated by the singer).

Song Text 8.2. Bahanarotu Curing Song, Section A, Gerónimo Velásquez, 6 August 1972 (Part 1, Olsen Collection 72.8-88; Part 2, 72.8-89)

Part 1:

oya oya yae yae yae yae ine hioko amawari ine yehebatu ine
oya oya yae yae yae yae
I am the one who calls Mawari

ine hioko aisiko diawarae, ine hioko nesabasaba
I was born with you, I am at your side

ine hioko ine, ine nesabasaba diawarae ine
I am like this, I was born at your side

ine hioko amawari ine, ine yehebatu ine, ine etuwaratu ine,
    owaeya
I am like Mawari, I call you, I greet you, *owaeya*

ine yakera diawarae ine, ine yakera diawarae ine hioko ine
I was born well, I was born well like this

ine hioko sabasaba diawarae, ine hioko sabasaba ine, oyae
    oyae oyae
I like this was born there at your side, I am like this at your
    side *oyae oyae oyae*

ine ine ine ine ine ine hioko amawari ine yehebatu ine
I, I, I, I, I, I am like Mawari and I call you

ine kasabukaha wituma ine? ine ahoka amawari yehebatu ine,
    owaya
Who am I? I am he who calls Mawari within me, *owaya*

ine tamaha aisiku amawari, ine tamaha amawari ine yehe-
    batu
I am this with Mawari, I am he who calls Mawari

ine ahoka amawari yehebatu ine, owaeya oiya oiya
I am he who calls Mawari within me, *owaeya oiya oiya*

ine ine ine tamaha hoka amawari; ine yehebatu ine, ine ahoka
    amarwari
I, I, I am like Mawari within me; I call you, I am Mawari
    within me

ine ahokarimatuma, ine nasaribamotuma

I am the father of them, I am the one who is talking with
   them

ahoka amawari ine yehebatu ine
I am he who calls Mawari within me

ine aisiko ine, ine tamaha simunuka ine
I am like that, I am exactly the equal of that

ine taimunuka ine, ine sabasaba taimunuka, owaya
I am one and the same, I am there along side like that, *owaya*

ine ahoko urusituma ine, ine kokotukane ine
I am naming the son within me, I am in everything

ine yehebatu ine, ine etuwaratu ine, owaya oya oya oya
I call you, I greet you, *owaya oya oya oya*

ine ine ine ine ine ine, owai owai owai
I, I, I, I, I, I, *owai owai owai*

ine ahoko amawari ine yehebatu ine, owayo
I am he who calls Mawari within me, *owayo*

ine amakaramuna, ine mawae makaramuna ine
I, my name is, I, this is my name

ine waekare waekare amawari
I am Waekare, Waekare Mawari

*ine yehebatu ine waekare ahoko amawari, yehebatu ine,
   owaya*
I call Waekare Mawari within me, I call you, *owaya*

*ine isetuwaratu ine, ine etwaratu yakera diawarae ine, ine ma-
   hoko arimasaba*
I greet you, I greet you, I greet you and was born well for you,
   I am for my father within

ine kahoko arimasaba ine, ine mamorabu towakore
I come to where my father is, I extend my hand

he abanae tane tiakorisa oya ine
when I touch with the son's hand, then it is placed there

oya owai owai, ine waekare, ine waekare ahoka amawari ine
oya owai owai, I am Waekare, I am Waekare within me
   Mawari, I

ine yehebatune ine etuwaratune ine, ine nisatune
I call and greet you, I, I am the grabber

ine nowatuwana, ine hebukatu ine ine nisatun
I am not afraid of it, I am one who snares and grabs it

ine iriyaha nowatuyana ine nisatu ine, owaya oeee
I am not very afraid and I grab it, *owaya oeee*

ine ine ine ine ine ine hioko ine oyo ine hioko isiko diawarae ine
I, I, I, I, I, I was born like that with him

owaya, ine ine ine kasabukaha waituma ine
owaya,
I, I, I, what are they?

ine ahoka amawari yehebatu ine ine, oya oya oya
I am who calls Mawari within me, oya oya oya

ine ine kasabukaha waituma, ine ahoka amawari
I, I, what are they? I am Mawari from within

ine tamahasike kahoko amawari yehebatu, ine kahoko arioso-
   tuma
I am this, I call Mawari from within me, I, within me, have
   spirits

ine ahoko amaware yehebatu ine, ine ahoko ariosotuma
I am who calls Mawari within me, I, within me, have spirits

Part 2:

ine hioko amawari ine, ine yehebatu ine, oyai
I am like Mawari, I am the one who calls, *oyai*

ine etuwaratu, ine yehebatu yakera, oyai
I am the one who greets, I call well, *oyai*

ine kasabukaha waitu ine? ine ahoka amawari yehebatu
What will this be? I am the caller of Mawari within me

ine mabataru ine, ine mabataru barawaida
I am in my place, my place is in the large river in the sea

barawa matana tatane
Along side of the sea I also have my place

mabataru bubu yariyawara kware sabuka ine ori kokanamatu
    ine ine ine
There, where the large hills were born, I am standing I, I, I

ine tatane yakera diawarae ine mabataru bubu tatane yakera
    diawarae
There, I was born well, at the top of the hills

owaya, ine mawae karamuna, ine domo yoromahore, ahoka
    amawari yehebatu, domo yoromahore
owaya, I, my name is this, I am brown pelican, called to be
    Mawari within, brown pelican

ahoka amaware ine yehebatu ine, ine tai ahoko ariosotuma, ine
    yehebatu ine
I am who calls Mawari within me, I, within me, have spirits,
    I call you

ine ahoka amawarituma, ine yehebatu yakera, oyae
I am the spirits within me, I call you well, oyae

ine domu ine domu yoromahore; ahoka mawari ine yehebatu
    ine

I am brown pelican; I am who calls Mawari within me

ine etuwaratu ine, ine abahana diawara, ine etuwaratu ine
I am who greets, I am who has arrived, I am who greets

oyaa, ine hioko aisiko diawarae, ine tamaha korisa
oyaa, I was born with you, I am the same as this

ine makaramuna domu yoromahore ariawara taimonuka,
* oya*
I am named brown pelican and was born for you, *oya*

ine iridaha nowatuwana ine; ine nisatu ine, ine bukatu ine
I am not very afraid; I am one who grabs, I am one who
  snares

ine hinuatuana ine oya oya oya oya
I do not frighten you, *oya oya oya oya*

ine hioko ine hioko amawari yehebatu ine, oya, ine hioko
* amawari yehebatu ine*
I am the one who calls Mawari, *oya*, I am the one who calls
  Mawari

ine makaramuna domu yekabane ariawara taimonuka
I am named yekabane bird and was born for you

taisi ahoko amawari ine yehebatu ine, oya; tamaha korisa
* hiwai karamuna, oy oy oy*
This is Mawari, I call from within, *oya*; this is your name, *oy*
  oy oy

ine hioko aisiko diawarae ine, oy oy oy, ine hioko aisiko ine
I am like that and I was born, *oy oy oy*, I am like that

ine yehebatu ine, ine yehebatu yakera diawarae ine, oya
I call you I call you, I am born to call you well, *oya*

ine bukatu ine, ine nisatu ine

I am one who snares, I am one who grabs

ine nowatuwana iridaha anisatu
I do not frighten anybody and have grabbed everything

ine hebukatu ine, ine henubaratu ine tamaha ahokwarosi
I am one who snares, I am your pusher with this rattle

aisiakwane ahokwarosi aisia ine bukatu ine naminaha
with this rattle I know how to snare

ine tane naminaha, ine nisatu ine, oya oy huay
I know like this, I am one who grabs, *oya oy huay*

ine ine ine ine ine hioko ine hioko amawari ine
I, I, I, I, I am like Mawari, I

ine yehebatu ine ine hioko amawari ine, ine etuwaratu ine
I am one who calls, I am like Mawari, I am one who greets

ine taisi ahoko amawarituma, ine yehebatu ine
I am like the Mawarituma within me, I am one who calls

This lengthy song text reveals that the bahanarotu Gerónimo and his spirit son are both referred to as Mawari, which the singer himself translates as el Señor or "the master." Mawari is the same supernatural entity that Wilbert (1972b, 65–72) calls the "Creator Bird of the Dawn," a bird of tobacco smoke with the shape of a swallow-tailed kite (Wilbert 1985, 147); although Barral (1964, 171) refers to Maguari (same pronunciation) as the spirit of the Supreme Wisiratu. The use of one word, Mawari, referring both to the bahanarotu and his spirit son suggests the oneness of father and son via the transformation of the bahanarotu into a supernatural entity. Gerónimo sings "ine ahoka amawari" (I am Mawari from within), also referring to the oneness of shaman and helping spirit (also Mawarituma, the plural form, is used). Likewise, Barral (1964, 171) quotes a wisiratu shaman from the Mariúsa subtribe in 1942 who explained the following: *"Maguari ma güisiratu i-namoninae. Eku ine Maguari bakaya:* Mawari is who has converted me into a shaman: I carry Mawari within me."

Next the bahanarotu calls Waekare, asking for his help in snaring and grabbing the evil bahana essence (object) to effect a cure. Although Waekare was not identified, it is probably one of the many avian spirit helpers (perhaps related to waimare, the gavilan culebrero or snake sparrow hawk, according to Barral 1969, 169). Then Gerónimo calls for the assistance of another helping spirit called Yoromahore, which he explains is a species of sea bird, also known as a bahana bird. This is probably the same as yoroa, the brown pelican (*Pelecanus occidentalis*), which, according to Wilbert (1981a, 50, f. 7), is one of the "three major avian companions of the Warao Creator Bird." Later Gerónimo calls another bird, yekabane, which neither I nor the scholarly literature has identified. (See Wilbert 1981a, 50; 1985, 181, for other birds associated with bahanarotu shamanism.) With these powerful helpers, and by virtue of the fact that he is a powerful shaman, the bahanarotu is himself transformed into a spirit, as Gerónimo expresses when he sings, "I am Waekare." Also during section A, a dialogue takes place between the bahanarotu, his spirit son, and the helping bahana spirit bird.

Thus, in section A several spirit helpers are called through song to aid in the diagnosis and curing of the bahanarotu's patient. Gerónimo also sings about extending his hand, which is his spirit son's hand. (Recall what Menegildo said: "He who is touching with his hand is the spirit of the hand, or the hand of the spirit.") After the A section the bahanarotu touches the patient with his hands; and his spirit sons exit through the holes in his palms (seen only by the bahanarotu) and enter into his patient's body to assist in grabbing, snaring, and ultimately removing the object that is causing the illness (Wilbert 1972b, 71–72).

I witnessed the laying on of the hand during an actual curing ritual performed by Primitivo Sánchez on 5 August 1972. Before he removed the illness-causing objects, however, he sang a section B curing song that incorporated textual material from a typical section A. In other words, he omitted the section A song completely and did not mask his voice except for several vocables that seemed to emanate from the rafters of the house. These interjections were created with ventriloquism and were used to call forth his helping spirits.

The section B of the bahanarotu curing cycle is determined by expanded melodic use, normal tone production, and textual content. The melodic use in section B is indicated by the skeletal notations presented in music example 8.5 (from Olsen Collection 72.8-90 and 72.8-91). These emphasize a slightly lowered second degree of the scale, creating a neutral second between the principal tone and the supporting tone. This interval is the most prominent throughout the songs, while the ornamentations are infrequent. Music example 8.6 is a transcription of the beginning portion of Primitivo's curing ritual (section B song), and the opening minutes can be heard in recorded example 13.

Primitivo's section B song shows a variation in both his choice of words and melody, and his ritual performance incorporates textual elements of a typical section A bahanarotu curing song (see song text 8.3). During his performance he used a hebu mataro rattle and employed ventriloquism occasionally to project masked vocal interpretations of "owai," "owaya," and similar vocables, which seemed as though they were coming from the roof or the rafters. According to Gerónimo, these strategically placed muffled and guttural words were spoken by the illness-causing spirit who was present during the curing ritual. (In Warao belief these words are spoken by a spirit rather than the bahanarotu.) In song text 8.3 Primitivo's song is transliterated and translated in full, and the ventriloquized words of the illness-causing spirit appear in parentheses.

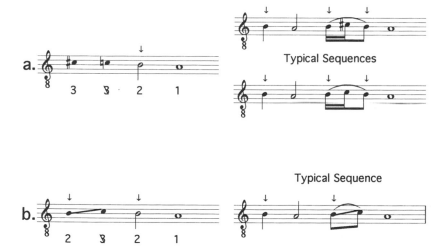

Music Example 8.5. Bahanarotu curing song, section B, tone systems and typical sequences: (a) Primitivo Sánchez (Olsen Collection 72.8-90); (b) Gerónimo Velásquez. Olsen Collection 72.8-91.

*Song Text 8.3. Bahanarotu Curing Ritual, Section B Song,
Primitivo Sánchez, 5 August 1972, 8:15 P.M.; contextual
ceremony with continuous hebu mataro rattle
(Olsen Collection 72.8-90)*

(*oya oya oya oya oya oya oya oya*)

ine yehebatu ine (*oya oya oya*) *ine yehebatu yakara* (*oya oya
   oya)*
I am the caller (*oya oya oya*), I am a good caller (*oya oya oya*)

hisaba diawarae, ine yehebata yakara hisaba diawarae
I am born for you, I call well and was born for you

*ine yehebatu ine, ine makaribetuma abahana diawara yehe-
   batu ine*
I am the caller, I am the one who calls the Carib spirits who
   appeared

*ine sabasabamu yehebatu ine, ine yehebatu ine, ine etuwaratu
   ine*
I am next to them, calling, I am the caller, I am the greeter

ine etuwaratu yakera saba diawarae, ine mabahana diawara
I am the good greeter who appears next to them, I was born
   for the bahana

*ine makaribetuma ehibaratu ine, abahana diawara natokotu
   ine*
I am the greeter of the Carib spirits, I am the puller of the bahana that appeared

(*oyeo oyeo oyeo*)

ine yehebatu ine, ine natokotu ine, yae, ine nisatu ine
I am the caller, I am the puller, yae, I am the one who grabs

ine nisatu yakera saba diawarae
I am the one who was born there to be a good grabber

ine makaramuna daesarana, ine makaramuna waekare
I, my name is none other, I, my name is Waekare

ine waekare abahana diawara
I am born as the bahana of Waekare

In this song Primitivo addresses Waekare but not Mawari; and he
sings, "I am the caller, I am the puller, I am the grabber," referring to
his skills at laying on his hand and the supernatural removal of objects
within the patient. While these textual elements recall ideas found in A
sections of bahanarotu curing songs, the B section has characteristics
suggesting that the bahanarotu is speaking as a transformed entity
who has achieved power through oneness with his spirit son. Although
the lack of voice masking (except for ventriloquism) may suggest that
the bahanarotu is the speaker, Gerónimo explained that a helping
spirit is itself speaking in the second half of Primitivo's song. This is
additionally verified by the dialogue between the shaman and a spirit,
when the latter says, "I am born as the bahana of Waekare." Therefore,
a spirit can speak through a bahanarotu shaman's voice even though
the shaman's voice is not masked. Portions of the text also refer to the
transformed bahanarotu's oneness with his powerful spirit helpers,
making the bahanarotu himself powerful. The most important characteristic of section B, however, is to name the spirits that have caused
the pain and anguish in the patient. Primitivo, for example, names
Carib Indians as the evil bahanatuma. Singling out another culture as
the cause of suffering may seem unusual; but as Barral (1964, 164)
writes, "anyone who knows something about American history would
not find it strange that the Warao consider the Caribs not as people but
as evil spirits and ogres, owing to the atrocities that they committed
and the concept of cannibalism that they practiced . . . the terrible concept of the fierce Carib Indians hunting slaves has been conserved and
kept alive throughout the years, transmitted from fathers to sons." The
Spanish term caribe translates into English as "savage" (Velázquez de
la Cadena 1966, 144) and is also the name for the Venezuelan piranha
fish found in many waters of the Orinoco Delta. These meanings—
"savage" and "flesh eater," as in the case of the caribe fish—reinforce
the concept of fear among the Warao. The Barama River Carib Indians
of Guyana, traditional enemies of the Warao, have a similar shaman

capable of shooting magical arrows from holes in his hand (Gillin 1936, 173; Wilbert 1972b, 72). This supernatural attribute has undoubtedly inspired the Warao bahanarotu shamans to be prepared for foreign magical arrows from Guyana if not cannibalistic slave hunters as in the past. An interesting paradox in bahanarotu shamanism is that while the Carib Indians are themselves considered evil by the Warao, the term Mawari is Cariban for spirit (Vaquero 1965, 132); and Mawari epitomizes the good power of the eastern cosmic realm. Here we perhaps see evidence of intertribal trade resulting in spirit role reversal.

After Primitivo finished singing his ritual, he extracted several physical objects from his male patient. He began his extraction by grunting, growling, slurping, gagging, and making other sounds implying suction and regurgitation. Because it was dark, those of us present could not see what was happening; we could only hear. After the sounds ended, however, Primitivo and others turned on their flashlights so we could view the objects he had just removed from his patient. These included a small piece of nylon rope and a nail that were respectively causing his patient's fever and headache, according to Primitivo. We were all amazed, and the Warao observers remarked, "No wonder he was ill." For the Warao, such causes of illness and the consequent curing processes are a part of their belief system and are therefore understandable to them through faith. For the non-Warao (outsiders) it is perhaps possible to understand the phenomenon if we think in terms of the material object also having a spiritual essence that becomes transformed into a magical arrow. In wisiratu shamanism as well, the hebu removed from a patient during curing is a spiritual essence rather than the material form of an animal or object. Likewise, the Hoa removed from a patient by a hoarotu shaman (see chapter 9) is a spiritual rather than a material essence. All these shamanic essence concepts are very real to the Warao; they do not make the Western distinction between spiritual and material. Thus, when Primitivo extracted a rusty nail and a nylon rope from his patient during the total darkness of the evening and subsequently passed the objects around for all of us to feel and for those of us with flashlights to see, I thought of them as material objects whose spiritual essences had been removed from the patient and were properly returned to their material shapes. To the Warao observers, however, they were the actual material objects that were removed. The bahanarotu himself believes that

Music Example 8.6. Bahanarotu curing song, section B (Primitivo Sánchez). Olsen Collection 72.8-90.

even if the material object is taken from his basket or bag, it is not the complete object until its spiritual essence has been restored to it. Thus, the bahanarotu must not be considered a deceiver or a charlatan (as Spanish missionary scholars such as Barral and Turrado Moreno have maintained in their writings) but as a skilled practitioner whose specialized and unique type of knowledge helps to maintain a proper balance within the Warao belief system.

Gerónimo's section B curing song (sung noncontextually) includes a solicitation for assistance from Mawari, as the first part of song text 8.4 reveals. The following is a transliteration and translation by the shaman himself of the first part of his section B curing song.

Song Text 8.4. Bahanarotu Curing Song, Section B, Gerónimo Velásquez, 6 August 1972 (Olsen Collection 72.8-91)

ine yemawari ine, ine hioko ine
I am Mawari, I am like this

ine hioko amawari yehebatu, ine etuwaratu ine, ine ahoko amawari
I am the caller of Mawari, I am the greeter, I am Mawari within

ine yehebatu ine, ine etuwaratu ine, ine hioko ine ine hioko amawari yehebatu ine
I am the caller, I am the greeter, I am like this, I am the caller of Mawari

ine sabasabamo ine, ine sabasabamo diawarae ine
I am at your side, I am born at your side

ine taemonuka ine, ine ahoko amawari yehebatu ine
I am the same as this, I am who calls Mawari from within

ine mawae karamuna ine, ine mawae karamuna kasabukaha yana
I, my name, I, my name is not this

ine mawae karamuna hebu amerikanotuma

I, my name is hebu of the Americans

ahoko amawari yehebatu ine
I am he who calls Mawari from within

Gerónimo named an American spirit as the cause of illness in his make-believe patient: "ine mawae karamuna hebu amerikanotuma" (I, my name is hebu of the Americans). Gerónimo explained that the American hebu was the same as a Creole or Carib spirit. The fact that these are considered the same becomes more clear after living in a traditional Warao village and experiencing the Warao's world. The word "American" is known to them only by way of an occasional knife or hatchet bearing the stamp "Made in America" (Hecho en Amerika), which has been purchased in the Creole towns of Tucupita or Barrancas. To a Warao, anyone who is not a Warao is an outsider (a hotarao or person of the hill); and an outsider is generally known as a Creole, a Venezuelan, a Carib, or an American—all meaning the same thing: one who does not understand, one who is in Warao reality "a savage," or one who seemingly cares little or nothing for Warao culture.

Just as a malevolent illness-causing wizard (brujo in Spanish) can be an outsider, he can also be an insider—a member of the same sub-tribe. Perhaps out of jealousy one bahanarotu will turn on another and accuse him of bringing illness or death to someone. I personally witnessed such an occurrence when Primitivo accused his companion, Gerónimo, of bringing severe illness to Luís Jiménez, the prominent tribal leader who had suffered a stroke (see also chapters 7 and 9). Primitivo's divination was reported to the Warao governor (appointed by the Venezuelan government) who set up a committee to judge the accused. Gerónimo asked me to write a letter to the governor. I agreed, and he dictated the following: "How could I, a human being, do such a thing to my beloved uncle? I am a man." Accusing a particular person rather than generally naming a Creole or a Carib is done because the bahanarotu believed to be responsible for the evil deed of shooting the magical arrows has been revealed to the curing bahanarotu in a dream. The underlying motive may perhaps, but not necessarily, be jealousy. Bahanarotu shamanism has grown in popularity among the younger Warao generation to a level where it has surpassed wisiratu and hoarotu shamanism in membership. This is partially due to the rather easy and relatively short initiation period necessary to become a bahanarotu today, in contrast to the lengthy and physically difficult initiation of the wisiratu and the hoarotu. On the other hand, because the wisiratu is associated with ancestor spirits and Kanoboism, and the hoarotu with all the fears of death and darkness, the bahanarotu is involved with a seemingly less difficult and dangerous type of shamanism yet one that gives the practitioner a high status in his society and assures him a happy life after death (Wilbert 1975a). Thus, jealousy seems to play a part in this popular shamanistic office and may subconsciously cause one bahanarotu to have negative dreams about another.

When sections A and B fail to bring relief to the patient, section C is sung. Musically this is the most complex section and usually lasts longer than the others. In the two examples I recorded (Olsen Collection 72.8-92 and 72.8-94), the melodic use of section C in bahanarotu curing reveals only slight variations. The noncontextual renditions were sung by two different shamans and are melodically similar except for one note. The song by Gerónimo is based on five pitches (see music example 8.7). Two excerpts from this song are also transcribed as music example 8.8a and 8.8b, showing the results of a microtonal rise in pitch. The section C song performed by Antonio Lorenzano consists of four pitches (see music example 8.9). An excerpt from the end of this song appears in music example 8.10. This is basically the same melodic naming motive shown in the previous notation, without pitch 5. Musically, the lack of pitch 5 is a very slight difference that can perhaps be explained by the fact that Gerónimo is also a hoarotu who may be blending curing song styles. As we shall see in chapter 9, a hoarotu curing song consists of the motive 5 4 3̣ 1, which is similar to Gerónimo's section C song. That Gerónimo is indeed a hoarotu as well as a bahanarotu is evidenced by the two hoarotu curing songs that he

Music Example 8.7. Bahanarotu curing song, section C, tone system (transposed to D as the principal tone) (Gerónimo Velásquez). Adapted from Olsen Collection 72.8-93.

The singer continually rose in pitch and ended his song with the following:

Music Example 8.8. Bahanarotu curing song, section C, a and b (Gerónimo Velásquez). Olsen Collection 72.8-93.

Music Example 8.9. Bahanarotu curing song, section C, tone system (transposed to D as the principal tone) (Antonio Lorenzano). Adapted from Olsen Collection 72.8-94.

sang in trio with two other hoarao for the purpose of curing Luís Jiménez. Even the text of his bahanarotu song suggests that it is for hoarotu curing rather than bahanarotu curing, although Gerónimo himself said its function is to remove a bahana.

Gerónimo named two objects in his section C curing song: a type of bear that lives in the rain forest (oso palmero, actually one of two types of anteaters because there are no bears in the delta) and an iron chain. The first object, said to be tied around the patient like a collar, did not make the pain-inflicted area in the patient move when it was named. Therefore, it was not causing the illness. The second object, believed to be tied inside the neck of a woman, also did not move when named. Here the singer ended; but during an actual curing ritual he would continue singing and naming objects until the inflicted area moved, when he would suck out the object that caused the movement. If the inflicted area of the patient did not move, the bahanarotu would normally stop singing after thirty or forty-five minutes, having named many objects in the process. Following a short rest he would resume singing and, if still not successful, would explain that something other than bahana was causing the illness.

Section C of a bahanarotu curing cycle is sung when the pain-causing object inside the patient has been put there by the Bahanarao, or the wizards of the arrows living in hokonamu. This material object was "thought" (el pensamiento) by an evil bahanarotu and with the help of the Bahanarao in hokonamu was placed within the body of the malevolent bahanarotu's victim. The only way a benevolent bahanarotu can remove the object is to name it through song. When properly named, it vibrates and is then physically and spiritually (which are the same in Warao belief) removed through suction with the help of the curing bahanarotu's spirit sons. Song text 8.5 is from Antonio's section C bahanarotu curing song, translated into Spanish by its per-

Music Example 8.10. Bahanarotu curing song, section C (Antonio Lorenzano). Olsen Collection 72.8-94.

former (included here in English only). Because Antonio is an elder, the illness-causing essence (the bahana) in his song is an object from Warao traditional culture—a hair—rather than a modern piece of nylon rope.

Song Text 8.5. Bahanarotu Curing Song, Section C, Antonio Lorenzano, 20 July 1972 (Olsen Collection 72.8-94)

You have chosen the words in order to know.
I have chosen the words of bahanarotu.
The head bahanarotu of the house put a bahana witch in you
    to kill you.

The bahana that a bahanarotu put in you, it must be loosened.

The words of the bahanarotu were transformed to make you ill.

This bahanarotu, with the thought of his words, spoke to make you ill.

The bahana must be loosened.

The bahanarotu put the bahana into the chest of a woman.

The bahanarotu spoke the bahana words to put the bahana into the woman beneath the ribs.

He also spoke to place the bahana into the back.

The bahana must be loosened.

The bahanarotu put the bahana in the stomach and in the intestines of a woman.

This bahanarotu thought for a woman, to make her ill.

The bahana must be loosened.

This bahanarotu thought hard and bad to make you ill.

With what object will it be that he made you ill?

This bahanarotu already knew what it would be.

This bahanarotu put the bahana in with as much knowledge as I have to remove it.

This is the bahana which the bahanarotu sent.

This bahana is from the Bahanarotu who is there at the beginning of the world in hokonamu.

Ah, with this the bahanarotu thought to place the bahana in you.

This bahana must be loosened.

Even though I do not know you very well, I will choose your words.

This is a very small hair.

You are the bahana made from a small hair which was sent by the Bahanarotu where the sun rises.

This is what was sent to be shot into you.

Thinking about this hair, the bahanarotu transformed it into a bahana.

This bahana that a bahanarotu put in you must be loosened.

This is what you named [speaking to other bahanarotu] to be shot.

This bahana must be loosened.

You are a very small hair, the bahana, which was sent by the Bahanarotu where the sun rises.

We are not acquainted with this hair, it is very strange to us.

You are a bahanarotu and I, as much as you, am a bahanarotu.

For this reason, I know what the bahana is that you sent.

You put the bahana into this woman so it would produce a very sharp pain in her stomach.

I am loosening the bahana which you, woman, have in your stomach, and later I will remove it.

[To the woman] This is how the bahanarotu thought and chose the words to make you ill.

With the placing of my hand over your body I will cure you and take out the bahana.

Upon removing it from you I will put it outside of you.

This was thought by a bahanarotu saying your name, in order to place the bahana in you.

The bahanarotu was the one who thought this bahana in order to place it in you. With the placing of my hand over your body, I will cure you and take out the bahana.

With the point of my finger I took you out.

After finishing section C, Antonio explained bahanarotu curing and how song is used to name the pain-causing object:

This is to take out the bahana which one has inside of him [or her]. When a person gets sick, the people call a wisiratu to cure him. The wisiratu, with his hand, touches the belly, the chest, the foot, and any other part of the patient that hurts. Then the wisiratu says, "It is not hebu which is making the patient ill," and the people call a hoarotu to come and cure this man or woman. They do not want him or her to die, and say, "Touch him to see what it is that he has."

So the hoarotu touches him. He also says, "This is not Hoa."

Finally they call a bahanarotu and say, "Look, bahanarotu, come here, touch this sick person. What is it that he has? We asked a wisiratu, but he does not have hebu. Then we asked a hoarotu, but he does not have Hoa either. Now, what do you say?"

The bahanarotu sits down, lights a wina cigar, begins to make smoke, and starts to touch the patient. "Where do you hurt?" he asks.

"I hurt here," replies the patient.

The bahanarotu touches him a while. "Ah, this is neither hebu nor Hoa; this is bahana, bahana of a hair."

"Oh, good," the husband (or father) [or other family member] says, "you are a companion of mine. I do not want this woman of mine to die," or "this is my son, I do not want him to die. So, cure him. You said that he has a hair—take it out. I will pay you one of these days when I am able to work. If not, take whatever you see, whatever thing you want for payment if you cure my boy (or woman) well."

So, the boy or woman is sick, does not eat, and the family is afraid. Thus, the bahanarotu takes out bahana, four, five, six, ten times, and it does not do any good. The patient is still feeling pain [the bahanarotu has sung or in some other manner carried out the function of sections A and B, without success]. So he thinks, "What could this be? It will have a name, so I am going to sing." He sings the following like he does to take out Hoa: "Already I know the spirit who did you damage [referring to section B]. What will it be?"

You know that far away in the country, at the beginning of the world [at the eastern edge], there is a small settlement where the wizards of the arrows, the Bahanarao, live. Thus, another bahanarotu, in his dream, asked of him [them], and he thought bad. He thought the following: "When I ask for something, such as dinner, clothes, hatchet, whatever, when I ask I don't get it. You didn't give me anything [speaking to his victim]. I was very hungry and you didn't give me anything; that was very bad of you. Now I am going to shoot arrows in you, and in a few days you will feel bad." This is how the malevolent bahanarotu, this wizard, would think.

The curing bahanarotu says the following: "So now I am going to sing because your master, your father, sang like that. I am going to remove the bahana, and cure you." Thus, he begins, and if the patient is an elder, if he is master of the house, if he is chief, if he is the captain, if he is the fiscál, if he is the governor, the bahanarotu sings exactly like I sang.

Afterward, the patient may say, "I don't hurt there, I hurt in my belly, in my ribs."

So the bahanarotu sings by the chest, by the ribs, by both sides; after this, by the belly, he sings "Where is the hair? There it is." Since he knows bahanarotu shamanism he touches, and when he touches he has the bahana. Therefore, the bahanarotu begins to sing, singing, singing, "Your father thought evil. You are a hair. He thought evil to you. I am going to name a hair that I have never seen here, never have I seen it around here. This hair comes from the beginning of the world [hokonamu], very far away. From there I am going call it." Thus, with the song of the bahanarotu, he calls it and it comes, and it is with that hair that the woman, man, or boy was pierced. This is the way another bahanarotu sings to take out an object; singing, singing, already he sees the object moving. His hand is over the belly or the chest where the pain is, touching, touching, singing, singing, and naming, naming, naming. Thus, the object, the bahana, moves; that hair, which the wizard put into the belly of his victim, moves. And when it moves, the bahanarotu sings, "I am going to take it out with my finger, with my hand: I know what it is that is damaging this poor woman."

Thus, the hair says, "Okay, you are the same as my father, already you are taking me out." And the bahanarotu answers, "Yes, I am taking you out. I take you out, and I call your father and ask him why he did harm to this lady friend. This is bad. You understand that we all still want to live in this world. We are all brothers, we are all children of God. So why did you do this like this?" This is what one bahanarotu said to the other. Thereafter, the bahanarotu who did the damage is silent. So the man keeps singing, "I will take you out. I take you out because you cannot do this to me, but I can do this to you." Thus, he sings and passes over all the points of the hair inside the patient's stomach, where the pain is. So, moving, singing, moving, singing, he takes one hair out. How many are there?

There is another, so he begins to sing again, and sings as he sang the first time, singing, "Why did you do this? Why? It is a bad thing: you thought evil. Don't do this, because we are brothers, we are children of God, we want to continue to live in this world; you did a bad thing." He is singing, but he is not talking with the master who put the hair there or who harmed the man; he is talking to the hair itself which is inside the stomach or chest of the patient.

Then the hair answers, "If it is you, you can take me out because you know, just like my father. My father knows, and likewise you know. Therefore, I cannot resist you, and you can control me. So, take me out." Thus, the bahanarotu takes out the hair, and in a few days the patient is better, is relieved, he or she eats, the pain subsides, and above all, the family is happy. It is true that the bahanarotu took it out, he did not deceive. The people say that if this bahanarotu had not taken out the arrows of the other bahanarotu, the patient would have died. Now, since this man came, sang, and took out the object, this poor person is today much better. This is the way that he or she is saved. This is the end, my friend.

Antonio's explanation that the pain-causing object answers the curing bahanarotu and that it is succumbing to the shaman because the shaman is as powerful as the object's father (the malevolent bahanarotu) is unique, and the song text does not indicate that this occurs. His explanation may refer to what is occurring subconsciously between him and the evil spirit while in his Theurgic State of Consciousness.

Another teacher (José Antonio Páez) explained that a bahanarotu sings section C only to extract objects that are long and flexible (kaidoko), such as string, nylon rope, hair, and so forth, but not to extract nails or other nonflexible objects. In bahanarotu shamanism, however, so much depends upon the individual shaman that curing methods vary. We have seen, for example, that some bahanarao sing to extract nails and other objects from a patient, while others do not. Antonio sang every song he knew, but this did not include a song for the extraction of any object other than a hair.

Antonio's explanation of his song text refers to two other characteristics that are important in Warao shamanistic curing: the shaman's pensamiento (thought) and the animate qualities of a normally inanimate object, in this case a hair. Warao shamans refer to the supernatural process of attaining power that occurs during TSC as pensamiento. Antonio suggests that, in the case of the malevolent bahanarotu, evil power is attained by evil thought with assistance from the ancestor wizards in the bahanarotu's cosmic world. The curing bahanarotu speaks directly to the illness-causing object that has been placed into the patient's body; and it answers him, acknowledging the curing shaman's power. This living quality of an inanimate object is also an important characteristic in the successful curing of hoa maladies (see chapter 10). Additionally, as the previous song text indicates, the curing bahanarotu names "all points of the hair," a technique whereby all parts of the object must be named before the curing power is complete. Among the Warao, prefatory, step-by-step, and ultimately complete naming is the essential power technique for curing all intrusion illnesses as well as causing them in hoarotu shamanism (see chapter 9). Moreover, naming is the essential power technique in the hoa curing songs (see chapter 10), the magical protection songs (see chapter 11), and the magical love songs (see chapter 12).

Changes, such as those described with Gerónimo's learning experience and the modern objects extracted during Primitivo's curing ritual (nail and nylon rope), occur more in bahanarotu shamanism than in other types of Warao shamanism. A bahanarotu today, for example, seldom extracts magical arrows that have been transformed into pieces of hair, thorns, or natural objects. Rather, he removes nails, pieces of nylon rope, batteries, and other objects from the industrialized world.

The Song of the Creator Bird of the Dawn

I have made several references to birds in this chapter. These include a large black bird, perhaps the magnificent frigate bird (in the context of the Mother of Seizure story), a bahana bird with the name Yoromahore that is probably the brown pelican (in bahanarotu curing song 72.8-89), and the Creator Bird of the Dawn (domu hokonomana ariawara), which is like a swallow-tailed kite with the name Mawari (songs 72.8-88, 89, 91; stories of bahana cosmology). The most important of these is the Creator Bird of the Dawn, the hokonomana bird, who is associated with the supreme deity of the eastern cosmic mountain and is the most important power source of bahanarotu shamanism.

In Spanish, Antonio called the hokonamana bird *pájaro tijeras* or scissors bird because of its long, bifurcated tail. Wilbert (1985, 180n. 3) explains that this bird is known in Venezuela "as *gavilán tijereta:* scissor-tailed kite (Waraoan: *hokonomana* or *hokono kahamana*)," although he refers to it as a swallow-tailed kite (*Elanoides forficatus*), "a shamanic tutelary spirit of highest rank" among many South American Indians (1985, 151). The scissors bird is the subject of the most important and most ancient song belonging to bahanarotu shamanism. Antonio mentioned the song of the hokonomana creator bird many times in his story about the origin of bahanarotu shamanism, which he related to Wilbert (1972b, 66–70). Several of those musical references from Antonio's story, which Wilbert entitles "The House of Tobacco Smoke," are included here:

> One day the youth who had arisen in the East spread out his arms and proclaimed his name: *Domu Hokonamana Ari-awara,* "Creator Bird of the Dawn." With his left wing he held a bow and two quivering arrows, and his right wing shook a rattle. The plumes of his body chanted incessantly the new song that was heard in the East. The thoughts of the Bird of the Dawn fell now on a house—and immediately it appeared: a round, white house made of tobacco smoke. It looked like a cloud. The singing Bird walked inside whirling his rattle.
>
> Next he wanted to have four companions. . . . Black Bee arrived with his wife. They transformed into tobacco smoke and chanted the song of the Bird of the Dawn. . . . The red Wasp arrived with his wife, transformed into smoke, and joined in the singing. . . . Termite . . . and . . . his wife . . . transformed into smoke, and learned the new song. . . . Honey Bee . . . transformed into tobacco smoke and joined in the chanting. . . . They chanted and smoked cigars.

In a more recent publication Wilbert (1985, 147–48) includes the same story with several updates.

> At the foot of the eastern World Tree-Mountain there is a hollow that contains two eggs. From it emerged a youth, the

son of the avian god of origin. Upon leaving the cave the youth adopted the form of a swallow-tailed kite, spread his wings, and pronounced his name, "Mawari." With his left wing he held a bow and two quivering arrows, and with his right wing he shook a rattle. The plumes of his body rang out the new song of bahana. Through the power of his thought, Mawari created an egg-shaped house northeast of the zenith. Made of tobacco smoke this "Cosmic Egg" looks like a cloud. . . .

To occupy his house Mawari invited four couples of insects: the black bees came to live in the black room, the wasps in the red, the termites in the yellow, and the blue bees in the blue room. Teaching them the chant of bahana, Mawari ranked his new companions below him. . . . All the inhabitants of the birthplace of bahana were changed into tobacco smoke.

Antonio sang me the song of the singing bird, which is included as recorded example 14. It is very different from all other Warao songs, and Antonio himself refers to it as a "beautiful song" in his story (Wilbert 1972b, 68): "Now teach me your beautiful song," asks the Warao youth who becomes the first human bahanarotu. The "Song of the Creator Bird of the Dawn" (chant of bahana) possesses the most extensive tone system of all Warao theurgical music, consisting of the ten pitches notated in music example 8.11. Music example 8.12 is a transcription of the complete song. As you see, hear, and follow the song text, it is clear that this song does not have a melodic pattern like most other theurgical songs but is somewhat strophic. (I have suggested strophes or verses by double spacing in the song text.) It is clear, however, that the strophic technique is not similar to European-derived music but an individually determined mixture of strophic and "through composed." It is also sung very personally and softly, as if in

Music Example 8.11. Bahanarotu "Song of the Creator Bird of the Dawn," tone system.

a dream. Indeed, in a dreamlike TSC the hokonamana bird appears to the bahanarotu apprentice and teaches him (via his mortal bahanarotu teacher) this most sacred song. The complete text of the "Song

Music Example 8.12. Bahanarotu "Song of the Creator Bird of the Dawn" (Antonio Lorenzano). Olsen Collection 72.8-96.

of the Creator Bird of the Dawn," transliterated and translated by the singer, follows as song text 8.6.

Music Example 8.12 (*continued*)

Music Example 8.12 (*continued*)

Music Example 8.12 (*continued*)

Song Text 8.6. Bahanarotu "Song of the Creator Bird of the Dawn," Antonio Lorenzano, 21 July 1972 (Olsen Collection 72.8-96)

Kasabukaha mawari domu domu sanuka, kasabukaha mawari domu domu sanuka, domu sanuka mawari mawariwitu.
This is Mawari little bird, bird, this is Mawari little bird, bird, little bird, Mawari, great Mawari.

Domu sanuka ihi hane, domu sanuka ariawara, domu sanuka ariawara hane.
You are the little bird, little creator bird, you are little creator bird.

Taisi kayukane taisi kayukane, domu sanuka ariawara, yakure hane.
With him, with him, little creator bird, it is good.

Taisi kayukane ihi naru, ihi naru ihi naru, taisi kayukane hiawihi hiawihi.
With him you go, you go, you go, with him great bird, great bird.

Arima tanukane, hiawihi hiawihi, ari arima tanukane, ori orisaba tihi tano tanonae, tane tianehe.
The father together, great bird, great bird, the father together, all together it was made, it is.

Taisi kayukane, hetehore, nohi sabukane, hia hokono, ari dokotananae, tane tiane domu sanuka.
With him, your body, substantial torso, great white bird, born with a clamor, it is little bird.

Domu sanuka ariawara, kao kwarika, kao kwarisaba, domu ariawara.
Little creator bird, wasp, for wasp, creator bird.

Domu sanuka ariawara, taisi kayukane, kamiana domu domu sanuka.

Little creator bird, with him, our spirit bird little bird.

Ihi rakate bahanarao, bahanariawara taisi ariawara, taisi-monuka.
You are like that Bahanarao, this is born bahana, it is little honey bee.

Ihi rakate, hiesia hoibuna karamunae karamunae, domu sanuka, kamiana, kao kwarika arotu.
You, like that, you are black bee, you are, little bird, our spirit, owner of wasp.

Domu sanuka, kao kwarika arotu, kamiana, utuida, kao kwarika kabo.
Little bird, owner of wasp, our spirit, in the very center, for the wasp.

Kao kwarisaba kabo, kao kwarisaba kabo, utuida ariawara tata, arotuhane.
For the wasp, for the wasp, there in the very center you are born, the true owner.

Domu sanuka ihi, tatawituhae ori nokoruba kane, hoi hoi-buna, karamuna ya nehae, karamuna ya nehae, domu sanuka domu sanuka.
You are little bird, there together in your house, black bee, the noise made clear, the noise made clear, little bird, little bird.

Ine hiesiawitu, ine hiesiawitu, ine nasaribu dibu karamuna yakore.
I enter greatly into you, I enter greatly into you, I spoke and made clear.

Maribu eku, mahoko, mua ebe tane; ihi rakate, hoibuna; kara-munao domu sanuka hokonamu
According to my word, my whiteness, it is termite; you are like that, black bee; you are little bird of the dawn.

yata yama kao kwarika, kao kwarisaba, kabo; kamiana tata di-
  awaratu; domu sanuka, tane hikaramuna, ariawara hokono-
  mana, hokonomana.
Now for wasp, for the wasp, umbilical cord; our spirit there is
  born; little bird, there you became clear, born of the dawn,
  the dawn.

Tane tianene tane tiane tane tiane, diawara hinihi diawara
  hinihi, domu sanuka domu sanuka.
It is, it is, it is, you are born, you are born, little bird, little
  bird.

Domu sanuka hokonomana, hane bahanariawara, taisi
  amawari monuka hane.
Little bird of the dawn, you are born bahana, this is Mawari
  honey bee.

Yae ye yae ye yae ye ye, amawari ye, amawari ye ye.
Yae ye yae ye yae ye ye, Mawari ye, Mawari ye ye.

The "Song of the Creator Bird of the Dawn" can be paraphrased this
way:

This is Mawari, the little bird. You are Mawari, the little creator bird. It is good with him, the little creator bird. You go together with the great bird, the father. With the father, together
it was made. It is with him that your body and the substantial
torso of the great white bird were born with a clamor. With
the little creator bird, is wasp. The little creator bird is for
wasp, and wasp is with him. Oh little creator bird, our little
spirit bird, we are Bahanarao just like that. This is born bahana. Also with him, just like that, is little honey bee, and just
like that, black bee. Oh little bird, our spirit and owner of
wasp. Oh little bird, our spirit in the very center. Little bird
also exists for wasp. There in the very center you are born. Oh
little bird, you are the true owner, and there together in your
house is black bee. The noise (of the rattle) made it clear. Oh
little bird, little bird, I enter into you. I spoke and made clear,

according to my word. My whiteness is termite. You are like that, termite. You are black bee. Oh little bird of the dawn, you are for the wasp. With the umbilical cord our spirit is born there in the center. Oh little bird, there you became clear, you, born of the dawn. It is born, it is born. You are the little bird, the little bird. Oh little bird, little swallow-tailed kite, you are born bahana. This is Mawari. Oh, oh, oh, oh Mawari. Oh, oh, oh.

After he finished singing the "Song of the Creator Bird of the Dawn," Antonio enthusiastically commented about its extreme importance and great antiquity:

This is about the history of the Warao, of the song of the Warao. This is not known now. It is very ancient. From the beginning, when the world began, this story, this song, was born. This song is about a bird that is not found around here. From the very beginning of the Warao, the spirit scissors bird appeared, and it was also there that this scissors bird which we see in this world was created. This song is about the father of the scissors bird. Nobody sees it. It is in all of the middle of the sky of the world. This bird lives there above the middle of the center of the sky. There he has his house, his bed. There he eats, sleeps, and has all his little things. And there he will have his family. Now, this bird begins to sing as I sang. He sings in the night, at about midnight. He sings only once, and does not sing during the day because he does not like to. He sings every night at twelve midnight. He said, "I am not made to sing during the day. I am made here in the middle of the center of the sky to sing only at night, at twelve midnight. When I have a dream, then I begin to sing. If I sleep and do not have a dream, then I do not sing. I am the father of the scissors bird." This scissors bird that you see in this world was created for me. I am a great bahanarotu, and the bird is also a bahanarotu. When you see the bird flying above you can see that he has a white chest with a slightly dark back. The feathers look white on its chest and on its back they look rather dark, slightly greenish. This bird is called the hokonomana bird in

Warao. Now, a person, when he learns bahana, also sings with
the hokonomana bird. You have to talk to this hokonomana
bird so that he helps you to sing. Every bahanarotu does this.
That is all, my friend.

The text of the song introduces several important aspects in bahanarotu shamanism. First is the union of the father bird with the son
bird, who were created together according to the song. The father bird
is given the name hiawihi, which, according to Barral (1957, 112), consists of two parts. The first, hia or jía, is a bird commonly called cagón
in Venezuela, a vulgar term for a person afflicted with diarrhea. This is
symbolically important in bahanarotu shamanism when we recall that
the "big pains" are the basic disorders that a bahanarotu cures. Because the cagón bird releases big stools (judging from its name), it is
the metaphoric bird of diarrheal diseases among the Warao. The
second part of the father bird is wihi (uíji), which is a gray wild pigeon
with a white neck known as paloma torcaz in Spanish (Barral 1957,
205). The bird is symbolically used in this song for the father bird because its color resembles the tobacco-smoke abode of the supreme
lord of the east.

The previous translation of the names of the four insects differs
somewhat from the Warao terms used by Wilbert (1985). For example,
simonuka is "little honey bee," from simo arao sanuka (Barral 1957,
188) or "little owner of honey," a "bee." Wilbert (1985, 161), however,
obtains his translation from asebe, meaning "blue bee," and derives
wasp from the Warao term for honey, included as tomonoho-simo. I
interpret wasp from kao kwarika because Barral (1957, 223) translates
kuajene as wasp (jene means "yellow," according to Barral). The term
tomonoho does not occur in my version of "Song of the Creator Bird."
In my translation termite is the meaning of mua (Barral 1957, 152),
while Wilbert (1985, 160) derives termite from ahi simo. According to
Barral (1957, 26), ahi (aji) is a shortened form of ahi-mu, while simo
means "honey" (p. 188). Finally, both Wilbert's source and my recorded
version of "Song of the Creator Bird" use hoi, meaning "black bee."

The habi sanuka rattle is implied in my translation by the Warao
word karamuna, meaning "noise" (Barral 1957, 127). The bahanarotu's rattle is referred to many times in Wilbert's versions of the bahana myth; and he relates its shape, rustling interior noise, and repro-

ductive power symbolism to the termites' oval home or nest built around a tree branch (1985, 155–58) (see also chapter 4).

The Warao term kabo (kabu) is translated as "umbilical cord" (Barral 1957, 125) and refers to either the axis mundi of the Warao cosmic vault or "the rope-bridge that connects the Cosmic Egg with the zenith and the central world axis" (Wilbert 1985, 160). Through this cosmic umbilical cord the original bahana family was born, as the song implies.

Bahanarotu songs are unique because of their melodic variety and functional diversity. We have seen and heard curing songs with narrow ranges, and dream songs with very wide ranges. We have even heard the aesthetic word "beautiful" (*bonita*) applied to one of the dream songs by the singer himself. The next chapter pertains to another type of Warao shaman, the hoarotu, also noted for his extensive use of song; the hoarotu, however, sings as a matter of death and life.

9   Hoarotu Shaman Songs

Hoarotu shamanism is the most feared of the three Warao shamanic divisions because of its association with the westernmost cosmic realm of darkness. Wilbert (1972b, 73) refers to it as "dark" shamanism because of its association with the absence of light and its preoccupation with death.

The Hoarotu Teachers

José Antonio Páez, from Moriki Hana on the lower Winikina River, was my primary teacher in hoarotu shamanism. His people consider him to be the most knowledgeable hoarotu in the Winikina area. According to him, he studied two years to become a hoarotu. By contrast, his elderly friend Jaime Zapata, who sang several songs with him during our recording sessions, studied hoarotu shamanism for only three days. I also recorded another elderly singer, Francisco, from Hana Kahamana on the upper Winikina River, a master shaman with the combined knowledge of a wisiratu, bahanarotu, and hoarotu. Although the village of Hana Kahamana is only a few miles upstream from Yaruara Akoho (see figure 1.3), the people there have little to do with their neighbors on the Winikina River. Nevertheless, both Francisco and his younger brother, Miguel, were brought in to try to cure Luís Jiménez. Three shamans from Yaruara Akoho were also hired to sing together to cure Luís, including two hoarao named Gabriel Sánchez and Biwa Tovar, and my bahanarotu teacher, Gerónimo Velásquez, who, I then discovered, is also knowledgeable in hoarotu shamanism. I was permitted to record their complete late-night rituals.

Hoarotu Shamanism

At the western terminus of the world where the sun dies, according to Warao belief, is Hoebo, the lord of death, the Supreme Hoa, embodied as a scarlet macaw (*Ara chloroptera*) with the color of the setting sun and dusk. It is the hoarotu's mission to provide human food for Hoebo and the Hoarao or souls of dead hoarotu shamans who live with him. (Hoarao is the plural form of hoarotu. When lowercased, the word refers to living and practicing hoarotu shamans; capitalized, Hoarao refers to the spirits of the deceased hoarotu shamans living with Hoebo.) Wilbert (1972b, 73) writes about Hoebo's supernatural abode, which is also known as the hoebo:

> The stench of human cadavers and clotted blood saturates the air, and the stream of *hoarotu* shamans who come from all parts of Warao-land with cadavers hanging head down from their shoulders is endless. It has to be endless if the Supreme *Hoa* and spirit companions, called *hoarao,* are to continue living: the former by eating human hearts and livers, the latter by devouring the bodies. All *hoarao* in the *Hoebo* drink human blood from a gigantic canoe made of human bone.

If no food is provided, the Warao believe, these lords of the western-most cosmic realm will bring death and destruction to the world. This death is not swift, and it is metaphorically related to diseases that fea-ture loss of blood, as Wilbert (1983, 360) explains: "The cannibal god of the West, the Scarlet Macaw, kills by means of hemorrhagic diseases like bloody dysentery, amoebic and bacillary. He is a strangler who overpowers his victims with a snare of tobacco smoke. Typical of this slow death by asphyxiation is 'the incurable cough' (pulmonary tuber-culosis), when the blood-coughing patient is slowly consumed by the god before the very eyes of his terrified family and friends."

All this began long ago in mythological times; and it was guided by song and instrumental music, as the following story makes clear (Wilbert 1972b, 73–74):

> There was an old man by the name of Miana (Without Sight). As his name implies, he had no eyes. He lived alone in the zenith and begot a son whose name, like that of the Abode of Darkness, was Hoebo. Hoebo had learned to sing like his fa-ther, in order to activate the search for blood by the celestial umbilicus. One day Hoebo wanted to visit the Supreme *Hoa.* Father and son set out on their journey. They heard the hum-ming chant of the Spirits of the West when they had gone

only half way. They also beheld the bright lights of white and yellow penetrating the darkness of the *Hoebo*. "See the *hoa ahutu* artery," said Miana to his son. "Listen to its humming." The youth became very anxious to reach the Supreme *Hoa*. Then his eyes fell on a beautiful girl below him in the Warao village. He decided to marry her, but when he lowered himself head first from the *hoa ahutu* umbilicus to the dancing platform in the center of the village, a jealous rival for the girl cut off Hoebo's head. The sphere at the end of the blood duct fell to the ground and disappeared. All the people present suddenly felt sick with a sharp pain in their stomachs. The elastic blood duct snapped back to the West.

Another narrative suggests that the humming that attracted Hoebo are the sounds of Warao aerophones such as the isimoi, the hekunukabe, and the muhusemoi, as related in the following story (Wilbert 1969, 58–60, "Origin of the hoarotus"):

A Warao man had a younger sister who was a very beautiful girl. She had a young male friend with whom she made love. They were very happy, and the young man behaved with her as if she was his wife. . . . But at the same time this woman talked with another man whom she also took as a lover and whom she entertained. This second man did not know about the first man.

But her brother saw them, and he said to her: "What are you doing, sister? If your first lover finds out about this he will become very angry. You, my sister, are behaving badly." It is true that his sister entertained herself too much with the second young man: it became bad. Therefore, the brother decided to organize a festival. When all was prepared, he said to his sister: "Little sister, I have prepared a festival: be careful that you do not ruin it. When the first young man arrives, nonchalantly go and meet and greet him kindly. But, when the second young man comes do not look him in the face. Only look at the first man and have a good time with him, but do not take the opportunity to play with the second man. Precisely for this reason I am preparing my festival, and I want it to be a great festival. Be careful you don't ruin it for me."

These were the bits of advice that the brother gave to his little sister.

The day of the festival arrived. . . . Once more the brother advised his sister: "Be very careful. . . . If you are truly my sister, pay attention to what I say: You must dance well at my festival and not look into the face of that second young man; do not give him the eye. Pay attention to what I have told you, and be careful you do not forget it. . . ." That is what the brother said.

Then the dance began. A large quantity of Warao danced the [habi sanuka] dance of the little maracas. Still the brother of this woman came to give her advice: "Careful, little sister, don't forget what I have said. Now I am going to dance."

Now the second young man came. He heard the sounds of the festival from afar, and he saw that the Warao were already dancing. Seeing him, the brother of the girl began to tremble. This second young man came playing an isimoi, and the isimoi said: "If those who are before me behave well I will do them well." This young man had many wind instruments, and he began to play another isimoi which said: "If they behave well I will do them well." Then he played a hekunukabe flute, and it said: "If those who are before me behave well I will do them well, if they behave badly I will do them badly." He put that flute down and took another, the muhusemoi. This deer bone flute said the same thing: "If those who are before me behave well I will do them well, if they behave badly something bad will happen to them right now." Upon hearing this, the brother of the woman turned and said to her: "Be careful, little sister, and do not forget that which I said to you; do not ruin the festival." Meanwhile, as the Warao danced the first youth, whose name was Hoebo, arrived. Hoebo was already above the Warao when they danced, but he lowered himself down even more from above. At that moment the other young man (the flutist) appeared and immediately sat down in a hammock with his machete. He tried to force the girl to look him in the eye, but she turned her glance from him and looked at Hoebo instead. Then the ungrateful young man became very angry and, with his machete in hand, raced toward the center of the area where the Warao were dancing. There he swung his machete at Hoebo who was just lowering himself down from above, and he cut him completely in half. As soon as he split Hoebo in two, all the Warao who were dancing felt ill. They remained like that in their misfortune.

This young male musician-butcher was named Abajera (scarlet macaw = lit. "he of painful death" . . .). The youth who had been cut in half with the machete was called Hoebo ("spirit owner of all the Hoatuma"). Half of Hoebo's body went off to the West on its own volition to be in the middle of the western Warao; and, for that reason, there are many hoarotu shamans among them. The other half of his body went eastward, and because of that there are many hoarotu shamans among those Warao as well. If this marvelous body of Hoebo had remained intact here, all the Warao would be hoarotu shamans, even the children and the women; everybody would understand about Hoa. But because of their capriciousness, all the Warao from around here remain disgraceful and ignorant.

Today's Warao explain that Hoebo remains in his abode of darkness at the place of the western cosmic mountain in the aitona, the end of the universe, cut off from the rest of the universe. His soul, however, remains on the lesser mountain at the western end of earth. Only hoarotu shamans can traverse this lonely road on their celestial journeys to the hoebo. On their way they hear musical sounds that are perhaps the macabre remnants of Abajera's clarinet and flute playing. Wilbert (1975a, 173–74) writes, however, that what the hoarotu travelers hear is "the continuous hooting of the trumpet of the Macaw . . . in this case . . . made not of a conch shell but of a human skull. The piercing sounds of a clarinet can also be heard. The instrument is made of long human bones and has a skull as its resonance chamber." These are the calls of Hoebo and the Hoarao, aerophonic signals and identifiers, calling out to the cosmic travelers who bring human food.

What is a Hoa? Using a capital *H*, I make a distinction between the Hoa found in hoarotu shamanism and the hoa power songs discussed in chapters 10 through 13. The Hoa of hoarotu shamanism, like the hebu of wisiratu shamanism and the bahana of bahanarotu shamanism, is a spiritual essence of something that causes illness when it is activated by a hoarotu. Among the essences in Warao shamanism, the Hoa is the most deadly because hoarotu shamanism is associated with death. Its entire existence, paradoxically, depends on death. A Hoa is the spiritual essence of any object, animal, or intangible entity that has been named and, therefore, given great destructive power, either by a mortal hoarotu or by an immortal Hoarotu living in the hoebo.

As "owner of Hoa" (Hoa arotu), the hoarotu shaman has two Hoa spirit "sons" dwelling within his chest, which he acquires during his strenuous initiation. Through dreams the spirit sons communicate with their hoarotu father, mediating between him and the hoebo with the purpose of telling him when Hoebo or the Hoarao need human food. These spirit helpers then aid the hoarotu in inflicting illness and death upon his victims in his malevolent role as provider of human food for the Hoebo and the Hoarao. Paradoxically, they also help the hoarotu to cure Hoa-caused illnesses in his benevolent role as healer. While the hoarotu is similar to the wisiratu and the bahanarotu because he has spirit helpers living within his chest, the relationship between the hoarotu and his spirit sons differs from the other relationships. The hoarotu, for example, is not in communication with his spirit helpers and does not use voice masking while inflicting or curing. Likewise, his relationship with his spirit sons is not one in which he asks them for their help; on the contrary, they ask *him* for help by begging for food. The hoarotu must provide his spirit sons with food as any father must feed his children. Their food, however, is human blood. Four times the hoarotu feeds his spirit helpers tobacco, but the fifth time when they "demand their proper food—human blood—he can no longer turn them away unsatisfied" (Wilbert 1972b, 77).

A hoarotu acquires his inflicting and curing powers during an extensive initiation period that includes fasting, smoking tobacco, and learning the song formulas for both types of power. During this time he receives his spirit sons in his chest who will assist him with his kaidoko tobacco-smoke snares and his deadly magical arrows. In the shaman's inflicting and curing roles, the spirit helpers manipulate the hoarotu's kaidoko snares; and in the curing phase they search out the illness-causing essence within the patient's body. The hoarotu's kaidoko tobacco-smoke snares are activated during inflicting and curing when they sinuate from the corners of the hoarotu's mouth like tendrils or tentacles. In his malevolent role the hoarotu's kaidokotuma (plural form) wind out from his mouth and reach toward his victim, ultimately wrapping themselves around the latter's neck to weaken him or her through strangulation (Wilbert 1972b, 76). At this point the hoarotu sings mentally to name the Hoa, which can be a transformed object, animal, or intangible entity whose essence he shoots off as a magical arrow that travels through the air via the smoke of his wina cigar to be lodged into the victim's body. The Warao say that a victim "está flechado," meaning that he "has been shot with arrows" (Spanish flechar, "to shoot arrows at").

The cure for this type of illness can be effected only by another hoarotu who, by singing aloud, must name the transformed object, animal, or intangible entity whose essence has been shot into the body of the victim by the malevolent hoarotu. In this benevolent role, the curing hoarotu's own kaidoko tobacco-smoke snares wrench the illness-causing Hoa from the patient's body after the Hoa has been named through song (Wilbert 1972b, 77). Because the object, animal, or intangible entity has been transformed by the power of Hoa, it is itself referred to as the Hoa. The hoarotu, for example, will sing "this is Hoa," referring to the entity that he has just named. Once properly named, the essence will vibrate within the patient; and the hoarotu will remove it by massage. When it is finally in his hands, he makes a fist and blows forcibly into it, sending the Hoa into the cosmos from whence it came.

The hoarotu uses unaccompanied song for both inflicting and curing illnesses, with a repertory consisting of more than five hundred curing songs for an accomplished practitioner, according to José Antonio. Because he used song to mean the words of the song, however, the number of songs is actually infinite because the number of entities that can become Hoatuma is also infinite. These hoarotu songs can be placed into two broad categories—inflicting and curing—which are almost as different musically as they are functionally.

Hoarotu Inflicting Songs

According to José Antonio, a hoarotu must sing his inflicting song mentally, facing the person or object he will kill or destroy. While he is singing to himself, he continually smokes a long wina cigar and fixedly glares at his victim. And as he sings and glares, his tobacco-smoke kaidokotuma leave the corners of his mouth to strangle and weaken his victim. After the recipient is properly weakened, the shaman then mentally sings to send the Hoa arrows into the victim for the kill. José Antonio explained that a hoarotu shaman sings his inflicting songs aloud only when he teaches them to an apprentice or when he is alone in his house or canoe and feels the need to practice them.

This malevolent function of the hoarotu is accepted by other Warao, who realize that the Supreme Hoa must be fed so the world does not come to an end. In 1972, José Antonio and Jaime Zapata noncontextually sang eleven inflicting songs for me without hesitation. The songs were all incomplete, however (a fact I did not realize until I had returned to Los Angeles); I returned to the delta in the spring of 1973 to find José Antonio and have him teach me several complete hoarotu inflicting songs. He explained that the complete songs must only be sung contextually, and to do so can cause great harm. He agreed to teach me several complete songs and allow me to record them, but only if I would become his apprentice and pay him the same amount he had paid his teacher to learn the songs. After agreeing on terms (which included money, a new miner's head lantern and batteries to use for hunting, several pants and shirts, and cloth for his two wives), José Antonio pondered on what to kill or destroy, explaining that he no longer kills humans and that he naturally did not want to kill his dogs or destroy the moriche palm tree behind his house. At that point I suggested he destroy my tape recorders, to which he quickly agreed. I then added that perhaps he should only destroy my inexpensive Concord cassette recorder rather than the expensive Nagra III, which was not mine but loaned to me by UCLA's Institute of Ethnomusicology. He thought for a minute and then said no, explaining that he could not destroy just one machine without destroying the other because the magical arrows could not tell the difference between the two. I consented, and José Antonio sang two complete songs to destroy both my and UCLA's tape recorders (recorded example 15). These complete versions are each at least fifteen times the length of the longest incomplete song that he recorded for me months before. The outcome of that afternoon of magical tape recorder destruction is a story in itself, and I will relate it after we first musically and textually analyze the songs.

Of the 1972 excerpts, six were sung by José Antonio and five by him and Jaime singing together. Although the songs were sung in duet fashion, José Antonio explained that two shamans would sing together to inflict illness, death, or destruction only on very rare occasions, and then mentally rather than aloud. In such a situation they would have to be brothers or extremely close friends. In an actual inflicting ritual the two would sit together, concentrating on and mentally singing about their victim; glaring at or in the direction of him, her, or it; and continually smoking their long wina cigars.

A hoarotu inflicting song consists of two sections that I call A and B because they can be differentiated musically, textually, and functionally. As a hoarotu begins to inflict illness, kill, or destroy, he first lights a wina cigar and begins to sing mentally, the latter action immediately activating his kaidoko tobacco-smoke snares. As the kaidokotuma wind their way to the victim, the hoarotu continues to think-sing the A section of his inflicting song while mentally naming the animal or object whose essence he will later shoot through the air and into the victim's body via his magical arrows. The animal or object, as it is being named, is becoming the Hoa. Section B, mentally sung without pause after section A, occurs when the Hoa (animal, object, or intangible entity) has been properly named and the kaidoko snares have weakened the hoarotu's victim. In section B the hoarotu names the person or object to be destroyed and also asks Hoebo and other spirits to assist him with the magical arrows.

The melodic contour of a hoarotu's section A inflicting song is descending. Therefore, like all other Warao shamanistic music we have studied so far, its tone system is written in a descending order of pitches (see music example 9.1). The range of section A is relatively narrow and is very similar to that found in section A of wisiratu curing music. As in most Warao shamanistic music, the minor-third interval is prominent, as shown in music example 9.2—a typical hoarotu inflicting song, section A pattern. (Listen to recorded example 15, part A.)

Music Example 9.1. Hoarotu inflicting song, section A, tone system.

Music Example 9.2. Hoarotu inflicting song, section A (José Antonio Páez). Olsen Collection 72.8-79a.

Section B of a hoarotu inflicting song (the most essential part, according to José Antonio) is based on two pitches, a principal tone and a supporting tone, plus a downward glissando following each supporting tone. Because the melodic pattern of section B ascends, the tone system is written in an ascending manner (see music example 9.3). This is the only type of Warao shamanistic music that ascends rather than descends; and the result, partially seen in the transcription as music example 9.4, is a very emphatic and intense contrast to Warao curing music. Much of the intensity results from the singer's conscious or unconscious use of microtonal rises in pitch (upward drift). The inflicting song, section B, sung by José Antonio and partially notated as music example 9.4, contains an upward drift of 664 cents, a rise of nearly a fifth. The only way to experience this musical phenomenon fully is to hear it in recorded example 15, especially in part B, which includes beginning, middle, and ending portions of the song. The upward drift is almost imperceptible unless it is compared to a nonfluctuating standard, such as a Korg tuner, or unless the listener has perfect pitch. A visual representation of the upward drift can be made with Western notation, although it is most useful when combined with the recording. Music example 9.4 is notated in three parts (a, b, and c), reflecting the beginning, middle, and ending of José Antonio's inflicting song, section B. Upward drift is indicated by the "key" signatures, which should be interpreted as signifying a gradual and microtonal rise in pitch. (The upward arrows indicate an approximate quarter tone sharp.) At the beginning of the except in part a, the first pitch (D) is 11 cents flat and the second pitch (E) is 15 cents flat. Part b represents the same song 7 minutes, 36 seconds later, after the shaman rose in pitch approximately a major third. In part b of music example 9.4, the first (F sharp) and second pitches (G sharp) are 20 cents flat. At the song's end, represented by part c, the hoarotu singer rose in pitch to his maximum level: the final two pitches in the transcription (G sharp and A sharp) are respectively 53 and 49 cents sharp. The possible significance of such microtonal rising during theurgical singing is discussed in chapter 15.

Music Example 9.3. Hoarotu inflicting song, section B, tone system.

During the course of the thirteen performances of section A that I recorded, my hoarotu teachers named creatures, spirits, objects, and a variety of intangible entities, all of them essences appearing in the spirit world of hokonamu, in the easternmost part of the cosmic world. Because hokonamu is conceived of as the beginning of the world where the sun rises, it has an association with dawn. The presence of hokonamu is extremely important in the shamanic world of the Warao, for the wisiratu and the bahanarotu also appeal to the spirits in the east. The hoarotu, although directly associated with the spirit world in the west, also obtains many of his Hoa essences from the

Music Example 9.4. Hoarotu inflicting song, section B (José Antonio Páez). Olsen Collection 72.8-79a.

ta-ma-ha sa-ba i-ne   ta-ma-ha wi-tu-ma sa-ba i-ne

ma-hi-na   ko-bo-ka-ne   ma-hi-na   he-ko-bo-ka-ne

he-ko-bo-ka-ne   ko-bo-ka-ne   ma-hi-na   i-ta-ta-ba-ne

ka-sa-bu-ka-ha ya-na i-ne   ka-sa-bu-ka-ha ya-na i-ne

ta-ma-ha   ha-te-ko-re   ma-ki-na   o-bo-no-na ya-ka-ra

ya-ka-rai-da   wa-ro-ra ya-ka-ra   ya-ka-rai-da

ta-ma-ha sa-ba i-ne ma-hi-na   ko-bo-ka-ne   continues

Music Example 9.4 (*continued*)

Music Example 9.4 (*continued*)

powers in hokonamu. The hokonamu animals that my hoarotu teachers chose to become Hoa are a baba (a small species of crocodile, *Caiman crocodylus*), a water snake, a hebu bird, a humpback cow, a dog, and a domesticated bird. The Hoa spirits of the west that were selected include a hebu who is a leader of darkness, a small hebu, and a bachelor hebu, while the chosen Hoa objects of another realm were a hebu mataro rattle, a hebu's small house, the burning tip of a hebu's cigar, the hebu's sweat when he smokes his cigar, the hebu's fire, a foreign iron, the earth and its essences, and a white-haired horse of the Creoles. The numerous intangible entities that were named include peritonitis of the sea; the clouds of twilight; the coldness and vapor of the clouds of twilight; the silence of hokonamu; the words of a tape recorder; the prettiness of the lights on a hill in hokonamu; the vapor of a power generator; the movements of a horse's tail; and the essences of the earth such as its ornaments, silence, coldness, teeth, large body, and movement.

The essences of secondary objects are named before the naming of the final or complete essence. For example, the tail, waist, skin, scales, and neck of the baba as well as the sound that it produces with its scales must be named before the complete object, the baba itself, can be named. Similarly, the movements of the dog, such as its standing, walking, looking, arriving, and tail wagging, must be named before the dog itself can be named as Hoa. It is easy to understand how a hoarotu can have a repertory of more than five hundred songs because they are differentiated by the content found within their song texts. Indeed, there are as many different texts as there are objects, animals, and intangible entities whose essences can be named. The Warao believe that so many of their people die because the hoarotu has an almost unlimited quantity of essences he can name to help him kill, destroy, or cure; and their fear of hoarotu shamanism is strong because of its great danger. During curing, time is always of the essence because the patient is dying a slow and painful death.

As incredible as these objects and animals may seem to the outsider, they are very credible to the Warao because they exist as Hoatuma in the spirit world, their other reality. Many of the animals, of course, are everyday creatures such as the baba and the dog, while others are not commonly found in the delta, such as the horse and the humpback cow. But the reality of the animals, objects, and other entities in Warao shamanism is in the supernatural world. José Antonio explained that the humpback cow, for example, could be replaced by a horse or a bull and that one of those animals comes to look for and carry off a wisiratu when he dies. The animal is, in other words, a psychopomp, a supernatural guide that leads a soul to the afterlife. The hoarotu knows only in his pensamiento (literally "thought"; his trance or TSC) what each Hoa entity is.

The use of the essence of a machine as Hoa is of recent origin, arriving with the introduction of Creole and Western technology into the delta. One can easily imagine, for example, how a machine such as generator, capable of producing electric lights at a mission or a sawmill, becomes a power symbol in hoarotu shamanism, especially because a bright light existed long ago in the hoebo or "Abode of Darkness," according to Warao mythology (Wilbert 1972b, 73–74). Even today, artificial light causes fear among some Warao elders. Another machine-related power essence is the ability of a tape recorder to "grab" human words. José Antonio explained that in the song to destroy my tape recorders, he named not only the words of my machines but also the words of *all* the tape recorders of the Creoles. Lacking a Warao term for tape recorder, the shaman uses the Spanish-derived word makina (máquina), as shown in the song text of my transcription of his inflicting song (music example 9.4, parts a and b) and clearly heard in recorded example 15 when he sings the words "aya-makina" (literally, "well-dressed machine," glossed as "high-quality tape recorder with the good voice").

Section B of a hoarotu inflicting song is used to name the victim and indicate the exact area of the human body or object that will be inflicted by the Hoa. In it the hoarotu speaks directly to the Hoatuma, commanding them to kill or destroy. Song text 9.1 is a translation of the complete text of the inflicting song sung by José Antonio to destroy my tape recorders. (It was translated by the singer with assistance from Cesáreo Soto.)

Song Text 9.1. Hoarotu Inflicting Song, José Antonio Páez, March 1973 (Olsen Collection 73.3-1)

A.

This is the Hoa.

This is the hebu that belongs to the Creoles who live on the hill.

It is a hebu of the ornaments of the hill that belongs to the
   Creoles.
This is the white-haired horse that is standing on top of the
   hill next to the Creole's house.
This horse produces a great fright.
This is the white horse of the Creoles.
This white horse has its hoofs upon the hill.
This horse that is standing there is quiet and silent.
This horse that is silent has a large stomach that is hanging.
This white horse is pregnant with a colt.
Inside the stomach of this horse she has her small son.
It is the movement of the son inside the horse's stomach.
After the son was born, blood came out from the horse's
   stomach.
After the birth the hill was covered with blood.
After the birth, visitors came to see the horse.
All of the movements of the horse's tail are named.
The movement of the horse's tail that is hanging down is
   named.
This is the Hoa.

B.
Oh Hoa, I am for the foreign machines.
It is this, the large horse of the Creoles.
With the white hair of the horse I name the insides of these
   foreign machines of high quality.
Oh Hoa, destroy these foreign machines of high quality,
   which speak well.
Destroy the entire bodies of these machines, together with
   their insides.
I am the one who is saying all this in order to destroy them.
   Destroy them, break them to pieces, and inside of them, let
   all of their parts be lost.
Oh great scissors in hokonamu, you will destroy them.
Together with your body and the movements of your sharp
   blades, I will destroy the machines of the foreigner.
I say to you, oh scissors, so you will cut and destroy these ma-
   chines.

With the scissors of hokonamu I will destroy the machines inside their bodies.

With all of the body of the scissors, with the sharp blades and
the handle, I am going to destroy the high-quality machines
of the foreigner.

The scissors of hokonamu will destroy with its sharp blades
all of the cables and wires that are inside the machines.

With my sharp and filed teeth, I will destroy all of the cables
and wires of the machines.

Inside of you, oh foreign machines with the good voices, I am
going to place the Hoa.

It is with the white plate that is in hokonamu. This is a large
clay plate.

With this I am going to destroy the bodies and the throats of
the machines.

Prepare yourself, oh Hoebo, get ready, together with your
body, your chest, and your throat.

Hear my words, oh Hoebo, and prepare yourself.

I call you for nothing else than for these foreign-made machines.

Oh Hoebo, with your breath—I, with all of this, am calling
you for these foreign-made machines.

With all of your breath I ask you, Hoebo, to send the Hoa in
order to grab and destroy these well-made machines of the
foreigner.

For these machines I am going to send off my breath.

My breath is for the well-made foreign machines which have
well-made throats.

I send off all of my breath. This is Hoa.

As the bahanarotu shaman at times extracts objects from the industrialized world, so the hoarotu shaman is also influenced by industrial-
ization. In this complete inflicting Hoa sung to destroy my Nagra III
tape recorder and Concord cassette recorder, José Antonio first mentions "the hebu of the ornaments of the hill that belongs to the Creoles." Hills play an important role in Warao cosmology (see chapter 2).
When Wilbert and I visited the southern world mountain, Karoshima,
in the summer of 1974, we recognized it as a slight hill that houses a

mine, visible for several miles. In the evening it is possible to see lights
on the hill, the "ornaments of the hill" as the song text says. Such an
industrialized phenomenon has a great affect on the Warao, and it
easily becomes a power object. Another object of acculturation in this
inflicting Hoa is a white-haired horse standing on top of a hill. Horses,
of course, are not a part of Warao culture; therefore, the shaman uses
the Spanish-derived word "akawayo" (caballo) when singing about the
white horse on the hill. The development of the horse theme (that is,
its hoofs upon the hill, its silence, its pregnancy, the movement of the
colt while in the mare's womb, and the afterbirth) are all prefatory to
the final naming of the movement of the horse's tail. It is this last
essence, the movement of the horse's tail, that was named as a Hoa to
destroy my tape recorders. José Antonio's appeal to and command of
a "great scissors in hokonamu" is another example of acculturation because scissors are not an aspect of traditional Warao culture. He calls
upon a scissors spirit to cut all of the cables and wires inside the bodies
of the machines. Then, in a grand effort as a transformed shaman, José
Antonio himself becomes the Hoa and sings that he, with his sharp,
filed teeth, will destroy all the cables and wires of my machines.

In a manner similar to the prefatory naming of the Hoa to cause an
infliction, the hoarotu must also name all the parts of the person or object to be destroyed before naming the complete entity itself as the
final statement. Unfamiliar with the inner mechanisms of a tape
recorder, José Antonio speaks of the bodies and throats of the
recorders much as if he were naming the voice-producing parts of a
human. He then solicits the help of a large white clay plate from
hokonamu to aid him in the destruction of the machines. Finally, he
commands Hoebo himself, the son of Miana, who together are the
most powerful Hoarao in the land of the living dead and eternal darkness at the westernmost edge of the world, to send the Hoa via José Antonio's breath into the machines to destroy them. The hoarotu, master
of the Hoa and transformed by the power of Hoebo, sends off the Hoa
arrows himself with his breath. "This song," explained José Antonio,
"is so powerful that both tape recorders will be completely destroyed
within two weeks." Had he desired to destroy the machines immediately, he would have smoked a long wina cigar and at the end of the
song glared and growled at the machines, all the time blowing tobacco
smoke at them. Fearful, however, of destroying me as well because of

the power of the additional arrows and my proximity to the machines (I was sitting next to them), he refrained from doing so.

Now that many years have passed I can tell the complete story about José Antonio's inflicting songs sung to destroy my tape recorders. When I returned to UCLA in the spring of 1973 I explained to the sound technician in the former Institute of Ethnomusicology that the Nagra tape recorder I had borrowed had a musical spell cast upon it in order to destroy it. Being very familiar with the supernatural power of music because of his research in Bali, the technician asked me to place the tape recorder in the corner of a particular storage room; he wanted nothing to do with a cursed tape recorder. Shortly thereafter I received my doctorate and moved to Tallahassee, Florida. The Institute of Ethnomusicology at UCLA soon lost its funding and was dissolved, resulting in the early retirement of many of its staff members, including the sound technician. Several months later the Nagra III tape recorder was taken into the field by a student who soon discovered that the machine would not function. Suspecting faulty batteries, the student opened the back of the Nagra's case only to discover that the 12 D-cell batteries (they had never been removed since the hoarotu's song of destruction) had leaked acid that had corroded and eaten away all the internal wires and many parts of the machine, just as José Antonio had said (personal communication with Andrew Toth). Moreover, my Concord cassette recorder ceased to function after about six months. It began to "eat" tapes and one day had to be forcibly opened with a pliers, which destroyed it. Both these incidents are perhaps the result of neglect or planned obsolescence—but then, José Antonio never really described the precise details of the machines' demise.

Hoarotu Curing Songs

While curing, a hoarotu sits next to his patient's hammock, lights a wina cigar, and begins to sing, trying to name the illness-causing Hoa. When he names the correct Hoa, it begins to vibrate within the body of the patient, causing an outward movement of the patient's body that is visible to the hoarotu. The shaman then sings, saying that he will take out the Hoa and save the patient. The Hoa is removed by massaging the inflicted part of the body and squeezing out the evil spirit, which is then blown away by the hoarotu's breath. During the actual removal, the shaman does not sing.

During a curing ritual more than one hoarotu may sing at a time, depending on the severity of the illness or the social status of the victim. Multipart singing took place in Yaruara Akoho during the summer of 1972, when Luís Jiménez suddenly became seriously ill. After several days the local Catholic missionary, Padre Damián del Blanco, arrived and diagnosed Luís's ailment as a stroke. Very soon after the stroke occurred, wisiratu, bahanarotu, and hoarotu shamans were brought in to try individually to effect a cure; however, all three failed. Next, two hoarao tried and later that same evening three shamans sang together, first for forty-five minutes and then for thirty minutes. None of them had any success. The next day I discussed the past day's events with my friends, who explained that as many as five hoarotu shamans can sing together on certain occasions. When multiple hoarao perform together, each sings different words, trying to name the Hoa that is causing the illness. Time is very short in Hoa illness, and in extremely serious cases multiple hoarotu shamans have a greater chance of naming the illness-causing Hoa.

One of the specialists hired to cure Luís Jiménez during the first day of his illness was Francisco, a powerful combined wisiratu, bahanarotu, and hoarotu from Hana Kahamana. At 10:30 in the morning on 27 July 1972, Francisco sang alone to attempt a cure; you can hear his solo performance as recorded example 16. As you listen to his curing song, you can tell it is a daytime ritual because you can hear the chickens and roosters. Usually hoarotu curing is done at night, as are the curing rituals of the wisiratu and bahanarotu. Luís Jiménez, however, was both a very sick man and a wealthy, important political figure. Therefore, curing ceremonies for him were nearly continuous, day and night. Francisco's solo performance was followed a few minutes later by a ritual curing duet when he was joined by his younger brother Miguel. As you listen to their duet on recorded example 17, you hear an incredible phenomenon—Francisco sings an upward drift while Miguel maintains a precise pitch level. There is no musical transcription of this performance because it would be impossible to render faithfully such microtonal rising; it has to be heard. In spite of their complex polyphony, however, their musical therapy had no effect on the patient; and they immediately returned home. Several evenings later, on 30 July 1972, three shamans from Yaruara Akoho were called in to sing together to cure Luís: Gabriel Sánchez, Biwa Tovar, and Gerónimo Velásquez. Gabriel began the singing, and one minute and twenty seconds later he was joined by the other two singers. Once the polyphony was established, Biwa and Gerónimo sang a fifth above Gabriel. An excerpt of their lengthy performance, which began at approximately 8:30 P.M., can be heard in recorded example 18.

Hoarotu curing songs are the most complex of Warao shamanistic curing songs because they have the largest vocal range. Additionally, unlike wisiratu and bahanarotu singers who mask their voices much of the time, the hoarotu always sings with a full, unmasked voice. The basic melodic pattern (5 4 ♭3 1) is nearly identical to the wisiratu and bahanarotu melodic patterns used for naming, as shown by the typical hoarotu curing melodic pattern notated in music example 9.5. An excerpt from a noncontextual hoarotu curing song sung by José Antonio Páez is transcribed in music example 9.6. During an actual curing ritual, a hoarotu may sing with a range that exceeds an octave, although his basic spread remains approximately a fifth. Of the thirteen curing songs recorded noncontextually, twelve are based on the intervallic span of a fifth, while the other example, sung by a wisiratu knowledgeable in hoarotu shamanism, expands that basic range to a raised seventh. Two of the three recorded solo performances sung during actual curing, however, employ the range of an octave or more. Moreover, during five consecutive nocturnal hoarotu curing sessions performed by José Antonio on 2 August 1972 (which I did not record; nevertheless, I notated the pitches as I lay in my hammock several houses away), he sang one song with a range of an octave while he sang another with an expanded range to an approximate minor ninth above the principal tone. Other wide ranges used during actual hoarotu curing include approximate major and minor sixths, minor sevenths, major sevenths, and octaves. An attempt to explain the psychological significance of this intervallic expansion is not possible through folk evaluation because Warao shamans have no words for intervallic relationships as we understand them. I believe, however, that such melodic expansion is the result of the shaman's continually deepening trance state. Gabriel, for example, expanded his melody to an octave one minute and thirty seconds into the ritual, after a muffled "oya" emanated from somewhere, as if triggering his trance (see music example 9.7 and listen to recorded example 18). I elaborate on this hypothesis about melodic expansion and trance in chapter 15.

Music Example 9.5. Hoarotu curing song, tone system.

Music Example 9.6. Hoarotu curing song (José Antonio Páez). Olsen Collection 72.8-54.

Music Example 9.7. Hoarotu curing ritual, part 1 of trio (Gabriel Sánchez). Olsen Collection 72.8-67.

no-ti-wa-ka-ne he-wi-si-ba-ka-ne hi-ya-ba-nae o-wai o-wai

o-to-no-ma-ri be-ho-to a-we-ku-ya ne-mo-ni-bu-ne

ne-mo-ni-bu-ne hi-ya-ba-ne-ra hi-ya-ba-na-wa-si-ne

hi-e-ko-ka-ne ko-ne-ba-ka-ne ho-ko — ne

ba-ra-ne ko-ne-ba-rae o-wai o-wai o-wai

continues

Music Example 9.7 (*continued*)

Unlike all other Warao shamanistic curing songs, and unlike hoarotu inflicting songs, hoarotu curing songs consist of only one musical section; that is, thematically or melodically the music is the same from beginning to end except for the individual shaman's own melodic variations. This melodic fixity or consistency is unique to the hoarotu. Likewise, voice quality is fixed throughout; and there is no alternation between unmasked and masked vocal production.

Textually, however, hoarotu curing songs consist of two parts. Part 1 of the text functions as an introduction because it explains what has happened, tells the sex of the patient, diagnoses what and where the pain or infliction is, asks the question "What will it be?" and responds "It will be this," and finally explains how the Hoa will be removed. Although these functions do not always appear in this exact order, the sequence I present is their most common arrangement. Part 1 is followed directly by Part 2, which is the main body of the song because it prepares to name the Hoatuma, specifically names them, points out

other areas of pain (optional), and explains how the Hoa will be removed (optional). Part 2 is essentially the search for the correct illness-
causing Hoa. Table 9.1 classifies the contents of the hoarotu curing
songs in this study.

Table 9.1 also lists the numerous Hoatuma that are found in the
main parts of the curing songs that I recorded. The hoarao naming of
animals has been mentioned by various scholars, including Turrado
Moreno (1945, 153–54) and Wilbert (1970, 24). The naming of the
essences of numerous humans, objects, and intangibles, however, is
unique, and the frequency with which these essences occur indicates
their importance as Hoatuma. With a few exceptions the line between
the four categories is very thin because all the Hoatuma belong to the
spirit world of the Warao. Nevertheless, for purposes of description,
the Hoatuma grouped in table 9.1 as "animals or humans" and "objects," unique and poetic as they are, might be thought of as tangible to
the non-Warao mind. The Hoatuma grouped as "hebutuma" and "intangibles," however, defy any shape or form that is tangible. The majority of the Hoatuma are derived from the spirit worlds of hokonamu,
including the sky, beneath the water, or beneath the earth. These
cosmic worlds are very shamanistic and so are the many animals that
traverse the known world and the heights and depths of the unknown.
The earth itself is a source of great power, as Turrado Moreno (1945,
154) writes: "[A shaman] receives a virtue from the earth, an incom-
municable power to shoot arrows into an enemy." And the cosmos, as
we have already seen in chapter 2 and elsewhere, is the greatest source
of power for the Warao.

The significance of the Hoa concept can be best understood by an
analysis of the songs used during actual curing ceremonies. The illness of Luís Jiménez again provides for such a study. I followed his
condition closely because he lived just a few houses away from me and
I had daily contact with shamans and other musicians and friends
who visited him. Padre Damián's medical diagnosis specifically noted
that Luís suffered a stroke of apoplexy caused by the rupturing of a
blood vessel in the left side of the brain, resulting in paralysis of the
right side of the body. Further characteristics of the patient's illness
were difficulty breathing, swallowing, and talking, plus coughing up
phlegm. The texts of the hoarotu curing songs sung for Luís reveal that
the shamans named Hoatuma that "metaphorically" (to the outside

Table 9.1. Functions of hoarotu curing songs

Telling the sex of the patient (location in parts 1 and 2)
  Noncontextual performances mention man 3 times
  Noncontextual performances mention woman 9 times
  Contextual curing sessions are to cure a man

Giving location of pain and Hoa
  Head (brain)
  Eyes
  Tongue
  Throat (back of tongue, back of jaw)
  Neck
  Chest
  Heart
  Back
  Ribs
  Stomach
  Waist
  Intestines
  Leg

Telling symptoms of illness
  Pain
  Loss of weight
  Loss of blood
  Bleeding from stomach
  Wildness or craziness
  Stomach pain (eating the flesh inside stomach)
  Lame leg or inability to walk
  Weakness and withering away
  Sick blood
  Sadness
  Crying and yelling
  Quietness
  Strangulation or suffocation
  Loss of sight
  Paralysis
  Heaviness
  Vomiting and salivating
  Loss of speech
  Fever and perspiring
  Incoherent speech

Table 9.1 (*continued*)

Naming the Hoatuma
  Animals or humans
    Thin morocoto fish
    Armadillo which is resting on the root of a tree in Hokonamu
    Young boy who looks around
    Sea turtle
    The girl beneath the earth when she has her menstrual flow
    Stuttering foreigner who lives alone
    Tan colored tiger in Hokonamu
    Tiger
    Body of a water horse
    Group of angoleta birds
    Large toad sitting in Hokonamu
    Little crabs
  Objects
    Objects which an outsider has in his store
    A car that is driven—one that races and stops, over and
      over, as if delivering mail
    Iron shaft of an automobile
    Rib of a morocoto fish
    Kareko stones that are fastened in the bottom of the water
    Ornament of the earth
    The infertile earth
    The earth that uses a comb to comb itself
    Iron cane of the earth
    Iron pipe beneath the earth
    Sun
    Collar of bone from a young boy
    Hokonemu's small chest (thorax)
    Metal hat of the sun
    Large collar
    Large silver collar of the sun
    Large hat with wide wings that is in the middle of the sea
    Hat of a stuttering foreigner
    Clothes of a stuttering foreigner
    Large hat of the large sea in Hokonamu
    Large hat of the hebus from the hills next to the sea
    Large motor of the foreigners
    Gasoline of the foreigner's motor
    Collar of the young Hoebo
    Hat of Hoebo
    Sweat produced by the hat of Hoebo
    Wide brimmed hat of the foreigners

Table 9.1 (*continued*)

Naming the Hoatuma (*continued*)
 Objects (*continued*)
  Motor on a canoe
  Sticks and branches of the rain forest at the bank of the river
  Leaves of the trees that move when the breeze blows
  Flesh of a horse's head
  Paper-making machine of the Creoles
  Lighthouse on the Orinoco River
  Dolls or images of the Creole
  Iron collar
  Bone collar
  Collar of iron clouds
  Money buried beneath the earth

Hebutuma (spirits or Hoatuma): a. Hebu of the earth b. Silent hebu c. Hebu señora d. Good hebu of the machine that is inside its case e. Evil hebu like the menstrual blood of a woman f. Maisikiri that swims beneath the water g. Hebu like the blood lost by the maisikiri when it gives birth in the water h. Hebu born in the bottom of the water i. Hebu from Hokonamu j. Spirit that has the form of a type of dog k. Maisikiri l. Hoa born in the earth m. Hebu whose breath sounds like he is dying n. Good God of the Creoles o. Hoa who sits on the hill on the other side of the sea p. Female hebu from Hokonamu q. Hoa of Hoebo r. Stuttering hebu s. Young Hoebo that lives in the clouds of twilight in Hokonamu t. Crazy hebu beyond Hokonamu u. Hebu of a large mirror of the Creoles v. Hebu that remains near the sun w. Hebu of the gods of the Creoles

Intangibles: a. Type of odor that passes over the earth at night b. Odor during the night and early morning of the blood lost by the maisikiri after it has given birth c. Songs of a frog which lives in Hokonamu d. Puffing of the earth when it walks e. Wind f. Large breeze g. Vapor of the fire from Hokonamu h. Smoke of the cigar from the hill on the other side of the sea i. Silence of the early evening which rises in Hokonamu j. Opening of an umbrella k. Vapor of the foreigner's motor when it is started l. Vapor of an outboard motor when it is started m. Noise of an outboard motor n. Silence of the Creole's machine when it sits o. Silence of the man who is manipulating the machine and who is looking around p. Illness of the sun q. Silence and sadness of the sun when it is ill r. Illness of the sick and crazy hebu s. Coldness of the Orinoco River t. Vapor in Hokonamu u. Clouds, vapor of twilight v. Rising up of the clouds observer) coincided with the characteristics of the patient's infliction. Such diagnosis is the essence of Warao shamans' skill as medical doctors. Table 9.1, for example, specifically lists the areas of the patient's body from the chest up to the brain and lists Luís's major symptoms as suffocation, fever, and lack of control over muscular movement resulting in an inability to speak, swallow, move certain limbs, and see. The section in table 9.1 labeled "Naming the Hoatuma" signifies that the curing hoarotu shamans tended to name types of collars or similar encircling objects, the sun or items related to either the sun or heat, and objects or characteristics of noise. Hoatuma that are collars or similar encircling objects, such as a hat and the brim of a hat, are "symbols" of suffocation relating to the difficulty that Luís had in breathing, talking, and swallowing because of the phlegm in his throat. The Hoatuma that refer to the sun or are related to it "symbolize" the patient's fever, and the Hoa of the coldness of the Orinoco River "symbolizes" his accompanying chills. The Hoatuma that are related to noise are "symbolic" of the grinding sound of the patient's breathing (created by the phlegm) and his coughing, while the patient's incoherent speech is reflected in Hoatuma such as a "stuttering foreigner who lives alone," a "group of angoleta birds" whose chattering is incoherent noise, and a "stuttering hebu." Finally, the patient's loss of speech and unconscious state are "symbolized" by the Hoatuma that refer to silence. These words relating to particular physical states of the patient were *not* described by the Warao as symbol or metaphor. To them, what we may call symbol or metaphor is a diagnostic/curing technique that is reality because the Hoatuma are (or can be) those very objects, animals, or intangibles that are causing the illness. In this sense, the idea of symbol or metaphor is only an outside concept for analysis, and the terms are not to be applied to this realm of Warao music in the same way that Seeger (1986, 1987) has done for the Suyá, Seitz (1981) for the Quichua, Feld (1989) for the Kaluli, and Roseman (1991) for the Temiar. Among the Suyá, Quichua, Kaluli, and Temiar, the teachers themselves speak about their own music (or speech) as metaphor.

Song text 9.2 was sung by Gabriel Sánchez, the lead singer of the hoarotu trio that performed twice one evening to cure Luís Jiménez (see Olsen 1976, 114–22, for song texts of the second ritual). Shortly after Gabriel began singing, the other two shamans, Biwa and

Gerónimo, began to sing different words using different pitches in their attempt to name the correct illness-causing Hoa (listen to recorded example 18). Only Gabriel's words have been translated, however, because of the difficulty in distinguishing the song texts once the polyphony began.

Song Text 9.2. Hoarotu Curing Song (the text of Gabriel Sánchez), 30 July 1972 (Olsen Collection 72.8-67)

Part 1

This is for you that it was named. This was named for you.

It was left for the inside of the head [in the skin] of a man.

It was placed there by the words of the hoarotu which fell upon you.

The Hoa that was placed underneath the skin of your head, I will loosen it and remove it.

He put this Hoa inside you so you would lose your sight.

It is for the area beneath your jaws where it fell.

He put the Hoa inside your throat, and thus he sang to place it there.

The hoarotu placed the Hoa in you, the head of the household, to make you ill.

Naming this Hoa he put it in you.

This Hoa was sung to be placed beneath your throat and beneath your chest, and also so you will have difficulty breathing.

It is the Hoa from the master's mouth.

This is the Hoa which is winding itself around like a snare, and was placed in you so you would rock back and forth [in your hammock] as a sick person.

He put a heavy and strong pain inside your throat.

All of this pain that you have beneath your throat because of the Hoa, I will loosen and remove it from you.

The hoarotu put the Hoa beneath your ribs.

He placed the Hoa beneath your protruding ribs.

I will loosen, remove, and send off the Hoa which was placed into you.

The hoarotu placed it inside the good skin in your back.

I will loosen and send off the Hoa which the hoarotu sent off
for you.

He placed the Hoa inside the bones of your spinal column, so
you would not be able to move and so you would have pain.
This Hoa that was put into you with a kaidoko snare, I will
loosen and send it off.

A hoarotu sang the Hoatuma, and all of the Hoatuma that are
binding you in the back, I will loosen a little.

The hoarotu prepared his breath and sent off the Hoa so it
would tie up your back.

The Hoa which the hoarotu sent is in order to give you a huge
weight, so that you will never get up, and will remain quiet.

The Hoa of Hoebo was prepared to make you ill.

I will loosen you from it.

He sang and placed it in you, there, inside your head.

What will this be?

Part 2

It will be the sun which has risen above us, which is sitting on
top of its chair.

This is a metal hat of the sun, made by the Creoles.

It is this that is placed in you.

A metal hat of the sun made by the Creoles was named.

This metal Creole sun hat was named to be placed into your
head to make you heavy.

All of this which was named I will loosen and remove.

This is a large collar that was placed in your throat to give you
the weight and the heat of the sun which is sitting above us.

Inside your throat a large silver collar of the sun was placed.

It was put tied and suspended inside your throat.

This is the collar which is stopping up the inside of your
throat.

This is the Hoa that was placed inside your throat, so you
would be ill.

This is a large toad that is sitting there in hokonamu, somewhat beneath hokonamu.

Just like he is sitting there, he is also sitting in the throat of
this man, making him vomit and produce saliva, and
making him nauseated.

This is the Hoa of the little crabs that are inside your throat to
   make you unable to speak.
Thus sang the hoarotu to make you ill.
This is a large hat of wide wings that is in the middle of the
   sea.
It is of the stuttering foreigner.
This is what was placed in your head to weigh you down.
This is of a foreigner who lives alone.
He, together with his hat and his clothes, was named.
The clothes were left in your back, and the hat in your head.
I will loosen and send off all of this which was placed in you.
This is the large hat of the large sea that exists in hokonamu.
It has an umbrella made with metal ribs.
This is what was placed in your head to produce heat.
This is like the opening of the umbrella, which was sung by a
   hoarotu for you.
This is the large hat of the hebutuma from the hills next to the
   sea.
It was this hat which was placed in this man's head, and this
   is how the hoarotu sang.
This is the hat of the hebu from the hill next to the sea.
It produces a heat like the sun inside your head, makes you
   unable to speak, and makes you sweat.
I will loosen and rid you of all of this.
This is the large motor of the foreigners which runs inside the
   canoe which is floating and stopped.
The Hoa is together with the gasoline and the vapor produced
   when the motor of the foreigners is started.
All of this was placed inside your spine.
I will loosen all of this and send it off.

After several days of attempted curing by Warao shamans, Luís
Jiménez was taken to a hospital in Maturín. Because of the permanent
damage caused by the stroke, he never showed outward signs of im-
provement and was returned to his home after several weeks. I visited
him eight months later, and he was able to talk slowly and walk hesi-
tatingly with a cane. According to him and his family, the two weeks
spent in the hospital had no curative value. He was often not fed (his
Warao friends who visited him in the hospital considered intravenous

feeding virtual starvation; consequently, they smuggled in soft drinks and crackers for him to eat) and was not treated with much care and respect. He owed his recovery to the work of the many shamans and even to himself, for at times he sang powerful curing songs to himself as he gradually gained strength. There was no doubt in Luís Jiménez's mind that his illness and near death were caused by Hoa and that he was lucky to be alive. Indeed, very few Warao survive Hoa sickness.

The last three chapters have examined the ethnomusicology of Warao shamanism. The large array of curing songs of the wisiratu, bahanarotu, and hoarotu, however, does not constitute all of the musical healing practices of the Warao. Another large category, a nonshamanistic type known as *hoa* (as distinct from Hoa), is discussed in the next chapter.

10 hoa Curing Songs

The Warao hoa is a broad theurgical song and magical power genre that is used for a multitude of purposes. A Warao shaman is not required for its successful use; therefore, I write the word with a small *h* to distinguish it from the shamanistic Hoa of the hoarotu. The Warao use the same word to identify the formidable power realm of the hoarotu and the lesser power realm used by anyone who has the proper knowledge (the songs and techniques). This has caused some misunderstanding among scholars with regard to the hoa for healing. Turrado Moreno (1945, 157, 305), for example, explains that the wisiratu shaman sings hoa curing songs to take out hebu illnesses; but he also says that all shamans sing hoa curing songs for curing (1945, 170). Barral (1964, 129) says that hoa curing songs are sung by hoarotu shamans only, and other writers also discuss hoa only in connection with the hoarotu (Aretz 1991, 288). The Warao, however, make a distinction. They recognize the song type called hoa, which is sung by anyone to cure ailments inflicted by supernaturally inspired natural causes—for example, flesh wounds, animal bites, insect stings, snakebites, swelling, birth complications, and so forth. It is a non-shamanistic song type distinct from the power songs sung by hoarotu shamans to inflict and cure direct supernatural Hoa illnesses (see chapter 9). Turrado Moreno (1945, 170) seems to be aware of this distinction when he writes the following:

> "Joa" is the prayer, the psalm, the oration which these wizards pray, sing (or better said) low, in order to cure diverse illnesses and pains. There are "joas" that are prayed and others that are sung, according to the solemnity with which they are applied. I know of many "joas" used for taking out "jebu": against the sting of a sting ray, of a scorpion, or against snake bites. These "joas" are also called by the name of "tenoy" [*sic*] meaning blow, puff, or breath.

Turrado Moreno's first criterion for distinguishing between the two types is musical—the hoa is lowed (berrear), and the Hoa is sung. This, as we shall see, is not a valid distinction. His reference to blowing, however, is valid. The word *temoy* (which Turrado Moreno later spells correctly) was given to me as part of the title of a hoa for a hatchet cut—"hima a temoy." Barral (1957, 113) translates hima (jima) as iron tool; he does not include temoy in his dictionary, although he does include temoya ("insufflate, to blow") in his article "Vocabulario teurgico-magico de los indios Guaraos" (1958, 35). Among the Mariusa-Warao, the nonshamanistic hoa is called ahitemoi (pain-blow), according to Briggs (1994, 142).

According to my Warao teachers, the word hoa has two meanings: (1) hoa for curing, whereby a person sings and blows on the patient; it refers only to the body, not to a spirit; and (2) Hoa of the hoarotu, a spirit like the wind that, when named, can kill or injure someone. A further verification of this distinction is the frequent explanation that the hoa can be sung by anyone. As Antonio Lorenzano said, "this is not a wisiratu song; it is a song of hoa for a woman who gives birth." Bernardo Jiménez Tovar explained that "anyone can cure by singing a hoa, by blowing smoke; he does not have to be a wisiratu." I should add, however, that "anyone" also includes any type of shaman. In many cases a wisiratu, bahanarotu, or hoarotu is called upon to sing a hoa because he is believed to be more knowledgeable than a non-shaman. But when a wisiratu shaman does cure by singing a hoa, he never uses a hebu mataro rattle. As Bernardo explained, "any person can sing this, including a wisiratu, who would sing it without a rattle to cure a person." Among the Mariusa-Warao, the curer is a specialist called ahitemoi arotu (Briggs 1994, 142).

An injured person may sing a hoa to his or her wound to relieve the pain. One afternoon, for example, Bernardo's son Felicisimo, then a child of fourteen, bumped his previously injured knee while playing. Immediately it began to swell. As he was carried into my room, he began to sing a hoa amid his tears; and later I could hear him singing it often as he lay in his hammock. Several years before this bump, Felicisimo's knee was severely cut by a hatchet. Gangrene set in, and he nearly died because his father, who does not believe in Western medicine, would not allow him to be taken to the hospital in Maturín. After singing hoa curing songs for many days, Bernardo finally allowed Felicisimo to be taken to the hospital where antibiotics saved the boy's life. Today, Felicisimo still limps because of permanent damage done to his knee.

A hoa curing song is addressed to the patient's affliction and to the physical cause of the affliction, which is believed present within the patient as an essence. Sometimes the wound-causing object or animal is addressed directly. While explaining a hoa for a machete cut, Chano Rivero said that "the hoa for curing means prayer; however, it is not sung to a spirit; it is sung only to the cut." While not sung to a spirit at the same level as shamanistic songs are, the hoa is very theurgical. The hoa is a form of musical therapy that employs the theurgical power of singing, the psychological power of suggestion, and the physical power of blowing.

hoa As Musical and Physical Therapy

What is the therapeutic affect of the hoa curing song? Dieter Heinen (1973, personal communication) suggested that the vibration of the sounds produced in the song match the vibrations of a particular person's body and that this aids in the curing of external wounds. Given the varied vibrations of human vocal chords, however, and the unscientific data relating to body vibrations, it is unlikely that the singing of a hoa assists healing in a musically physiological sense. Rather, it may work in a musically psychological one—hoa singing soothes and relaxes the patient, thus accelerating nature's own healing process. This hypothesis is suggested by a consideration of the kinds of external wounds and illnesses for which hoa musical therapy is used: they are almost all ailments that would normally heal with proper rest and the passing of time, such as cuts by a machete, hatchet, or knife; an abscessed tooth; a wound inflicted by an animal bite; the pain and swelling caused by an insect or stingray; the discomfort caused by a snakebite; swelling created by some internal misfunction; and so on. Of course, the singing of a hoa is not always successful, as we have seen in Felicisimo's case.

The medicinal effect of blowing tobacco smoke over the afflicted part of the body is unknown and should be explored further. Antonio Lorenzano explained that when he blew tobacco smoke on the blood that was flowing from a wound on a man's foot, the blood stopped: "The next day you could not see anything, for the wound was completely dry," he said to me. Another time he discussed a hoa for curing an abscessed tooth: "Now, when you sing you have to blow on the patient with smoke from a wina cigar made from [black tobacco within] a rolled up manaca palm leaf. You blow the first time and already the patient is a little better. You blow again and he is a little better still. After the third and the fourth times his pain has now calmed down." When the Warao explain the power of hoa curing songs, they often emphasize the freshness of the breath and sometimes the saliva, which is like a fine mist. Both have a physiologically cooling effect on the patient, especially when the patient has a fever; and their soothing quality perhaps momentarily distracts the patient from the pain. Fuller Torrey (1972, 68–69) considers spray to be a form of shock therapy: "Mild forms of shock therapy are widely used by therapists in many cultures. It is common, for instance, to spray or throw water in the patient's face, thereby producing a mild shock, raising the level of emotion, and encouraging the patient to give up his symptoms. Such an approach is widely used by Mexican *curanderos.*" The very small amount of saliva used by a Warao healer, however, weakens the possibility of the shock-therapy hypothesis in hoa curing.

hoa Curing Songs and the Singers

I recorded twenty-three hoa songs performed noncontextually for curing eleven disorders: hatchet cut, knife cut, machete cut, peccary bite, snakebite, stingray wound, scorpion sting, thorn in foot, birth complications, abscessed tooth, and pain in a woman's breast. All twenty-three songs were coincidentally sung by shamans (thirteen by wisimo, seven by a bahanarotu, and three by a hoarotu). Even though the genre is not shamanistic, the hoa is magical, its function is theurgical, and there is a substantial level of supernatural communication involved (see Briggs 1994).

Melodically, hoa curing songs consist of one or two sections, sung continuously, sometimes with repeats or slight pauses. They do not employ voice masking. Thus, outward musical contrasts may exist during a performance of a curing hoa. There are, moreover, at least two distinct types that differ musically, textually, and functionally: hoa for healing external wounds or internal disorders, and hoa for eliminating birth complications.

hoa for External Wounds or Internal Disorders

This type of hoa is the most common because of the large number of afflictions it can cure. It is melodically very similar to the A and B sections of a wisiratu curing song cycle. The principal interval, for example, is approximately a minor third; and the complete melodic pattern usually includes additional subsecondary tones, as shown in the representative tone systems notated in music example 10.1. Music example 10.2 and recorded example 19 are from a hoa curing song to stop the bleeding of a man's wound caused by a hatchet. The singer is Bernardo Jiménez Tovar, a wisiratu. While his example is melodically typical, he makes extensive use of vibrato and dynamic contrast, alternating constantly from *f* to *p*. Because these techniques are not used by everyone who sings this type of hoa, I interpret them as the aesthetic choices of the singer. Music example 10.3 is an excerpt from another portion of the same hoa, in which Bernardo names the sharp edge of the hatchet that cut a man. These two segments of the same hoa (not sung consecutively) show the singer's use of variation, as indicated in the tone systems notated in music example 10.1.

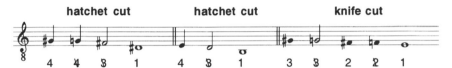

Music Example 10.1. hoa for external wounds or internal disorders, tone systems.

Most of the textual content and format of the hoa for external wounds or internal disorders indicate that there are three steps or concepts used by the singer to make the curing song effective. The first is to name all the attributes of the wound-causing object or animal, whose essence is believed to be within the patient, ending at inner phrases with the precise wound-causing part (such as the cutting edge of a hatchet or the fangs of a snake) or with the complete object or animal. Naming all the object or animal's spiritual and physical attributes is prefatory to pinpointing the actual damage-causing agent or total entity, a concept that is similar to the naming sequences found in the shamanistic inflicting and curing songs discussed in previous chapters. It is, in fact, the way in which naming is usually conducted: that is, saving the most important element until last. Sometimes certain parts of the objects are described metaphorically during the naming process. For example, the rivets in the handles or the lettering on the

Music Example 10.2. hoa for hatchet wound (Bernardo Jiménez Tovar). Olsen Collection 72.8-1.

Music Example 10.3. hoa for hatchet wound (Bernardo Jiménez Tovar). Olsen Collection 72.8-4.

hatchets, machetes, or knives are their "eyes." In addition, proper names (or magical proper names) for certain objects or animals are used during naming; and the singer will address them directly in the hoa curing songs. During some hoa naming, the object or animal is discredited. In one hoa, for example, a wound-causing hatchet is called "a nothing"; in another, a snake that bit a Warao is called "a nothing, a little ant." The healer thus shows his power over the corporeal aspect of the wounding agent. Briggs (1994, 153–54) refers to these steps in the naming process as the "path" or "road" that is necessary so the essence within the patient will let go of the patient's flesh.

In the second step, the healer orders the object or the animal that caused the wound to stop the bleeding. Additionally, he will sing to the blood itself, demanding that it stop flowing. If there is no blood involved, as in the case of a snakebite, the healer will order the snake that did the biting and caused the pain to stop the pain; or he will order the swelling and pain themselves to go away.

During the third step, the healer sings about blowing on the wound, specifically about one of three actions: blowing smoke, blowing only the breath, or blowing a fine spray of saliva. This is followed by physical blowing.

The three steps of the hoa musical therapy, then, are theurgical, psychological, and physical. The entire action of singing is musical therapy; the discourse in the texts indicates theurgical and psychological therapy, as we shall see; and the action of blowing is physical therapy. The following hoa for a hatchet cut (song text 10.1) is representative of this type of hoa curing genre. It was sung by Antonio Lorenzano and translated by him into Spanish.

Song Text 10.1. hoa Curing Song for Hatchet Cut, 12 July 1972, Antonio Lorenzano (Olsen Collection 72.8-3)

This is your name, your name, your name . . .
We have never seen this.
The hebu was born far away.
The hebutuma did this.
It was put this way in the hatchet by hebu.
Oh hatchet, hatchet, hatchet, hatchet.
It is in the head of the hatchet.
From the head to beneath it, it is the line over the hatchet.
These are the eyes of the hatchet.
You are hatchet.
It is a hatchet.
The flesh parted where the cut goes across.
A hatchet cut.
This is the flat body of the hatchet, from the edge on one side
    to the other.
You did it. You are a nothing.
This is the sharp edge.
The sharp edge which cuts, oh hatchet, hatchet, hatchet . . .
    this is your name, your name, your name . . .

This has happened to a man, in his leg, above his foot.
In the front of his leg is where the hatchet cut.
It cut the skin, and beneath the skin it cut flesh.
Where it is cut, there it is bleeding.
The blood is spilling out where the sharp edge cut.
The blood is spilling.
Much blood is coming out.
Hatchet, stop the bleeding!
Hatchet, with your sharp edge, stop the blood right now!
It is bleeding, spilling blood.
Oh hatchet, hatchet.
Stop now—no more bleeding!
There now, the blood stopped.
Oh hatchet.
But, just in case of more bleeding, I am going to blow on you.
Yes, now I blow on you, and my breath is soothing.
I blow with freshness.
Stay there, blood, remain stopped.
Oh hatchet, hatchet.
It is someone's fault.
I am blowing.
Stop, blood.
Oh hatchet, hatchet, hatchet, hatchet.
This is your name, your name, your name.

Antonio explained this hoa in great detail. The following is his complete commentary about the way in which danger can exist within common material possessions, how danger seems to lurk in unknown places, how the naming process functions, and about the way in which he applies psychological and physical therapy:

We never know where a hatchet is made. We do not know the people who make the hatchets, the machetes, the knives, the pails, the pans, the plates. Concerning everything that is made of iron, we do not know where the people are who made those things, and we have never seen them. So, these people put these objects inside a box, they nail the box shut, and we buy them, use them, and cut a foot, for example. The head of the hatchet, near the top where the hole is, has some letters on it. This is either the proper name of the hatchet, or the letters can be the eyes of the hatchet. After this there is the point of the hatchet, and after this you can see a line, a thin line. After this comes the sharp edge that cuts. This is how I called the name of the hatchet in the song I just sang.

Now, in order to stop the blood you have to sing a hoa. You sing and sing, and blow like this. [He blows.] After four, five, or six times the blood stops. Then you ask, "Does it hurt?"

"Yes, it hurts," is the reply. Then you have to sing and blow four or five times more to take away the pain, to calm down the pain.

We can see where the sharp cutting edge of the hatchet cut someone's foot. The skin and the flesh have parted and there the blood is spilling out. In order to stop this blood I have to say, "Good, now you are becoming quieter, blood." "You have to stop, blood." Blood is spilling from the place where the hatchet cut.

When we were in Tucupita on a trip, Llora, a young girl, got cut. Her dad said to me, "Lorenzano, she's cut; you can see the bone."

"How did it happen?" I ask.

"A hatchet fell on her foot and cut it," her dad responded.

Then, this hoa is sung with the following words: "You have to stop. I am saying to you, hatchet, that where you cut this person in the foot, you have to stop. Stop the blood of this person."

If it's possible, brother, I'll do it. I have to blow with my breath, with my spit, in order to stop the blood which is flowing. Above all, the blood which is flowing has to stop, in the bone, in the vein, all that is spilling, so that tomorrow the person will be better. Thus, I blew on the blood and it stopped. The next day you could not see anything; it was completely dry.

In this hoa for curing a hatchet cut, Antonio clearly sings that the real cause of the infliction is supernatural. A hebu caused a hatchet to cut a man's foot, and the hebu-possessed hatchet has to be named. To name it Antonio uses a term for the sound a hatchet makes when chopping wood. "Baro, baro, baro," Antonio sings, or "bao, bao, bao," according to Barral (1957, 46), who calls the term an "onomatopoeic interjection that imitates the sound produced by a hatchet when a person is cutting a tree or chopping wood." Therefore, hoa curing songs are theurgical because wounds are believed to be caused supernaturally even though the objects or animals that cause the physical damage are real rather than spiritual. If we recall the meaning of hebu given in chapter 7, we can understand why this should be so because everything except people can be possessed by hebu. The difference, however, between a hebu illness as cured by a wisiratu shaman and a hebu affliction as cured by anyone knowledgeable in hoa curing, is that the former is caused by an unknown metaphysical essence that has been placed within the patient's body by a hebu (and is considered to be the hebu itself) and the latter is characterized by either an external wound or the malfunctioning of the human body (as in a toothache or childbirth complications), that is caused by a known object or an animal possessed by hebu and whose essence is within the patient's body, causing pain. Because the material entity has the visible shape of an object or an animal, it can be controlled by any knowledgeable Warao who sings a hoa directly to the entity and blows tobacco smoke over the wound or afflicted part of the body. There is generally no communication with the outer spirit world while in trance or ecstasy, as in Warao shamanism; nor is there a need for spirit helpers. Nevertheless, the hoa curing song is a type of theurgical therapy because it is sung to the harmful essence believed to be within the patient's body, and to its cause.

Material objects that cause wounds are not always tools from the outside; they can also be natural things. Antonio sang a hoa for curing a wound caused by a sliver in the foot and explained it this way:

> This is the hoa of the trees of the sandbar. In Warao we call these trees nabaru. They have many roots, and it is impossible to step around them because they give off many splinters. When a person gets a sliver in the foot, then someone who knows how to sing this hoa about the roots of this tree sings three or four times and the person can walk again. This is a prayer for when a person gets a sliver in his foot. That's how it is, my friend. That's all.

A hoa for curing a snakebite, partially notated as music example

10.4 and heard in recorded example 20, was sung in 1972 by Isaías Rodríguez, the most powerful wisiratu priest-shaman in the Winikina
area. His hoa (song text 10.2) was translated by the singer himself in
1973 from ritual Warao into current Waraoan and then translated into
Spanish by Cesáreo Soto.

Music Example 10.4. hoa for snakebite (Isaías Rodríguez). Olsen Collection
72.8-13.

Song Text 10.2. hoa Curing Song for Snakebite, Isaías Rodríguez (Olsen Collection 72.8-13)

Cure yourself, wound. Mr. Snake.
Cure yourself. Mr. Snake.
You, wound, are going to cure yourself. Mr. Snake.
You will come, curing. Mr. Snake.
By curing you will be cured. Mr. Snake.
Cure yourself. Mr. Snake.

Stop, pain, and alleviate yourself. Mr. Snake.

There, pain, stop yourself. Mr. Snake.

You are going to stop. Mr. Snake.

You will stop hurting. Mr. Snake.

Come and calm down the pain and stop it. Mr. Snake.

There you will disappear, venom. Mr. Snake.

Disappear, venom. Mr. Snake.

Calm down, venom. Mr. Snake.

Disappear, venom. Mr. Snake.

You will come and alleviate the pain. Mr. Snake.

Calm down. Mr. Snake.

Go away, venom. Mr. Snake.

There you will receive the freshness of my breath, wound. Mr. Snake.

Refresh yourself, wound. Mr. Snake.

Cure yourself completely so the pain will go away completely. Mr. Snake.

Refresh yourself, wound, and make the pain disappear. Mr. Snake.

Oh venom of your fangs, go away. Mr. Snake.

Go away, venom. Mr. Snake.

Saliva of your teeth, go away. Mr. Snake.

Calm down, wound. Mr. Snake.

Cure yourself completely. Mr. Snake.

Calm down, pain. Mr. Snake.

You are not large for me. Mr. Snake.

You are as small as an ant, Snake. Mr. Snake.

Calm down, wound. Mr. Snake.

You are a small ant. Mr. Snake.

You are like a very poor little ant. Mr. Snake.

You snake, your wound is not to kill. You are nothing for me. Mr. Snake.

You are a nothing, nor are you a hebu. Mr. Snake.

You are not a hebu. Mr. Snake.

With my breath, calm down pain. Mr. Snake.

With the breath from my mouth, go away pain. Mr. Snake.

With the blowing from my mouth, you will calm down, wound. Mr. Snake.

Disappear, poisonous saliva. Disappear with my blowing. Mr.
Snake.
Make the pain go away, saliva of your fangs. Mr. Snake.

As you can hear in recorded example 20, Isaías respectfully sang this
song very softly. He also sang some of the time with slight dynamic nuance, as the principal tones are occasionally lower in amplitude
(softer) than the higher secondary pitches. Generally, these kinds of
hoa curing songs are prayerlike. They are individual and familiar musical expressions for relieving pain. In addition, you can hear the constant musical and textual repetitions. The name of the snake, ihi
makao or "Mr. Snake," occurred nearly every other sung phrase. If the
act of naming the cause of the affliction releases the essence within the
patient's body and alleviates the pain, then why not repeat the name
many times until the pain and the affliction are gone? Naming is
power, and repetition (musical and textual) is power.

The name for the snake, ihi makao, is not the common name for
snake (huba) in Warao. Rather, it is the power name for the snake
essence that caused the infliction, and which is lodged within the patient, as Briggs (1994, 153) writes about the stingray (I have substituted snake for ray): "The [snake] would not hear the song if it were in-
toned in the everyday lexicon; such words do not travel very far, and
they are comprehensible only to humans. Utterances that combine
musical prosody with curer's lexicon, on the other hand, can extend in-
definitely in space and time. . . . The audience for this objectification is
the [snake], *not* the patient." While the patient does not (ideally) understand the name given to the pain-causing agent, he or she does
(generally) understand the words used during the process for allevia-
tion and removal of the essence. In this way immortal and mortal
powers are combined—the ihi makao essence loosens its grip because
it has been named and ultimately removed, and the patient's own curative energies are employed through power of suggestion.

Through the process of repetitive magical naming, the singer of a
hoa has complete control over an object or animal that caused the ailment. This is shown in another hoa to cure a snakebite (song texts 10.3
and 10.4) sung by Jaime Zapata, Isaías's brother. Jaime's lengthy hoa is
performed in two sections (which I call A and B). Section A is based on
the melodic motive 5 4 ₹ 1, the musical naming formula found in

wisiratu, bahanarotu, and hoarotu curing songs. Like those shamanic curing examples, the function of this section is also spiritual naming. Jaime Zapata names the angry spirit that possessed a snake, made it wild, and caused it to bite its victim. Section A uses the melodic theurgical naming motive because there *is* direct communication with the spirit world. While this section is also musically similar to the Hoa of the hoarotu (see chapter 9), the basic melodic formula of 5 4 ᶾ 1 is developed differently, as a comparison of the two skeletal notations in music example 10.5 demonstrates. (Both are sung by Jaime Zapata.) The section A of Jaime's snakebite hoa discussed here has two unique musical characteristics: an extension of the basic naming motive into 5 4 ᶾ 4 ᶾ 1, which is rhythmically altered; and a more frequent use of tones of short duration. Music example 10.6 is a transcribed excerpt from section A of the hoa, and it can be heard in recorded example 21. This section of the hoa involves direct communication with the supernatural force that caused the snake to attack and wound a person. In song text 10.3, Jaime names spirits called the "grandfathers of the ancient people," also called the "masters" or "carpenters who make canoes," commanding them to remove the pain of the wound they caused.

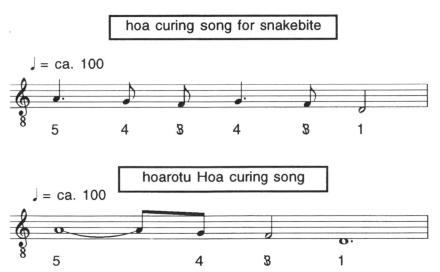

Music Example 10.5. Comparison of tone systems for hoa curing song for snakebite and hoarotu Hoa curing song (both sung by Jaime Zapata).

Music Example 10.6. hoa for swelling from snakebite, section A (Jaime Zapata). Olsen Collection 72.8-10.

Song Text 10.3. hoa Curing Song for Snakebite, Jaime Zapata (Olsen Collection 72.8-10)

Swelling, you did this. The swelling itself is doing this.

You made heat, that which you are doing.

You arrived and stayed there to swell.

There you attacked, and I name you.

What is your name? There, swelling, this is your name.

You swelled up for the body of my companion.

You are doing this.

That which you are doing I will put to one side.

This is your name.

You swelled all the skin. I say to the skin, go down.

From the stem in the middle of a leaf is where it was born in the earth, there below. Inside the stem in the leaf, in the heart of the leaf, there is the snake. With the jaw of the snake the wound was caused.

Go away, leave.

There, where you came from, there, go back there.

Your name is what I speak, I speak your name.

It relied upon the sun, from there is where it arrived. From there you came, to swell, to make me hot. From there it caused swelling in the skin.

You need our grandfather.

You attacked to make me hot. He went to make me hot. He arrived. Thus, you are there. That which you had, you needed. You both attacked in front of me, and are making me hot.

This is your name, our grandfather who needs it for me.

You are a snake, and you arrived, and struck me.

This is from the wound of the jaw of the snake who struck.

That is where your jaw made contact. You are doing this.

The leaf is from the beginning of existence, that is where it appeared.

Behind this very leaf is the snake, our grandfather origin snakes, this is you.

Our grandfather canoe builders who pass their hands as if measuring to make a canoe. This is it.

You are the masters who know everything.

All the work that was born was done for the master.

Now come the snakes. They are you.

There the pain was placed. May your skin calm down, calm down good.

The pain was placed in the blood. You are who have attacked for the blood.

This is what you needed to be master. The thought of the master is what you needed.

This section A of Jaime's snakebite hoa is extremely powerful because he names Hahuba, called ayubatuma or "snakes of being" in the song text. This deity, as you will recall, is the two-headed snake, the foundation of the world, whose heads face the east, the place of the origin of light (hokonamu). Jaime sings "ihi hae hikaramuna mahokonamu-tuma ayubatuma" (this was your name, snakes of being of the east). The all-powerful serpentine creature (or creatures because it has two heads, hence ayubatuma) is the metaphor of the snake that attacked a Warao man, causing swelling, fever, and pain in his leg. Jaime sings that the attacking snake needed help from the grandfather (kanobo) snake and the sun. The fever in the wound makes the sun metaphor obvious. Just as the hoarotu observes his patient's external characteristics and chooses what he names from his diagnosis, Jaime's choice of which spirit to name is similar. Likewise, his display of control over the hebutuma (snakes of being and the grandfathers of the canoes) recalls the power of the wisiratu, who is master of hebu.

In section B of his snakebite hoa, Jaime Zapata sings words that the snake spoke before it struck its victim, showing such complete dominance over the snake that he can re-create its thoughts. Having now reduced the serpent from Hahuba (snakes of being) to ihi makao (Mr. Snake), he demands that "Mr. Snake" (which he repeats incessantly) release his victim from the grips of pain. He then sings to the wound itself and to the pain, asking them to calm down.

Song Text 10.4. hoa Curing Song for Snakebite, 10 July 1972, Jaime Zapata (Olsen Collection 72.8-11)

"I am going to make myself born wild in the earth. I will be born wild in the earth. I will be born in my home. I arrived to my earth and I did what I said."

Mr. Snake, Snake.

"My words are what I said."

Mr. Snake.

It said: "My home is the earth where there is thick underbrush. I am making my body coiled in the center of the underbrush."

Mr. Snake.

It said: "I am going to coil my body. I am going to make my body silent and alert. Now I will be silent and alert. And for what reason am I silent and alert? I have made my body tranquil and coiled, and am going to remain here very quietly for those who walk on the earth. I am going to be wild for them. I am going to make myself wild and now I am wild."

Mr. Snake.

It said: "I am going to put my coiled body and my raised neck on the top of the earth. I am going to look around from the top. When I am looking around I will be waiting for those who come here; for them I am going to be wild."

Mr. Snake.

It said: "I am making my body wild, waiting for those that come, those that are born in the earth [the Warao]. I am not for him, I am for those who were born in the earth. For them I am wild."

Mr. Snake. That's how Mr. Snake spoke. That's how you were, Mr. Snake.

Your name, your name, your name.

It is for a woman and a man. There, in the leg, in the foot, in the skin of the foot, that is where you were wounded from the jaw of the snake. He did it from the jaw, wounding, as if he were eating. That's how you were.

You there, hear me, Mr. Snake. After you hear me, hear me again, Mr. Snake. Hear me well, Mr. Snake. After you listened, you heard, Mr. Snake.

Your name, your name, your name.

Now that you have heard me, go away pain.

Mr. Snake.

Remove yourself, pain, and stop.

Mr. Snake.

Remove yourself good, pain, calm down.

Mr. Snake.

Hear me, remove yourself, get out.

Mr. Snake.

Calm down.

Mr. Snake.

Your name, your name.

There, I knew it.

Mr. Snake.

There, I knew the venom from your fangs, and the saliva from
your teeth. I knew the fluid of your teeth, together with
your tongue, and with the saliva. I knew.

There, with my breath, with my mouth, with the freshness of
my breath, I am going to blow there. Calm down there,
where the wound is; there, where the bite of the jaw occurred; there, where the teeth were lodged; there, where the
fang marks are; there, calm down, calm down good.

Hear me, and calm down, pain. Calm down, there, in the
skin, and there, in the flesh of the leg.

Mr. Snake, Snake.

There, in the wound that you caused with your jaw; there,
where the fang marks are; there, where you grabbed with
your fangs. Calm down the pain. Mr. Snake, calm down the
pain.

Mr. Snake.

Your name, your name.

Textually, this section B of Jaime's hoa for snakebite is in two parts. In
the first part he conducts a dialogue by speaking directly to the snake
and by speaking the words that the snake spoke, using elaborate detail
to describe the snake and its actions. Because the singer is speaking to
the animal, this is a continuation of the theurgical therapy begun in
section A, in which he shows dominance over the animal. In the
second part, the longer of the two and the start of the psychological
therapy of the hoa, he begins by explaining who was bitten by the
snake (a man and a woman), where the bite occurred (in the skin of the
foot and leg), and how the snake did it (from his jaw, wounding, as if
he were eating). Jaime continues, singing alternately to the patient and
the wound and pain, with each phrase interrupted repeatedly by the
naming of the snake. Physical therapy is applied next, as the curer
blows on the wound, cooling it and providing relief. Finally, Jaime admonishes the snake itself to heal the patient by singing "Oh, Mr. Snake.
There, in the wound that you caused with your jaw; there, where the
fang marks are; there, where you grabbed with your fangs. Calm down
the pain. Mr. Snake, calm down the pain."

Jaime Zapata is a powerful spiritual leader of the Warao. He calls himself a novice hoarotu, and Wilbert (1981b, 1993) discovered that Jaime is also a naharima (rain father) or weather shaman. His most important ritual position, however, is as isimoi arotu or "keeper of the isimoi" (see chapter 4). He is truly a very powerful person and a man with great cosmological knowledge. His numerous religious positions and hoa knowledge provided him with theurgical power to cure many people. When listening to his hoa (section A) in recorded example 21, you will recognize a completely different approach to a curing song. Whereas the previous types are soft and prayerlike, this one is fast and staccato. Such musical characteristics are the sonic identifiers of the curing song types.

Certain internal complications are also believed to be caused by animals. A toothache resulting from an abscessed tooth, for example, is caused by a worm eating the tooth from within. Antonio Lorenzano sang a hoa for a pain in a molar and explained it in the following way:

> There is a pain in a person's molar, and inside the tooth, in the root, is a worm which is making a hole and causing the pain and the blood. This little worm is eating the molar from within, making a hole. There is no remedy for this little worm; there are neither medicines from the outside [Venezuela or elsewhere] nor doctors that can help. For this reason a Warao has to sing. (The person who really knows how to sing this is the husband of my daughter.) Now, if there is no one who knows how to sing the hoa for pain in the molar, the person goes around holding his jaw, moaning, with blood coming out of his mouth. He does not eat, during the day or at night. He just has pain in the molar caused by this little worm. When someone sings he has to blow on the patient with smoke from a wina. . . . After the third time, and the fourth, this pain that was preventing him from eating, talking, and drinking now has calmed down. This means that the little worm is finished; he is dead! Now he causes no more pain because he is deceased. That's all, my friend.

Only in this manner do the traditional Warao understand such an infection because they are unfamiliar with modern dental and medical practices.

Another internal disorder for which this common type of hoa formula is used is for curing an inflammation in a woman's breast:

Song Text 10.5. hoa Curing Song for Breast Inflammation, Antonio Lorenzano (Olsen Collection 72.8-25)

Your name, your name, your name.
You had no fever, and now you have fever.
Woman, in your chest, for all the upper part of your chest,
    from one side to the other, there it is planted in the breast.
It was not painful, and now it is painful in the breast, breast,
    breast.
Woman, in the breast, from one side to the other it is planted.
You were not angry, and now you are angry.
There where the pain is, with my fresh breath I will blow.
Blowing, calm down, breast, calm down.
With the fresh spray of my saliva, I am blowing.
Calm down pain in the breast.

Antonio then explained this hoa:

This is the prayer, the hoa, for when a woman gets sick in her breast. The sickness doesn't have to last very long, but if a hoa is not sung to the breast, it will be completely swollen in one day. This hoa is to make the swelling go down. Already the breast has pus in it, and if the hoa is not sung, the woman could die. This is our belief, my friend, here among us Warao. Now, a woman will tell me when she gets ill: "Look, my father (my brother, or my uncle), last night I began to get a pain in my breast." Then it is necessary to sing for a time. If you do not sing, she could die. You sing to the pus, the blood, the blood of the pus; the inflammation bursts. I sing, blow, sing, blow, about four times, and then it's better. That's what the song means, my friend.

Antonio made no reference to an essence within the woman's breast and did not precisely explain the physical nature of the sickness or affliction. The swelling, however, is likely to be near the surface of the breast in the skin because the action of his musical and physical therapy causes the inflammation to burst. Antonio's therapy for curing internal disorders is within the patient's conception, while European-derived medicine is outside it, as Lévi-Strauss (1967, 193) writes: "Once the sick woman understands, . . . she gets well. But no such thing happens to our sick when the causes of their diseases have been explained to them in terms of secretions, germs, or viruses. . . . The relationship between germ and disease is external to the mind of the patient, for it is a cause-and-effect relationship; whereas the relationship between monster and disease is internal to his mind, whether conscious or unconscious."

hoa for Birth Complications

The second musically and functionally distinct type of curing hoa is exemplified by three songs for eliminating birth complications. These hoatuma were sung on different days by three singers from neighboring villages: Bernardo Jiménez Tovar from Yaruara Ahoko, Antonio Lorenzano from Lorenzano Ahanoko, and Juan Bustillo Calderón from Hebu Wabanoko. All examples employ the tone system notated in music example 10.7. The hoa for birth complications is melodically and rhythmically unique in Warao curing music, as shown in music example 10.8, an excerpt sung by Bernardo, and music example 10.9, sung by Antonio. Bernardo's hoa can be heard in recorded example 22. As you follow the notation in music example 10.8 and listen to the recording, you can hear that the melodic contour is ⅔ 1 2⅞ 1, a melody completely different from the other hoa types.

Music Example 10.7. hoa for birth complications, tone system.

Antonio's song text (10.6) is typical of the hoa for eliminating birth complications.

Song Text 10.6. hoa Curing Song for Birth Complications, Antonio Lorenzano (Olsen Collection 72.8-19 and 20; sung as one complete song)

Go down, blood! The blood which you have rising in you, woman, go down!
Come out! The blood is clotting and it does not want to come out.

Music Example 10.8. hoa for birth complications (Bernardo Jiménez Tovar).
Olsen Collection 72.8-18.

mo - no mo - no mu - tu   mo - no mo - no mu - tu

𝅘𝅥 = 138

o - to - no - ma - ro a - ru - we - ru mu - tu   o - ri   e - nu - wa - rai

faster

o - ri   e - nu - wa - rai   o - ri   e - nu - wa - rai

o - ri   e - nu - wa - rai   mo - no   mo - no mu - tu

continues

mo - no mo - no mu - tu   mo - no mo - no mu - tu

Music Example 10.8 (*continued*)

The blood which is inside this woman, come out! Come out,
  blood!
It is in the woman's neck. Come out, blood!
It is in the other side of the woman's neck. Come out, blood!
It is in the woman's shoulder. Come out, blood!
It is in the woman's other shoulder. Come out, blood, clot of
  blood that is inside!
It is in the woman's ribs. Come out, blood!
It is in the other side of the woman's ribs. Come out, blood!
It is in the woman's stomach. Come out, blood!
It is in the woman's back. Come out, blood!
It is in the other side of the woman's back. Come out, blood!

Antonio's explanation of this hoa is very precise about the particular
parts of the woman's body:

This is a hoa for blood that is stopped inside a woman who
has given birth. Already it is clotting to kill this woman, to

Music Example 10.9. hoa for birth complications (Antonio Lorenzano). Olsen Collection 72.8-20.

o- ri e - no - wa - ra - ne   o- ri e - no - wa - ra - ne

o - ri e - no - wa - ra - ne   o - ri e - no - wa - ra - ne

mo - no mo - no mu - tu   mo - no   mo - no mu -

tu   mo - no   mo - no   mu - tu   continues

Music Example 10.9 (*continued*)

make her die. It doesn't come out, or spill out; it is stopped up. Therefore, the result is that you have to say the following to the blood in the neck of the woman: "Come on out. From the middle of the neck also, come on out. Blood of this woman, from the back, come out. Come out from the other side. Blood from the backbone, come out. Half of it, come out."

This is what I was singing: "The blood of the waist, come out. From the other side, come out. Blood from the liver, come out. From the other half, come out. Blood from the body of the woman, come out. From the other half, come out." And so on continues the hoa.

Thus, I blow into my hand, and another woman, the sister, prepares it and carries it, arriving to where the sick woman is, passing it over the back, or here. Thus, since I sang, singing all the words, the blood now has all come out, spilled, or fallen out.

That is all, my friend. This you have to learn well. I am teaching you. This is good. Everything that you need, I will sing in Warao and explain in Spanish, so that you understand it well.

The function of this particular hoa is to name all the parts of the woman's body where the blood is found, beginning with the neck and ending with the womb. It is essential that the blood (placenta) come out or the woman will die. Unique in Antonio's detailed commentary is the use of a female helper, a sort of midwife who carries the healer's breath and passes it over the patient's back. The reason is because the bahanarotu (or any man) must not touch a pregnant woman and risk coming into contact with her menstrual blood or placenta, for such contact will weaken the shaman's (or any man's) power and may even kill him (Wilbert 1972a, 101). So powerful is this song that Antonio, after singing about fifteen seconds of his hoa, stopped and ordered his pregnant sister-in-law out of hearing. He explained to me that if any pregnant woman were to hear this, especially someone in the beginning stages of pregnancy, she would have a miscarriage.

To summarize, let us look at music examples 10.2, 10.6, and 10.8 and sing them aloud, being sure to select the appropriate tempi. (If the words are difficult to pronounce, sing vocables such as "la la la.") Music must be both heard and performed so that we can fully appreciate how melody, rhythm, tempo, and dynamics are cultural identifiers. The Warao have carefully chosen these musical characteristics to fulfill particular functions. This is their native music theory.

There are no humanly controled preventive measures for the supernaturally caused intrusion illnesses studied in chapters 7 through 9, and accidents that cause wounds or natural bodily disorders as discussed in the present chapter are basically unavoidable. Certain musical techniques exist, however, for avoiding particular personal tragedies while traveling in the rain forest by foot or canoe. The next chapter will investigate some these preventive measures, which I call magical protection songs. Among the Warao these musical preventive measures are also types of hoa.

11 hoa Magical Protection Songs

It has always been essential for the Warao to travel the watery, swampy paths of their riverine tropical rain forest world, either in search of food, for work, to visit friends or relatives, or for religious reasons. After leaving the relative safety of their stilt houses, they must constantly guard against wild animals and, even more dangerous, malevolent spirit-possessed animals and other creatures from the supernatural world. Since primordial times, the Warao have probably sung hoa songs to protect themselves from supernaturally transformed animals and other ogres that they believe are capable of eating humans. All these supernatural beings are considered hebutuma, the designation also given to the ancestor spirits. During the Warao's travels, virtually any animal, from a normally harmless honeybee or moriche-palm grub worm to the already dangerous jaguar, can become transformed into a human-eating beast. Just as threatening are the ogres, which Barral (1964, 159–70; 1981, 123–32) calls *"los jebus duendes"* meaning elf, fairy, goblin, hobgoblin, or ghost hebutuma. The Warao have never seen several of the hebutuma described in this chapter. These are the unseen ogres, who are only heard singing—except for the silent one who occasionally gives off a few bumping sounds. The only protection from such supernatural creatures is the knowledge of hoa magical protection songs. The number of transformed animals or other hebu spirits for which the Warao have hoatuma or power songs for protection is far greater than those included in this chapter; indeed, the number is probably infinite. Nevertheless, during three field trips with the Warao I recorded and studied a representative number of magical protection songs for a variety of real animals, spiritually transformed beasts, and ogres.

The Warao magical protection song, called hoa by the Warao, is also a melodic formula. During the course of its performance a Warao singer names a malevolent hebu; protection is granted simply by the fact that the singer has identified the correct one and that its name is repeated many times. This functional-structural interpretation relates the protection hoa to all the other genres of Warao theurgical songs, each type having its own melodic formula.

Although they are capable of protecting a person from a transformed animal or a hebu spirit, Warao magical protection songs are not shamanistic because the singer does not undergo transformation while in a trance or TSC. The song itself has the power to remove the danger, and anyone who knows the song can sing it and thus reap its protective power. This hoa song type is distinct from the curing hoa discussed in chapter 10 and the shamanistic Hoa studied in chapter 9. Nevertheless, the relationship between this genre and the curing hoa is clear: both are sung to counteract a hebu spirit that has possessed or transformed something not necessarily dangerous (such as an animal or an object) into something very dangerous. Another similar characteristic is that the singer must blow out tobacco smoke to make the animal or spirit go away, just as the curing hoa singer's breath, often mixed with tobacco smoke as a visual power agent, is a common companion to song.

I collected twenty-one songs for protection against supernaturally transformed animals and other ferocious beasts and seven songs for protection against evil spirits that roam the deltaic rain forest (see Olsen 1980a, 1981). They were not recorded in their actual protection contexts but were sung to me in a teacher-student context, which is also traditional. It is customary, for example, for Warao young people to learn such songs from their elders, who often explain that many of their ancestors died because they did not know as many protection songs as the people know today. The usual answer to my question about the antiquity of the magical protection songs is that they are very ancient. Nowhere, however, have I found any other mention of this type of song style in the literature on the Warao. Collections of Warao mythology (narratives), for example, make no reference to any power songs for protection against spirits, animals, transformed animals, and ogres other than the use of a shotgun or a harpoon (see García 1971 and Wilbert 1972a). Most often, in fact, the narratives tell of Warao who wander through the rain forest and are confronted by spirits in the form of humans or animals, which either eat the people or directly or indirectly maim or kill them. This suggests either a more recent origin for the magical protection song or a scholarly disregard for the genre.

The singers of the twenty-one songs that I collected share several characteristics. First, they are all shamans, which suggests little more than the fact that shamans were always my most willing teachers. The Warao also considered these men to be the best singers. My friends mentioned several times, however, that anybody can sing these songs. A second characteristic is that all the singers were men, from which I also conclude that men were always my most willing teachers; women, in fact, were often reluctant to sing for me. Nevertheless, the men's explanations that *anybody* can sing the magical protection songs also includes women and children.

The Animals, the Ogres, and the Song Style

Table 11.1 lists the Warao animals appearing in the hoa magical protection songs in the Olsen Collection, including their names in English, Spanish, current Warao, ritual Warao (the names used in the songs), and zoology (scientific names) (Cervigon M. 1966). The table also lists the ogres appearing in the songs and includes a short description of each. I have selected several representative songs to discuss in detail.

In addition to the seven ogres listed in table 11.1, my teachers described two others, although they sang no songs for them. The first is a male hebu named Noböwerutu that is found in the rain forest and sounds like trees falling, although it does not have a voice. The second is a male hebu named Yebu Kamo, a creature that lives in the rain forest where it eats a fruit called hiorohi in Warao and camoare in Spanish. Swinging his arms, he picks the fruit and eats it. When a Warao sees a tree with this fruit scattered on the ground, he or she has to watch out for Yebu Kamo. Although it looks like a handsome man, Yebu Kamo is deadly; and when a Warao sees it, he or she is doomed.

The musical style of each magical protection song varies only slightly from singer to singer. The basic melodic pattern is centric, constructed on a tone system that usually consists of three pitches, one above and one below the principal tone at the interval of a major or minor second (usually 2 1 $\hat{7}$ or $\hat{2}$ 1 $\hat{7}$). Less frequently, it may consist of four pitches ($\hat{3}$ 2 1 $\hat{7}$). Another characteristic of many of the performances is dynamic nuance. Generally the beginning of each verse is sung loudly, but after a few seconds the singer suddenly drops in

Table 11.1. Topics named in Warao magical protection songs

Identification of animals

English	Spanish	Winikina Waraoan	Ritual Waraoan	Scientific
agouti	picure or acure	kahamuru	ayekurihi	Dasyprocta aguti
anteater	oso palmero		hiyayarakaba	Myrmecophega jubata
silky anteater	oso palmero	ana ibure arani	hehitu	Cyclopes didactylus
opossum	rabipelado or zarigüeya	nobu	hiatata	Didelphia marsupialis
jaguar	tigre	tobe	inamoso or ebobi	Felis onca
deer	venado	masi	koyara	Cervidae
tapir	tapir	naba or abitanaba	wayamo	Tapirus terrestris or Tapirus americanus
tortoise	morrocoy	hibahima, adoni, waku, daubaka, or araobaka	ahowama or wayamo	Geochelone denticulata
spectacled cayman	caiman or baba	duruduru or niarabaka	ahodura or akare	Caiman crocodylus
teju (lizard)	mato	mera	warisi	Tupinambis teguixin
anaconda	culebra de agua	wama	ahotutu	Eunectes murinus
boa constrictor	tragavenados	huba	yobamo	Constrictor constrictor
shark	tiburón or cazón: cazón chino, cazón trozo, cazón amarillo	ibute or banabana	yebuteri	Rhizoprionodon, Carcharhinus milberti, Carcharhinus acronotus
owl	lechuza	inanaid-arotu	tobesía	Strix passerina
larvae of moriche beetle	gusano de moriche or congorocho	ohiru amo	ayemo	Mauritia flexuosa
honeybee	colmena	simo-arotu	awanu	Apis mellifera
scorpion	alacrán	ayawaka	ayewaka	Scorpionida

Identification of ogre (hebu)

Waraoan	Description
Yorobiamo	Male ogre that lives in the trees in the northern rain forest, the husband of Yorokiamo
Yorokiamo	Female ogre that lives in the trees in the southern rain forest, the wife of Yorobiamo
Huramu	Male ogre of the west, who makes the sound "hu . . ." and is the husband of Ahiware
Ahiware	Female ogre of the east, who makes the sound "ah . . ." and is the wife of Huramu
Muyawana	Little one-eyed ogre in the sea
Hotuda Kamiana	Thunder ogre, born in hokonamu
Inareko Sanuka	Little silence ogre that is quiet except for making a few bumps and is invisible

amplitude and continues softly. This dynamic contrast is also found in some curing hoatuma and magical love songs and tends to reflect personal aesthetic choice rather than song style.

Music example 11.1 is a complete transcription in Western notation of a magical protection hoa for a transformed agouti. It is sung by José Antonio Páez, and can be heard as recorded example 23. The rhythm is quite free and determined somewhat by the text. Nevertheless, there is a slow pulse, as indicated in the notation. Similar to the curing hoa for wounds or natural disorders, the protection hoa is prayerlike.

hoa Magical Protection Song Texts

Seven songs are included for analysis, four pertaining to transformed animals and three to ogres (see Olsen 1980a, 131–61; 1981, 1–10). The animals are the agouti, jaguar, spectacled cayman, and owl, while the ogres are Yorobiamo, Yorokiamo, and Muyawana. Yorobiamo and Yorokiamo, who are husband and wife ogres, are discussed together. Because the singers explained their magical protection songs before actually singing them, I follow that order here.

The first example is for protection from a transformed agouti. In real life, an agouti is a rodent of the cavy or guinea pig family, about the size of a rabbit. It is a common animal in the South American rain forest and has great food value. Known as kahamuru among the Winikina Warao and called kuamare among the Wayo Warao further south, it has the ritual or archaic name of ayekurihi. In Spanish the animal is known as picure or acure. The singer, José Antonio Páez, explained his song this way:

> This is the hoa for when an animal converts itself into a large animal in order to eat a Warao (especially when a Warao is alone in the darkness while walking or hunting in the jungle). This is the knowledge we Indians have. Now I am going to sing. I am going to sing only a little because one knows only so much. This is so my friend will know how to scare away an animal which has been converted into a man-eating beast, so he will not be eaten. This is not a game. It is so when we are confronted by one of these animals we will not be eaten by it. It is so that when an animal comes, you can easily sing the hoa.

Music Example 11.1. Magical protection hoa (José Antonio Páez). Olsen Collection 74.7-1.

Music Example 11.1 (*continued*)

Music Example 11.1 (*continued*)

José Antonio's song is translated in song text 11.1, transcribed in music example 11.1, and heard in recorded example 23.

Song Text 11.1. Magical Protection hoa for Agouti, José Antonio Páez (Olsen Collection 74.7-1)

You are coming toward me, coming toward me, coming toward me.

I am really here alone, and you, hebu of the night, you hebu of the darkness, you are coming toward me, coming toward me.

This is your land, this is your name, this is your movement, this is your movement.

Hear your name, hear your name, hear your name, hear your name.

Yes, this is your name, yes, this is your name, a small land agouti, a small land agouti, a small land agouti.

Yes, this is your name, yes, your movement, yes, this is your name.

Go away from me, go away.

Go to where your house is in the earth, to your hole.

Go to your house, go to your house.

Take your thoughts away from here, to your house, and leave me, leave me, leave me.

Leave me, go away, make your path, go away, go away, go away, small agouti of the earth, small agouti.

The next hoa example is for protection from a transformed jaguar. The jaguar (*Felis onca*) is a large, powerful cat with brownish-yellow or buff skin marked with black spots. It is referred to as inamosoratu or ebobi in the ritual language of the Warao, known as tobe in current Warao, and called tigre (tiger) by local Venezuelans (even though true tigers are not found in South America). The hoa for protection against this animal is unique because it also makes use of a wooden stick that has a charm applied to it. José Antonio sang this song and explained it in the following way:

> This is a hoa. A person puts the hoa in a stick, and after singing the song he will throw the stick and the jaguar will run a little way and fall dead; or if the stick hits the jaguar (or

any animal the person meets) the animal will jump up and fall down dead. It is the song that has the power. After the animal dies the person can eat it if he first blows away the hoa and cuts off the part of the animal where the stick struck. If you know how to sing this song you do not need a gun. A person can kill birds or anything this way. One time a friend went hunting this way, saw two turkeys, and began to sing his hoa. He then threw his stick, but the stick missed and hit a branch instead. But still the two turkeys fell dead and the man had a good feast. Anyone knowing this song can hunt or protect himself in this way. It is only the song that has the power; it is not a spirit that hears the song, only the song. This song, by substituting different words, can kill any animal.

The words to his power song appear in song text 11.2. (The opening line, "Foot, run!" is an order to the jaguar's foot to make certain that the animal will run away.)

Song Text 11.2. Magical Protection hoa for Jaguar, José Antonio Páez (Olsen Collection 74.7-6)

Foot, run! Foot, run! Run away, foot, run! Run away! Run away!

Run away! Run, foot! Run away! Run away! . . .

I do this for the jaguar, *inamosoratu*.

Run away foot, run away! Run foot, run! . . .

I, by myself, with my stick will send you on your path.

Run away! Run, foot, run! . . .

I, myself, cut the stick only for the jaguar to give to him.

Run away! Run away fast, jaguar *inamasoratu*.

Run away, with your hair sticking up.

Run, run, with your hair sticking up . . .

O jaguar, with your tail raised and lowered again, run away, run away!

O jaguar *inamasoratu*, with your tail raised and curved, and with the fright that you have with your tail and hair raised, run away, run away, run away!

My voice and my breath are like this so you will run away. Run away!

The next hoa is a power song for protection from a transformed spectacled cayman. The spectacled cayman (*Caiman crocodylus*) is a reptile known as baba in Spanish, duruduru in current Winikina Warao, and noidu in Wayo. Another common Warao term for this reptile is niarabaka, especially in the Amacuro-Barima zone. The spectacled cayman is quite small when compared to its relatives in other tropical regions of the Americas. The singer, Jaime Zapata, gave the following explanation of the song:

> When the niarabaka gets wild he is transformed so he will eat us. This is the hoa of our ancients. A person does not forget this hoa; we all know it. When a person leaves in the canoe, going far from home, and when something bad comes we have to be ready. Surely, when this animal comes, it is to eat us. Thus, we have to sing this hoa. This is how I learned this hoa for caymans. One sings this so he won't be eaten by the caymans. Since a Warao is a man, so he won't cry, he has to be prepared to sing the hoa. If a person begins to cry and doesn't do anything, he will certainly die. This is very old, from the most ancient times. Before, when the Warao didn't know this hoa, they certainly died; but not now. One day we began teaching each other this hoa and, even though we live at the edge of the river, the caymans do not eat us any more. Maybe some people who still live in the jungle will die because they don't know this hoa. We have heard that transformed caymans do eat people if those people don't know this song. The transformed caymans have eaten many Warao. Why didn't they sing this hoa? Why did they let themselves be eaten? This is the end.

Jaime then sang the following text:

Song Text 11.3. Magical Protection hoa for Cayman, Jaime Zapata (Olsen Collection 74.7-12)

You are coming. You are coming.
Born in the river, you are born in the river.
This is your movement and your name.
Born in the river, born in the water.

You are coming, hebu of the night, of the darkness.

This is your movement and your name: a small spectacled cayman of the river, a small spectacled cayman of the rain forest.

Go far away from me, go far from here.

This is your name and your movement: a small spectacled cayman of the river.

This is your name, this is your movement.

Go away from me, far away.

The next example is a power song for protection from a transformed owl. The owl (*Strix passerina*) is known as lechuza in Spanish and imanaid arotu in current Warao, although the singer, Antonio Lorenzano, only used the word tobesia, its ritual or archaic name. The Warao fear the owl because of its association with the supernatural, as Barral (1957, 200) explains:

> *Tobesia—Lechuza.* "Chauro." The Warao call it *imanaid-arotu,* "senor de la noche avanzada" or "lord of the approaching night." The owl is one of the so-called witch birds. The Warao belief about the magical influence of this night fowl on them is the following: "If, when the owl is singing and a person imitates it, that mocking person will be converted into a jaguar." From this expression comes the name *tobesia* (tobe-isía, "with the tiger" or "in tiger").

Antonio explained his song before singing it: "This is a hoa of an evil bird. When a boy cries, then the bird also begins to cry. For us, from the most ancient times, this bird is also a spirit. During the day it sleeps, but during the night it does not. It comes looking for a house where a boy is crying; then it comes listening for the crying boy and it also begins to cry. It is bad, this bird." Song text 11.4 shows the words of his power song:

Song Text 11.4. Magical Protection hoa for Owl, Antonio Lorenzano (Olsen Collection 72.8-111)

You are coming toward me, you are coming, you are coming. . . .

You are coming to where I am.

Go far away from me, go far away, take your thoughts from
me.

I am in my house during the night, and you, oh hebu of the
darkness, are coming toward me when I am sleeping.

Take your thoughts from me and go away.

You do not know your name; this is your name, yes, this is
your movement.

Oh bird, bird, bird, bird, bird, bird, bird.

Oh bird, bird, small owl witch bird, small owl witch bird.

This is your very movement and name, so hear your name, oh
bird, bird, bird, small owl witch bird, small owl witch bird,
small owl witch bird.

Oh hebu of the night, you are looking for me near my house,
and you are sitting on a branch of a tree, mister bird, clearly
singing and speaking.

Oh bird, bird, small owl witch bird, small owl witch bird.

This is your movement, and I am singing.

Go away from me, go far away from me, return to your house
where you belong and go away from me, go far away.

Oh bird, bird, small owl witch bird, small owl witch bird,
small owl witch bird.

Oh bird, bird, bird, bird.

After Antonio finished singing his protection song, he further explained it:

A person (or the people in general), when he is sleeping here
or there, does not know when this bird comes inside the village from afar. It comes silently here, or here [he points],
wherever it wants. Where there are people, there it comes.
When it comes it stays near the house, silently waiting for a
boy to cry, or for the children to cry. Now then, it is silent,
right? But, when a boy in the house begins to cry, the bird
also begins to cry at the same time as when the child is crying.
Then, when the people hear this somebody asks, "Hey, why is
this child crying so much?"

"It is because there is an evil bird that arrived, and it is
also crying" is the answer.

Then the people say, "Well, then, light your candle. Get out of here, bird, go away from here!" This bird is very bad. This bird is the same as all the other evil spirits.

The next power song is for protection against two ogres named Yorobiamo and Yorokiamo. Although the hoa was addressed only to the hebu spirit Yorobiamo, singer Jaime Zapata explained that it was actually sung to nahakahotu, the name given collectively to the male and female ogres who inhabit the treetops in the northern and southern parts of the Orinoco Delta rain forest. Yorobiamo is the male ogre that lives in the north, while his wife, Yorokiamo, lives in the south. They are distinguished by their voices: the large voice belongs to the male and the small voice to the female. The Warao say they have never seen these ogres; but they know that if these hebu spirits draw near, they will eat the Warao. The nahakahotu always come to where the tallest trees of the rain forest are. They may approach when a Warao is walking or paddling his canoe, but they never come near a Warao house. The ogres may also appear up river, especially where the Winikina River becomes narrow. Jaime spoke about this song and the nahakahotu:

> I am singing for both the male and the female hebu spirits. When you sing for them both, it is the same hoa. Both these hebutuma sing—the woman's voice is finer and the male's voice is heavier. This is the hoa of the hebu nahakahotu. If you don't sing this you will die. A person has to blow like this with the hand [he blew through his fist] and then the spirits go away. The female hebu, Yorokiamo, is from the south; the male, Yorobiamo, is from the north. A person hears their singing. The woman has a fine voice, and she is found in the south during the day. Her noise is the same as that produced by a branch crashing in the jungle or by teeth rubbing together. She is found in the tops of the trees. The male is found in the north, in the top of the largest tree. His voice is harsher than that of the female hebu. At times they can be heard from afar, one calling to the other. This song has power so these hebutuma will not come. Everyone knows it, even the children. This is it; if you want to learn it, record it.

Here is the text from the power song that Jaime sang as protection from Yorobiamo:

Song Text 11.5. Magical Protection hoa for Ogres, Jaime Zapata (Olsen Collection 74.7-2)

Now he comes toward me.

This is your movement, hebu, hebu, hebu, hebu, hebu, hebu, hebu, hebu, hebu; this is your movement and this is your name.

This is your name, oh hebu Yorobiamo, Yorobiamo.

Remember your house is up in the sky.

Go away from me, remember your food.

This is your name, hebu, hebu, hebu Yorobiamo, hebu Yorobiamo, hebu, hebu.

Oh hebu, hebu Yorobiamo, hebu Yorobiamo, this is your movement, this is your name.

Remember your house, remember your food.

Remember the fruit that was born in the sky, oh hebu, hebu, little hebu Yorobiamo, little hebu Yorobiamo.

Jaime continued to explain that the fruit born in the sky, hiadehore (mentioned in the last verse of the song), is like an onion that grows on a tree in the sky. When he sings "remember your food" or "remember the fruit that was born in the sky," he means "I am not your food and I am not good to eat; eat the hiadehore fruit instead; it tastes better."

Antonio Lorenzano sang a similar song for magical protection from both Yorobiamo and Yorokiamo. In it he names both ogres, as the song's concluding passages show.

Song Text 11.6. Magical Protection hoa for Ogres, Antonio Lorenzano (Olsen Collection 72.8-110)

Your feet belong in your house. Go away to your hammock, go away from here with your canoe, your canoe, your canoe.

Oh hebu, hebu, hebu Yorokiamo, Yorokiamo, Yorokiamo, hebu, hebu, hebu Yorobiamo, hebu Yorobiamo, hebu, hebu.

Antonio then explained his song:

I will now explain in Spanish about this hoa that I just sang. For example, when my wife and I go walking in the rain forest, looking for honey or looking for the small fish of the

moriche grove, then this bad spirit presents itself to me. I can
hear it singing. Then I say to my wife, "Now, this is bad. An
evil spirit has made its presence known to us. This is hebu.
Well, don't worry because I know how to sing its hoa." So, I
start to sing this hoa and the spirit goes away. After you have
finished singing you must blow like this, into your hand, so it
comes out the other side. [He made a fist.] The name of the
male hebu, the husband, is Yorobiamo. The woman, its wife,
is called Yorokiamo. I learned this song from my old uncle, a
long time ago. This is all, my friend.

The final example of this genre is for protection from an ogre named
Muyawana. Muyawana Sanuka, the ogre's full name, translates as
"little one-eyed ogre." The singer of this power song, Jaime Zapata, explained it as follows: "Muyawana Sanuka is a hebu which has one
large eye that is like the moon. This hebu is found in the sea, and its
one eye is like a spotlight. When it gets close to a Warao, the Indian
loses his senses and is eaten by the hebu. Also, if a Warao finds a fish
or animal with one eye, he must not eat it because the hebu will come
and eat the Warao." This magical protection song was perhaps inspired by a lighthouse on the Orinoco River. Its song text is as follows:

Song Text 11.7. Magical Protection hoa for Ogre, Jaime Zapata (Olsen Collection 74.7-3)

Now you are coming toward me, here you come, you are ar-
   riving.
This is your movement, this is your name.
You are a hebu born on the hill, you are hebu, little hebu
   Muyawana, little hebu Muyawana.
This is your movement, so go far away from me, go to your
   house on the hill.
Oh hebu, hebu, hebu, little hebu Muyawana, Muyawana
   Sanuka.
Go far away from me, get out of here, go away to your house,
   to your house on the hill, oh hebu, hebu, little hebu
   Muyawana, Muyawana Sanuka.

The major element of power in the hoa magical protection songs, besides the song itself, is the process of naming the dangerous trans-

formed animal, ogre, or spirit. Unlike the shamanistic curing songs, however, there is no patient-specialist relationship because the singer sings for his or her own protection (and perhaps that of his family). Nevertheless, the singer is a specialist who has considerable (and, the Warao hope, sufficient) knowledge to ward off dangers from transformed animals, ogres, or spirits. The singer's special type of knowledge, however, cannot be as clearly explained in medical or psychological terms as can the shaman's knowledge. But the protection that the singer receives from the knowledge of his or her protection songs can perhaps be explained in two ways. First, if the transformed animals are actually real animals that have been transformed by the singer through his or her own fear, the real power of the song may be to overcome that fear. In a sense, then, the singer is both the patient and the curing specialist. The second viewpoint, an emic interpretation rather than an etic one, is that the spirit (that is, the transformed animal or ogre, ergo the danger) disappears when properly named (see Basso 1985, 245). This Warao interpretation is based on their belief that the supernatural context is real and that the power of the magical protection songs is a real supernatural power. To the Warao, of course, there is no doubt that the spirits are real and that the magical protection songs provide genuine protection.

12 hoa Magical Love Songs

There are two types of hoa for magical love: nisahoa for courting and marriage and marehoa for lovemaking. Exclusively the property of men, the songs are often sung by shamans, although being a shaman is not a requirement for the songs to have power.

Nisahoa

The nisahoa is sung by a young man or by a father for his son to make a girl fall in love and marry the young man. According to Barral (1957, 167), nisa means "to gather, to hold out your hand to something, to buy, to marry." The ceremony of marriage among traditional Warao amounts to little more "than overtly moving one person's hammock next to that of another" (Wilbert 1972a, 100). This act implies sleeping together, making the nisahoa and marehoa a matter of degree. In fact, none of the magical love songs that I recorded were called nisahoa by my teachers.

Marehoa

The marehoa is also sung by a young man or by a father for his son; however, it is performed to make a woman of choice unable to resist the male's sexual desires. José Antonio Páez explained that the marehoa is to make a girl go crazy with sexual desire: "When this is sung the woman goes crazy and takes off her clothes. She doesn't eat and will die unless the same man cures her, or another who knows." Mare translates as "joy," and the word marehoa can be glossed as "magical song for sexual gratification." Pedro Rivero explained that the marehoa "is happy. Whichever man who wishes to fall in love sings this hoa. It is to make the woman fall in love with him. After, if they want to marry, they marry. If the woman doesn't want to fall in love, then the man continues to sing this hoa." Menegildo Paredes explained the concept this way: "This is the hoa that we use, the hoa that many people around here sing for a woman who doesn't want to court a man.

Thus, whenever a man begins to sing this song, immediately the woman begins to look for him. This is a Warao prayer, a marehoa."

According to my Warao teachers, the marehoa is not shamanistic and does not require a shaman to sing it, contrary to what Wilbert (1972a, 101) writes: "a man who is attracted to a woman will make his intentions known by staring fixedly at her. Should such overt courting fail, he may secretly ask a shaman to sing a particular chant that is supposed to have an aphrodisiac effect." Likewise, Turrado Moreno (1945, 172) writes that the marehoa *does* require the aid of a shaman:

> When a Warao in love wishes to possess the heart of a girl whom he desires, after exhausting all the recourses that love invents in these cases, he asks the assistance of a famous wizard to apply the powerful remedy of the marejoa. By way of another female, he communicates to the selected girl who, from that moment, cries and trembles with fright.
>
> For the bewitching ceremony the wizard builds a hut out of temiche palm fronds and cazupo leaves not far from the house of the girl. The idea is so she will hear the marejoa, if he desires it.
>
> The Warao lover, the wizard, and an assistant, move into their hut. Once there, the wizard makes a very long wina cigar . . . and inhales a great amount of smoke which he blows toward the house of the girl he wishes to make fall in love. Immediately he begins to sing the marehoa . . . and when finished, the wizard leaves his hiding place and throws small particles of yuruma flour towards the girl. Later the assistant who is present at the ceremony tells all of this to the girl who ordinarily, for fear of death, renders herself to the male suitor.

Turrado Moreno does not specify the particular type of specialist in his analysis of the marehoa but simply uses the Spanish term brujo (wizard). It is likely that the marehoa that he knew and described was sung by a shaman. Nevertheless, the marehoa does not seem to require a shaman today, at least in the Winikina area, a fact suggested by an interview with Antonio Lorenzano:

> *A.L.:* This is a marehoa. Luis Mariano, who died, taught me this.
> *D.O.:* Can you explain it to me?

A.L.: Sure. Like the lullabies, this is long and difficult. I sang it complete, from the foot to the hair. Talking and writing, as before, I can explain it, little by little.

D.O.: What is the function of a marehoa?

A.L.: This is so a man and woman will fall in love. It is so the woman will be in heat for a man. She is afraid to, and it is difficult for her to do so. Thus, singing, I blow, and she would come to me. It would be like that.

D.O.: Therefore, if a person wants to marry a woman. . . .

A.L.: Yes, it is so a man can marry a woman.

D.O.: And if she doesn't want to marry, what do you do?

A.L.: If she doesn't want to marry, then you begin to sing so she will want to marry. If you do not sing the marehoa at her, nothing happens.

D.O.: You yourself can sing this?

A.L.: Yes, I myself can sing this in order to get a woman.

D.O.: You do not need a wisiratu?

A.L.: No, no, no. Since I know the marehoa, I myself have to sing.

Like the hoa for curing wounds and other physical ailments and like the magical protection songs, the marehoa can be sung by any man, according to my Warao teachers. The key to its success is naming—not a spirit directly but a woman and all the parts of her body. When properly named, she will behave as if she is in heat for the man, according to Warao belief.

Marehoa Music and Song Texts

The musical formula or melodic pattern used for the marehoa is similar to the naming motive of Warao shamanistic curing music. The basic tone system is 5 4 ₹ 1, which is used with several variations. Pedro Rivero, for example, begins his song with some fluctuation, but in several seconds he settles into the melodic pattern. (Listen to recorded example 24.) As his song progresses, however, the fundamental tone (1) occurs rarely; and when it does, it is very soft and nearly inaudible. Instead, the pitches 5 4 ₹ are emphasized, as the transcription in music example 12.1 indicates—even to the extent of terminating on pitch 3 at the end of musical phrases. Bernardo Jiménez Tovar also uses this technique in his curing hoa style (see music examples 10.1 and 10.2), as does José Antonio Páez in his magical protection songs (see music example 11.1). The technique is, therefore, individually determined. Pedro Rivero also rises in pitch, perhaps another individually determined technique, as the beginning and ending excerpts of music example 12.1 reveal. In addition, the marehoa is very rhythmical, as you can hear in recorded example 24.

The text of Pedro Rivero's marehoa is reproduced in full in transliterated Warao and English. In it the naming process is clear, as are the repetitions of the things named. Along with naming, both word and musical repetition are important characteristics that give a singer power through song. In spite of the length of Pedro's performance, he stopped short of completing the song; therefore, not all the parts of the woman's body are named.

Song Text 12.1. Marehoa, Pedro Rivero
(Olsen Collection 72.8-100)

hotonomaro hotonomaro hotonomaro hotonomaro hotono-
maro hotonomaro hotonomaro hotonomaro

Oh woman, woman, woman, woman, woman, woman, woman, woman

miana miana hotonomaro miana hotonomaro nami miana
miana miana miana

The hoa, the hoa, oh woman, the hoa, woman, nami, the hoa, the hoa, the hoa, the hoa

hotonomaro hotonomaro hotonomaro hotonomaro hotono-
maro ayomu ayomu mokomoko hatehore hatehore hatehore
hatehore

Oh woman, woman, woman, woman, woman, in the feet, in the feet and toes, this is it, this is it, this is it, this is it

hotonomaro hotonomaro ayomu ayekobe aribuhu tane
hatekore hatekore hatekore

Music Example 12.1. Marehoa (Pedro Rivero). Olsen Collection 72.8-100.

Oh woman, woman, in the feet and sole of the foot, for the movement, this is it, this is it, this is it

tamaha wituma hotonomaro ayomu mokomoko mokomoko mokomoko mokomoko ayomu mokomoko aribuhu tane
It is for these, oh woman, in the feet and toes, toes, toes, toes, in the feet and toes, for the movement

ine mauwara aribu naya hotonomaro ayomu mokomoko aribuhu hate ine aribuhu hate ine
I and my song, for the movement, oh woman, in the feet and toes, this is for the movement, I am for the movement, I

miana miana miana miana hotonomaro hotonomaro hotono-maro hotonomaro
The hoa, the hoa, the hoa, the hoa, oh woman, woman, woman, woman

ayomu matana mokomoko aribuhutane tanewitu ayomu mokomoko aribuhu tane
In the feet, in the other foot and toes, for the movement of the feet, in the toes, this is the movement

abate ine hotonomaro saba mawara aribute ine hotonomaro hotonomaro
That is where I put it, oh woman, for her is my song, I am for the movement, oh woman, woman

ayomu ayekobe ayekobe mokomoko horo mokomoko aribuhutane, tamaha wituma
In the feet, the sole of the foot, the toes, and the knuckles of the toes, for the movement, it is for these

ine kamiana kamiana miana hatekore utuya utuya bubuwata hatekore hatekore hotonomaro
I, our hoa, our hoa, the hoa, this is it, from afar, from afar, from the high land, this is it, this is it, oh woman

*ayomu aribuhutane hokonamu wata hatekore kamianare
hatekore hatekore hatekore miana*

In the feet, for the movement, from hokonamu, there, this is
it, our hoa, this is it, this is it, this is it, miana

*hotonomaro hotonomaro awaba awaba awaba mokomoko
aribuhutane aribuhutane tamahasi wituma ine*

Oh woman, woman, death, death, death, for the toes, the
movement, the movement, it is for these, I

*hotonomaro ahowaba aribuhutane aribuhate ine miana
miana miana miana miana hokonamu wata ayekobo
hatekore taisi*

Oh woman, for the leg, for the movement, the movement, I,
the hoa, the hoa, the hoa, the hoa, the hoa, from hokonamu
there, there it is, it is this

*ayewihi hatekore hatekore hatekore domusanuka hatekore do-
musanuka hatekore awai karamuna domu hatekore akara-
muna domu hukuhuku hatekore*

In the wings, this is it, this is it, this is it, it is the little bird, it
is the little bird, calling and singing, it is the little bird, this
is the name, hummingbird, this is it

*hotonomaro hotonomaro amaretane amaretane amaretane
amaretane amaretane amaretane*

Oh woman, woman, it is truly for love, truly for love, truly for
love, truly for love, truly for love, truly for love

*abane abane miana miana miana miana miana miana
hokonamu*

I put, I put the hoa, the hoa, the hoa, the hoa, the hoa, the
hoa, from hokonamu

*ayerauna ayekuahaya ayanoakatu domu sanuka taimonuka
wituma hotonomaro hotonomaro ayebihitane*

In the trees, at the very treetops, that is where it is, it is the little bird, it is these, oh woman, woman, that which is in the wings

abane abane abate abate miana miana miana miana miana miana miana, hatekore hatekore hotonomaro hotonomaro hotonomaro

I put, I put, put, put the hoa, the hoa, the hoa, the hoa, the hoa, the hoa, the hoa, this is it, this is it, oh woman, woman, woman

ayebihitane ayebihitane orimatanane orimatanane orimatanane, hotonomaro ayebihitane abane abane miana miana miana miana miana miana miana miana miana

In the wings, in the wings, in both wings, in both wings, in both wings, oh woman, in the wings, I put, I put, the hoa, the hoa, the hoa, the hoa, the hoa, the hoa, the hoa, the hoa

tamahasebetuma hotonomaro hotonomaro atehorina aribuhutane abate ine

These are it and nothing more, oh woman, woman, for the body, for the movement, I put

hokonamu wata ayebebe anaibaribari hatekore hatekore, hotonomaro hotonomaro amaretane

From hokonamu, the leaves shimmer in the wind, this is it, this is it, oh woman, woman, truly for love

anaibaribarinatane anaibaribarinatane kayukane kayukane kayukane kayukane

It is in the wind they shimmer, it is in the wind they shimmer, with that, with that, with that, with that

amorabu ekukwane amorabu ekukwane ayereba ayereba ayereba hatekore hatekore

The hand, inside the hand, the hand, inside the hand, the food, the food, the food, this is it, this is it

ayerebatane ayerebatane hotonomaro ayerebatane tamahisebe-
tuma tamahisebetuma ine

It is for the food, it is for the food, oh woman, it is for the
food, it is these, it is these, I

hotonomaro awabatane awabatane miana miana miana
miana miana miana amaretane amaretane

Oh woman, it is like death, it is like death, the hoa, the hoa,
the hoa, the hoa, the hoa, the hoa, it is truly for love, it is
truly for love

anaibaribaritane ayekotibutane tobatane diana maribu dibu
narute hotonomaro saba miana miana miana miana

It is when they shimmer, the method of this game is thus,
now, my word, word goes, oh woman, looking, the hoa, the
hoa, the hoa, the hoa

miana miana miana miana miana miana miana miana

The hoa, the hoa, the hoa, the hoa, the hoa, the hoa, the hoa,
the hoa

Pedro's lengthy song text can be paraphrased in the following manner:

Oh woman, this hoa, this prayer I sing for you, woman. Oh
woman, I sing this hoa and name your feet, your toes. Oh
woman, I name your feet, inside your feet, and your toes. Yes,
this is being named for you, oh woman, in the sole of your
foot, and in the other foot, and for the movement of both feet.
For this I am singing and naming, oh woman. This is where I
place the hoa, and for you I sing. I sing this hoa and I name
your feet, the sole of your feet, your toes, the knuckles of your
toes, and the movement of your feet. For this I sing and this
is it.

I am naming as hoa that which is from afar, from the high
land far from here, and it is for you, oh woman, for your feet
and the movement of your feet. From way over there in
hokonamu, the eastern part of the world, from there comes
the hoa. I have never seen this, and this is the hoa for you, oh

woman. It is like death, and it is for your toes, for the movement of your feet, and this is it. Oh woman, I name your leg,
and the movement of your leg, and I name as hoa that from
the eastern part of the world, from the dawn. There, there it
is, and it is this.

The hoa is in the wings of the little bird in the east. Yes, it
is is coming in the wings of the little bird. I call its name, I call
your name, oh hoa in the wings of the little bird. The little
bird is singing, and this is its name—hummingbird. This is
the hoa for you, oh woman. It is truly for love, yes, truly for
love. I name as hoa and put as hoa the hummingbird from the
eastern part of the world, from the dawn, from there, at the
very tops of the tree where the little bird is. Yes, it is just like
that, oh woman, woman, just like that which is in the wings
of the little bird. I name this and place this as hoa. Yes, this is
it, this is it, oh woman—it is that which is in the wings, in
both wings—and I name it and place it as hoa for you. This is
it, oh woman, for your body, and for the movement of your
body.

I call the hoa from the eastern part of the world, from
hokonamu, and I place it in you. The hoa is the leaves that
shimmer in the wind. Yes, this is it, this is it. Oh woman, it is
truly for love. The hoa is the shimmer of the leaves that is
caused by the wind. It is in the wind that they shimmer, and
this is the hoa.

I name your hand, oh woman, and inside your hand. The
hand is used for food, and this is it. Oh woman, I name the
hand used for food, for eating food. This is it, nothing more.
Oh woman, it is like death, but it is truly for love. I am
naming as hoa the shimmer of the leaves in the land of the
dawn.

This is the method of this game of love, and these now are
my words that go looking and naming the hoa for you, oh
woman. Oh hoa, be named. Oh hoa.

The power of the marehoa is achieved by naming all the parts of the
woman's body and, in the process, naming and calling upon supernatural elements to work, step by step, on the singer's behalf or on behalf

of the lovesick person whom the singer is helping. The choice of supernatural entities or elements named as hoa metaphorically (for us) relate to the parts of the woman's body that are being named. For example, when the singer finishes singing about the woman's feet and toes, he names the wings of the hummingbird as hoa. Both the woman's feet and the hummingbird's wings are appendages. Likewise, when he names the movement of the woman's body, he names the movement of the leaves in the treetops, whose shimmering or swaying movements in the wind are a metaphor (for us) for the swaying of the woman's torso. This metaphoric relationship is also clear in the hoarotu's choice of entities named during his curing songs—for example, when his diagnosis of the patient reveals physical characteristics that are matched by hoatuma that have similar characteristics (see chapter 9). This type of textual conjugation is vital for the song (or, more specifically, the naming process) to have curative or causative power.

Another marehoa, sung by José Antonio Páez, is very explicit in its intent. Song text 12.2 is his translation of his hoa for magical love:

Song Text 12.2. Marehoa, José Antonio Páez (Olsen Collection 1974.7-1)

hotonomaro hotonomaro; obonona yakara hatekore; tamaha witu tamaha ine otonomari obonona yakarawitu ine
Oh woman, woman; it is the good knowledge, this is it; I am a man with very good knowledge.

hotonomaro ayiyaka yakara ayahoro yakarawitu hane ihi; mahiyaka tane abane
The woman is dressed very well and her undergarments are good; give your clothes to me.

ine wite mayeyaka hatehore yakarawitu; hatekore hotonomaro; ahiyaka tane abane yabane witu
I remove these good clothes from you; this is it, woman; I take your clothes for me always.

hotonomaro obaru obaru obaruya, hatekore; ine wite maobaru yakara witu; tane abane yabane

Woman, I surrender my hammock to you, this is it; I give my
personal good hammock to you; I give it to you.

waetu ine ine wite maobaru yakara witu hatekore hotonomaro;
aobaro tane abane waetu ine hotonomaro hotonomaro
I left my very good hammock for you, this is it, oh woman;
my hammock is good and I give it to you, oh woman,
woman.

obonona aikwarana witu hatekore witu hotonomaro hotono-
maro obonona nanisane nisane witu; hotonomaro obonona
mehoroko obonona
There is a lack of passion of the woman, woman, and I take
away the sense that you have; the passion of the woman is
pensive like the earth is quiet.

aenare tane abane waetu ine obonona yakara hatekore
kasabukahawitu maobonona yakarawitu tane
I put this hoa this way into her, so she will have this good desire for my good desire.

tamaha hatekore domu hatekore hatekore domu namu-
natekoho hatekore tamaha wituma; obonona yakarawitu
hatekore hotonomaro
This is a bird, this is, this is a bird, this is a mockingbird, this
is it; this is the good thought for the woman.

obonona abane abane yabane waetu hotonomaro ayiyaka
akobukana; ayakara witu katakore hekobukane
The thought I put, I put this this way so the woman lifts up
her dress; suddenly, when the dress is up it is good.

taisikayukane kasabukaha wituma ine hotonomaro obonona
aikwarana tane; abane abane waetu ine tamahawitu
hatekore
This I will put to you woman, so you will lose your sense; I
put this, I put this to you, this is it.

barawaida ekukwane hatekore owaraka ariawara; hatekore tamahawituma hotonomaro obonona aikwaranatane aburetane; heburetane waetu ine

There is a sea within the sea, this is where a monkey was born; this is it, there, woman, to make you lose your sense and make you crazy; I make you crazy.

The intent of this marehoa is clearly sexual gratification, although the outcome may be marriage, as suggested by the male's giving up his good hammock. José Antonio names two animals to assist him with his conquest: a black mockingbird (arrendajo in Spanish) and a monkey. While he did not provide specific information about them or suggest a double meaning for the black mockingbird, he explained that the monkey is no ordinary monkey—it is owaraka, an animal that has the form of a Warao. Because it names a monkey, this marehoa may be similar to a powerful magical love song called nakumare, about which Turrado Moreno (1945, 172) writes the following:

> The *nakumare*—from naku—monkey, and *mare*—happy in love: it is the most powerful and infallible marehoa, to enamor a woman.
>
> When, for whatever cause, circumstance, or motive, the marehoa does not have an effect, then the wizard applies the nakumare in the same way, manner, and form explained before with respect to the hut, the wina cigar, the tossing of yuruma flour, etc.
>
> The nakumare is distinguished from the marehoa only in that the knowledgeable wizard repeats, various times, with the same words, with the same gentle, feigned, entrancing, and sensual voice, the powerful and infallible song of the nakumare.
>
> The word "hoa" signifies chant, prayer; "marehoa" is the prayer of the enamored man, of happiness when enamoring a woman: "nakumare" means "happy monkey," that is, chant to make one happy, like the monkey which, upon being content, jumps, grins, and is amusing.

Whether or not José Antonio's marehoa is a nakumare is unclear because neither he nor any other singer gave me that term. In addition, the type of monkey is not specified; and the term owaraka does not appear in any Warao dictionary. Nevertheless, this magical love song differs from those sung by Antonio Lorenzano and Pedro Rivero because the parts of the woman's body are not named—only the assisting supernatural forces that are placed in the woman to drive her crazy. This resemblance to a Hoa inflicting song is not coincidental because José Antonio Páez is a powerful hoarotu. Here the inflicting power, however, is not to provide human food for Hoebo but sexual gratification and perhaps a spouse for the singer.

Another type of hoa is discussed in the next chapter, and it is related to the marehoa because sexual intercourse is one of the intended results of its power. The desired sexual relations, however, are not physically with a mortal woman, but supernaturally with a divine being, the mother of the forest, who is the cachicamo tree from which a Warao canoe is made.

13 Magical Songs for Canoe Building

Canoe construction is a very important process for the Warao. The watery world of the "canoe people" makes sturdy crafts a necessity; and to accommodate their needs, the Warao construct two types of dugout canoe—large and small. The larger craft, which is intended for open water and regional use and is fitted with a large outboard motor, requires an elaborate ceremony using magical songs for its construction. Ritual and power songs, also called hoatuma, are necessary because the cachicamo tree from which a large craft is made is believed to be the embodiment of Dauarani (mother of the forest), the first wisiratu shaman-priest (Wilbert 1977, 23). The entire process, from cutting the tree to finishing the canoe, includes a ritualistic act of sexual intercourse between her and the master canoe craftsman, or moyotu. The smaller craft, for regional use with paddles only, requires elaborate construction techniques but no ritual. The construction processes of both canoes have songs associated with them, but only the building of a large canoe requires the use of magical songs sung directly to the supernatural.

Large Canoe Construction: The Song Style and the Ritual

My sole teacher for the ritual construction of a large canoe was Antonio Lorenzano, a bahanarotu. His songs for building a ritual canoe are based on the minor-third foundation interval (3 1), and the complete tone system includes only one pitch above that interval (see the notation in music example 13.1). Like the Warao shamanistic and other theurgical songs, melody is subservient to the words, with certain points of rest emphasized by elongated tones. Music example 13.2 is an excerpt from a lengthy ritual canoe construction song, which Antonio performed noncontextually. When he finished singing, he gave the following explanation:

Music Example 13.1. Large canoe construction song, tone system.

This is what the song means. Last night I dreamed, and the dream told me, "You have to chop down a cachicamo tree to make a canoe." I thought, "We don't have a large and pretty canoe. Nor do we have a small canoe. We don't have a large one for a thirty-three horsepower motor. We are always borrowing a canoe from afar, from other people, from the master, from Renaud" [the Creole owner of the sawmill]. The dream said, "Now, you are my brother, my son, my grandson, already you are everything. You are understanding that which I am speaking." Thus, I need a large cachicamo so that we can have a well-built canoe for a thirty-three horsepower motor. Thus, we (the sons, the sons-in-law, the grandsons) know how, and the next day we have to get our cutting tools. I get my hatchet and we get prepared and sharpen the tools, very sharp. I dreamed in the night, another night, that when it dawns we should go. We should go to where the cachicamo is. Upon arriving at the cachicamo, everyone goes up into the tree. Someone yells, "Hey, is it good?"

"Yes, it is good!" responds another.

Others arrive and go up. They say the same: "It is good."

"Where will this cachicamo fall?"

"Well, it will fall here. Here we are going to cut, here we are going to let it fall, along here." So that the tree doesn't go into the ground, we cut small trees to form a crisscross, so that the main tree doesn't stick into the ground, so that the trunk doesn't stick into the ground. Now, if the cachicamo is large and if nothing is done, when the cachicamo falls its branches will become buried and you cannot cut them. For that reason, when there are enough people, we cut smaller trees around the location. During the winter we cut the tree, cutting the trunk of the cachicamo. This is what the song is about.

The tree fell. Then an older man, like me, cuts a meter stick. How many meters are we going to cut? We are going to cut twelve meters. In barras that is fourteen; twelve meters calculates into fourteen barras. That is a good length. Therefore, I say, "Here it is too little, here it is good." You see, one person is in charge, one person sings. Others come and cut.

Now, when the cachicamo maiden comes she also says

[sings], "Half of me is male, and the other half of me is female." That is what the cachicamo says. The song which I just sang says that. Then, at the same time she says, "I am a wisiratu. With the breeze, with the wind, you will speak [sing] to me, along with the movement of the leaves. Just like the rest of the little trees, when the wind blows all the branches and the leaves move. In the same way all my branches and leaves move, because I am worth more than the rest of the trees." The cachicamo is worth more than the rest of the trees. The cachicamo is a big stick of wood, we could say, like a chief, a leader. It yells, announces, and so forth; it is a stick like us. Well, this is the red cachicamo. The white cachicamo, we can say, is like the leader of the trees. For that reason, there is a song for felling the tree. A person begins to sing, joyfully.

Now then after this, when the tree is felled we ask, "Where are we going to make the road?"

"Here we are going to open a road, here we will make a trail like a little canyon." We take manaca palm trees to make the cañaote [corduroy road]. We do this because at this moment the tree trunk is very, very heavy. Wow, is it heavy, because the tree trunk is still solid. There is still lots of wood there. To transport the tree trunk you need many people, the men pulling from the front and the women pushing from behind. Little by little the tree is moved, little by little until it reaches the river. When the tree trunk reaches the river it is floated to the house of the master craftsman. It is put between two rafts. We have to be careful not to kill a fish, and be careful that the blood of fish that comes in the water does not touch the trunk. It is said that the blood of a fish is bad, and also the blood of a peccary and the blood of an acure. So, the blood of those animals must not come in the water and reach the trunk. This is the belief of the ancients. Now then, if we do not take care, and blood from any type of animal reaches the tree, we can get sick. I, my wife, my son, or another child can get sick and die. Therefore, we have to be very careful with this trunk.

Wherever I construct a canoe, over there or there behind

us (and I always make the canoes) I bring the mud and the trunk here by myself; at first, when you cut the tree, however, there are helpers. After two or three days the work is ready to begin. Then, when the trunk is brought here with the mud, and when I work alone, it takes me thirty days. If it is a large and pretty cachicamo it takes me thirty days. I take a break at 11:00 in the morning, or noon. I am old, but I am not as old as some. I am still a new master. The Warao people say that I am still a new master. Therefore, I am not a completely old man. They say, "You work a large cachicamo until 11:00 or 12:00, and you do not come by here. You are going to get sick, because the strenuous work is dangerous. You will get sleepy from making the canoe. If you fall with the danger of becoming sleepy, you will not have many more years to live. You will get sick and die. Which is stronger, the cachicamo that you work or you? Don't pass the hour." Thus I work from 7:00 or 8:00 to 12:00. Now, I am an old man. I am an old master canoe maker. I have many years experience. I work from 7:00 to 12:00, and again until 4:00 or 5:00. Now the sleepiness has passed. Now it won't do anything.

My friend, this is what the song I sang is about. This is a good and important song. This I sang for Wilbert about three years ago.

The text of Antonio's ritual song is consistent with his explanation, except the latter goes into much greater detail. Wilbert (1976, 1977) has written extensively about the text of Antonio's song, which he collected several years before me. In this chapter I use portions of Wilbert's translation for comparison with the translation that Antonio made for me during my fieldwork.

Antonio's explanation tells us that a master canoe maker receives a calling in a dream to build a large canoe. To construct such a craft is a task that the master builder and his sons, sons-in-law, and grandsons have been ready for; the younger helpers know how to do it because they have seen it done or have already done it themselves. The morning after the dream, just before dawn, the master craftsman sings from his hammock a song of announcement about the construction that will soon begin. (The short musical excerpt transcribed in music example 13.2 is the beginning of his song.) Song text 13.1 is the announcement section of the master's song, translated from Warao into Spanish by Antonio:

u- ba- no- a- e   ka - na - mu - na - hi - da   o - ho - ko - to - tu

no- ko- ro - tu   ka - na - mu - na - hi - dao   u- ba- no- nae

u- ba- no- nae   u - ba- no- nae   no- ko- ro- tu   continues

Music Example 13.2. Large canoe construction song (Antonio Lorenzano). Olsen Collection 72.8-104.

Song Text 13.1. Ritual Canoe Construction Song: The Announcement, Antonio Lorenzano (Olsen Collection 72.8-104)

I had a dream. I am a young man. I am the head of this house. I am the head of this house. I am a young man. I had a dream, I had a dream, I had a dream. I am the head of this house.

I am not the chief, I am not the chief. I am who was. I am a young man. I am me. I had a dream.

When I was a young man, I had a dream. When it was, when it was dawning, it spoke.

You are speaking. How did you speak? What do you say? What are you saying? What do you say?

You cannot speak. What do you say? I am head of the house.

I am head of the house. Speaking just like that, my thought, I am thinking.

Just like that, the young men, my son, brothers, I am leading. I had a dream. My thought, I am thinking.

It is younger brother who spoke and clarified. Just like that,
   talking, clarifying.
Eredede eredede eredededede.

Wilbert's (1977, 31–32) translation of this section of the song differs
considerably from the version I collected, as the following excerpt
from his text reveals. (The spacings, line lengths, and capitalizations
are Wilbert's.)

THE ANNOUNCEMENT
Our young sapling had a dream.
Dawn spoke to him.
Our young sapling,
owner of the house and,
oh, master canoe-maker,
when he speaks these words,
he raises his voice.

Eh! Our young sapling,
owner of the house and,
oh, master canoe-maker,
had a dream.
Dawn spoke to him.
At sunrise
our young sapling and,
oh, master canoe-maker,
speaks these words.

What is he saying?
Listen closely,
my younger brother:
Listen well!

The word is sounding
for you, my women, and
for our saplings.
The words were given at sunrise
by the owner of the house.
His smoked-upon thoughts—

what could they be set upon,
my little brothers and sisters?

Wilbert's version, which uses the second person, is distinct from the version I recorded several years later. There is no suggestion in the translation that Antonio gave me of anything other than the first person.

After the announcement the master craftsman must prepare his sacred hatchet for the canoe construction that he and his workers will soon undertake. Antonio's ritual continued with the following song about the preparation.

Song Text 13.2. Ritual Canoe Construction Song: The Preparation, Antonio Lorenzano (Olsen Collection 72.8-104)

I am first the thought. I thought. I am standing in front of
  you, younger brothers.
You are behind me, also with your thoughts. I thought.
You are behind, also to go, my younger brothers, my younger
  brothers.
I am the eldest, and ahead. I thought. I am standing.
Tomorrow the sun, my grandfather the sun, just like that.
We are the thought, we are one to act.
For this reason you are waiting to go. You, yourselves, also.
What will the sickness be? What will it be? We cannot say.
This is the sickness.
The name: hatchet, the hatchet. The name, the name.
I am your elder brother. I spoke; I clarified.

The master craftsman emphasizes his knowledge, thought, and power and the collective power (the thoughts) of his helpers. Wilbert (1976, 340) writes about the illness-causing potential of the hatchet (or adze, as he calls it) and the care with which it must be stored, prepared, and kept away from children, menstruating women, and kitchen fumes. If an illness caused by the spirit of the tool weakens a Warao, only a wisiratu shaman can effect a cure with his hebu mataro rattle. Thus, unlike a superficial wound (a cut) that is cured by a hoa curing song for hatchet cuts (see chapter 10), an internal illness caused by the master craftsman's hatchet is a task for a shaman's curative power.

After the announcement and preparation, the important day comes for selecting the proper cachicamo tree. The master craftsman stands, holds his heresemoi conch-shell trumpet, and greets the sun with the following song (Wilbert 1976, 341):

> Sun, my grandfather, we are coming to you. We will take the right road at the fork, the one that leads to your house. It is dry like sand, and clean, and without danger. The left road is boggy, covered with thorns and infested with toads and snakes and jaguars. I have seen your house in my dreams, . . . I will come to talk in your house.

The men sharpen their hatchets and, with their families, head into the rain forest in search of the large, supernaturally chosen cachicamo tree. They are led by the master craftsman who "alternately blows his conch trumpet and chants, addressing the cachicamo tree selected to be transformed into a canoe" (Wilbert 1977, 26). Antonio addresses the cachicamo tree in his song, using the Warao power practice of naming, as the text of his song reveals.

Song Text 13.3. Ritual Canoe Construction Song: The Naming, Antonio Lorenzano (Olsen Collection 72.8-104)

I am singing. I am speaking. I am clarifying. I am the head of the house.

In the earth, you grow, you are born. Over the earth you grow in the body of the tree. You grow in the trunk. You know the body.

You are Baberi, the white cachicamo; this is your name. Yes, this is it; this is your name, your name: Baberi, the white cachicamo.

In the earth, in the hill on the earth. There, exactly, you are in your house.

Babe, the first part of the name Baberi, is the Warao term for white cachicamo (Barral 1957, 44). The suffix (-ri or -re) is often used by singers to make the words of the song sound good (Barral 1957, 181). Antonio continues his song by singing about the process of singing. He translated the term siribanu as "sing," although Barral (1957) includes no such Warao word.

Song Text 13.4. Ritual Canoe Construction Song: The Singing, Antonio Lorenzano (Olsen Collection 72.8-104)

Brother, go ahead of me.

You, yourself, dream and sleep; and, when it is dawning, sing.

This is a large dawn. Sing.

Brother, go ahead, sing.

This section is followed directly by what I perceive as a dialogue between the craftsman and the cachicamo maiden. Wilbert (1977, 33–34) refers to it as "arrival at the chosen tree" and says that it is sung by the "tree maiden." My version, however, makes no clear distinction between who is singing, although Antonio's tenses suggest a dialogue. In song text 13.5, I indicate this dialogue by placing the tree maiden's words in parentheses.

Song Text 13.5. Ritual Canoe Construction Song: Arrival at the Chosen Tree, Antonio Lorenzano (Olsen Collection 72.8-104)

For this is your body. (Half is male.) I want to learn to be.

You were born and this is your body. (Half is female.) You were born.

(The leaves, your body, the leaves, the breeze; they flutter. Just like that they move, they move, they move. They move.

The leaves, from the smallest, in the breeze, they flutter just like that.)

Wilbert's poetic translation is included here for comparison (1977, 34). In it he indicates that only the tree maiden is speaking. (The line lengths are his.)

Also I had one part
of my body born male.
With the wind in my leaves
I am swaying,
swaying and bending,
back and forth,
with the wind in my leaves
with my grandfather:
the breeze,
the breeze.

> With the wind in my leaves
> I will be bending.
> I will be moving gently
> with my young branches.

As the cachicamo tree has sexual bimorphism, so the completed canoe will also have a male half (right side) and a female half (left side) (Wilbert 1977, 33).

After the ritual selection of the white cachicamo tree, the master canoe maker seeks the aid of an accompanying wisiratu priest-shaman who has the power to communicate with Dauarani, the mother of all trees. It is she who "has to release a tree before the workers may put an axe to it. This ritual death must be executed only with the explicit consent of both the goddess and the victim herself. In order to obtain this permission, the . . . [wisiratu] communicates with the spirit of the cachicamo in a special séance. . . . If the shaman receives agreement from the tree maiden, she will appear in the dream of the master and invite him to carry out his plan" (Wilbert 1977, 31). The master craftsman sings in dialogue with Dauarani and the cachicamo maiden, both of whom sing through the voice of the wisiratu. Wilbert (1976, 341–42) details portions of the ritual process. In his transcription of the verses, the master sings the following words when the maiden appears: "Don't become upset. Be happy and smile at me. I am like your own offshoot. I am the one you accepted. I am fond of you. I came to touch your body, to caress you lovingly."

The cachicamo maiden responds through the shaman's voice: "You are a neophyte master builder. I can tell from your new ornaments. Do with me according to your vision: Kill me and thrust me down on the very soil that raised me."

The master builder continues: "What I carry in my hand is called an axe. You will feel it at your waist, it will consume you."

The cachicamo maiden replies:

> So this is what you call an axe. It will eat my flesh, it will make me fall down to the ground that gave birth to me.
>
> Poor me. Your hands will examine my body and my roots. Looking at my body, do you like what you see? You will notice that I also have adorned my body. This I did while awaiting your arrival.

Now that it is done, come take my measure. You possess
the measure in your hands.

The master continues to sing: "Yes, indeed, I am the one with knowledge. I can tell you how long you are; your stretched out body measures 16 arms exactly. I make the mark so the men can cut off your head."

This is how the master canoe builder and the wisiratu sing throughout the first day of felling. The master builder continues into the night, singing to pacify the tree maiden. Wilbert (1976, 342) explains that the cachicamo maiden is "upset and disturbed. Her home is now in the stump of the tree and she vacillates between it and the fallen trunk. The master must pacify her through his chanting." He also sings magical protection songs (see chapter 11) to protect himself and his sleeping family and workers from wild beasts, transformed animals, and ogres of the rain forest. The most dangerous "is the jaguar. He [the jaguar] comes during the night to the camp and to the building site to jeer at the quartered tree maiden. The master's chant keeps him at a distance" (Wilbert 1976, 342). Incidentally, this reference to chant is the only reference outside of my research to a magical protection song among the Warao.

After the master craftsman spends several days and nights singing for each phase of the canoe construction, the women and older children help to prepare a corduroy road consisting of many small trees placed on the jungle floor over which the large, hollowed, hull-shaped trunk is dragged. As the tree is about to be taken to the water, the wisiratu sings the tree maiden's farewell song (Wilbert 1976, 343; in 1977, 34, Wilbert writes that "the artisan intonates the chant of the tree maiden's farewell"). In the song the maiden herself uses the technique of naming, as the following excerpt from the text reveals (Wilbert 1977, 35; spacings, line lengths, and capitalizations are his).

THE TREE MAIDEN'S FAREWELL

. . .

I shall advise you,
my poor stump,
my poor one, there
with my shavings,
all my shavings and

all my bark:
I am leaving without you.
I am leaving without you
to be dragged away.

I am leaving without you,
I am leaving without you,
all my branches,
my little branches,
with all my waiting leaves,
my poor piled-up leaves.
Goodbye, to all of you.

Wilbert (1976, 344) writes about this song and the master craftsman's remaining tasks before floating away the dugout tree:

> The cachicamo takes leave of her branches and of the many birds who formerly lived in her crown. She says goodbye to the animals and to the stump remaining behind as abode of her soul. She also bids farewell to the bark and the excavated chips. The master signals when his sentimental chant comes to an end and the arduous task of pushing the log to the river is to begin. He walks ahead of the workers chanting and forcefully blowing the conch shell trumpet down to the river.

At the master craftsman's village, the construction process lasts for weeks and sometimes months, with workers chipping, smoothing, firing, and shaping the hull while the master sings his power songs for protection and to continue his dialogue with Dauarani (Wilbert 1977, 22). On the day of the hull's firing, a fire is built beneath the open cavity to temper the craft. This moment has special ritual importance, involving songs and offerings of yuruma (sago or moriche palm) cakes. Wilbert (1976, 345) explains it as follows:

> On the morning of the day when the boat is burned, the master orders the women to begin baking sago cakes. He intends to invite the sky serpent to an agape of moriche bread and tobacco and then send her back to her celestial home. . . . The offering of the gifts is performed by the . . . [wisiratu]. In fact, he and the master builder arrive at the work place early

in the morning before anyone else in order to start calling the sky snake and the spirits of all the predecessors of the master who have died. It is they who have spent their lives in the service of Dauarani and now, after death, enjoy their afterlives in her divine company. All of the *moyomotuma*—that is, the serpent protector spirit and the souls of the defunct master craftsmen—respond to the invitation of their young colleague. They come to admire his boat, to eat the sago, and to smoke the ten cigars he offers them for their pleasure. "Are you satisfied?" asks the shaman. "Yes, this is the right way. We are very pleased." Then the shaman urges the spirits to leave the clearing and to return to their home. There will be many women and children arriving soon, and spirit presences could be harmful.

This concludes the musical aspect of Warao canoe construction. Following the elaborate ritual and months of magical songs are special songs for the canoe launching. These include the master craftsman's farewell song to the moyomotuma spirits, "who have permitted him to complete the arduous task of successfully making a large canoe" (Wilbert 1976, 345), and songs about Haburi, the culture hero and the first canoe sailor. Wilbert (1977, 40–41) explains the launching:

> Readying the boat took two weeks. . . . There was much excitement in the air during this period of preparation, with everybody singing the characteristic *erere* song of seafarers. . . . The bowman was attired like Haburi on his first crossing to Naparima. Behind the man the two women sang *erere*, the song sung by Haburi's mothers, from whom the Warao adopted it.

The middle and final parts of Antonio's song for canoe building use the vocable "erere," which also appeared more elaborately in the announcement portion as "eredede eredede eredededede." Antonio never gave a meaning for them, nor did he ever sing a separate song that he called an "erere" song.

Few Warao rituals with song have been so carefully documented as Wilbert has done with the canoe construction ritual. His keen anthropological sensitivity has captured its profundity and beauty. My analysis has only slightly penetrated the religious depths of the ritual, emphasizing in the process the continued importance of song as the Warao expressive vehicle for supernatural communication.

Small Canoe Construction: The Song Style and the Process

José Antonio Páez sang two canoe construction songs for me in 1974, giving brief explanations of them. Because the length of the songs and the depth of the explanations do not compare with Antonio's songs and stories, I assume that they are for small rather than large canoe construction.

José Antonio sang two songs related to canoe building: the first for cutting the tree and the second for making the canoe. Both songs were sung to one pitch only, and each contained slight microtonal rising or upward drift.

> This song I am going to sing right now is about the following: it is for when a single man is chopping down a cachicamo tree, so the work will go as fast as possible, so he does not have to force himself. When one man rapidly finishes chopping the trunk, then another man comes and asks him if he cut it alone. The cutter says, "Man, I cut it by myself."
>
> "How did you finish it so fast?" asks the other man.
>
> "I did it because I sang the hoa. That is how I finished my work so fast," replies the cutter.

The following song texts were translated by the singer himself, speaking Warao and some Spanish to my Warao guide and assistant, Cesáreo Soto, who completed the Spanish translation. Song text 13.6 is intended to make the cachicamo tree easy to cut.

Song Text 13.6. Canoe Construction Song: Cutting the Tree, José Antonio Páez (Olsen Collection 74.7-2)

Where will the desires of my older brothers be, where will they be?

The good owner of the desires of my older brother and of the carpenters, where will the desires of my older brother be?

The desires of the men and their descendants, their getting up and their desires, where are they?

The look that one gives around the trunk of the cachicamo
 tree, and around the roots.
The good view that we give with our eyes to the length of the
 tree, in order to cut it down.
The force that one needs to chop down the tree, the force of
 our bodies and our hands and our arms.
The noise of the chips and the tree as they fall on the earth.
The falling down to the surface of the land.
The good straightness of the length of the cachicamo.
For the carpenter's ax, so it has a sharp edge to cut the tree.
So that I will put my vision on the top of the tree.
For the good thoughts of the cutter, towards the tree.
For our work on the top of the tree.
So the tree will not be tough to cut.
For the wood of the cachicamo, so that the entire cachicamo
 wood will be soft for me.
Soft, soft.

Then José Antonio explained his next canoe-building song (song text
13.7): "This is a song in which the tree cutter has to name a brother to
help him carve the tree; it is also so that the canoe will go rapidly in the
water."

Song Text 13.7. Canoe Construction Song: Building the Canoe, José Antonio Páez (Olsen Collection 74.7-3)

The desire and rapidity of my older brother's hand, for mea-
 suring very well [with accuracy].
The cutting of the log [with an ax] so the canoe will be light.
My older brother will pass his hand to measure so it will be
 good.
I remember the work of my older brother.
This is a bird called hummingbird, which goes very fast over
 the river.
May the speed of my brother's work be the same as the flight
 and the noise of the bird's wings.
I will put it in the river over the surface of the water so it will
 go fast.

José Antonio refers to these two songs as types of hoa. Insofar as they are prayerlike and employ the naming technique used in other Warao magical songs, they are sources of power for the canoe builder. In his two songs he names his ancestors, specifically his older brothers and canoe carpenters, followed by the various steps for cutting the tree. Then he names a bird whose fast flight and noise are metaphors (to us) for the rapidity and ease of the canoe craftsmen's work. While the bird is translated as a hummingbird (picaflor in Spanish), the Waraoan term is dekwamoidya, which is not found in Barral (1957). Instead, he gives the term hukuhuku for hummingbird. Finally, José Antonio names the launching of his boat, assuring its ability to go fast over the water.

The preceding seven chapters have stressed the importance of naming as a power technique in Warao shamanistic songs for inflicting and curing illnesses, and in the nonshamanistic songs for curing, protection, love, and canoe construction. The following chapter examines another large body of Warao supernatural music— instrumental and vocal music for Warao religious festivals—in which naming does not play an important role. In addition, a distinction between music for power and pleasure cannot be clearly made during Warao religious festivals, as the areas of shamanism, Kanoboism, and entertainment are overlapped and even fused.

14 Religious Festival Music

Warao religious festival expressions include two main musical and dance types that are part of a ritual complex known as nahanamu, a religious cycle that celebrates the kanobotuma. The two festivals are nahanamu, a harvest celebration that is the main event of the cycle, and habi sanuka, a fertility festival. Both Turrado Moreno (1945, 234–39) and Barral (1964, 57–123) have written extensively about these celebrations—the nahanamu led by the wisiratu priest-shaman, the habi sanuka overseen by the bahanarotu shaman. I attended a nahanamu festival in 1972, recording and photographing almost the entire day's event. Additionally, I recorded several nahanamu songs out of context. Although I have never seen the habi sanuka festival, I recorded several habi sanuka songs noncontextually, including lengthy explanations of them.

Nahanamu

The nahanamu ritual complex includes several segments that together function as a religious event to propitiate a Warao kanobo, one of the cardinal gods of the north, east, or south depending upon which deity is the patron of the community (Wilbert 1975a, 179). The supreme god is honored by the preparation and presentation of yuruma starch collected and processed from the pith of the moriche palm tree. In addition to its religious importance, "the *nahanamu* feast fulfills an important economic function by preventing the immediate consumption of large quantities of starch . . . [;] by causing it to be stored in the *hebu ahanoko* (home of the kanobo) temple structure for many months, the *nahanamu* ensures distribution of the starch precisely in those months of greatest scarcity" (Heinen and Ruddle 1974, 120). Furthermore, the nahanamu ritual "has a significant influence on the social life of the tribe, since it regularly unites and then disperses the bands" (Heinen and Ruddle 1974, 121).

Because it depends on the availability of moriche palm starch, the ritual complex varies throughout the Orinoco Delta, where ecological conditions that support the growth of the moriche palm also vary. Heinen and Ruddle (1974, 125) define two situations that determine the abundance of moriche palms and, consequently, the presence of nahanamu festivals. The first includes fast-flowing fresh water, which allows moriche palms to grow close to the shores of the caños (small connecting rivers in the delta), making the palms abundant and accessible. In those areas the storage of moriche starch is not necessary, and the nahanamu festival does not exist as an important ritual. In the second situation, however, many of the caños are nonfunctional distributary rivers (such as the Winikina River); and the islands of the central delta have seasonal stands of brackish water, causing the moriche palms to grow far from the river shores in groves known as morichales. Because gathering starch is a major operation, the Warao store it for distribution during June through August when supplies are normally low. Reflecting this situation, the nahanamu ritual complex developed as a religious phenomenon in the central Orinoco Delta only. "This difference in microenvironment . . . is one of the decisive factors determining the peculiar Central Deltaic form taken by the offering of yuruma starch and the corresponding Kanobo cult" (Heinen and Ruddle 1974, 124).

The complex includes four major stages, which I call dream preparation, nahanamu anamunaya, preparation gathering, and the nahanamu festival itself. Dream preparation usually begins during the dry months of February and March, and the nahanamu festival usually occurs during the rainy season of July, August, or September (Heinen and Ruddle 1974, 128).

The guardian of the kanobo, the wisiratu priest-shaman, receives a dream in which the kanobo speaks the following message: "I am coming amongst you all. Now prepare yourself and make an isimoi . . . to get a nahanamu out. If you pay no attention, fevers (hebu) and other illnesses will come over the people and you will be eaten by the vultures" (Heinen and Ruddle 1974, 129). The kanobo tells the wisiratu that he is hungry for yuruma cakes and tobacco smoke. Upon awakening, the wisiratu explains his dream in song to his people, initiating the primary gathering and preparation of yuruma for the first stage of the ritual cycle. After the elders and other initiates eat yuruma cakes, the cycle advances to the nahanamu anamunawa, a smaller version of the nahanamu festival that uses dance and the religious paraphernalia of the festival such as the hebu mataro rattle and the daunona staffs that represent the hebuwitu (the suffix *witu* is superlative), the spiritual sides of the kanobo (Heinen and Ruddle 1974, 130). During this portion of the ritual complex, young initiated men formally promise the deity that they will collect yuruma for him.

The preparation-gathering stage lasts for several weeks following the pre-festival. It is a time for building the mapire baskets (woven containers for carrying items) and strainers, making and sharpening the chopping tools, and constructing the sacred isimoi clarinets (see chapter 4). This last task is accomplished by the isimoi arotu (owner of the isimoi) who is, after the wisiratu priest-shaman, the most important elder in charge of the nahanamu ritual complex. Playing his isimoi, he follows the workers into the moriche grove (Barral 1964, 46); and at predetermined times, when large mapire baskets are full of yuruma, he again plays his instrument for general rejoicing (Heinen and Ruddle 1974, 130). According to Antonio Lorenzano, only the women sing as they travel to and from the morichal, while the isimoi player (or players) take up the rear. Antonio explained the nighttime excursion into the morichal and the leaders and players of the isimoi clarinets:

> The head cutter, the leader of the people felling the moriche, is called naharuto ahabara in Warao. This leader of ours plays the longest isimoi. There can be several naharuto ahabara numbering two, three, four, five, or six men. They are prepared to fell the moriche but they do not chop out the pith. They have to very carefully fell the moriche and cut off the tops well. But first they ask, "How many people are going?" and "How many moriche trees will have to be cut for the people to chop out tomorrow?"
>
> They say, "Many, maybe ten." They know already. Then, at three o'clock in the morning they place torches around, and first the women leave. Then the men go, and since my son, Brigido, is the leader, the first naharuto, the leader of the others, he is also the cutter. He plays the first notes. And the others, all of his people, take torches made from dry moriche palm leaves in order to make light—one torch there, one here, one over there, so that there will be enough light. It is

very dark. Then, little by little the dawn starts and finally the people arrive to the morichal, and each one is ready. Already the first, my son, is ready. The other people of my son's village, they begin to work. This road is inside the morichal and is well made. This is how it is, my friend.

Antonio continues to explain that there are no songs for the felling of the moriche palms and that only the women sing during the yuruma preparation stage:

> You asked, "Is there a song about moriche, cutting moriche, or felling a tree?" No, there is not a song.
>
> Now, among the women there is a song for the preparation of the yuruma, but it consists of only four or five words. The men do not know how to sing the yuruma preparation song for the kanobo; it pertains only to the women. Nothing is known by any man—not me or anybody.
>
> There in the morichal it is a pretty sight, my friend. The women are wearing their appropriate dresses for making yuruma, and are making the moriche tree to resemble a canoe, all the women in a line. Now, my sister is the leader of all the other women. She works less than the others, and the others work more than she. She works less because she is the leader. It is because she knows how to sing. The other women bring baskets full of yuruma.

The playing of the isimoi clarinets (by the men only) continues during the preparation, and the isimoi music is of the utmost importance to assure a bountiful harvest of palm starch. If the playing is not done properly and in the strictest good faith, the kanobo may become angry and bring illness to the players and the workers, as Antonio explains:

> You asked about the isimoi; yes, it is played. The isimoi is played for cutting, for felling moriche, and for gathering yuruma. It is not just for anything. Because it is for the kanobo it has to be played. It is played so that the pith of the moriche will be cut out well, and so that nothing is wasted. This is played by Jaime. He plays so there won't be any mistakes with the yuruma. Now, if one tries to work only with a hatchet, he will not get any yuruma. And when another person tries, he

also doesn't get any, and another, and he also gets nothing. He says, "Now I am tired, I do not want to cut more." Sometimes a Warao cuts four, five, or six clusters of moriche, but he is cutting moriche without isimoi. Now, if it is for the kanobo, he plays isimoi. This is so that none of the clusters of moriche will be wasted, and no yuruma will be wasted. When the isimoi is played, he has yuruma.

Now here, they say, they are gathering yuruma today for the kanobo for this village. This kanobo, who is Warowaro, pertains to Mateo. He is playing the isimoi, and the other men who are playing isimoi are José María and Alejandro. Three isimoi clarinets are now being played during the cutting and preparation. Then, they argue and fight for the yuruma. When they got three baskets, Alejandro brought it for Isaías who made a large basket for the yuruma. Now, Mateo and Alejandro are brothers, and they got mad and fought. "Why do you do this, brother? How is it possible? Why did you do it, don't you know the kanobo will get mad at us? This is bad what is being done, bad because it is thought. This yuruma that has been put into the basket, this is for our kanobo." Thus, the younger brother got mad, swung his machete and struck at all the yuruma. Why? Now, the kanobo got hot, they say, and the young brother died with an attack, the other brother is dying, and the third man is also sick. A dream from a wisiratu living around here revealed that Alejandro died because the men's arguing and fighting angered the kanobo. For this reason they say that you have to be very careful when gathering yuruma for the kanobo.

Although Antonio did not sing the song of the women during the yuruma preparation stage, he did sing songs that offer protection during that process. Similar to the time of felling the cachicamo tree for building a canoe, and like any occasion when the Warao are in the rain forest, hebu spirits are a constant threat. Antonio sang a song of vital importance to the yuruma preparation process because it offers protection against several hebutuma. Notated as music example 14.2, it is based on a major-second interval like the other magical protection songs (chapter 12). Unlike them, however, it employs a tone system

consisting of three descending approximate major-second intervals
with no raised seventh below, as indicated in music example 14.1.

Music Example 14.1. Nahanamu protection song, tone system.

In the text of this protection song, presented as song text 14.1, Antonio sings about isibutu akohoko (a long-eared temblador spirit fish
called himabaca in current Warao); domu sanuka (little spirit bird);
and wakusimu sanuka (little red morocoto spirit fish called mehukware in current Waraoan).

Music Example 14.2. Yuruma gathering song (Antonio Lorenzano). Olsen
Collection 72.8-133.

Song Text 14.1: Nahanamu Protection Song, Antonio Loren-
zano (Olsen Collection 72.8-133)

> *amitikamo amatikamo manokonai tiane isibutu akohoko;*
> *mate ine miane*
> From there, from there, hear me, long-eared temblador fish; I
> myself am doing this

*domu sanuka anakonoko tane ubakwatakore hinakonoko
tane; mate ine miane*

Little bird, where you are going to bathe yourself day after
tomorrow, there where you bathe; I myself am doing this

*kemusaba sabaka oriabano manokanai tanu; mate ine hisaba
miane hinakonoko tane*

Go away from me, stay and hear me; I myself I am making
food where you bathe

*wakusimu sanuka mate ine miane; hisaba miakore tatukamu
maweremu manokonai tanu tanu wakusimu sanuka*

Little red morocoto fish, I myself am doing this; food from
there, close to me, hear me, little red morocoto fish.

Antonio then explained his song:

This is a song that can be sung while the yuruma for the
kanobo is being prepared. When I am chopping moriche the
little spirit bird hears me doing my work. Day after tomorrow,
if I am here, or if I go to another place, it may come here.
"Little bird, you come to bathe in it. You come to bathe here,
where I prepare the moriche and make yuruma. I am making
a trough so that you can bathe in it. It is when we all spit."

And another thing: while I am working here the long-
eared spirit fish quietly sneaks up on me. This long-eared temblador fish is a spirit, according to what we say; it is like a
person. It is a spirit called himabaca [to have a hatchet] in
Warao. He has a hatchet with a long handle. If the people act
badly, if the women act badly, and the spirit doesn't like it, he
brings a fever; he brings it with the horn of the hatchet,
because it is long; he brings it to a part of the body, such as the
head or the stomach. Thus, a person is hot, that is to say, if the
people act badly towards him, it is a bad spirit that has the
power to bring fevers to people. It is a prosecutor [fiscal, in
Spanish] for the kanobo. It is called himabaka in Warao—
oreja temblador or long-eared fish. To continue, I am working
here for the kanobo. When we spit, day after tomorrow, then
it comes to bathe here. This is a little red morocoto spirit
fish. This can kill a person. It is an erect and wild morocoto

fish. For this reason one sings, "I am doing work for the kanobo. Now stop, hear me. I am working. Little morocoto, get out of here." There is no water during the summer; there is no water because it is dry. Now, where I work, where I chop with ax, there is always rainwater. "So, get out of here, little red morocoto." This is called mehukware in Warao. "The only thing we do, little morocoto, is bathe and drink water where I work. Don't come here where we work, morocoto." This morocoto always arrives here because it likes to eat worms. It is a wormer, we can say. For this reason, it is aware of where people are working. There one finds the morocoto. This little red morocoto fish is bathing, and eating worms. This is it, my friend, and nothing more.

Antonio's use of the Spanish term escupe (spit) refers to the thick, white, watery substance (made by forcing the moriche pith through strainers with water) that accumulates in the trough of the opened moriche palm. When the liquid evaporates from this mass, the yuruma starch is left. The worms he refers to are edible and savored moriche larva, commonly found in the crotches of the moriche palm fronds. (While I never ate them, it is said they taste like soft cheese.)

The preparation of the yuruma palm starch is complete when numerous baskets are full; the exact number depends on the ritual leader. As Antonio explains, "it is said that Isaías Zapata, when he has filled four or five baskets of yuruma, concludes that that is enough to have a nahanamu festival for the kanobo." The preparation completed, the yuruma-filled baskets are taken to the Kanoboist temple where the starch is transferred into a large basket. It will remain there for several months until the nahanamu festival. Again Antonio explains:

> The right time for both parts of the festival are determined. For the first part, if there are five baskets of yuruma, then they celebrate the festival. Then we will make a naha, a large vat, into which we place the contents of the four or five baskets of yuruma. All will be placed inside the vat. Now, the vat is ready for the kanobo. This is for the kanobo, so he can see the vat and will be content and happy. The kanobo from above looks down and says, "Now they have the vat ready. Wow, it is for me, already." [Antonio laughs.] Good, filling the

vat is good. Now, if it is not full, the kanobo will be angry. Yes, for the festival we must put it all in. This is the first part of the festival. Then, the leaders are called, the fiscals, the captains, the commissaries, all of them. Then, the others are called, and all the people come together. The scene is set for the kanobo, and the table is set. "Good," the leaders say, "here is some for you, you, and you." Twenty men require twenty baskets. Each one has to have a basket of yuruma, even if there are twenty or thirty or more men. Now, my people have all come, and we can make a large festival.

Before this, however, the hohonoko or dancing platform is constructed, followed by all-night dancing.

The kanobo appears to the wisiratu once again in a dream in which immortal and mortal have the following dialogue (Heinen and Ruddle 1974, 130):

> KANOBO: I have eaten already; now you may eat. I have taken a bath [in the yuruma starch] already. I need tobacco.
> WISIRATU: Very good [thank you]. I am going to eat.

When the wisiratu has finished announcing his dream to his people, the dates for the nahanamu festival (feast and dance) are set to coincide with the next full moon. When the proper time arrives, the wisiratu and selected initiates sing and smoke wina cigars in the temple during an evening vespers, feeding tobacco smoke to the kanobo. In the morning the yuruma is distributed to the people, followed by the long-awaited dance. This is the portion that I personally witnessed and recorded in 1973, accompanied by Dr. Heinen.

Heinen and Ruddle (1974, 131) explain that "the sequence in which the dancers perform is of great political importance, because it establishes the power ranking and prestige of office holders for the remainder of the year. After the dances of the elders, the workers involved in the extraction of yuruma dance. This is an important confirmation of their standing in the community, which is partially based on their work capacity." In sequence, the dances include the following types: *dance of the akabatu* (the household heads, the fellers of the moriche palms); *dance of the anahurumu* (the young men who chopped out the pith and removed the pulp); *dance of the anamumo* (the women who sifted the pulp into flour); and *dance of the wayabatu* (comic dance of women and men).

At the center of the hohonoko, several daunona or wooden-staved ceremonial images are erected to represent the kanobo. During the dance of the anamumo, the women who participated in the yuruma starch preparation come individually onto the platform and dance before the daunona staves. Ceremoniously adorned by the wisiratu with a special cloth, each woman dances in front of the staves by bouncing up and down in place, on her toes, with her arms straight down. Meanwhile, the male dancer-musicians perform four counterclockwise circle dances around each female dancer, pausing for a few minutes between each cycle so a different woman can enter and dance. The dancer-musicians play several hebu mataro rattles, one or more small habi sanuka rattles, two isimoi clarinets, one or more muhusemoi flutes, and sewei strung rattles on their legs and on top of a pole. The four circle dances in each cycle consist of two parts for each dance (I call each part A and B), making a total of eight sections (A B A B A B A B). The second part (B) has about twice as much energy as the first. During both parts of each cycle, the featured woman dancer is very stiff and erect while the men dance with energetic movements. Each woman dances her little hops without making a sound, but the rattle players emit yells that function as signals between the four continuous dances and their individual A and B sections. Music example 14.3 is an excerpt (the second circle dance from the cycle of four) from the music for the nahanamu ritual dance of the anamumo (listen to recorded example 4).

In contrast with the other three, the final wayabatu dance is devoted solely to the women, who let themselves go, so to speak. This segment, called carnaval in Spanish, is festive, jocular, and ritually emasculating as the women dancers, dressed with humps in their backs, attack the male dancers one by one with sticks and clubs, aiming for the groin. The blows stop short of contact, but the message is clearly that of emasculation, all done in jest. Heinen and Ruddle (1974, 131) succinctly describe this portion of the festival: "In this dance the women jokingly attack whichever male is carrying the rattle, pretending to hit him hard with their fists and to tear out his penis." This is the end of the dancing part of the festival. The music for the wayabatu dance is similar to the B part of the dance of the anamumo, only it is longer in

Music Example 14.3. Nahanamu dance music. Olsen Collection 72.8-306.

Music Example 14.3 (*continued*)

duration because the women need more time to carry out their mock attacks on the men.

The nahanamu ritual complex continues during the night as the wisiratu, the isimoi arotu, and the other initiates sing additional religious songs, including the song of the howler monkey, described as kanobo arokohotu (song of the kanobo), "in which the organization of the howler monkey band represents that of Warao society" (Heinen and Ruddle 1974, 132). Talejo Tovar, a wisiratu from Juan Mata Ahanoko, sang several howler-monkey songs for me and explained that he was imitating the arawato or howler monkey. Music example 14.4 is a complete howler-monkey song in which the minor-third foundation interval is emphasized during most of the performance except for the beginning, which favors the major third and an occasional sixth below the principal tone. Talejo had difficulty translating much of the text because of its archaic Warao words; he explained, however, that the first words of the song, "he (ihi) tehore ihitawaetu monika," means "your body [the howler monkey's body] is the same as this." Then "yabarata bonetu" means "howler monkey, wake up." The term yabaratu translates as "people," meaning "howler-monkey people." Talejo concluded his explanation by stating, "I don't know where this song comes from, or who first sang it, or what it means. It is sung like this because that is how I learned it. This is how it was passed on to me."

After the songs of the howler monkey, the isimoi arotu plays for the last time; then he ritually breaks his instrument (Heinen and Ruddle 1974, 132). As I explained in chapter 4, however, the isimoi arotu saves certain parts of his instrument because they belong to the kanobo.

Habi Sanuka

Habi sanuka (habi = rattle, sack; sanuka = small) is the Warao term for a dance ritual that Barral (1964, 75) translates as "dance of the little sacred rattles." It is also the name for the little rattle itself, the sacred sound instrument of the bahanarotu shaman (see chapters 4 and 8). Wilbert (1972a, 113), who calls the habi sanuka ritual a fertility dance, writes the following (1985, 155):

> The "Dance of the Little Rattle" features rites to secure fertility in man and animals. Animal pantomimes are performed by means of steps, postures, and the little rattles, until at one

Music Example 14.4. Nahanamu arawato song (Talejo Tovar). Olsen Collection 72.8-126.

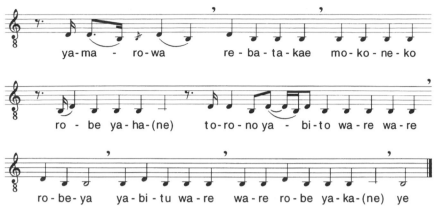

Music Example 14.4 (*continued*)

point enormous straw images are presented of a vulva (by men) and of a phallus (by women). In the ensuing melee the bearers of these effigies are clawed by members of the opposite sex who will not rest until the images are shredded and destroyed.

During the ritual . . . the affinal kin ties between spouses become suspended and replaced by ritual bonds known as mamuse. Husbands agree to exchange wives, and upon payment of a substantial price, called *horo amoara,* "skin payment," the partners are free to engage in dancing and sex. *Mamuse* relationships are considered honorable and are believed to exercise a fortifying influence on the woman's offspring.

Additionally, the dance is seen as an extension of the nahanamu ritual complex, as Turrado Moreno (1945, 237) writes: "The Warao have the custom of dancing the habi sanuka as a continuation of nahanamu; that is, during the day they dance the nahanamu and during the corresponding nights they dance the habi sanuka, as a crowning finish to the ritual cycle." This contrasts with the finish of nahanamu that Heinen and Ruddle described, who explain that the wisiratu and the initiates gather to sing sacred songs. This inconsistency can perhaps be interpreted as regional or temporal variation. Heinen and Ruddle, for example, are writing about the Winikina region, while both

Turrado Moreno and Barral are describing other subtribes in the central delta. Because several days and nights make up the temporal aspect of the ritual complex, certain evenings pertain to certain parts of the ceremony. Antonio gives the following explanation of the ritual complex in his village in Winikina:

> Two festivals are made continuously, the nahanamu and the habi sanuka, both at the same time. First is the celebration of nahanamu. After four or five [small baskets of yuruma] are used up, that part of the festival ends. Then, after that, if there are two baskets of yuruma left, they pertain to the dance of habi sanuka that follows during the night just before dawn. The habi sanuka maracas are inside the little house where they have to be. All the cakes are made, about forty, fifty, sixty cakes. That is good. Now, for the rest of the men there are often onions, turkey, cow, deer, and other types of food for the habi sanuka feast. This is how it is, my friend.

Barral (1964, 1981) provides the most detailed description of the habi sanuka dance ritual, its music, and its place within the larger nahanamu ritual complex. While his words refer to the Mariusa-Warao (he explains several times that there is much variation from one village to another and even more from one Warao subtribe to another [1964, 66, 76]), his is the only published in-depth analysis of this important music-dance event for which I recorded more than twenty songs out of context. Therefore, I will summarize his description of the festival.

Although the habi sanuka dance ritual is said to be a continuation of nahanamu, coming as the final part of the entire ritual complex (Barral 1964, 75; Turrado Moreno 1945, 237; Lorenzano, interview), the two dance contexts are somewhat dichotomous. For example, the nahanamu dance is a daytime affair, while the habi sanuka dance belongs to the night of the full moon. Nahanamu is in honor of Kuaimare, the great hebu or creator of the Mariusa subtribe, while habi sanuka is in honor of his mother, Yajuna (Barral 1964, 36, 75). The officiating shaman of the nahanamu dance is the wisiratu who uses a large hebu mataro rattle, while that of the habi sanuka dance is the bahanarotu with his small habi sanuka rattle (Wilbert 1972a, 112–13). The nahanamu dance and feast of yuruma cakes and crabs celebrate the products of conjugation or life itself (the supreme being, yuruma, and crabs), while the habi sanuka dance celebrates the process of conjugation or fertility (through the supreme mother figure and the repeated fertility symbolism of the multiple habi sanuka rattles). Finally, the nahanamu ritual is overtly religious, while the habi sanuka festival has today become a secular dance (Wilbert 1956, 14).

The evening of habi sanuka consists of many dances performed by men and women, with only the men shaking the rattles and singing the songs, according to Barral. Wilbert (1956, 16), however, claims that women also shake rattles. They are led by the music master known as dokotu moyotu (Barral 1964, 76). This man (who may be the same as the bahanarotu, although neither Barral nor Turrado Moreno specify this) guides the rhythm of the singing and dancing with the beats of his long staff topped with a sewei strung rattle, another symbol of fertility (Wilbert 1985, 174), and his habi sanuka.

Before the dancing begins, the habi sanuka rattles must be purified and prepared in the hebu ahanoko or temple of the kanobo. This solemn ritual involving men only includes baptism of the rattles with river water or moriche palm wine, depending on the subtribe (Barral 1964, 76), followed by the ritual painting of the calabash heads of each instrument. Every step of this predance ritual is accompanied by sacred songs. Following the purification-preparation of the habi sanuka rattles, and after sunset, the men leave the temple with their sacred rattles, heading for the hohonoko dancing platform. There they are met by the women and children who remain off the platform as spectators only for the first groups of dances. When the women finally join the men on the hohonoko, they never sing but only dance, each behind her man and joined to him by placing her right hand on her man's right shoulder (Barral 1964, 80). At this time children may also join the dance, staying close to their mothers' skirts.

Barral (1964, 75–76) interprets the habi sanuka dance as theater ("representaciones escénicas"): "The most interesting pictures represented in the habi sanuka dances . . . are the following: 'the taste of the bees,' 'the customs of the monkeys,' 'the description of the flight of the vultures,' 'the elaboration of the yuruma,' 'the canoe race,' and others." As Wilbert concurs, these scenes or dances interpret the actions of animals, according to their titles.

The songs sung by the men while dancing are short, with few if any translatable words, as Barral continues to explain (1964, 81–82):

> The texts of the habi sanuka songs are short and nearly unintelligible. According to what I have been able to observe, these habi sanuka texts . . . are not simply . . . words devoid of meaning, nor are they vocables taken from foreign languages used by the priests and shamans to create more mysteries for the Indians. They are, rather, ancestral prayers and songs, transmitted by tradition, in an ancient Waraoan language that today is no longer spoken . . . nor understood by contemporary Warao. . . . The habi sanuka songs are ancestral songs that are the same as those sung by ancient Warao, and precisely because they are considered sacred they have been scrupulously conserved without corruption, in spite of the evolution of the Warao's spoken language.

Whether or not the present habi sanuka songs are the same as those sung by the ancient Warao, a point that is not provable, Antonio Lorenzano said the following during his attempt to translate the twenty songs he sang for me: "Each group of words for each habi sanuka song is the name of the song itself. The words mean nothing in Spanish." Of those twenty songs, only one word in one song is translatable, and that is kawayo, coming from caballo, the Spanish word for horse.

Musically, the habi sanuka dance songs that Antonio sang feature the minor-third interval (♭1) so common in Warao theurgical music. Occasionally, a downward glissando is used at ends of inner phrases. The songs are rhythmical and accompanied by the habi sanuka rattle. I have transcribed one song as representative of Antonio's habi sanuka songs: music example 14.5 is a song about a horse (kawayo). In the transcription I have used a triple meter derived from the downbeat of the rattle and its relationship with the words.

Numerous habi sanuka songs notated by Barral (1964, 87–107) also feature the minor-third interval, although others use additional pitch relationships, again indicating subtribe and village diversity. None of his song transcriptions are in triple meter, although he occasionally indicates triplets. Such diversity may again be explained by regional and

individual preference or may be due to the way in which the songs
have been rhythmically interpreted by the investigators.

According to Antonio, the patron of the habi sanuka ritual is a headless snake (perhaps Hahuba), a deity that lives beneath the earth in a
cave or hole. The supernatural snake is without head, mouth, tongue,
eyes, and ears; yet it sings, sees, and hears. The song of the headless
snake (culebra sin cabeza, in Spanish) differs from the habi sanuka
dance songs because it lacks meter and contains microtones. Furthermore, it is not used for dancing and is sung unaccompanied, without
the habi sanuka rattle. The song of the headless snake is part of the
dream sequence of the wisiratu (not the bahanarotu) shaman for the
preparation of the habi sanuka festival. Melodically the 3 1 interval is
again employed, as shown in the excerpt transcribed as music example
14.6. Antonio himself could not translate the text, but he commented
after each section of the song (condensed as follows).

> The headless snake is large. She is from the beginning of the
> world and she lives where the sun rises. There she has her
> house. She is not outside, but is beneath the earth in a hole.
> In this hole she lives. She, the headless snake, has no head, no
> mouth, no tongue, yet she has a body. And, nevertheless, she
> speaks and sings. She sings like this [Antonio sings, music ex-
> ample 14.6].
>
> She sings, this headless snake, without mouth and tongue.
> She knows, she is wise. She is in her hole, and you can see her
> point sticking out a little. Her entire body, however, is still in-
> side this hole. Thus, she begins to sing [Antonio sings].
>
> And she continues, singing the following: "I am singing, I
> am a great singer, I know everything. I will move my body.
> And I see, as I am singing. I have my body, but I have neither
> a head, mouth, tongue, eyes, nor ears; nevertheless, I see
> everything, and I see everyone of you." Thus, she sings [An-
> tonio sings].
>
> Then, with this song the entire headless snake leaves her
> hole and goes outside. Now she sings more, completely out-
> side. Looking around at us, looking off to where the sun sets,
> she once again sings [Antonio sings].
>
> Now, she goes back and forth, back and forth, back and

Music Example 14.5. Habi sanuka kawayo song (Antonio Lorenzano). Olsen Collection 72.8-119p.

♩ = ca. 72

ku-ra-yo-ka-no   i-ne   ku-ra-yo-ka-no   i-ye ye

i-ye - ye ye ye ye ye   ku-ra-yo-ka-no   ye   ye

i-ye - ye ye ye ye   ra-yo-ka-no   ye   ye   ye

i-ye - ye ye ye ye   ra-yo-ka-no   o-ye ye ye ye

continues

ku-ra - yo-ka-no   ta-ye

Music Example 14.6. Habi sanuka headless snake song (Antonio Lorenzano).
Olsen Collection 72.8-136.

forth. That is how she slithers. She slithers along for two
hours. Since she is wise and knows everything, she is not like
a Warao; we can say she is a spirit, this headless snake, this
serpent. She sings, "This world is not large. For you who live
in this world the world is large and enormous. But, for me,
the world is small. I, slithering back and forth in two hours,
arrive to the other part. Then, going back, I return to my cave
to rest, but always singing, singing my song" [Antonio sings].

And the last thing the snake sings is this: "Everyone who
lives in this world will look for me when they need me, will
sing my song, will sing my song. And I also, just like them,
will sing my song. Just as they sing my song, I will accompany them, singing my song" [Antonio sings].

This is all, friend.

Antonio continued teaching me, going into great detail about the headless snake. Throughout his commentary he used the words singing and speaking interchangeably when referring to the communicative process of the headless snake. In fact, at one point he used the word wara (warará el canto mio, "you will sing-speak my song") in his translation (rather than decir or cantar). This type of ritual conversing through song is just another example of Warao singing for power. Here is how Antonio continued his description of the headless snake:

> Now, the habi sanuka ritual comes, and the festival belongs to the headless snake, and her song is sung not by a wisiratu but by a bahanarotu. She hears everything that is being sung.
>
> Why is it like that? Well, I don't know for sure, but according to what is said it is very old, from the first of our grandfathers, and their grandfathers, and before that from the beginning. They said that because they knew. For this reason, in this form, the song about the headless snake continues to be sung.
>
> Now, this snake leaves her cave, her hole, for short times to get some fresh air. It's not that she is always in her cave, in her hole. At times, at midnight, she leaves to refresh itself. During the day she does not leave, only at night, at midnight. When the snake leaves from her cave she comes up to the top of the earth, here, and looks around. They say that although she is without a head, ears, mouth, and eyes, she still sees. She looks around at us.
>
> Above all, this is what is important about the snake without a head, tongue, and mouth—it knows all the songs of habi sanuka. We say that she is the "chief of the dance." In Warao she is ahoto ho aidamo, oriwaka arotu, or oriwaka aidamo. Translated this means "the chief, the sovereign of the chiefs" of the habi sanuka dance. Now a Warao, when he is dancing and singing, knows that the chief of the dance is also among us.

The second term used by Antonio for the headless snake, oriwaka arotu, is also used by Wilbert (1975a, 167), who translates it as the "God of the Dance." Rather than living in a hole in the ground as a headless snake, however, the God of the Dance dwells "at the point of

midwinter sunset in the northwest and is related to the Mother of
Moriche Flour (Aruarani) who dwells "at the rising point of the midwinter sun in the northeast." Together with "the Natue, the Grandmothers, patronesses of the moriche palm," they constitute the pan-
theon of Warao fertility deities (Wilbert 1975a, 167).

Although the bahanarotu sings the song about the headless snake,
the deity appears to the wisiratu requesting that the habi sanuka festival be celebrated, as Antonio explains:

> Now the wisiratu remembers that which he dreamed in the
> night. The dream of the wisiratu says, "Look, now the head-
> less snake is seeing." Because he is wisiratu and had a dream,
> he knows that the chief of the habi sanuka dance is watching.
> Then the chief of the habi sanuka dance speaks to him in the
> dream, "Look, I want to hear my song. I wish that you will be
> happy, and that you dance." This is what the chief of the habi
> sanuka dance says. This is the dream.
>
> Then, the wisiratu awakens and speaks to the others—his
> brothers, his grandchildren, his children, his nephews, all his
> companions who live in his house, in his area, and who can
> hear him. "Listen everyone, last night I had a dream," says
> the wisiratu. "The dream said to me that we have to prepare
> to dance. Why? Because the dream says we have to dance."
> Now, when the people heard everything, they understood.
>
> In addition, there are other Warao who also have knowl-
> edge, who think like the wisiratu, and they say, "Yes, this is
> the truth. The dream said the truth, it did not deceive us, be-
> cause it came to the wisiratu."

Antonio's detailed explanation of the habi sanuka festival reveals an interesting contradiction to the order of the dances in the nahanamu
ritual complex. According to Barral (1964, 75), Turrado Moreno (1945,
237), and Antonio himself in a different interview, the habi sanuka
dance occurs after the nahanamu proper. But Antonio's following
commentary teaches us that the order is not fixed; rather, it depends on
the spiritual guidance of the wisiratu who was given instructions in a
dream. In his description Antonio also provides great ethnographic details about the preparations for the habi sanuka festival:

So, we have to go to the morichal to prepare yuruma and fill up our mapire baskets. If nothing bad happens to us we will fill up two or three mapires, or perhaps four or five baskets, so that we can have sufficient yuruma to dance the habi sanuka. Someone says, "It will take two or three days for us to prepare yuruma, so let's go to the morichal so we can later dance the habi sanuka. We are going to dance habi sanuka, let's go." Thus, everybody, the youths, the elders, all of the people, go to the morichal, taking mapire baskets with them. When they arrive at the morichal the women begin stamping their feet to scrape sangrito for facial paint, and the men, chopping with their hatchets, cut down moriche palm trees for the yuruma starch. The youth play the muhusemoi flutes if they know how, while others who know how play the ehuru, the howler-monkey skin drum. Everyone, all the people, are contented while preparing yuruma—preparing, preparing, until finally someone asks, "How many baskets do we have filled now?"

"Now we have five, we lack one for six," is the reply. Thus, they complete six.

"Now let's quit because we have to go to our leader, the wisiratu, to find out what to do next. We will listen carefully when he talks."

Thus, everybody is ready to return to the village. Upon arriving they say, "Look, you know you are a wisiratu, you are our leader. We have now filled six baskets of yuruma for the dance. Now what do you say? You know you are our leader."

Then the wisiratu says, "Six baskets, wow, that's a lot."

The people say, "That will be enough for us to dance. We will dance the isimoi [nahanamu]."

But the wisiratu answers, "No, no! It is better if we dance the habi sanuka like I said. It is better that we dance with korokoro, the small maracas, so that we don't get sick, so our children and families do not get ill."

When the baskets are filled with yuruma they are not taken home, but rather the people have to make a place in the jungle for them, near the village, because the yuruma is for the habi sanuka dance. If the yuruma cakes are to be served with crabs, however, then the mapires of yuruma go directly to someone's house because they are going to be put together with the crabs. Generally, however, the mapires of yuruma have to be placed in the jungle place near the village for the habi sanuka dance, and they have to be divided, just in case. This is because the chief of the habi sanuka dance, the headless snake, is watching those mapires of yuruma. Why? Because they are for her.

Then, another person says, "Well, when are we going to dance? We should dance now because the moon is good, it is full. We have to take advantage of the full moon because when it is too dark we cannot dance, there will be many stories, much horseplay, fights, rompings with the women, and so forth. When it is too dark there will be many undesirable things happening. Therefore, with a full moon, a pretty moon, you can see very clearly and nothing bad happens. There are fewer stories and just mostly habi sanuka dancing. For this reason then, let's dance tomorrow night."

The wisiratu pays attention to what the people are saying, and everything is prepared for that night of the dance. Then he says, "Good, now it is ready. We are going to dance habi sanuka because my dream told us that we have to dance habi sanuka."

Another Warao man says, "When we finish dancing the habi sanuka if you, wisiratu, have another dream later, much like the dream you had for habi sanuka, then we can start to prepare as much yuruma as we need. We can prepare enough for all of the people, as much as twenty or thirty baskets of yuruma so we can dance the isimoi dance of nahanamu. And the women can dance with their arms raised up, and the men with their arms raised up." This is the dance of isimoi.

This is how we do it. We have to do it this way because at this moment we have only six baskets of yuruma for dancing habi sanuka. We have to complete the dream of the wisiratu so that we conform well with the lord of the dance, the ruler of habi sanuka. Now, if we dance the nahanamu before the habi sanuka, we risk the possibility of our children, men, or women getting ill. We could get sick. Someone could die, or we could cry, and this we do not want. We have to complete the dream like the dream which first came. Thus, the wisiratu says, "That's good. Yes, my friends. Now, if the dancing platform is still to be prepared, make it good. When we celebrate the festival of habi sanuka we will all dance."

Thus, on that day when the dancing platform is ready, the people will dance the habi sanuka hane or dance of the little rattles of the jungle until the dawn. It's as if all the little rattles of the jungle come to celebrate all night long.

Now, a wisiratu who is the first to dance gives us the following admonition: "Look, friends, sons, brothers, you know that all of us wisimo give two cigars to the chiefs of the dance." Then, the wisiratu begins to sing. He gives two cigars to the chiefs of the owner of the habi sanuka dance and says, "Therefore, be good. Be careful, dance well, with much justice, and be careful of the blood of the young girls so the dance will go well and we can all celebrate. I will accompany the dancing unless you dance in the presence of the blood of the young girls who are having their periods. I will be there but you will dance alone. I will always sing, but I will not be happy. In addition, your body will feel bad and you will be tired and lazy. This is what happens when a man is dancing and a bleeding woman or girl is among you. Therefore, behave yourself, dance well, celebrate everything, and let the songs be good. Now then, we will begin; all of us will celebrate the entire festival with dancing all night long."

Then, on the day after the dance comes the feast. If a river is nearby somebody will have been instructed to go catch fish. If not, someone will have gone to the morichal to look for moriche grubs. If it is during the winter, someone will have gone to make hoko liquor, or moriche palm wine. This is so that in the afternoon of the festival the habi sanuka feast can be celebrated. The wisiratu says, "We have to do this, my friends. It is good like this; yes, it is good." Thus, the leaders, the captains, all the elders are content; the women comb their hair, the men also, everybody primps, and the custom is for the men, women, and children to paint their faces. Everybody is happy, children, women, men, the leaders, everyone is contented because they are going to the feast. Finally the yuruma is prepared. The people who fished have returned, the people who went to the morichal to obtain moriche grubs have returned, and those who went to make palm wine have also returned. All the people celebrate with the afternoon habi sanuka feast.

Reading like an anthropologist's ethnography, Antonio's lengthy explanation elaborates on several points already made and introduces new information. I have extracted the following details and interpretations related to Warao music from his story:

1. During the yuruma preparation stage the people hope that nothing will go wrong and the mapire baskets will be filled as planned. Earlier in this chapter I discussed Antonio's magical protection song so that the yuruma preparation (for nahanamu or habi sanuka) would go well. There is always a concern that something could happen, such as visitations by dangerous spirits that would make the journey into the rain forest hazardous and the yuruma preparation unsuccessful. With the joint power of song and word, however, the work will be accomplished successfully and without incident. The entire event is built on the Warao's traditional faith that everything will go well, and this belief is strongly reinforced by the security that their music offers them.

2. The trip to and from the morichal and the work of felling the trees, preparing the yuruma starch, and collecting the ingredients from the sangrito trees for making facial paint is a community event. It is a happy time of collective cooperation when the bone flutes and ehuru drum are played and songs are sung.

3. Young boys are entrusted with playing the muhusemoi flutes and the ehuru drums, undoubtedly assisted by the more knowledgeable men such as those who were my flute-playing and drum-beating teachers (see chapter 4). Informal musical training begins at an early age, and boys are thrust into performance situations during times of rituals.

4. The community's main consultant for the habi sanuka festival is the wisiratu, the religious leader of the village, as Antonio's lengthy description makes clear. The role of the bahanarotu is not mentioned in his exposition except as the singer of the song about the headless snake. Nor does he mention the "presence of a *dokotu moyotu* (song leader), a type of master of the ritual whose office is like that of the ancestors, passed on from fathers to sons" (Barral 1964, 76). The dokotu moyotu's total absence from Antonio's lengthy discourse suggests that the musical office does not exist among the Winikina-Warao.

5. The wisiratu often tells of sickness that will befall the Warao if the habi sanuka dance is not performed to the liking of the headless snake lord of the festival. This emphasis on the supernatural aspect of the dance through its ritual spirit owner contradicts Wilbert's secular interpretation of the dance. Indeed, while the ritual yuruma placation is not as large as it is for nahanamu proper, the preparation of the flour, the cakes, and the feast are indications of a certain level of religious profundity.

   Additional illness may befall the men if any of the female dancers are participating while menstruating, which the wisiratu warns of before the first dance. It is a common belief among the Warao that menstrual blood will weaken the supernatural powers of male shamans in particular and have a negative effect on other men as well (Wilbert 1972b, 101). This is perhaps a time of frustration for the menstruating woman because both menstruation and the habi sanuka ritual are related "to the Moon, who, as a young man, had an incestuous relationship with his sister and was punished by transformation" (Wilbert 1972b, 101). If both moon-related events occur simultaneously, they may have symbolic fertility significance for a woman.

   The moon again figures in Antonio's story when he says that the best time to dance is during a full moon. Several scholars also mention that an evening with a full moon is the proper time for the habi sanuka dance (Barral 1964; Heinen and Ruddle 1974); and Barral (1964, 36, 75) relates the festival to Yajuna, the mother of the kanobo Kwaimare and who, because of male-female dichotomy, is perhaps symbolic of the moon. But there is a practical reason for dancing during the full moon, as Antonio explains:

"With a full moon, a pretty moon, you can see very clearly, and nothing bad happens," meaning there will be no inappropriate behavior.

6. According to Antonio, the collection of the yuruma for habi sanuka and its brief storage differs from the lengthy storage of the starch for nahanamu, as explained by Heinen and Ruddle (1974, 120). Whether or not the jungle storage site is the same as the hebu ahanoko temple is unclear. Similarly, no information is given about the actual preparation of the yuruma cakes that are eaten during the habi sanuka feast.

7. Antonio's description of the habi sanuka preparation suggests an almost democratic approach to ritual behavior, as the people say, "That will be enough [yuruma] for us to dance. We will dance the isimoi [nahanamu]." This example of a decision-making attempt is somewhat reminiscent of Kuna society, which is known for its strong democratic way of life. The Warao speakers, however, quickly experience the hierarchy of authority in ritual matters when the wisiratu says, "No, no! It is better if we dance the habi sanuka like I said." His mandate comes from the kanobo itself and must be followed.

8. Finally, we learn from Antonio's description that during the day following the all-night habi sanuka dance, the people prepare their bodies with facial paint and gather food and drink for the ritual dinner. Yuruma cakes, fish, crabs, grubs, and unfermented moriche palm wine constitute the perfect habi sanuka menu.

After this chapter about collective music making for power—power shrouded in entertainment—and the previous chapters about individual music making for similar purposes, we will now explore how music enables the Warao to maintain their traditional culture. As we have seen, music is diversion, stability, protection, and power for the Warao, although the various forms of music making have their uniquenesses about them. The next chapter will collectively analyze the Warao concepts of music as power and power as music by synthesizing all the analyses and conclusions from preceding chapters. Its purpose is to support the hypothesis that music is power among the Warao.

15 Power As Music, Music As Power

Warao music and musical instruments, including those associated with shamanism, other theurgical song forms, lullabies, and some of the original uses of the dance songs, differ in purpose, essential meaning, and performance style. Yet all survive as sonic manifestations of power: that is, music as power. Perhaps they also survive because they and their performance media are Warao tools of power (that is, power as music), continuing into the present as abstract and material entities, activities, and forces that help the people maintain their traditional culture. Additionally, many Warao musical genres share functional and musical similarities. A primary functional similarity is wara speech-song conversation with nonhuman entities that involves naming; another, more occasional similarity is voice masking. Musical similarities include a predominance of a thirdness melodic foundation, nearly constant repetition, occasional alteration in the form of increased melodic span, and frequent microtonal rising (upward drift). These characteristics are among the most important Warao metaphors of transformation (Metzner 1987, 242) and musical icons for and identifiers of power.

Power As Conversation: Naming

Curing songs of the wisiratu and bahanarotu have two power functions: communicating with good and evil spirits, and naming the illness-causing essence. In contrast, hoarotu curing song texts do not include conversation with spirits but do have naming. The song texts reveal that during the spirit conversation sections the wisiratu and bahanarotu shamans are expressing loyalty to, identifying with, and soliciting the aid of their respective helping spirits and are expressing domination and control over the negative spirits that are believed to be causing the illness. One basic functional difference between the wisiratu and the bahanarotu is that the former invokes his spirits directly with tobacco smoke and masked guttural sounds, while the latter invokes his through song. These actions are followed by the most

important part of Warao shamanistic curing music—the naming section—in which each shaman names or labels the illness-causing spirit
or essence that is believed to have intruded into the patient. Naming
occurs in B sections of wisiratu curing songs, C sections of bahanarotu
curing songs, and in part 2 sections of hoarotu curing songs. The song
texts reveal that the essences are from the spirit world, coming from either the eastern realm of hokonamu, the western realm of hoebo, or
the upper firmament of the celestial dome. Through the action of either a supreme spirit or a malevolent shaman aided by his helping
spirits, tangible objects (animals, parts of animals, plants, parts of
plants, human-made materials, and so on) and intangibles (such as
spirits, movements, sounds, temperatures, and vapors) can be transformed into essences and placed into Warao victims, causing illness
and death. The curing shaman must attempt to name these essences to
effect a cure. When the correct essence is named, the shaman sees it
move within the patient and removes it by physical manipulations
such as touching, sucking, massaging, or blowing. Naming also occurs
in the variety of hoatuma used for curing nonintrusion maladies, providing magical protection, enamoring a young woman, felling a tree,
and many other areas of life where individual increase in power is
required.

Naming, therefore, occurs in two ways. In the first situation, within
shamanistic and nonshamanistic curing, the healer has to search for
the proper name of the intruding spirit essence within the patient. If
the healer cannot name the illness-causing agent, he cannot capture
and remove it and there will be no cure. The naming process employed in the nonshamanistic hoatuma differs slightly: the singer obtains power only when he or she has access to the proper combination
of melody and words. When armed with the proper song formula—
that is, when able to warakitane (speak-sing) the proper hoa—the
singer has sufficient power to overcome any adversary or accomplish
any task.

Speaking about what he calls "emotional trance," Rouget (1985,
315) writes: "From what source does the music draw this power? From
the meaning of the words and from the perfection of their relation
to the music . . . this power is indissociable from that of the words—it
is the 'union of poetry and music.'" Likewise, discussing the ecstati-
cally transformed shaman as healer, Lévi-Strauss (1967, 194) writes

about the power of song: "This is the function of the incantation proper. But the shaman does more than utter the incantation; he is its hero, for it is he who, at the head of a supernatural battalion of spirits, penetrates the endangered organs and frees the captive soul." Rouget and Lévi-Strauss are writing about widely divergent cultures (Rouget writes about Arabic culture, Lévi-Strauss about the Cuna); nevertheless, the proper union of words and music creates the power in both situations. This phenomenon is close to being a universal in shamanism; and, in general, "melodies and words are inseparable, and the very power of the song depends on their proper union" (Olsen 1980b, 365). Similarly, Rouget (1985, 319) writes that "the shaman is a magician, and his singing brings to life the imaginary world of the invisible. Without song, the shamanic imaginary system would be inconceivable." Among the Warao, this singing evokes not the imaginary world but the *real* world of the supernatural (not a contradiction but an emic view). The transformed shaman (since he is one with his spirit helpers) enters the body of the patient and, after determining the proper name of the illness-causing intruding spirit essence, is able to capture it, bring it to the surface of the patient's body, and blow it back to its place of origin. As we have also seen in the other theurgical songs (for example, the magical protection hoa, marehoa, canoe-building songs, and the curing hoa songs), the naming process, the proper union of text and melody, creates the power to protect, enamor, fell a sacred tree, and reduce swelling or stop bleeding.

Power As Music: Voice Masking

How the musical conversation is delivered is an important indicator of power in wisiratu shamanism and, to a lesser degree, bahanarotu shamanism. As we have seen in chapters 7 and 8, Warao shamans use two contrasting styles of vocal tone production. For lack of better terms, I have called these styles "masked" and "normal." By normal, I refer to a vocal tone quality (also called timbre) that is close to the singer's everyday speaking quality. Masked, on the other hand, requires a conscious alteration of that everyday quality. (I am not referring to vibrato.) In Warao shamanism, the basic functional reason for the two vocal productions is to provide a contrast during curing rituals between mortal shamanic speech-song (the wara of the shaman) and immortal shamanic speech-song (the wara of the spirit). Chapters 7 and 8 include many examples of this contrast, including textual analysis and interviews with musical consultants and teachers. To reveal more clearly the contrast between masked and normal voice production in Warao shamanism, a scientific analysis is essential. (See Briggs 1993 for a spectral analysis of Warao ritual wailing and Olsen 1973 for a spectral analysis of Warao shamanistic curing songs.)

Let us review what Warao shamans believe and say about voice masking. Briggs (1991, 21) explains that the wisiratu's initial masked sounds during a curing ritual are the acoustical verifications of the participation of spirits (see chapter 7). My bahanarotu teachers explained that the shaman's masked voice is the collective singing voice of the benevolent spirit helpers residing within his chest and that voice masking through ventriloquism is used for the exclamations of the malevolent illness-causing spirits who are present during curing rituals (see chapter 8). Gerónimo said that, for him, the masked singing voice is a reverent one. He explained that the bahanarotu's helping spirits speak without a masked voice in the B section of a curing song cycle. What seems like a contradiction is not: during the A section the shaman is transforming, and during the remaining parts he is transformed. After his transformation into a spirit, the shaman does not sing in a masked voice because he and the spirits are one. Voice masking does not induce trance, but it does indicate power. As one of the voices of the supernatural—its singing voice—it is a musical identifier of the shaman's power and control over the supernatural.

Power As Music: Thirdness Foundation Interval

Musical analysis has revealed a very important characteristic in Warao music theory: certain melodic formulas or patterns are reserved for particular power functions. For example, the terminating pattern of Ȝ 1 at the approximate interval of a minor third is the basic foundation of curing music as well as most traditional music. As table 15.1 shows, this thirdness foundation is emphasized most often in two sections of wisiratu and bahanarotu curing song cycles. It is the basis for hoarotu curing and much of the inflicting music, appears exclusively throughout the nonshamanistic hoa curing songs, and is used elsewhere in Warao theurgical performances. Additionally, it appears

in the instrumental music (isimoi and muhusemoi) during the nahanamu festival and is the foundation for ritual wailing among
Winikina-Warao women. (Although I occasionally heard Warao
women in Yaruara Akoho perform ritual wailing after a death, I was
never able to record it because it occurred late at night several houses
away; I was able to make a transcription of the tone system of the
genre, however, which is based on a 5 4 ♭3 1 melodic scheme [see
Lavandero 1972, 340–41 and Briggs 1993].)

Acoustical and philosophical explanations for the origin and predominance of the approximate minor-third foundation interval as a
terminating pattern in many preindustrial cultures have given rise to
the search for the "Ur-song, a basic human melody or chant" (Gardner
1981). Two questions, in particular, concern researchers: (1) where
does the minor third come from acoustically, and (2) is there any
meaning attached to its frequent use?

Leonard Bernstein, addressing the origin of music in his series of
Charles Eliot Norton Lectures at Harvard University in 1973, notes the
frequent occurrence of the descending minor-third interval in simple
children's songs throughout much of the world (Bernstein 1976, 16).
As this book has revealed, the phenomenon of the descending minor-
third interval is not restricted to children's songs; rather, it is often the
fundamental basis of an entire culture's musical system. Bernstein
(1976, 17–27) relates its frequent occurrence to the overtone series,
which is often considered a universal law of physics. The minor third,
he explains, is the interval found between the fourth and fifth over-
tones of any given fundamental tone. For example, a fundamental of
C^1 produces a minor third between its fourth overtone, E^3, and its fifth,
G^3. Nevertheless, this position in the overtone series neither accounts
for the interval's widespread use nor explains why earlier intervals in
the series (such as the octave, the fifth, the fourth, and the major third)
are not used before the minor third. Another system must exist.

The Fibonacci series is useful for mathematically showing why the
minor third may be the foundation interval of the so-called Ur-song.
The Fibonacci series is an arithmetic sequence that was first described
by the Italian mathematician Leonardo Fibonacci Pisano in his book
Liber Abaci, published in 1202 (Maxfield and Maxfield 1972, 80). He developed the pattern while solving a puzzle concerning the reproduction
of rabbits. In the sequence the first term is 1; consequent terms are

Table 15.1 Warao Melodic Patterns in Lullaby and Theurgical Songs (transposed)

Hoerekitane lullaby	Olsen Collection
Wisiratu curing song section A	Olsen Collection
Wisiratu curing song section B	Olsen Collection
Bahanarotu curing song section C	Olsen Collection
Hoarotu curing song	Olsen Collection
Hoarotu inflicting song section A	Olsen Collection
Hoarotu inflicting song section B	Olsen Collection
Magical protection hoa	Olsen Collection
Curing hoa: hatchet wound	Olsen Collection
Curing hoa: snake bite	Olsen Collection
Curing hoa: birth complications	Olsen Collection
Bahanarotu apprenticeship	Olsen Collection
Magical rain making song	Wilbert 1981, 139
Habi sanuka song	Barral 1964, 90, no. 21
Nahanamu song	Barral 1964, 71, no. 6

found by summing the previous two, beginning by summing the first, 1, with 0, generating another 1. The third term is obtained by adding the first and second (1 + 1 = 2) and so on, eventually generating the following first twenty terms: 1, 1, 2, 3, 5, 8, 13, 21, 34, 55, 89, 144, 233, 377, 610, 987, 1597, 2584, 4181, 6765. The importance of this series was not fully realized until the nineteenth century, when scholars discovered that the further up the series one goes, the closer the ratio between any two consecutive terms approaches the Golden Section (also known as the Divine Proportion, the Golden Ratio, and the Golden Mean). The Golden Section is based on the proportion 1.618 ∞, known as the *phi* factor (written as Ø, from the first letter of Phidias, a Greek sculptor who used the ratio). Although my assertion is not provable because of the individual and variable nature of musical performance, I suggest that the minor-third interval could be the musical version of the Golden Section and that the Fibonacci series could explain its existence, albeit unconscious among the Warao and others. Several studies (Huntley 1970, 51–56; Knoll n.d.; anon. 1981, 46) have shown that when this ratio is applied to musical tones, the result is an approximate major sixth. When inverted, this interval is an approximate minor third that is actually closer to a neutral third, a result consistent with the way in which the thirdness foundation interval of the Warao often microtonally fluctuates between minor and major thirds. Huntley (1970, 55) writes about the consonant nature of the major sixth: "There are three emotionally potent musical intervals which stand out from all others by virtue of their consonance: they are the unison, the octave and the major sixth. These are aesthetically pleasing because . . . these pairs of tones produce no beats between their harmonics." If this adequately explains why some cultures prefer the sound of the major-sixth interval, it still offers no explanation about why its inversion to the minor third is so common among the Warao and many other cultures (more common, in fact, than the major-sixth interval). Perhaps the smaller skip from 1 ♮1 is simply an abbreviation of 1♮1 (that is, the flatted third is an octave lower, creating a major-sixth interval) and is easier to sing. While the Warao employ only the former interval, other related cultures such as the Yanomamö use both forms in their shamanistic songs.

   The second question (is there any meaning attached to the frequent use of the minor third?) is much more difficult to answer. The Golden

Section as a geometric proportion was well known in ancient Greece and probably earlier among the ancient Egyptians. The Greeks, for example, determined that architecture employing the Golden Section was the most aesthetically pleasing; and many of the important dimensions of the Parthenon, such as the ratio of the height to the width of its facade, reflect that proportion (Makeig 1981, 38). The same height-to-width ratio applies to the facade of the Great Pyramid of Gizeh (Makeig 1981, 37). Additionally, Virgil and other Roman poets used the Golden Section in the structural proportions of their poems as did many other literary, artistic, and musical giants (Huntley 1970). The proportion is also found in innumerable natural phenomena— from the behavior of subatomic particles (Wlodarski 1963, 61), to the arrangement of leaves on certain plants and petals in certain flowers (anon. 1981; Huntley 1970, 39), to the spirals within conch shells and the order of the moons of Saturn (Reed 1970, 428), to the spiral formation of the galaxies.

The Golden Section as manifested in the approximate minor-third interval is much more abstract and has not been clearly studied. Makeig (1981, 38), for example, writes that "the 'golden mean' has only very rarely been involved in tuning theory—and never in the ancient world, so far as is known—for the simple reason that it cannot be expressed in terms of whole numbers. (Furthermore, it generates intervals which don't sound very good!)." If we put aside his parenthetical ethnocentrism (which contrasts with Huntley's previous quotation), we discover that the Golden Section *is* found musically (in its inversion) throughout much of the living ancient world. Why it is preferred over other intervals, however, cannot be answered, as an analogous analysis of the Golden Rectangle suggests (Huntley 1970, 52):

> Why this particular rectangle, which we may call "the golden rectangle," is preferred even to the square, or to the double square or to any other, is not understood. And when a matter is not understood; when, as in this case, no conceivable grounds for the preference are apparent; when a rational explanation is not even in sight; then scepticism concerning the facts arises. Accordingly, it is not surprising that many writers have dismissed the whole subject as nonsense. Nevertheless, it is difficult to believe that the alleged superiority of

the golden rectangle, incorporated in ancient art, endorsed by Kepler, who wrote about "the divine proportion," and supported as it is by many modern experiments, is entirely without substance. It is wiser to regard this difference of opinion as just another example of the notorious difficulty of finding a rational explanation for aesthetic preferences. But the difficulty of accounting for a phenomenon does not invalidate its reality.

My Warao teachers have given no reason for preferring certain melodic intervals, noting only that particular melodies are used for specific functions. As we have seen, most of their melodies employ the thirdness foundation; and for them it appears to be the ultimate source of melodic power.

Power As Music: Repetition

Repetitions of melodic patterns, notes, words, and vocables are essential characteristics in Warao theurgical music (see chapters 7 through 13). Repetition is widely employed throughout the world for communication with both the supernatural and groups of people. In a matter of life or death (the reasons for illness curing and inflicting, protection against harm, fertility, and other life events), it may be instinctive to be repetitive. The Warao themselves do not elaborate upon repetition, and little space is given to the topic in scholarly sources except with regard to drumming (Rouget 1985). My analytical evaluations of Warao music show constant musical and textual repetitions, and these have been discussed as methods for achieving power among shamans and other singers of theurgical songs.

Some discussion has been presented in the literature about interruption, acceleration, and increase in dynamics of repeated rhythmical patterns as devices that may trigger trance (Rouget 1985, 80–91). The Warao wisiratu shaman uses all three of these techniques when he plays his hebu mataro rattle during a curing ritual (see chapter 7). When you listen to recorded example 11, for example, you can hear how the wisiratu shakes his rattle with repeated starts, stops, single motions, circular movements, up-and-down thrusts, fast and furious energy, acceleration, and increases and decreases in loudness.

These performance techniques do not trigger trance among Warao shamans (although they may induce trance among the listeners during a curing ritual); rather, they indicate ceremonial curing activity and are linked to specific spiritual functions within the curing ritual.

Power As Music: Multipart Singing

As I described in the chapters on wisiratu and hoarotu shamanism (chapters 7 and 9), Warao shamans occasionally sing together in order to increase their power to cure. Im Thurn (1883, 339) also records such an instance among the Macusi Americans (Carib speakers) of Guyana:

> As soon as an Indian is ill he sends for the peaiman [shaman]. . . . If the first peaiman fails, a second is sent for; and the two fill the second night with their noise. Sometimes, in a very obstinate case, three peaimen perform on a third night.

In general, shamanistic curing is a solo art. Nevertheless, when time is running out and no cure seems imminent, multiple shamans are called upon. In the contextual example described in chapter 9, the nature of Luís Jiménez's illness (a stroke) did not lend itself to a rapid cure. Therefore, multiple shamans were hired because of the need for increased power: a larger number of shamans can name more illness-causing essences through song.

The intervals used by Warao singers for their multipart free canons seem to be randomly chosen. The wisiratu duo, for example, was based on a major second. The hoarotu trio began at the interval of a major second for each part, creating a cluster of one, two, and three scale degrees—this expanded to a major third and remained there as the lead hoarotu sang his melody and the other two sang a major third higher in unison. The hoarotu duet also began at the interval of a major second, but slowly expanded as the second singer drifted upward to a fourth. My attempt to understand the intervallic choice of Warao singers failed because of a cultural communication gap, as inferred from the following experiment I conducted with Gerónimo Velásquez. When I asked him to sing a naming motive, I joined in at a major second interval. His response was "muy bien" (very good). The second time I entered at a minor third; "muy bien" was again his response. Next I entered at a major third, getting the same "very good" answer. I continued at a fourth, a fifth, a sixth, and so on, each time with the same positive reaction by Gerónimo. I could only conclude that either all intervals were acceptable, he liked my singing, he was reacting favorably to my use of the words, or he was being polite. An emic discussion was not possible because he could not understand the Spanish words *intervalo* (interval), *tono* (tone), or *nivel del sonido* (level of sound)—these were not words in his Spanish vocabulary, and Warao music theory does not include such verbal analysis. I can only conclude by folk evaluation that any interval will do (although beginning at the major second is most common), and that power is not achieved by interval choice, but by the act of singing in parts.

Power As Music: Melodic Expansion and Microtonal Rising

Another musical characteristic shared by the three Warao shamanistic curing genres occurs in the naming sections: all emphasize the span of a perfect fifth in the melodic pattern of 5 4 ♩1. A wisiratu occasionally expands to ♭1 and 6 1; and a hoarotu sometimes uses 6 1, 7 1, i 1 (same as 8 1) and 2 1 (same as 9 1). It is significant that what seems to be the most important function of shamanistic curing—naming—is characterized by the widest melodic span.

Another type of alteration is microtonal rising or upward drift, a gradual and continuous rise in pitch that occurs most frequently in the naming sections of Warao shamanistic curing songs, hoarotu inflicting songs, and other theurgical songs such as the magical protection hoa and the marehoa. Upward drift in Warao curing songs often indicates direct communication between the transformed shaman and the spirits, while its use in nonshamanistic music occasionally indicates theurgical closeness between the singers and the supernatural world. Other writers have explored the significance of microtonal rising among native South American cultures (Seeger 1987, 88–103; Hill 1985, 1–30; Hill 1993, 97–130); and I first wrote about it among the Warao in 1975 (Olsen 1975, 24–33). None of these explorations have resulted in emic answers because the native practitioners did not talk about the phenomenon.

An etic acoustical explanation for the upward drift that occurs while the Warao sing the naming melodic formula is hypothetically based on two phenomena: (1) the stable nature of the perfect fifth, and (2) the instability of the neutral-third foundation interval. When a Warao singer of theurgical song is in deep concentration during his performance, his common minor-third fluctuation causes him to raise the pitch of his principal tone. This rise in the foundation pitch then causes the perfect fifth of the naming melodic formula to be slightly higher in pitch each time it occurs. As a consequence, the entire performance tends to rise microtonally. It seems as if the music is being lifted up, perhaps just as the shaman's alter ego is being lifted up during his Theurgical State of Consciousness (TSC).

Both increased melodic span and upward drift are types of expansion: the first is an expansion of melody, the second an expansion of vocal intensity and pitch. These types of expansion indicate, and may even measure, the importance and profundity of the musical section. In addition, they may reflect the level of involvement or ecstatic trance of the singer; TSC is the singer's desired level of awareness.

Music As Power: States of Consciousness

Throughout this book I have refrained from using the adjective *altered* to modify "state of consciousness." Instead, I have used *certain, particular, desired*, or no modifier at all. My hesitation reflects this observation: what may seem altered to the outside observer may not be considered altered to the practitioner. Arnold M. Ludwig's (1969, 11) definition of "altered state of consciousness" is somewhat sympathetic to this problem. (My brackets distinguish between the subjective practitioner and the objective observer.)

> An altered state of consciousness is any mental state induced by various physiological, psychological, or pharmacological maneuvers or agents, which can be recognized subjectively by the individual himself [or by an objective observer of the individual] as representing a sufficient deviation in subjective experience or psychological functioning from certain general norms for that individual during alert, waking consciousness.

Many cultures, especially Asian ones, do not consider certain religious states of consciousness to be altered. In Japanese Zen Buddhism, for example, the desired mental state, *satori* (enlightenment), is often misunderstood as trance or hypnosis. Japanese scholars, however, explain that satori is not an abnormal mental state but one's everyday mind in the Zen sense (Kasamatsu and Hirai 1969, 205). Michael Harner (1980) introduced the term "shamanic state of consciousness" as part of the new-age interest in shamanism as a technique for anyone. But the term detracts from the cultural specificity of shamanism and dilutes it into a new-age version of a profound ancient practice. The term "theurgical state of consciousness" is perhaps the best one for the Warao practice, for shamans are not the only Warao singers who experience some degree of trance while singing; nonshamans also exhibit characteristics of involvement while singing hoa songs.

Charles Tart (1969, 3) writes that in many preindustrial cultures the people believe that "almost every normal adult has the ability to go into a trance state and be possessed by a god; the adult who cannot do this is a psychological cripple." In the same book Arnold Ludwig (1969, 12–14) discusses five general methods often involved in the production of so-called altered states of consciousness: (1) reduction of exteroceptive stimulation (motor activity), (2) increase of exteroceptive stimulation or emotion, (3) increased alertness or mental involvement, (4) decreased alertness or relaxation of critical faculties, and (5) presence of somatopsychological factors.

I would like to relate Ludwig's categories to the religious practices and music of the Warao and other cultures. The first category, for which Ludwig includes the examples of solitary confinement, highway hypnosis, and extreme boredom, does not seem to correlate to belief systems or music. This is only a subjective observation, however; certain non-European–derived circumstances may, in fact, be related. For example, a native American sweat-lodge ritual may be an analogue of solitary confinement, and particular quiet meditation rituals such as *zazen* (Zen Buddhist sitting meditation) may create altered states analogous to extreme boredom. In other words, Ludwig's examples seem to deal with modern American life. Certainly, similar non-European–derived rituals cannot be ruled out, for they may relate to belief systems and music (perhaps mental song, such as exists among Warao hoarotu shamans).

The second category is associated with numerous African and African-American cultures that use drumming (or other percussing) or dance for spirit contact and possession during trance states that involve nondrumming or nondancing participants. Likewise, various native South American cultures employ drumming, rattling (or other percussing), or dance as a shamanistic tool for contacting the supernatural. They include the Mapuche of Chile, the Yekuana of Venezuela, and others.

The third category involves a technique of focused hyperalertness in which music may play an important role. The total mental involvement in performing music may stop the internal dialogue of the performer and induce trance. This seems to be the technique employed by the Warao and perhaps other native South Americans who do not use hallucinogenic drugs.

The fourth category is a technique of defocusing in which goal-directed thought ceases. The zazen technique of Japanese Zen Buddhist meditation is perhaps the best example of defocusing: the internal dialogue of the performer is stopped, thus producing satori. Music as a performer's activity involves minimal defocusing (musical sound is always in focus), but it can be used as a defocusing technique for listeners who are totally absorbed in listening to soothing musical sounds.

The fifth category involves mental states that result from alterations in body chemistry. Among many South American Indian cultures this involves the administration of narcotic or psychotropic drugs. The drug users usually employ song after their body chemistries are altered, as among the Yanomamö.

Thus, the desired state of consciousness for the Warao shaman who is functioning as a religious practitioner seems to correspond to Ludwig's third category: focused hyperalertness. The shaman's state of ecstacy is associated with his focused hyperalertness or extreme involvement with the ritual task assigned to him. Neither the physiological characteristics of singing nor the acoustical attributes of the song induce a shaman's trance; rather, his desired state of consciousness is induced through cultural conditioning. Music does not trigger neurophysiological changes in the performer as psychotropic drugs do; it is comparable to chemical mind-expanding agents only insofar as it stops the shaman's internal dialogue because he wills it to. Rouget (1985, 319) concurs when he writes about shamanic trance: "But the power of music alone cannot be held responsible for the shaman's entry into trance. . . . This trance must still be willed."

It is tempting to correlate a wisiratu's trance state with the shaking of his hebu mataro rattle (see chapter 7). Andrew Neher (1962), Rodney Needham (1967), and Anthony Jackson (1968) have written pioneering articles relating percussive sounds to trance states. While their musical sources are mainly membranophonic (that is, drums), Jackson (1968, 297) explains that the rattle "could be regarded as a drum beaten from within." Neher's study attempts to relate the auditory driving of drums to electrical impulses of the brain (brain waves), although he uses photic driving (flashing light) in his study because it is easier to control and measure. He writes the following (Neher 1962, 154):

> The range of individual differences in basic brain wave frequency is from around eight to thirteen cycles per second. This is thus the most effective range for obtaining responses to rhythmic light, although the laboratory part of this study indicates that slightly lower frequencies may be most effective for sound stimulation, due to the presence of low frequencies (theta rhythms) in the auditory region of the cortex.

I explained in chapter 4 how the number of shakes on the hebu mataro rattle can fluctuate from 96 to 210 per minute while the wisiratu is singing and can increase to 244 shakes per minute during the transitional sections when he is not singing. (The number transcribed in music example 7.9 was smaller.) These shakes per minute convert into 1.6 to 3.5 shakes per second during singing to 4.06 shakes per second during transitions. Not even the last number is high enough to be considered within Neher's reference frame for theta rhythms (which are slightly slower than alpha rhythms). Thus, the hebu mataro rattle cannot be considered a physiological producer of trance based on its auditory rhythms. The overall sound of the hebu mataro, however, consists of a nearly continuous pulsation rather than precisely differentiated individual strikes of the quartz pebbles within the calabash. As the shakes speed up during the wisiratu's singing phase and the overall pulsation increases, the effect can be related to Neher's observation that "if the frequency . . . is shifted somewhat, the brain rhythm changes to the new frequency" (1962, 153). This heightened agitation may affect the shaman and the patient within the wisiratu's curing complex. Nevertheless, the wisiratu with his rattle is the only example of percussion-related curing among the Warao (except when a baha-narotu also used the hebu mataro; see chapter 8); and all the Warao shamans, as well as nonshamans, experience a theurgical state of consciousness.

Another characteristic of the hebu mataro does have importance within Neher's study—its use as a photic driver rather than an auditory one. Neher writes (1962, 156–57) that there "are a number of stimuli which increase susceptibility to rhythmic stimulation. . . . Rhythmic light stimulation is not used probably because there is no practical way of achieving it outside the laboratory." The light produced by the hebu mataro as it is shaken by the wisiratu is an ethnographic example of rhythmic light stimulation coupled with auditory stimulation. As I explained in chapter 4, however, this light has not been scientifically recorded but only observed (Wilbert 1993, 137).

Rouget (1985, 318) considers yet another aspect of musical instrument use and trance in shamanism—its symbolic meaning:

> The shaman's musical instrument is endowed with symbolic meanings related to his journey, or, more precisely, to the world or worlds he visits during his trance. If the drum . . . plays a role in triggering trance, this is not . . . the result of some mysterious neurophysiological action specific to that instrument . . . nor of some kind of "obsessive" monotony that also exists only in the imagination of certain authors. Musically, the shamanic drum—or any other instrument used in its place—essentially functions to support his singing, to provide the rhythm that is the primary support of his dancing, and to dramatize or punctuate the action. In short, its role is precisely the same as the one it plays in theater music of any kind, with the single exception that here it is charged with symbolic meaning, and that this symbolic meaning is in turn charged with a certain emotional power. But even in this case we are still in the realm of psychology and cultural conditioning.

This is clearly the situation with hebu mataro use among Warao shamans, although I will later argue that the realm of spirituality is another level to be considered along with psychology and cultural conditioning.

Another musical factor relative to Warao shamanic trance is the singer's pitch alteration. Can melodic expansion and microtonal rising (upward drift) be correlated with reaching a heightened state of ecstasy among Warao musicians? A comparison of noncontextual and contextual performances indicates that these two musical characteristics occur only occasionally out of context but often within it. Nevertheless, according to song texts taken from both situations, communication with the supernatural takes place during noncontextual performances as well as shamanic rituals. While we may assume that spirit communication during actual curing is more profound than during the noncontextual performances, we can only speculate that a correlation exists between melodic expansion, upward drift, and a heightened state of awareness. Definite conclusions could be determined only if physiological measurements of the singer's pulse, heartbeat, salivation rate, and brain-wave activities were made. Nevertheless, I believe that melodic expansion and upward drift *do* reflect increases in the meditative states of Warao musicians (Olsen 1975). Melodic expansion can be a measure of the TSC of Warao shamans, while upward drift occurs in some Warao nonshamanistic musics as well. As we have seen with the analyses of numerous examples of the two secular genres of Warao music—dakoto dance songs and hoerekitane lullabies—microtonal rising does not occur in the former but does occasionally occur in the latter. An initial response to this might be that upward drift is associated with not only a theurgical state of consciousness but also a secular state of awareness because it is found in lullabies. Because theurgy is a broad term meaning "supernatural communication," however, the concept can also apply to Warao lullabies. An analysis of the hoerekitane texts reveals that every time the singer microtonally rises in pitch, he or she is telling the child to be quiet; otherwise, some supernatural creature will hear the child and carry off him or her to be eaten. These supernatural beings are (1) a hebu; (2) a mythological tiger whose head is pure flesh, without bones, and who has the ability to learn and speak Warao; (3) an animal from Our Grandfather (hebu); (4) an evil spirit who lives in a tree and consists of pure bones without flesh; and (5) another evil spirit, made purely of bones, who is capable of eating the Warao from within. Even the mother collecting grub worms is in a potentially dangerous environment (song text 6.1). In contrast, the lullabies without upward drift are about real tigers, deer, other animals of the forest, and birds. Therefore, although the songs are not shamanistic (that is, there is no direct communication with the supernatural), lullabies with upward drift often mention the supernatural element (that is, they have indirect communication with the supernatural). The singer, although perhaps not in a trance comparable to the shaman's, is in a highly meditative state of involvement because various dangerous spirits are either mentioned or inferred in song. Thus, upward drift is directly associated with involvement resulting from communication with or concentration upon the supernatural.

Music As Power: The Belief System

Within the Warao belief system, the totality of music gives humans the power to communicate with the supernatural, as many of the singers have explained. The song text itself is the message, and the music is the vehicle for transporting the words. They must always be performed together to create wara (theurgical communication) and achieve power. So important is wara to the Warao that as a culture they could be called Wara-arao (Wa[ra-a]rao)—owners of song-speech communicative powers. Thus, the Warao are not only the "canoe people" but also the "song people."

Then how does the music have the power to restore health to a sick patient? Boilès (1978, 147) writes that "the individual's belief system provides the basis for successful curing," and Lévi-Strauss (1967, 162) delineates three criteria for magical powers to occur:

> There is . . . no reason to doubt the efficacy of certain magical practices. But at the same time we see that the efficacy of magic implies a belief in magic. The latter has three complementary aspects: first, the sorcerer's belief in the effectiveness of his techniques; second, the patient's or victim's belief in the sorcerer's power; and, finally, the faith and expectations of the group, which constantly act as a sort of gravitational field within which the relationship between sorcerer and bewitched is located and defined.

Among the Warao there are at least two ramifications of these statements with regard to victim and patient. The first is what Boilès calls thanatomania, or "death induced through psychological attitudes." Certain illnesses may also be cured by psychological attitudes involving relaxation and peace and the consequent healing brought about by the soothing and hypnotic effect of songs that the patient believes are making him or her better. The patient believes that the illness-causing object that has intruded into his or her body is indeed being removed by the curing shaman. Again, the shaman's action of naming the illness-causing object helps to effect the cure. Torrey (1972, 18) writes that therapeutic success in non-Western and Western cultures alike is based on the assumption that the curer "knows the right name to put on the disease . . . and in order to know the right name the therapist must share some of the patient's world-view, especially that part of the world-view concerning the disease itself." I call these concepts—thanatomania and naming—physical psychological attitudes.

The other ramification, the second part of the entire culture's belief system, I term the spiritual psychological attitude. This is the belief that shamans and certain other singers have the ability to change successfully the behavior of the illness-causing spirit or spirits by using powerful words that are affectively transmitted by equally powerful music. To the Warao this is the *real* attitude; it is not psychological but actual. This spiritual attitude subsumes the physical psychological attitude because all illnesses, most dangers, and many life-cycle events are of the spirit world. Whether the so-called object that has intruded into the patient's body can be discussed as a material object or not, it has been placed there supernaturally, can be supernaturally captured when its name is pronounced through song, and is supernaturally sent off to the spirit world when it is successfully removed. Thus, illnesses are spiritually caused and spiritually cured by the transformed shaman with his spirit helpers. Music is the vehicle for spiritual communication because it is a language not used for normal human discourse (Smith and Stevens 1967). It is pleasing to the spirits, and its power is derived from the fact that the spirits relate to (like) it, just as they also like incense and tobacco smoke.

Grim (1983, 25) stresses the importance of a religious interpretation of shamanism: "The shamanic experience has yet to be given adequate religious interpretation. Recent studies have moved beyond facile rubrics, such as primitive religion, occultism, or psychopathic aberration, but they still tend to be reductionist, as they reduce the role of the shaman to a realm that is void of the mystery of power. They often concentrate exclusively on data that support only an anthropological, sociological, or psychological interpretation." Achterberg (1987, 104) writes, "We should not forget that the shamans are likely to regard the scientific interpretation of their work as either grossly in error or just plain foolish." Likewise, a religious interpretation of the power of music is valid, and several scholars have taken such an approach in their studies. Erlmann (1982, 54), for example, has found that among the Hausa of Niger, human praise songs are so powerful and the spirits like them so much that they cannot resist them. Underhill (1938, 5), writing about the Papago of Arizona, explains that "song was not simply self-expression. It was a magic which called upon the powers of Nature and constrained them to man's will." According to Guss (1989, 66), the Venezuelan Yekuana believe that their songs "are capable of successfully communicating with the spirits attached to each object. This power derives in part from the special secret language in which all *ademi* and *aichudi* are composed, a language of the invisible, like those to whom it is directed." And Kalweit (1988, 146), writes in general about shamanism: "A song is not simply a string of words to which a melody has been added. Rather, it is the expression of a . . . spiritual transformation which makes the shaman into a representative of another physical dimension."

Derived from the Warao shamans' interpretations and my own etic understanding, the following is a spiritual interpretation of the power of music among the Warao: direct communication between mortal (the shaman or another singer) and immortal is possible because the spirits cannot resist the power generated by the proper union of Warao words and musical sound. Numerous examples have been presented throughout this book that support my hypothesis that, for the Warao, music (and especially song) is power. Likewise, they support the spiritual interpretation that Warao spirits are placated by the irresistibility and perhaps the beauty of singing.

While native Warao mortal/immortal musical aesthetics and the power of song (wara) are culturally determined, the spirit world of the Warao, including the magical power of song, is real. Nevertheless, it manifests itself almost entirely on the belief of the Warao themselves. Without their belief it would still exist but would not become manifest.

I was convinced of this fact one evening in 1972 in the village of Yaruara Akoho. At about six o'clock P.M., I was reading from "Paul's First Letter to Timothy" in *Good News for Modern Man* (1966, 467). Felicisimo, the son of the village's most powerful wisiratu shaman, came to visit me. He lived in the house next to mine, which was separated from my back door by a fairly large creek. (My back door, incidently, led only to the outhouse situated at the end of a bridge forty feet long and six feet above the swamp; see figure 1.6.) He observed the modern drawing of the crucifixion and asked if I was studying the catechism. I said no and explained the basic differences between Catholicism and Protestantism. He in turn explained the traditional Warao beliefs that he had learned from his father and went into some detail about hebu spirits in particular. Several hours later he returned to his house and I retired into my hammock, my head filled with his interesting stories about hebu spirits. The wind had begun to blow slightly and, although almost asleep, I was suddenly startled by three loud knocks on my back door. Knowing that the door led nowhere except to the outhouse and that no person or animal could or was likely to climb six feet out of the mire onto the bridge, I was terrified. I prayed harder than I had ever prayed before; and suddenly a great peace and well-being came over me, I was no longer afraid, and I went immediately to sleep. The next morning Felicisimo came again to visit (via his canoe and my front door), and the first thing he asked me was if I had heard the three knocks on my back door. (He had also heard them.) I answered yes, and he asked me if I knew what had produced the knocks. I said perhaps a dog (although I did not believe it was a dog or any animal), but he replied no: it was a hebu. This experience confirmed my belief in the reality of the Warao spirit world and helped me to understand the Warao people's belief in it as well. A hebu had approached me that evening because my mind was open to it. My thoughts were with its existence and it became manifest to me. For protection against the hebu spirits the Warao have their power songs, which they sing directly to the dangerous spirits, telling them to go away. My power source is God, my own form of warakitane is prayer, and my protection is my guardian angel. As we have seen, the Warao have hundreds of songs for protection against transformed rain-forest beasts, ogres, and other supernatural forces capable of killing them. Without these powerful magical protection songs the Warao believe they would surely die.

Likewise, without their powerful curing songs they believe that many more would die than actually do.

Music As Malevolent Power: The Myth

So far music has been shown to have benevolent power. Except for the inflicting songs of the hoarotu shaman, which are sung mentally, all singing yields good results—curing, protection, fertility, and so on. The power of music among the Warao can also have a malevolent side, however—at least in myth. The narrative entitled "The man changed into a beast" (Wilbert 1970, 140–42, narrative 53) is presented here in its entirety because of its reference to the negative and detrimental (indeed, deadly) power of music:

> Two brothers set out in their corial to shoot *morocoto* (*Myletes*) fish, after telling their old father where they were going. The younger, who was steering, started singing. "Don't do that," said his brother. "If you make that noise, we shall get no fish and father will be disappointed." But he would not heed, and went on making a disturbance, so the elder one said, "This won't do. I will leave you on shore." The latter evidently had no objection, and with an "All right; leave me here," stayed on the bank where his brother left him, still continuing his singing, which, if anything, he now raised to an even higher pitch. The elder brother then recognized that it was a token of something that was about to happen, and paddled on by himself to shoot. He shot one *morocoto*, then a second, and then a third, now that there was no noise about. Having shot enough, he went to pick up his brother at the riverbank where he had left him, but found him singing even "more high" than ever before: indeed, so deafening was the noise—such a rolling and a roaring—that, becoming frightened, he went home without him.
>
> The father asked him where his brother was, and when he was told that he was screaming loud and that there was something wrong with him, he would not believe it, but said he would go to see for himself. So the two returned to the spot where the younger brother had been left; the old man heard

the awful noise in the distance and followed the tracks from
the waterside. The tracks were very prominent and the leaves
on each side were much crushed and damaged, showing that
a big carcass must have passed that way. At last the father
came upon his son, and said, "Come! Come!" but all the reply
he received was a terrible roar, which frightened him so
much that he turned back, his son following. The latter had
now been changed by the *hebu* into an evil beast, which was
ready to kill anybody and anything. On reaching the waterside again, the father told his elder boy his experiences with
the younger one, that he was on the road behind, and that
they must both be prepared to shoot as soon as he put in an
appearance. At last the latter came out into the clearing and
they shot him. It was lucky they did so, because he was already changed into a beast from the neck downward, with
two big teeth on his belly. Had he kept quiet when his brother
warned him all his trouble would not have happened.

In his summary of this narrative Wilbert writes that "the younger son
. . . has been changed by the *hebu* into a beast as punishment for his
loud singing." Given the nature of music's power among the Warao,
however, and my assumption that the supernatural forces enjoy and
communicate via music, this narrative does not suggest singing as
something that causes punishment but rather something that either
entices spirit possession or identifies spirit transformation. The idea
that singing entices spirit possession is strengthened by the fact that
the singing takes place at the edge of water, the natural abode of sirens
and other enticing spirits (Turino 1983, 111). The idea that singing
identifies spirit transformation is supported by many Warao narratives
in which singing, flute playing, and whistling are used as identifiers of
particular mortals and immortals and the transformation of human
into ogre. These etic and emic analyses support my hypothesis that,
among the Warao, music is power—and, conversely, that power is
music.

16 Conclusion: "Ah, such beautiful music!"

As I mentioned in the preface, ethnomusicology is the study of a culture's music undertaken to learn something about how that culture thinks about itself and the world in which it lives in. The ethnomusicologist must ask, What can music tell us about a civilization, a nation, a tribe, a village, a person that nothing else can tell us? The definition and the question are essentially the same idea: both suggest that music can explain culture. Let us consider some of the ways in which the musical knowledge presented in this book has explained several general and particular aspects of Warao culture. Even more broadly, how has it helped us to understand the human side of the rain forest?

First, let us return to my primary hypothesis—that Warao existence is held together by their traditional music. If cosmology is the heart of Warao culture, then music is the blood that nourishes it and flows to, from, and within its multifaceted chambers. Music gives Warao cosmology its life and vitality and gives the people a way of existing. Without music there would be no Warao belief system or life as they know it because neither immortal nor mortal could exist. Thus, for the Warao, music *is* culture.

Australian aborigines occasionally sing their creation, history, and existence along physical paths known as songlines (Chatwin 1987). The Warao, by contrast, sing to maintain their daily existence along the physical waterways and pathways of the Orinoco Delta's rain forest; the celestial highways of their cosmic world; and the raised floors of their dancing platforms, piling houses, and sacred temples. From these musical venues spring forth songs for pleasure, utility, and power—music that reveals a great deal about particular aspects of the culture that produces it.

Specifically, Warao music provides us with certain details about Warao culture, which can be arranged according to the four overlapping subsystems for viewing culture established by Beals (1967, 250–51): "economic, social, political, and belief systems" (Otterbein 1972, 3). Unlike Boas (1955, 355), who views music as one of the "arts in time," and Otterbein (1972, 122), who classifies it under "World

417

View and Life Cycle" within the Beals belief subsystem, I see music as a form of language among the Warao. Like their spoken language, it communicates across these arbitrary classification layers. Therefore, let us observe how music provides us with knowledge from all the subsystem areas outlined by Beals and summarized by Otterbein (1972).

"An economic system consists of the means by which the physical environment is exploited technologically and the means by which the products of this endeavor are differentially allocated to the members of the culture" (Otterbein 1972, 3). This definition is narrow because of its emphasis on the physical environment and how it is technologically used. For example, Warao shamanism employed for curing illnesses can also be considered an economic practice because human patients are part of the physical environment. Moreover, the shaman's tools (hebu mataro and wina) and his use of laying on hands, blowing, sucking, and singing are all forms of Warao technology. The songs and the explanations have taught us how a shaman can be economically better off when he personally cures his family and friends and does not have to depend on an outsider (chapter 7).

"A social system is composed of the relationships between kinsmen and the groups formed by kinsmen" (Otterbein 1972, 3). Among the Warao these relationships include personal, family, and local group. There are several ways that music has taught us something about personal relationships. First, we learn from the origin myth of the seke-seke (chapter 4) that music among the Warao is a means by which personality is measured. Consider the jaguar who says to the monkey, "Ah, such beautiful music! . . . I thought you were a brute, that you didn't know anything about music." Music (instrumental music, in this case) has the power to pacify the animals and alter brutish behavior. The jaguar (tiger), perhaps the biggest brute of the rain forest, uses the music of the violin to measure the behavior of the monkey. Music also teaches us about personal relationships in shamanistic apprenticeship. We can conclude, for example, that Gerónimo Velásquez, who studied only to become a bahanarotu, learned hoarotu shamanism by imitation rather than initiation. Once entry into any form of shamanism has been established, a bahanarotu can also become a part-time hoarotu simply by singing the curing songs in action. This personal learning and group practicing behavior is acceptable, as verified by the shamans' curing séance to cure Luís Jiménez. Gerónimo never revealed to me whether he conducted hoarotu curing séances alone or not, but perhaps he was practicing toward that end. Such a person skilled in all levels of Warao shamanism is known as a dau-narima in Warao, and to have reached that high level of knowledge gives great economic reward as well as community prestige.

Information about family relationships is also learned through Warao music. Antonio Lorenzano explains in chapter 8 how "above all, the family is happy" when he successfully cures a family member. Likewise, Warao lullabies teach us much about family life and relationships, such as parental and other kinship roles. As lullaby song text 6.5 (chapter 6) explains, the Warao family often has to go to sleep without eating because the quest for food is so difficult.

A Warao narrative collected by Barral (cited in Wilbert 1970, 243, narrative 116, "The Warao complex") explains why the Warao are poor and the Creoles are rich. A portion of that story is presented here:

> Beside them there was a store and God said to the Indian, "Would you like to have all this?" "No," answered the Indian, "there are many things there and I couldn't take care of all of them." "What do you want then? A little empty house?" He asked him. "Yes," responded the Indian, "that's what I'd like.". . . "Let's see now. Wouldn't you like a boat with a motor so you wouldn't have to paddle?" "I don't like them," responded the Indian, "because they make too much noise." "How about a big boat then?" "I'd like that even less, because it couldn't go into the little streams." He gave him a horse to ride, but the Indian began to yell from fear. He showed him cows and bulls, but he did not want any of them because they were too big. He gave him a dog, and he liked this so he kept it.
>
> Then God called the Creole and offered him all that he had offered to the Indian and the Creole accepted everything, the filled-up store, the motor boat, the launch, the schooner, the horses and the cows.

Contrary to the poverty theme of this narrative, however, we learn from Warao music, specifically the song texts of several curing songs, that the Warao are not poor in spirit and power. They may not possess the material goods of the Creoles, but they possess power over such material goods when the items cause illness to the Warao. "You are a nothing," the Warao healer sings to the hatchet (chapter 10). Thus, the local group feels itself to be self-sufficient, in control, and even prosperous as a rain-forest culture.

"A political system consists of organizational units, their leaders, the relationships which leaders have with members of their units, and relationships between units" (Otterbein 1972, 3). The numerous explanations of Warao musical events—shamanistic curing and apprenticeship, ritual canoe building, nahanamu and habi sanuka preparation and celebration, and others—delineate many leadership roles that make up the traditional Warao political system (not to be compared with the outside system established by the Spanish missionaries and the Venezuelan government for Indian regions within the Delta Amacuro Federal Territory). The wisiratu reigns as the supreme human authority within traditional Warao culture because of his role as priest in Kanoboism (including nahanamu and habi sanuka yuruma preparations, as Antonio Lorenzano's explanations have made clear). Antonio's commentaries are particularly telling because, even though he is a bahanarotu, they contain no shamanistic chauvinism. Within the nahanamu preparation of yuruma, however, two other leaders also emerge whose authority even the wisiratu cannot dispute: the female head of the yuruma preparation and the male isimoi arotu. Women's leadership roles in matrilocal societies are important but usually remain covertly so; meanwhile, men appear to be dominant in most overt affairs such as hunting, warfare, and religion. Yuruma starch preparation, however, is an activity that belongs solely to the women, and the ritual songs are theirs alone. These are sung by a female leader who does not have to work because she is the musician (chapter 14). The situation is similar with the owner of the isimoi (chapter 14), whose status as a musical-religious-political leader during nahanamu (and hence throughout the year) is very high. To be a Warao musician in religious affairs means high status, political leadership, and eternal bliss.

"And finally, a belief system is composed of the knowledge which people have of the world around them and the practices and customs by which people utilize that knowledge" (Otterbein 1972, 3). Within this subsystem, music has revealed most about Warao culture. We have seen, for example, how song is supernatural communication itself and how power is acquired through music and speech modes within that communication. From the music within the belief system we learn about structure and organization that are as complex and diverse as the belief system itself.

When viewed within the four subsystems outlined by Beals and summarized by Otterbein (1972), music largely has a functional role for the Warao. Nevertheless, while the Warao themselves use the term *wara* to differentiate communication music from *dakotu* (songs for pleasure) and *hoerekitane* (songs for utility), aesthetics is also an important consideration. Throughout this book, the song people themselves have discussed both secular and sacred musical performances as both aesthetic and functional. *How* music is performed is just as important to them as what, when, and why it is performed. These two concepts, music as function and music as aesthetics, form a foundational continuum that gives support for and cohesion to Warao existence. As I stated in chapter 1 and have argued throughout this book, "nearly all aspects of Warao life include music, and many of them would be unthinkable without it. For the Warao, music is diversion, stability, protection, and power."

While writing these words and thinking of the great diversity and complexity of the musical language of the Warao and other native South Americans, I also think of their worst enemy—the "progress" of Western civilization. As more and more transjungle highways, gold mines, oil fields, and frontier villages are being constructed in Venezuela, Brazil, Colombia, and elsewhere in the rain forests of the world, more traditional indigenous cultures disappear. As the owners of the sawmills in the Orinoco Delta continue to pay the Warao pennies to cut down hardwood trees and float them to the mills to be cut up and shipped out of the area, more native Warao houses collapse into the rivers because only softwoods are left to be used for foundation pilings. As the Venezuelan government continues to give the Warao rice to plant in the fragile wetlands of the Orinoco Delta's islands, using indiscriminate slash-and-burn agriculture, more ecological damage is done to the area. As rum and other alcoholic beverages become easier to purchase with money earned at the sawmills and from rice planting, more Warao are tempted by these destructive pleasures. Even the least susceptible native South American subtribes are subject to the invasion of transistor radios and cassette tape recorders and their great acculturative influences on traditional culture. Because of these rapidly occurring circumstances, any recent study of any aspect of traditional native South American culture may very well be the last of its kind. Of the original 1,492 South American indigenous languages and major dialects (Loukotka 1968, 17), only a small fraction remains today. Likewise, the cultures that continue their traditional belief systems and the music associated with those beliefs are rapidly disappearing. While many people lament the destruction of the rain-forest ecosystems because of the potential loss of yet undiscovered disease-controlling fauna and flora, few express equal concern for the loss of the rain-forest people and their traditional musics. As the rain forests disappear, however, the native inhabitants and their unique oral traditions are silenced forever. Such a lack of concern is a continuation of the racism that began in 1492; and the lack of interest in native South American music is caused by the common Western-influenced social, commercial, and religious attitudes about music in general: it is either entertainment, big business, or part of a religious fervor-degeneration dichotomy.

The music of the Orinoco Delta rain forest is one of the greatest healing forces and communication systems known to humankind. But first we have to listen.

References

Achterberg, Jeanne. 1987. "The Shaman: Master Healer in the Imaginary Realm." In *Shamanism: An Expanded View of Reality*, edited by Shirley Nicholson, 103–24. Wheaton, Ill.: Theosophical Publishing House.

Ackerknecht, Erwin H. 1971. *Medicine and Ethnology*, edited by H. H. Walser and H. M. Koelbing. Baltimore: Johns Hopkins University Press.

Anon. 1981. "The Golden Ratio: Formula for Transcendence." *Coming Revolution* (Fall).

Aretz, Isabel. 1991. *Música de los aborígenes de Venezuela* [Music of the aborigines of Venezuela]. Caracas: FUNDEF—CONAC.

Barral, P. Basilio María de. 1957. *Diccionario guarao-español/español-guarao* [Warao-Spanish, Spanish-Warao dictionary]. Caracas: Sociedad de Ciencias Naturales La Salle.

———. 1958. "Vocabulario teúrgico-mágico de los Indios Guaraos" [Theurgical-magical vocabulary of the Warao Indians]. *Antropológica* 4:27–36.

———. 1964. *Los Indios Guaraunos y su cancionero* [The Warao Indians and their song repertory]. Madrid: Consejo Superior de Investigaciones Científicas, Departamento de Misionología Española.

———. 1969. *Guarao a-ribu* [Spoken Warao]. Serie Lenguas Indígenas de Venezuela No. 1. Universidad Católica Andres Bello, Facultad de Humanidades, Venezuela.

———. 1972. *Mi batalla de Dios* [My battle for God]. Burgos, Venezuela: Artes Gráficas Galicia, S.A.

———. 1981. *La música teúrgico-mágica de los Indios Guaraos* [Theurgical-magical music of the Waro Indians]. Caracas: Universidad Católica Andres Bello, Instituto de Investigaciones Históricas, Centro de Lenguas Indígenas.

Basso, Ellen B. 1985. *A Musical View of the Universe*. Philadelphia: University of Pennsylvania Press.

Beals, Alan R. 1967. *Culture in Process*. New York: Holt, Rinehart, and Winston.

Bernau, Rev. J. H. 1847. *Missionary Labours in British Guiana: With Remarks on the Manners, Customs, and Superstitious Rites of the Aborigines*. London: John Farquhar Shaw.

Bernstein, Leonard. 1976. *The Unanswered Question: Six Talks at Harvard*. Cambridge, Mass.: Harvard University Press.

Boas, Franz. 1955. *Primitive Art*. New York: Dover.

Boilès, Charles Lafayette. 1978. *Man, Magic, and Musical Occasions*. Columbus, Ohio: Collegiate Publishing.

Bolingbroke, Henry. 1947. *A Voyage to Demerary (1799–1806)*. Georgetown, Demerara, British Guiana (Guyana): Daily Chronicle, Ltd.

Brett, William Henry. 1868. *The Indian Tribes of Guiana: Their Condition and Habits*. London: Bell and Daldy.

Briggs, Charles L. 1991. "The Effectiveness of Poetics." Unpublished MS, July.

———. 1993. "Personal Sentiments and Polyphonic Voices in Warao Women's Ritual Wailing: Music and Poetics in a Critical and Collective Discourse." *American Anthropologist* 95/4:929–57.

———. 1994. "The Sting of the Ray: Bodies, Agency, and Grammar in Warao Curing." *Journal of American Folklore* 107/423:139–66.

Cervigon M., Fernando. 1966. *Los peces marinos de Venezuela* [The marine fish of Venezuela]. Vol. 1. Caracas: Fundación La Salle de Ciencias Naturales, Estación de Investigaciones Marinas de Margarita.

Chase, Gilbert. 1959. *The Music of Spain*. New York: Dover.

Chatwin, Bruce. 1987. *The Songlines*. New York: Penguin.

Cruxent, José M., and Irving Rouse. 1963. *Venezuelan Archaeology*. New Haven: Yale University Press.

Dark, Philip J. C. 1970. *Bush Negro Art: An African Art in the Americas*. London: Alec Tiranti.

Deery de Phelps, Kathleen. 1954. *Aves venezolanas* [Venezuelan birds]. Caracas: Creole Petroleum Corp.

Dobkin de Rios, Marlene. 1972. *Visionary Vine: Hallucinogenic Healing in the Peruvian Amazon*. Prospect Heights, Ill.: Waveland Press.

Eliade, Mircea. 1972. *Shamanism: Archaic Techniques of Ecstasy*. Princeton: Princeton University Press.

Ellingson, Ter. 1992. "Transcription." In *Ethnomusicology: An Introduction*, edited by Helen Myres, 110–52. New York: Norton.

Erlmann, Veit. 1982. "Trance and Music in the Hausa *Boorii* Spirit Possession Cult in Niger." *Ethnomusicology* 26/1:49–58.

Feld, Steven. 1989. *Sound and Sentiment: Birds, Weeping, Poetics, and Song in Kaluli Expression*. 2d ed. Philadelphia: University of Pennsylvania Press.

Furst, Peter. 1965. "West Mexico, the Caribbean, and Northern South America: Some Problems in New World Inter-Relationships." *Antropológica* 14 (June):1–37.

García, Monseñor Argimiro. 1971. *Cuentos y tradiciones de los Indios Guaraunos* [Stories and traditions of the Warao Indians]. Caracas: Universidad Católica Andres Bello, Instituto de Investigaciones Históricas, Seminario de Lenguas Indígenas.

Gardner, Gerald W. 1980. "Physical Working Capacity of the Warao." In *Demographic and Biological Studies of the Warao Indians*, edited by Johannes Wilbert and Miguel Layrisse, 152–59. Latin American Studies, vol. 45. Los Angeles: UCLA Latin American Center Publications, University of California.

Gardner, Howard. 1981. "Do Babies Sing a Universal Song?" *Psychology Today* (December): 70–76.

Geertz, Clifford. 1988. *Works and Lives: The Anthropologist As Author*. Stanford: Stanford University Press.

Gillin, John Philip. 1936. *The Barama River Caribs of British Guiana*. Cambridge, Mass.: Papers of the Peabody Museum of American Archaeology and Ethnology of Harvard University, 14, No. 2.

Good, Kenneth, and David Chanoff. 1991. *Into the Heart: One Man's Pursuit of Love and Knowledge among the Yanomama*. New York: Simon and Schuster.

Greenberg, Joseph H. 1987. *Language in the Americas*. Stanford: Stanford University Press.

Grim, John A. 1983. *The Shaman: Patterns of Religious Healing among the Ojibway Indians*. Norman: University of Oklahoma Press.

Gushiken, José. 1977. *Tuno: el Curandero* [Tuno: the curer]. Lima, Peru: Universidad Nacional Mayor de San Marcos.

Guss, David M. 1989. *To Weave and Sing: Art, Symbol, and Narrative in the South American Rain Forest*. Berkeley: University of California Press.

Harich-Schneider, Eta. 1967. *Anthology of the Orient*. UNESCO recording.

Harner, Michael. 1973a. *Hallucinogens and Shamanism*. London: Oxford University Press.

———. 1973b. *Music of the Jívaro of Ecuador*. Ethnic Folkways Library Record Album FE 4386.

———. 1980. *The Way of the Shaman*. Toronto: Bantam.

———. 1987. "The Ancient Wisdom in Shamanic Cultures." Interview conducted by Gary Doore in *Shamanism: An Expanded View of Reality*, edited by Shirley Nicholson, 3–16. Wheaton, Ill.: Theosophical Publishing House.

Haro Alvear, Silvio Luis. 1973. *Shamanismo en el reino de Quito* [Shamanism in the kingdom of Quito]. Quito: Editorial Santo Domingo, Instituto Ecuatoriano de Ciencias Naturales.

Heinen, H. Dieter. 1972. "Residence Rules and Household Cycles in a Warao Subtribe: The Case of the Winikina." *Antropológica* 31:21–97.

Heinen, H. Dieter, and Kenneth Ruddle. 1974. "Ecology, Ritual, and Economic Organization in the Distribution of Palm Starch among the Warao of the Orinoco Delta." *Journal of Anthropological Research* 30/2 (Summer):116–38.

Hilhouse, William. 1834. "Memoir on the Warow Land of British Guiana." *Journal of the Royal Geographical Society of London* 4:321–33.

Hill, Jonathan D. 1985. "Myth, Spirit Naming, and the Art of Microtonal Rising: Childbirth Rituals of the Arawakan Wakuénai." *Latin American Music Review* 6/1:1–30.

———. 1993. *Keepers of the Sacred Chants: The Poetics of Ritual Power in an Amazonian Society*. Tucson: University of Arizona Press.

Hoppál, Mihály. 1987. "Shamanism: An Archaic and/or Recent System of Beliefs." In *Shamanism: An Expanded View of Reality*, edited by Shirley Nicholson, 76–100. Wheaton, Ill.: Theosophical Publishing House.

Huntley, H. E. 1970. *The Divine Proportion: A Study in Mathematical Beauty*. New York: Dover.

Im Thurn, Everard F. 1883. *Among the Indians of Guiana*. London: Kegan Paul, Trench, and Co.

Isaacs, Tony. 1969. *Comanche Peyote Songs, vol. 2*. Indian House recording IH 2402. Taos, N.M.: Indian House.

Izikowitz, K. B. 1970. *Musical and Other Sound Instruments of the South American Indians*. Yorkshire, England: S. R. Publishers Ltd. (reprint of 1936 edition).

Jackson, Anthony. 1968. "Sound and Ritual." *Man* 2/3:293–99.

Jensen, Adolf E. 1963. *Myth and Cult among Primitive Peoples*. Chicago: University of Chicago Press.

Josa, Rev. F. P. L. 1888. *"The Apostle of the Indians of Guiana" A Memoir of the Life and Labours of the Rev. W. H. Brett, B.D.* London: Wells Gardner, Darton, and Co.

Kalweit, Holger. 1988. *Dreamtime and Inner Space: The World of the Shaman.* Boston: Shambhala.

Kasamatsu, Akira, and Tomio Hirai. 1969. "An Electroencephalographic Study on the Zen Meditation (Zazen)." *Psychologia* 12/3–4 (December): 205–25.

Katz, Fred, and Marlene Dobkin de Rios. 1971. "Hallucinogenic Music." *Journal of American Folklore* 84/333:320–27.

Kirchoff, Paul. 1948. "The Warrau." In *Handbook of South American Indians,* vol. 3, edited by Julian H. Steward, 869–81. Washington: U.S. Government Printing Office.

Knoll, Mark William. 1982. "The Minor Third and the Fibonacci Series." Unpublished MS, School of Music, Florida State University, December.

Lavandero, P. Julio. 1969. "Iboma takatira, como si fueren muchachas" [As if they were girls]. *Venezuela Misionera* año 31, No. 365 (September):247–49.

Lessa William A., and Evon Z. Vogt. 1965. *Reader in Comparative Religion.* 2d ed. New York: Harper and Row.

———. 1972. *Reader in Comparative Religion.* 3d ed. New York: Harper and Row.

Lévi-Strauss, Claude. 1967. *Structural Anthropology.* New York: Basic Books.

Loukotka, Cestmír. 1968. *Classification of South American Indian Languages.* Los Angeles: Latin American Center, University of California, Los Angeles. Reference Series, vol. 7.

Loven, Sven. 1935. *Origins of the Tainan Culture.* Göteborg, Sweden: Elanders Boktryckeri Aktiebolag.

Ludwig, Arnold M. 1969. "Altered States of Consciousness." In *Altered States of Consciousness,* edited by Charles T. Tart, 11–24. Garden City, N.Y.: Doubleday.

Makeig, Scott. 1981. "Means, Meaning, and Music: Pythagoras, Archytas, and Plato." *Ex Tempore* 1/1 (January):36–62.

Maxfield, John E., and Margaret W. Maxfield. 1972. *Discovering Number Theory.* Philadelphia: W. B. Saunders Co.

McCosker, Sandra. 1976. "San Blas Cuna Indian Lullabies: A Means of Informal Learning." In *Enculturation in Latin America: An Anthology,* edited by Johannes Wilbert, 29–66. Latin American Studies, vol. 37. Los Angeles: UCLA Latin American Center Publications, University of California.

Merriam, Alan P. 1964. *The Anthropology of Music.* Evanston, Ill.: Northwestern University Press.

Métraux, Alfred. 1944. "Le shamanisme chez les Indiens de l'amerique du sud tropicale" [Shamanism among South American Indians]. *Acta Americana* (México) 2/1:197–219; 2/2:320–41.

———. 1946. "Ethnography of the Chaco." In *Handbook of South American Indians,* vol. 1, edited by Julian H. Steward, 197–370. Washington, D.C.: U.S. Government Printing Office.

———. 1949. "Religion and Shamanism." In *Handbook of South American Indians,* vol. 1, edited by Julian H. Steward, 559–99. Washington, D.C.: U.S. Government Printing Office.

Metzner, Ralph. 1987. "Transformation Processes in Shamanism, Alchemy, and Yoga." In *Shamanism: An Expanded View of Reality,* edited by Shirley Nicholson, 233–52. Wheaton, Ill.: Theosophical Publishing House.

Morton, David. 1980. "The Music of Thailand." In *Musics of Many Cultures: An Introduction,* edited by Elizabeth May, 63–82. Berkeley and Los Angeles: University of California Press.

Murphy, Yolanda, and Robert F. Murphy. 1974. *Women of the Forest.* New York: Columbia University Press.

Myres, Helen, ed. 1992. *Ethnomusicology: An Introduction.* New York: Norton.

Needham, Rodney. 1967. "Percussion and Transition." *Man* n.s. 2:606–14.

Neher, Andrew. 1962. "A Physiological Explanation of Unusual Behavior in Ceremonies Involving Drums." *Human Biology* 34/2:151–60.

Nettl, Bruno. 1983. *The Study of Ethnomusicology: Twenty-nine Issues and Concepts.* Urbana: University of Illinois Press.

Nicholson, Shirley, ed. 1987. *Shamanism: An Expanded View of Reality.* Wheaton, Ill.: Theosophical Publishing House.

Oficina Central de Estadística e Informática. 1985. *Censo indígena de Venezuela* [Indigenous Census of Venezuela]. Caracas: Taller Gráfico de la Oficina Central de Estadística e Informática.

Olsen, Dale A. 1973. "Music and Shamanism of the Winikina-Warao Indians of Venezuela: Music for Curing and Other Theurgy." Ph.D. diss., University of California at Los Angeles. Ann Arbor: University Microfilms.

―――. 1975. "Music-Induced Altered States of Consciousness among Warao Shamans." *Journal of Latin American Lore* 1/1:19–33.

―――. 1976. "The Function of Naming in the Curing Songs of the Warao Indians of Venezuela." *Anuario: Yearbook for Inter-American Musical Research* 10 (1974):88–122.

―――. 1979. "Musical Instruments of the Native Peoples of the Orinoco Delta, the Caribbean, and Beyond." *Revista/Review Interamericana* 8/4 (Winter 1978–79):577–613.

―――. 1980a. "Magical Protection Songs of the Warao, Part 1: Animals." *Latin American Music Review* 1/2:131–61.

―――. 1980b. "Symbol and Function in South American Indian Music." In *Musics of Many Cultures: An Introduction,* edited by Elizabeth May, 363–85. Berkeley: University of California Press.

―――. 1981. "Magical Protection Songs of the Warao, Part 2: Spirits." *Latin American Music Review* 2/1:1–10.

―――. 1990. "The Ethnomusicology of Archaeology: A Model for the Musical/Cultural Study of Ancient Material Culture." *Selected Reports in Ethnomusicology* 8:175–97.

Olsen, Fred. 1974. *On the Trail of the Arawaks.* Norman: University of Oklahoma Press.

Oramas, Luis R. 1947. *En pos del dorado* [In pursuit of the guilded one]. Caracas: Tipografía Garrido.

Otterbein, Keith F. 1972. *Comparative Cultural Analysis.* New York: Holt, Rinehart, and Winston.

Pinilla, Padre Gaspar María de. 1943–44. "Etnografía Guarauno" [Warao ethnography]. *Revista Nacional de Cultura* 42.

Reed, B. A. 1970. "Fibonacci Series in the Solar System." *Fibonacci Quarterly.*

Roberts, Helen H. 1967. *Ancient Hawaiian Music.* New York: Dover.

Roseman, Marina. 1991. *Healing Sounds from the Malaysian Rainforest.* Berkeley: University of California Press.

Roth, Walter E. 1915. "An Inquiry into the Animism and Folk-lore of the Guiana Indians." *Thirtieth Annual Report of the Bureau of American Ethnology to the Secretary of the Smithsonian Institution.* 1908–1909, pp. 103–386. Washington, D.C.: U.S. Government Printing Office.

———. 1924. "An Introductory Study of the Arts, Crafts, and Customs of the Guiana Indians." *Thirty-eighth Annual Report of the Bureau of American Ethnology to the Secretary of the Smithsonian Institution.* 1916–1917. Washington, D.C.: U.S. Government Printing Office.

Rouget, Gilbert. 1985. *Music and Trance: A Theory of the Relations between Music and Possession.* Chicago and London: University of Chicago Press.

Schad, Werner. 1953. "Apuntes sobre los Guarao" [Annotations about the Warao]. *Boletín Indigenista Venezolana* 1:399–422.

Schultes, Richard Evans. 1957. "A New Method of Coca Preparation in the Columbian Amazon." *Harvard Botanical Leaflet* 17/9:241.

Seeger, Anthony. 1986. "Oratory Is Spoken, Myth Is Told, and Song Is Sung, but They Are All Music to My Ears." In *Native South American Discourse,* edited by Joel Sherzer and Greg Urban, 59–82. Berlin: de Gruyter.

———. 1987. *Why Suyá Sing: A Musical Anthropology of an Amazonian People.* Cambridge: Cambridge University Press.

Seitz, Barbara. 1981. "Quichua Songs to Sadden the Heart: Music in a Communication Event." *Latin American Music Review* 2/2:223–51.

Sherzer, Joel, and Greg Urban, eds. 1986. *Native South American Discourse.* Berlin: de Gruyter.

Smith, Huston, and Kenneth Stevens. 1967. "Unique Vocal Abilities of Certain Tibetan Lamas." *American Anthropologist* 69/2:209–12.

Stevenson, Robert M. 1975. *A Guide to Caribbean Music History.* Lima: Ediciones CULTURA.

Steward, Julian H., ed. 1963. *Handbook of South American Indians,* vols. 1–4. New York: Cooper Square.

Suárez, María Matilde. 1968. *Los Warao: indígenas del Delta del Orinoco* [The Warao: indigenes of the Orinoco Delta]. Caracas: Instituto Venezolano de Investigaciones Científicas.

———. 1971. "Terminology, Alliance, and Change in Warao Society." *Nieuwe West-Indische Gids* 1, April, 48ste Jaargang: 58–122.

Sullivan, Lawrence E. 1988. *Icanchu's Drum: An Orientation to Meaning in South American Religions.* New York: Macmillan.

Tart, Charles T., ed. 1969. *Altered States of Consciousness.* Garden City, N.Y.: Doubleday.

Torrey, E. Fuller. 1972. *The Mind Game: Witchdoctors and Psychiatrists.* New York: Bantam.

Turrado Moreno, Angel. 1945. *Etnografía de los Indios Guaraunos* [Ethnography of the Warao Indians]. Caracas: Lithografía y Tipografía Vargas, Interamerican Conference on Agriculture III, Cuadernos Verdes 15.

Underhill, Ruth Murray. 1938. *Singing for Power.* New York: Ballantine.

Vaquero, P. Antonio. 1965. *Idioma Warao* [The Warao language]. Caracas: Estudios Venezolanos Indígenas.

Vega, Garcilaso de la. 1961. *The Incas (The Royal Commentaries of the Inca),* edited by Alain Gheerbrant. New York: Avon.

Velázquez de la Cadena, Mariano. 1966. *Spanish and English Dictionary.* Chicago and New York: Follett.

Whitten, Jr., Norman E. 1979. *Soul Vine Shaman.* Sacha Runa Research Foundation Occasional Paper No. 5. Urbana, Ill.: Foundation Office.

Wilbert, Johannes. 1956. "Los instrumentos musicales de los warrau" [The musical instruments of the Warao]. *Antropológica* 1:2–22.

———. 1969. *Textos folklóricos de los Indios Warao* [Folkloric texts of the Warao Indians]. University of California, Los Angeles: Latin American Center, vol. 12.

———. 1970. *Folk Literature of the Warao Indians.* University of California, Los Angeles: Latin American Center, vol. 15.

———. 1972a. *Survivors of Eldorado.* New York: Praeger.

———. 1972b. "Tobacco and Shamanistic Ecstasy among the Warao Indians." In *Flesh of the Gods,* edited by Peter T. Furst 55–83. New York: Praeger.

———. 1974. "The Calabash of the Ruffled Feathers." In *Stones, Bones, and Skin: Ritual and Shamanic Art,* edited by Anne Trueblood Brodzky, Rose Daneswich, and Nick Johnson, 90–93. Toronto: Artscanada.

———. 1975a. "Eschatology in a Participatory Universe: Destinies of the Soul among the Warao Indians of Venezuela." In *Death and the Afterlife in Pre-Columbian America,* edited by Elizabeth P. Benson, 163–89. Washington, D.C.: Dumbarton Oaks Research Library and Collections, Trustees for Harvard University.

———. 1975b. *Warao Basketry: Form and Function.* Occasional Papers of the Museum of Cultural History, no. 3. Los Angeles: University of California, Los Angeles.

———. 1976. "To Become a Maker of Canoes: An Essay in Warao Enculturation." In *Enculturation in Latin America: An Anthology,* edited by Johannes Wilbert, 308–58. Latin American Studies, vol. 37. Los Angeles: UCLA Latin American Center Publications, University of California.

———. 1977. "Navigators of the Winter Sun." In *The Sea in the Pre-Columbian World,* edited by Elizabeth P. Benson, 17–46. Washington, D.C.: Dumbarton Oaks Research Library and Collections.

———. 1979. "Geography and Telluric Lore of the Orinoco Delta." *Journal of Latin American Lore* 5/1:129–50.

———. 1980a. "Genesis and Demography of a Warao Subtribe: The Winikina." In *Demographic and Biological Studies of the Warao Indians,* edited by Johannes Wilbert and Miguel Layrisse, 13–47. Latin American Studies, vol. 45. Los Angeles: UCLA Latin American Center Publications, University of California.

———. 1980b. "The Warao Indians of the Orinoco Delta." In *Demographic and Biological Studies of the Warao Indians,* edited by Johannes Wilbert and Miguel Layrisse, 3–12. Latin American Studies, vol. 45. Los Angeles: UCLA Latin American Center Publications, University of California.

———. 1981a. "Warao Cosmology and Yekuana Roundhouse Symbolism." *Journal of Latin American Lore* 7/1:37–72.

———. 1981b. "The Warao Lords of Rain." In *The Shape of the Past: Studies in Honor of Franklin D. Murphy,* edited by G. Buccellati and C. Speroni, 127–45. Los Angeles: Institute of Archaeology and Office of the Chancellor, University of California.

———. 1983. "Warao Ethnopathology and Exotic Epidemic Disease." *Journal of Ethnopharmacology* 8:357–61.

———. 1985. "The House of the Swallow-Tailed Kite: Warao Myth and the Art of Thinking in Images." In *Animal Myths and Metaphors in South America,* edited by Gary Urton, 145–82. Salt Lake City: University of Utah Press.

———. 1987a. *Tobacco and Shamanism in South America.* New Haven: Yale University Press.

———. 1987b. "Trance, Music, and Music/Trance Relations: A Symposium." *Pacific Review of Ethnomusicology* 4:1–38.

———. 1993. *Mystic Endowment: Religious Ethnography of the Warao Indians.* Cambridge, Mass.: Harvard University Press.

Wilbert, Johannes, and Miguel Layrisse, eds. 1980. *Demographic and Biological Studies of the Warao Indians.* Latin American Studies, vol. 45. Los Angeles: UCLA Latin American Center Publications, University of California.

Wilbert, Werner. 1986. "Warao Herbal Medicine: A Pneumatic Theory of Illness and Healing." Ph.D. diss., University of California, Los Angeles.

Wlodarski, J. 1963. "The Golden Ratio and the Fibonacci Numbers in the World of Atoms." *Fibonacci Quarterly* 1/1:61–63.

Index